A CONTEST OF IDEAS

THE WORKING CLASS IN AMERICAN HISTORY

Editorial Advisors
James R. Barrett, Julie Greene, William P. Jones,
Alice Kessler-Harris, and Nelson Lichtenstein

A Contest of Ideas

Capital, Politics, and Labor

NELSON LICHTENSTEIN

UNIVERSITY OF ILLINOIS PRESS
URBANA, CHICAGO, AND SPRINGFIELD

The Center for the Study of Work, Labor, and Democracy at UCSB
provided financial support for the publication of this volume.

Library of Congress Cataloging-in-Publication Data
Lichtenstein, Nelson.
A contest of ideas : capital, politics, and labor / Nelson Lichtenstein.
Pages cm. — (The working class in American history)
Includes bibliographical references and index.
ISBN 978-0-252-03785-6 (hardcover : alk. paper) —
ISBN 978-0-252-07940-5 (pbk. : alk. paper) —
ISBN 978-0-252-09512-2 (e-book)
1. Labor—United States—History. 2. Labor unions—United States—
History. 3. Working class—United States—History. 4. Capitalism—
United States—History. I. Title.
HD8066.L527   2013
331.0973—dc23   2013003507

To Richard Arneson, who has heard all of this in the mountains

CONTENTS

ACKNOWLEDGMENTS

Since the essays and interventions in this volume reach back, in some instances, more than thirty years, an acknowledgment of those who have helped along the way constitutes something close to a list of all who have influenced my view of history and politics during those years. Some have been in the academy and others not; some have offered a close, critical analysis of a particular essay, while others have shaped my worldview in a more general sense. Most are alive, but a few are gone. I owe a debt to Richard Appelbaum, Eric Arnesen, Richard Arneson, Eileen Boris, Howard Brick, David Brody, Charles Capper, Melvyn Dubofsky, Howard Erlanger, Leon Fink, Richard Flacks, Dana Frank, Steve Fraser, Joshua Freeman, Daniel Geary, Gary Gerstle, Martin Glaberman, Howell Harris, Meg Jacobs, Sanford Jacoby, Michael Kazin, Jennifer Klein, Robert Korstad, Joanne Landy, John Logan, Harold Meyerson, David Montgomery, Bruce Nelson, Alice O'Connor, Michael Parker, Christopher Phelps, Michael Rogin, Roy Rosenzweig, Reuel Schiller, Ellen Schrecker, Elizabeth Shermer, Alison Silver, Judith Stein, David Thelen, Jean-Christian Vinel, Alan Wald, Seth Wigderson, Karen Winkler, and Jonathan Zeitlin. University of Illinois Press editor Laurie Matheson encouraged my efforts on this volume and helped conceptualize its shape, while Joseph McCartin and George Cotkin gave the entire manuscript insightful readings. Jill Hughes proved an exceptionally fine copyeditor. Jim O'Brien once again demonstrated his craftsmanship as the indexer for another of my books.

And of course I had to eat and pay the mortgage while writing these essays, so a debt is owed to the National Endowment for the Humanities, to the Fulbright Commission, the Rockefeller, Guggenheim, and MacArthur Foundations, the Oregon Humanities Center, and to the three very different institutions—the Catholic University of America, the University of Virginia, and the University of California, Santa Barbara—that have provided me with an academic home.

INTRODUCTION

In 1983 I visited Clark Kerr, whom Governor Ronald Reagan had fired from his post as president of the University of California some sixteen years before. Kerr still had an office on Channing Way in Berkeley, in the building that housed the UC Institute of Industrial Relations, where I had done much research for my dissertation, which, as it happened, was critical of the industrial relations regime that men like Kerr had helped to construct.

I was not meeting Kerr to "interview" him. I had no agenda other than simply to talk with a celebrated figure whose writings, politics, and leadership I thought I knew all too well. After all, he had presided over the university's fight against the Free Speech Movement at Berkeley in 1964. Equally important for my purposes, Kerr had been one of the most influential theorists of postwar industrial relations, whose defense of managerial authority and advocacy of a bureaucratic and routinized collective bargaining regime had been subjected to a critical, historical analysis in my own academic work.

Likewise, Kerr thought he had me pretty much figured out as well. I was one of those bearded radicals who had bedeviled his presidency during the 1960s and given Reagan and other conservative regents the chance to get rid of a man who practically exemplified mid-twentieth-century liberalism. And while it is doubtful that he had read anything that I had written, he probably had me tagged, correctly, as one of those new labor historians who were contemptuous of his careful efforts to mediate and ameliorate conflict in industry and elsewhere.

So Kerr came on pretty strong. He made it clear that he really was a liberal who believed in trade unionism, something important in the years right after President Reagan's destruction of the union of air traffic controllers. And Kerr denied that he was a bureaucratic elitist: he was a liberal pluralist who defended the democratic governance of trade unions and other institutions of civil society. Most importantly, Kerr emphasized that a generation of New Leftists had been gravely mistaken to think that the greatest threat to their vision of the good society came from liberal administrators such as he. Instead it came from his own long-standing enemies: the corporate and political right, who had been gunning for him ever since he first defended Harry Bridges, the radical longshore unionist, forty years before.

This meeting with Kerr—there would be only one—hardly altered my views, but it did coincide with a transformation in the direction my scholarship would take. Postwar liberalism had many faults, but the American political right never made a settled peace with the New Deal values and institutions that Kerr imperfectly championed. It took time, but eventually most historians of my generation and those who would come afterward, took this lesson to heart. And perhaps even more important, Kerr did see the production and animation of ideas as a decisive lever that could transform society. After all, in his famous set of lectures, "The Uses of the University," delivered in 1963, Kerr called UC and other research universities a "knowledge industry" that had replaced the railroad transport of the late nineteenth century and auto production early in the twentieth century as the "focal point for national growth."[1]

I would never sign on to this sort of celebratory forecasting—this collection contains a critique of just this sort of wishful postwar liberalism—but Kerr and his generation of academic mandarins were nevertheless important intellectuals even as they functioned as bureaucratic managers, within the academy and without. Like all elite strata, they sought to generate and project an ideology that rationalized their rule both for themselves and for those subject to their authority. Their ideas had to be taken as seriously as the ideas of those who opposed them.

This collection of essays therefore takes as a starting point the idea that intellectuals, both those anointed by the academy and those who emerge in a more organic fashion out of working-class and other plebian experiences, play a decisive role in shaping the way men and women see the social and economic world in which they live. Without a set of ideas that explain, structure, and reify the utter complexity of social existence and workaday life, all is chaos and confusion. Although Marx proclaimed, "Philosophers have hitherto only interpreted the world in various ways; the point is to change it," the opposite is equally true. One cannot chart a course of social action without understanding the world in which one lives, works, and struggles.

Thus, it would be well for historians, especially labor historians, to banish the word "spontaneous" as a descriptive that presumes to explain the origins of a social movement or political eruption. Used in this fashion, spontaneity is a profoundly condescending marker that entirely eviscerates the sentiment, planning, ideas, and leaders that are always present when collective action becomes visible to outsiders who are not privy to the inner world of those whose discontent is finally made manifest.

To be efficacious, ideas must have an audience. My project and that of many in my generation has been to offer a historical analysis that explains why the very existence of a working class requires an understanding of the institutions and individuals who presume to speak on its behalf, as well as an understanding of those who seek to contain and delegitimize the many voices that arise out of labor's world. It is not just that a new vocabulary is necessary for this work, but in a world where many of the old social democratic markers have been obscured, the rationale for collective organization at the workplace and in the polity has changed dramatically in the last few decades. In a world of global corporations and weak states, working-class power has an exceedingly hard time making itself manifest. Both the strike and the ballot seem to have an increasingly anemic payoff in the face of the capital mobility that pressures contemporary states to subordinate social and economic regulation to the prerogatives of enterprise. This is one reason that the contest of ideas is so important and why intellectuals of whatever pedigree are essential combatants.

I came to this role because both of my parents were exiles of a sort. My father was a German-Jewish refugee from the Nazis, who came to own a five-and-dime store in sleepy Frederick, Maryland. There in the late 1930s he met my mother, a sometime journalist, whose self-exile from an established merchant family in Vicksburg, Mississippi, was propelled by a disdain for the vulgar racism of Mississippi Senator Theodore Bilbo and his ilk—a disdain no less intense than my father's fear and hatred of Herr Hitler. Neither my brother nor I were interested in running Dad's store when we finished our education, but perhaps some retail resonance continued to reverberate in the far recesses of my mind. When many decades later I began to write a history of Wal-Mart, some useful memories came flooding back: the long drives to the Baltimore wholesale houses where we picked up a deal on ten dozen blouses or sneakers; the visiting salesmen, some of them refugees from Eastern Europe; the lucrative excitement of the holiday rush as well as the growing competition from the chain stores and the suburban shopping centers; and the increasingly difficult racial terrain, which found my father stocking a set of dolls, both "colored" and white, even as he wrote small checks to the more militant civil rights organizations.

So I grew up in what I would later recognize as a family with liberal, social democratic values, although in Frederick during the 1950s there were few venues for putting those ideas into practice. The largest student organization at my high school was a branch of the Future Farmers of America; Fort Detrick, the U.S. Army biological warfare center, seemed like a friendly place: it had the largest swimming pool in town and sponsored the best Boy Scout troop. When a group of Quakers from Philadelphia conducted a silent vigil there in 1960, I remained entirely unmoved. I knew no one in a trade union nor any individual on a university faculty, though from my high school years on, I was convinced that anyone wishing to become an intellectual had to spend some time in New York, preferably in publishing. But when I visited Columbia University, to which I had been admitted, I found it all too urban and alien; instead I chose Dartmouth College, a leafier and more collegiate institution.

I was a history major at Dartmouth, active on the daily student newspaper, and, increasingly, a wannabe radical. My beat was often the civil rights movement, so I spent the summer right after my 1966 graduation as a reporter for the *Southern Courier*, an integrationist weekly funded by Northern liberals. I was posted to Selma and Mobile. I did not get jailed or beaten up, but on occasion, as when I watched Stokely Carmichael talk one evening in a rural Lowndes County church, I did catch a glimpse of the moral power and social radicalism near the heart of twentieth-century America's greatest social movement.

So it was only natural that I would find graduate school at Berkeley alluring. At the time it was probably the best place in the country to study African American history. Kenneth Stampp was there and also younger scholars like George Stocking, Lawrence Levine, and Leon Litwack. But I did not really go to Berkeley to study with those eminent figures. Instead, I knew that graduate school would keep me out of the draft—I shared a five-year deferment with the likes of Dick Cheney—and even more important, I was attracted to the East Bay, because the aura generated by the Free Speech Movement remained strong, confirming to me and thousands of other young people that something remarkable was on offer there, outside the classroom as well as within.

Stocking, Stampp, Samuel Haber, Michael Rogin, and Larzer Ziff were among those who did teach me how to write, but my real education came from Berkeley's radical student milieu, especially from my political sect of choice, then labeling itself the International Socialists, an anti-Stalinist formation whose most important figure was the Trotskyist intellectual Hal Draper. It was here in the late 1960s and early 1970s, off campus as well as on, that I encountered many of the concepts and ideological frameworks that would prove compelling and useful in subsequent decades: an understanding that capitalism is an ever changing, historically structured phenomenon, a moral and ideological critique of Communism, including its Cuban and Vietnamese variants, a feel for the dynamics of a social movement (learned from direct personal experience), and an approach to trade unionism and working-class consciousness that was equally appreciative of the radical potential and conservative reality.[2]

Indeed, the subject for my doctoral dissertation, on the industrial unions during the era of their World War II "no-strike pledge," emerged right out of the internal International Socialist debate that accompanied the organization's decision to "industrialize," our term for quitting school and getting a job in the unionized auto, steel, or trucking industries.[3] During World War II, Draper reminded us, Trotskyists had won much influence as shop floor militants who opposed the no-strike pledge. Would something similar be possible today if young radicals moved to Detroit, Gary, and Chicago to take blue-collar jobs and organize against a union leadership we thought all too conservative and collaborationist?

I never made that sojourn. I had no principled objection, though I did think teaching, health care, and municipal government might be a more natural and therefore a more advantageous venue for my college-educated, middle-class generation than heavy industry. I think history has proven me correct, but I take no pride in that foresight, because in the early 1970s none of us could foresee the deindustrialization and deunionization that would cast such a pall over shop floor militancy and radical politics in the rust belt. Still, I salute the accomplishments of those who recast their lives: they built sometimes potent oppositional movements in the Teamsters and the United Auto Workers (UAW); they founded and sustained *Labor Notes*, an exceedingly useful source of progressive information on union affairs; and many did in fact win local union leadership posts, though perhaps not on quite the radical, socialist platform first envisioned.

When I did get around to writing a thesis, later published as *Labor's War at Home: The CIO in World War II*,[4] I did not work closely with Berkeley's pioneering social historians Leon Litwack and Larry Levine, and I was largely oblivious to the work of Herbert Gutman, David Montgomery, and even E. P. Thompson. Litwack would have been an obvious advisor for my dissertation; during those very same years he was mentoring Nick Salvatore, who wrote a celebrated biography of Eugene V. Debs. But in my hyper-political circle there seemed something "soft" and structureless in the new social and cultural history; moreover, as Joanne Landy, my comrade, spouse, and tutor in all things political, reminded me, Litwack may well have failed to thoroughly repudiate the Popular Front politics of his youth. Far less contaminating as a dissertation advisor would be the more conservative business historian Richard Abrams, an academic who would be unlikely to have much interest or impact on my own narrative/analysis.

Given such a pedigree, it is not surprising that my academic career went nowhere in the years after I got my PhD in 1974. I could not land a permanent teaching post, and when I did finally spend eighteen months in New York City publishing, the fulfillment of this youthful ambition proved neither romantic nor stimulating. Meanwhile, no publisher, not even those well down the prestige hierarchy, wanted to turn my 750-page dissertation into a book. I gave few conference papers during the half decade following my graduation from Berkeley. My first, and for quite a while my only, "academic" publication came in a 1975 issue of the erstwhile Students for a Democratic Society journal, *Radical America*, devoted to labor in the 1940s.[5]

These failures had little to do with my lack of a mentor at Berkeley; rather, the field of post–Wagner Act labor history was no field at all. Labor economists were the arbitrators of this subdiscipline, and from their point of view I had neither the correct methodology—where were the equations and the data sets?—nor the appropriate theoretical outlook to grasp the dynamics of a collective bargaining regime that was inherently functional to modern industry. After all, I saw the system created during World War II as a tragic defeat for working-class empowerment; they saw it as a triumph of pluralist statecraft. Indeed, industrial relations was still a supremely self-confident and imperial field, which had probably supplied the academy and the federal government with more deans, presidents, and cabinet secretaries than any other academic field. The discipline's entire raison d'être was the resolution of conflicts once thought endemic to industrial capitalism. Thus it may be telling that the Industrial Relations Research Association was just about the only academic group that had escaped formation of a radical caucus during the late 1960s. Likewise, when it became painfully apparent in later years that corporate management was entirely prepared to eradicate trade unionism, some of the most distinguished industrial relations scholars and practitioners remained in a state of denial about this new reality.

My own relationship to the writing of labor history finally became more positive and rewarding at the end of the 1970s. Feminists proved a model of how to do it. After I married historian Eileen Boris, an activist scholar in her own right, in 1979, I came to appreciate the perspective of a young generation of women academics who saw themselves as radicals and revisionists but who were also determined to make their way forward within the historical profession itself. Indeed, they understood that the transformation of our understanding of the historical record, their recasting of the canon, their effort to win a presence within the faculty of leading colleges and universities was itself a battle feminists must wholeheartedly join. This proved a revelation for me, helping dispel the alienation and disdain that had been an unfortunate product of my otherwise salutary engagement with the New Left during my grad student years.

Even more important was a generational shift that took place round about 1980. By this point the founders of the new labor history, especially David Brody and David Montgomery, had begun to challenge the authority of the labor economists. And a younger set of newly minted PhDs, including Ronald Schatz, Joshua Freeman, and Steve Fraser, had begun to use the tools of the historian's craft to write a new account of labor's triumphs and failures during the Great Depression and afterward. Our coming-out party took place at a Rochester meeting of the Social Science History Association in 1979 when Steve, Josh, and I delivered long papers on our work to a packed audience. Melvyn Dubofsky was the commentator, with E. P. Thompson and David Montgomery paying close attention from the front row. Steve Fraser, whose political and academic career was even more checkered than mine, finally helped me break through on the publishing front. As the new history editor at Cambridge, and in a few years time the author of a stunningly original biography of Sidney Hillman, Steve understood where I was going. In one piece of editorial advice, obvious now but not so clear in that era, he remarked, "Tell us about the people and politics in the corridors of power, as well as on the shop floor." He helped shepherd into print *Labor's War at Home* as well as most of my other key essays and books. In 1996, as I discuss later in this volume, Steve and I were among the historians who organized a series of "teach-ins with the labor movement," designed to bridge the gap that had long divided the left academy from the AFL-CIO leadership. Steve was truly the academic mentor I never found at Berkeley.

For my next project I *had* to write a biography of Walter Reuther, one of the founders of the UAW and that union's most famous and influential leader. This was less a choice than an ideological and political imperative. For any student of the left and labor during the mid-twentieth century, Reuther was a lightning rod, a figure who evoked as much disdain as celebration. Upon one thing Trotskyists and Communists could agree: Reuther was an opportunist, a grave digger of the trade union left, an architect of the claustrophobic system endorsed by all those industrial relations scholars. But if I was to write a biography of this man and the union he did so much to create, I also had to figure out why he had been, and until his death in 1970 still remained, such an attractive figure for so many people, among them older radicals and intellectuals like C. Wright Mills, Michael Harrington, Harvey Swados, and Irving Howe. So, like any good biographer, I had to get inside the head of this man, to explore the battle there between the insurgent sensibilities that remained from his socialist youth and the capitalist realities, economic and political, that confronted any figure who sought to reform the work life of those millions who depended for their livelihoods on what was then America's largest and most powerful industry. As to his role in building the UAW, I called Reuther "a prisoner of the institution he had helped construct."

I had begun writing the Reuther biography in the mid-1980s, at the height of the cultural and linguistic turns in history. I was not hostile to the insights generated by this genre, but my political training at Berkeley and my engagement with the legal and political fate of the labor movement afterward have kept my work focused on political economy, on organizational structures, and on ideas and ideology. Thus I first came to appreciate C.L.R. James for his work on theories of state capitalism rather than his role as a pioneer in postcolonial studies. Likewise, I found the work of Charles Maier and David Abraham particularly useful insofar as they explored how capitalist elites confronted, contained, and defeated an interwar European working class that was far better organized and politicized than that in the United States. Howell John Harris and Sanford Jacoby would prove highly influential guides to the same process on this side of the Atlantic.[6]

When I finally got around to reading Herbert Gutman's pioneering 1973 essay, "Work, Culture, and Society in Industrializing America," I thought his description of how wave after immigrant wave of peasants and rural folk came into a stressful engagement with industrial capitalism was an amazingly rich and fruitful way of reperiodizing nineteenth-century working-class history.[7] But Gutman's quasi-anthropological schema did not provide much guidance to the contest for power in a unionized auto factory. Indeed, insofar as social historians like him thought that working-class radicalism arose more often among greenhorn and first-generation factory workers, I saw this view buttressing the outlook of that older generation of economists and social scientists, like Clark Kerr and W. W. Rostow, who saw radicalism as merely an epiphenomenon of the early industrialization process.[8] In the auto factories of the 1940s, I found that the wildcat strikers were frequently veteran workers and shop stewards, often skilled craftsmen from families with generations of industrial experience.

Given the perspective outlined above, it may seem puzzling that during these very same years I leaped at the chance to join the team of young historians who were writing and editing *Who Built America: Working People and the Nation's Economy, Politics, Culture, and Society.* That textbook, a product of the American Social History Project, had been inspired by Herbert Gutman himself and given guidance until his untimely death in 1985. Whatever my historiographic equivocations, I was delighted and excited to work with Gutman "students" like Steven Brier, Roy Rosenzweig, Bruce Levine, Susan Porter Benson, Joshua Brown, and Joshua Freeman. We were going to revolutionize the teaching of American history, putting the experience of working men and women, slave or free, immigrant and native born, in unions or out, at the very center of the nation's narrative. In the process presidents, elections, diplomacy, and elite culture would find themselves competing for space with the Knights of Labor, accounts of working-class leisure, and the internal politics of the unions and other insurgent organizations.[9]

I was one of the writers who stayed with *Who Built America* through all three of its editions. Since I was responsible for the post-1929 chapters, I did a lot of new writing on very contemporary issues. That was fun, but the effort to end the book on a hopeful working-class note in keeping with the textbook's overall ethos proved difficult. Indeed, as the editors and I came to see that high politics and the global economy were of increasing importance, I was tasked with a kind of "Nixon goes to China" sort of job: reducing the space devoted to the spirited strike narratives and analysis of working-class politics in several chapters of the book. I felt no sense of betrayal, because as the 1990s turned into a new century, it was apparent to everyone associated with the textbook that we had to take politics and political economy much more seriously.

When my biography of Walter Reuther appeared in 1995, it was well received within most of the academy. I was particularly gratified that my old Berkeley comrades also found that I had struck a reasonable balance between the classic Trotskyist critique of the Reutherites and the recognition that they faced an institutional set of dilemmas that no mere promulgation of a more militant strategy could overcome. However, I found the critics of the book even more validating than those who praised it. Martin Glaberman, an old radical who had spent much of his life in the Detroit auto shops battling Reuther, and Herbert Hill, the former labor secretary of the NAACP, both considered the book an apologia. They are now gone, but I can't help believe that they found particularly objectionable my failure to project the kind of hectoring, dismissive critique of Reuther and other union leaders upon which they had become politicized in their youth. Glaberman, for example, could not fathom why I felt it illuminating to subtitle my biography "The Most Dangerous Man in Detroit," which was a phrase taken from a 1945 comment by auto executive George Romney. And Hill, who had been a courageous and determined critic of labor's manifest failures on the civil rights front, ignored my own sharp critique of Reuther's foot-dragging on such issues, if only because I refrained from labeling him an outright racist.[10]

Irving Bluestone didn't like the book either. He had been Reuther's closest friend and collaborator during the 1960s and later a UAW vice president. A sometime proponent of various forms of labor-management collaboration, Bluestone, then retired, viewed the biography as just another New Left screed attacking a now embattled UAW. I found little persuasive in his critique, but I was impressed with the method by which Bluestone delivered his message. He reserved a room in a UAW local union hall in one of Detroit's blue-collar suburbs, put together a 1950s-style leaflet announcing his talk, and then proceeded to engage those unionists he could attract in what I imagine was a spirited denunciation of my book.

I had begun writing the Reuther biography when I taught at the Catholic University of America, where I spent most of the 1980s. I salute the late Monsignor George Higgins, one of the last of the great "labor priests" associated with CUA. A trusted figure, both in Reuther's UAW and in the United Farm Workers of Cesar Chavez, he ran interference for me in 1983 when the labor economists at the university, who apparently had some say in the matter, tossed a few obstacles onto my path toward tenure.

My 1990s were spent at the University of Virginia. There I was able to attract graduate students for the first time, encountering the deeply rewarding process by which one mentors cohort after cohort of young intellectuals. I have never had any sympathy for those colleagues who resent the time, effort, and emotional demands made by such apprentice scholars. What could be more thrilling than to see in the work of these young historians even a small slice of your own ideas propagated unto the next generation?

Virginia also had a large impact on my research agenda. There my ideas were shaped again as much by what was happening outside my study as within. As soon as I got to Charlottesville, I took an interest in efforts to raise wages and give workers a voice at Thomas Jefferson's university. But we quickly found that the trade union idea generated little traction in this right-to-work state. It was an alien concept and quite often a dangerous one as well. Virginia had never really had a New Deal, but the civil rights movement had worked a revolution, if not in the social structure itself, then certainly in terms of the meaning of rights and citizenship. By the last decade of the twentieth century, this conception of civic and social rights enjoyed considerable legitimacy at virtually every level of the university, as it did in the nation as a whole. This helped me reframe my understanding of both the rise and the fall of the solidarity principle that had undergirded the labor movement of the early twentieth century and the welfare state that it helped to sustain. Solidarity and collective action were ideological constructs, once highly legitimate in law and administrative practice during those midcentury years when unionism seemed but a naturalized element in a polity characterized by pluralist statecraft. The rise of the civil rights movement initially strengthened this New Deal project by bringing millions of white women and people of color into that social democratic fold. But a discourse of rights might also subvert the solidarity principle and in the process delegitimize the unions and the governmental apparatus that had once sustained them. In law and political rhetoric, American conservatives would soon take full advantage of this apparent contradiction.[11]

However, it would be a great mistake for scholars and citizens to think that the decline of labor and the rise of the right were mainly a function of conflict, social or ideological, within the world of liberalism. The study of conservatism and the economic and social transformations that advanced it has become of increasing preoccupation to historians and social scientists during the 1990s and after. Once again it became possible to study capitalism, or some slice of it, without the obligatory nod to the Marxist classics or, even more debilitating, to engage in a debate with those who thought modernity, industrialism, or some kind of organizational pluralism a more promising way to think about power, conflict, and economic transformation. Because I had always tilted toward structural explanations over those rooted in cultural or social history, and because I thought formal ideologies continued to have great motivational value in politics, business, and labor, I found myself and some of my students in the midst of this historiographical turn. Thus one of the first conferences that I organized when Eileen and I began to teach at the University of California, Santa Barbara, showcased the work of a new generation of scholars, many trained by David Hollinger and Howard Brick, who studied the way intellectuals had conceptualized the character and trajectory of twentieth-century American capitalism.[12]

And then things got down and dirty. During the fall of 2003 a large strike of grocery workers began in Southern California. Safeway, Albertsons, and other employers sought to slash wages and benefits so as to bring their labor costs into line with those of Wal-Mart, a company that had announced that it planned to build scores of big hypercompetitive stores throughout coastal California. I had had my eye on Wal-Mart for quite some time. What did it mean that a low wage, antiunion retailer, which prided itself on its rural Southern roots, was now a larger and more powerful corporation than once mighty General Motors? And why was this Arkansas-based company so efficient and its workers so loyal and so powerless? Political and economic theorists have devoted a great deal of ink to the definition and denunciation of "neoliberalism." Much of it seemed far too abstract and meta-historical for my taste. But here was an organizational and ideological phenomenon that seemingly exemplified the triumph on a worldwide scale of an unfettered market in goods and labor. So I organized a conference on the company, which turned into a book, and then into another. Soon I was a Wal-Mart expert.[13]

Along the way I took a couple of trips to China and began to get a textured feel for the real meaning of globalization in a world where a set of retail-dominated supply chains have displaced manufacturing capital from the world economy's commanding heights and squeezed labor at every node of value creation from South China to the checkout counter. Although finance and its failures have undoubtedly played the most dramatic role in world capitalism's recent crisis, the rise in the past few decades of this new configuration of capitalist power and production may well have an impact that is just as potent and pervasive. Capital and labor are still with us. Indeed, more people work on an assembly line today than at any other moment in world history, but the terrain upon which managers and workers clash is unlike that of the short twentieth century (1914–1989), when capital was less mobile and the state more powerful. Today borders seem more porous, and executive decisions of enormous economic and social consequence are now being made in once obscure places like Bentonville, Issaquah, and Cupertino. Traditional manufacturing languishes in the United States, but in China, Bangladesh, Vietnam, and Latin America a new industrial working class is coming into a consciousness of its own power and potential. A new generation of labor historians is just beginning to write that history.

This book is arranged in five sections, categorized by theme and interest rather than a chronological schema, either in terms of when I wrote the pieces or their ostensible subject. The collection is not designed as an archive, so I have corrected mistakes, updated the text, and added new material to make my meaning clear for contemporary readers. Most of the pieces were written during the last dozen years.

PART I

Shaping Myself, Shaping History

The essays in this section are biographical in orientation, exploring how I have written about the relationship between labor, capital, and politics and why my ideas have often changed over the years. "Writing and Rewriting Labor's Narrative" explains how, along with so many others in my New Left generation, I have reframed my understanding of those structures and social impulses that create the consciousness of the working-class as well its antagonists. At Berkeley in the early 1970s I was convinced that neither the law, religion, ethnicity, nor even race were as important as the work experience itself in shaping the consciousness of industrial unionists, whose sit-down strikes and wildcat strikes seemed to emerge directly out of a revolt against hierarchy and authority on the shop floor itself. The works of mid-twentieth-century sociologists like Alvin Gouldner, Donald Roy, and Reinhard Bendix were therefore important influences. Likewise I was inspired by Harry Braverman's deconstruction of the labor process under conditions of Taylorite management, and I found the work of David Brody, who truly understood work and authority among steelworkers and butchers, something of an academic model, even though he was far more of an "institutionalist" than the other new labor history pioneers.

But to put it rather crudely, I've come to the conclusion that the relationship of an individual to his or her work life is of less immediate importance than that person's capacity to identify with and then expound a set of ideas and aspirations that may or may not run parallel to what an outside observer—say, a historian of left-wing inclinations—might seem to think met the person's objective interests. This is the point Tom Frank made in *What's the Matter with Kansas?*, although I hasten to add that consciousness and behavior are not merely the product of a preexisting set of cultural tropes. Instead they are heavily influenced by what workers and citizens see as part of a struggle whose success is probable and useful. So in this section's inaugural essay, on writing and revising labor's Depression-era narrative, one can find a younger Lichtenstein and an older Lichtenstein arguing with each other. The former focuses relentlessly on working-class self-activity at the point of production; the latter offers equal weight to the larger ideological, cultural, and racial context within which the unions and their antagonists competed for power and prestige.

A second essay, which yanks the reader from mid-twentieth-century Detroit to early twenty-first-century Guangdong Province, recounts my discovery that the labor question can have many different configurations, especially when some of the most important and characteristic enterprises of our day are the big-box retailers, whose employee rolls and annual revenues now far outrank those of the largest manufacturing companies. To my sometime consternation, it now seems apparent that the essence of the twenty-first-century labor question no longer resides at the point of production in a struggle between workers and the owners of the factories in which they labor. Instead, the site of value production is found at every link along a set of global supply chains, in which the manufacturer and the warehouse operator, the ports and the shipping companies, as well as the retailers and their branded vendors jockey for power and profit. In this disaggregated system, legal ownership of the forces of production has been divorced from operational control, making accountability for labor conditions diffuse and knowledge of the actual producers far from transparent.

I have always been interested in putting ideas into practice, which is why I've included an essay here that ruminates on the meaning of the public intellectual. At Berkeley my comrades and I saw ourselves as standing in a revolutionary tradition that reached back almost to the first years of the twentieth century. The task was to put that ideology to work, here, now, tomorrow morning. At the time we crammed as much history and analysis onto a series of mimeographed leaflets—single spaced, double sided, and normally finished at 2:00 A.M.—which we distributed bright and early at Sather Gate. New and more effective forms of distribution would soon become available, but the impulse to reach a larger, animated public by deploying ideas generated in either the seminar room or the political caucus retains its potency. Indeed, such an impulse is a hallmark of good citizenship, which is the essence of what being a political activist or even a public intellectual is all about.

CHAPTER 1

Writing and Rewriting Labor's Narrative

In the years after 1970 my New Left generation inaugurated a remarkable probe into the character, meaning, and history of the working class and its institutions. Two events in particular seemed to crystallize my decision to write a history of unionism and the state during the 1940s. The first came on the evening of September 14, 1970, when a few dozen Berkeley students drove down to Fremont's sprawling General Motors assembly complex to support rank-and-file workers when the United Automobile Workers (UAW) struck the company at midnight. Hundreds jumped the gun and rushed out of the factory a couple of hours early. These youthful, boisterous, night-shift workers happily waved our hand-painted signs—"GM: Mark of Exploitation"—took over the union hall, and cheered militant speeches, both anti-company and critical of top UAW leaders. It was the beginning of the first coordinated, nationwide stoppage at GM since the winter of 1945–1946. We didn't know it at the time, but the 1970 GM strike, which would continue for ten weeks, came right in the midst of the last great wave of twentieth-century industrial conflict in the United States.[1]

While all of this was going on, the Berkeley branch of the International Socialists, a Trotskyist formation of New Left sensibility and "third camp" (i.e., anti-Stalinist and anticapitalist) politics, was in the midst of furious debate. Along with others radicalized on the campuses and in the anti–Vietnam War movement, a "turn toward the working class" had begun to propel thousands of student radicals into the nation's factories, warehouses, hospitals, and offices. From Berkeley, friends and comrades took off for Detroit auto plants, Chicago steel mills, Cleveland trucking companies, and all sorts of industrial jobs throughout the Bay Area.[2]

But what were they to do when they got there? If these "industrializers" began to work their way up through the trade union apparatus, they would be helping to build an institution that seemed positively anathema to many of us. The AFL-CIO remained a firm backer of the war in Vietnam; moreover, even the more progressive unions, like the UAW and the Packinghouse Workers, appeared so strapped by bureaucracy, law, contracts, and political allegiances that they hardly seemed an appropriate vehicle to advance the class struggle. C. Wright Mills, Stanley Aronowitz, Harvey Swados, C.L.R. James, and other radicals had taught us that the growth of the union bureaucracy and the government's intrusive labor relations apparatus had robbed labor of its radical heritage. By incorporating the trade unions into the structures of the American state, or at least the two-party system, these institutions were thought to resemble those of Stalinist or fascist regimes, where statist unions and labor fronts had been foisted upon the working class.[3]

Thus, in the debates that animated my generation of Berkeley students, older activists, like Hal Draper and Stan Weir, made much of labor's experience during the World War II mobilization era. Then the unions had offered the state and enforced upon their members a "no-strike pledge," even as wildcat strikes (i.e., those unauthorized by higher officials), union factionalism, and labor party agitation energized many of the rank-and-filers who had built the industrial unions during the great strikes that electrified the nation between 1934 and 1941. A new generation of working-class radicals, it was therefore believed, must keep a wary eye on the union leadership and build their own independent caucuses within the labor movement.[4] Indeed, I was beginning my research as a wave of spirited strikes, many of them wildcat, shattered the industrial relations routine in Detroit auto factories, Midwest trucking barns, big-city post offices, and throughout California agriculture. Between 1967 and 1973 the size and number of strikes reached levels not seen since the immediate post–World War II years.

This was the perspective put forth in my 1974 University of California dissertation, published in 1982 as *Labor's War at Home: The CIO in World War II*. The book was skeptical about the staying power of New Deal liberalism; saw the warfare state as a repressive institution; criticized Congress of Industrial Organization leaders, both "conservative" (i.e., social democratic) and Communist; and celebrated the World War II wildcat strike movement in the auto, rubber, and shipbuilding industries. It saw that the emergence of a stolid, bureaucratically insular postwar labor movement was a product not of some inherent "job-conscious" parochialism within the union rank and file, nor of McCarthyite repression after the war, but of the bargain struck between the government and cooperative, patriotic union leaders during World War II itself.[5] This kind of argument was anathema to the then dominant set of industrial relations scholars, many themselves trained while serving with the War Labor Board and other labor relations agencies of the wartime era. These influential scholars—some of whom, like John Dunlop, Clark Kerr, Archibald Cox, George Shultz, and James MacGregor Burns, had achieved high-visibility posts in government and the academy—saw labor's World War II experience as a gloriously successful one: the unions had matured by demonstrating their patriotism, doubling their membership, and stabilizing their relationship with employers and the state.

To their way of thinking, labor history really had come to an end near 1941, if not before; what followed was "industrial relations," a policy-oriented research enterprise that sought to fine-tune a depoliticized system of labor-management accommodation and conflict.[6] Their enormous influence blocked efforts to re-configure a twentieth-century history of class relations. Indeed the most influential labor historians of the 1970s, Herbert Gutman, David Montgomery, and E. P. Thompson, were all students of society and ideology in the eighteenth and nineteenth centuries. David Brody had written a pioneering social history of the 1919 steel strike, but in the 1970s there were still few conceptual tools at hand by which to examine a history of the working class or its institutions during the mid-twentieth-century decades. The "state" had not yet been "brought back in," to use a phrase coined by Theda Skocpol and her associates; nor had historians begun to deconstruct the twentieth-century working class into those categories, including race, gender, skill, and mentalité, that have subsequently proven so illuminating. During the early 1970s the left, even the academic left, still imagined an undifferentiated rank and file, which was itself the ideological product of a bipolar discourse that dichotomized a powerful set of labor leaders and a bureaucratically repressed or misled mass union membership. Thus, there were more studies written on the Knights of Labor in that decade than on the Congress of Industrial Organizations (CIO). For labor historians it seemed a lot easier to find a usable past in the conflicts that divided a late nineteenth-century mill town than among those contractual disputes and internal union fights that structured the production regime in a Detroit factory circa 1945.

Things are different today. Decades of union decline and labor-liberal defeat have transformed the questions historians choose to ask about the trajectory of organized labor during the New Deal and World War II years. Contemporary labor and social historians write more about the CIO than the Knights, or even the radical Industrial Workers of the World. In the early twenty-first century, when the proportion of all union workers hovers just above 12 percent, organized labor's incorporation into a claustrophobic state apparatus seems far less an issue than survival of those same unions, not to mention the revival of a socially conscious, New Deal impulse within the body politic. The postwar fate of New Deal liberalism has become a highly contentious issue, so an increasingly rich historiography on the "New Deal order" now stands embedded within a reconsideration of the postwar transformation of U.S. capitalism itself. We are becoming as interested in the ideas and institutions of those who fought against labor and the New Deal—the corporations, the various layers of the middle class, the anti–New Deal politicians of the South and West, the traditionalist conservatives within the working class itself—as we are determined to dissect the contradictions inherent in mid-twentieth-century labor liberalism and the Rooseveltian state.[7]

In this reevaluation the line that once divided the Depression decade from that of the war and the era of postwar politics now appears increasingly fractured. In part this stems from our understanding that the working class of the 1930s was hardly as radical as once conceived, or rather, that its presumptive militancy cannot be divorced from the state structures and institutions that are dialectically complicit in that advanced level of working-class mobilization. The nature of "militancy" and "conservatism" within the working class has become hugely problematic as questions of ethnicity, racism, sexism, homophobia, and regionalism have moved to the fore.[8] Thus the warfare state did not instantly make irrelevant the politics, the social ideologies, or the ethnocultural matrix that had structured class relations during the heyday of the New Deal itself. Continuity, not abrupt change, characterizes the political culture of the late 1930s and early 1940s. As I often tell my classes, December 7, 1941, is the most overrated day in U.S. history.[9]

Thus, historians now see that the political economy of World War II is part of a larger New Deal order that stretched from the early 1930s to the 1970s. This was an era characterized by Democratic Party dominance, Keynesian statecraft, and a trade union movement whose power and presence was too often taken for granted, not the least by historians of "state development." Industry-wide unions sustained both the dominance of the Democratic Party and a quasi-corporatist system of labor-management relations whose impact, far transcending the realm of firm-centered collective bargaining, framed much of the polity's consensus on taxes, social provision, and industry regulation. And, finally, the system of production, distribution, and social expectations that characterized both union strength and business enterprise was uniquely stable, resting on both a well-protected continental market and a technologically and ideologically dominant mass-production model.

In this context the economic power wielded by American trade unions was by its very nature political, for the New Deal had thoroughly politicized all relations among the union movement, the business community, and the state. The New Deal provided a set of semipermanent political structures in which key issues of vital concern to the trade union movement might be accommodated. The National Labor Relations Board established the legal basis of union power and a mechanism for its state sanction; New Deal regulatory bodies stabilized competition in key industries like trucking, coal, air transport, banking, and utilities; and the National War Labor Board provided a tripartite institution that set national wage policy and contributed to the rapid wartime growth of the new trade unions. Corporatism of this sort called for government agencies, composed of capital, labor, and public representatives, to substitute bureaucratic initiative and national economic planning for the chaos and inequities of the market.[10] The successive reappearance of such tripartite governing arrangements during the mid-twentieth century seemed to signal that in the future as in the past the fortunes of organized labor would be determined as much by a process of politicized bargaining in Washington as by the give-and-take of contractual collective bargaining.

This was neither "free collective bargaining" nor the kind of syndicalism that, during the era of the Great War, had informed phrases like "social reconstruction," "industrial democracy," and "workers' control."[11] To ensure industrial peace during World War II, the state sustained a coercive labor relations apparatus that policed not only recalcitrant corporations but also radical shop stewards, uncooperative unions, and striking workers. A generation ago the repressive character of this regime drew much attention. Thus Martin Glaberman celebrated the unstructured spontaneity by which new industrial migrants threw off the contract shackles and Wagner Act procedures forged by the New Deal state. George Lipsitz searched for the link that would unite in song and struggle many of those same working-class rebels, especially those white Appalachians and African Americans who were once thought marginal to the New Deal universe. And I condemned as a disastrous bargain the no-strike pledge that virtually all union leaders offered the nation. They won "union security" and a rising membership but advanced the union movement's internal bureaucratic deformities as well as its marriage to the Democratic Party and the warfare state.[12]

But in the early years of the twenty-first century, the potential payoff from the corporatist bargain of the World War II era looks much better than it did a half century before. Resistance to union organizing declined dramatically during the war as the union movement nearly doubled in size. In the South the work of the War Labor Board (WLB), not to mention the Fair Employment Practices Commission, generated something close to a social revolution. As Michelle Brattain, Daniel Clark, Michael Honey, and Robert Korstad have demonstrated, the WLB orders that mandated union recognition and collective bargaining opened up the organizational and ideological space that enabled workers, both black and white, to liberate themselves from three generations of paternalism and repression. In his study of Winston-Salem tobacco workers, Korstad rightly calls this the "Daybreak of Freedom."[13] Meanwhile, in the North the WLB socialized much of the labor movement's prewar agenda, thus making union security, grievance arbitration, seniority, vacation pay, sick leave, and night-shift supplements standard entitlements mandated for an increasingly large section of the working class. The government's World War II–era Little Steel wage formula, although bitterly resisted by the more highly paid and better-organized sections of the working class, had enough loopholes and special dispensations to enable low-paid workers in labor-short industries to bring their wages closer to the national average.[14] Thus black wages rose twice as fast as white, and weekly earnings in cotton textiles and in retail trade increased about 50 percent faster than in high-wage industries like steel and auto. By the onset of postwar reconversion, WLB wage policy was explicitly egalitarian. "It is not desirable to increase hourly earnings in each industry in accordance with the rise of productivity in that industry," declared a July 1945 memorandum. "The proper goal of policy is to increase hourly earnings generally in proportion to the average increase of productivity in the economy as a *whole*."[15]

The capacity of the state to reshape labor relations at the point of production has also been the subject of much debate and reevaluation. *Labor's War at Home* reflected the perspective of those union militants and dissidents who in the 1960s and 1970s saw the codification of routine industrial relations as a disaster for democracy and militancy inside the factory, mine, and mill. The Taft-Hartley–era labor law, much of which had been first deployed by the War Labor Board, became an increasingly restrictive straitjacket that constrained and suffocated the union movement's bolder and more progressive spirits. The routinization of industrial relations, the marginalization of shop floor activism symbolized and embodied in the wartime no-strike pledge, and the rise of a social patriotic ideology all devalued worker militancy and opened the door to the restoration of managerial authority. In the 1980s this perspective generated much support, especially from a new generation of legal scholars animated by the emancipatory spirit of the New Left. Christopher Tomlins thought that the increasingly intrusive character of the New Deal labor law generated little more than a "counterfeit liberty." James Atleson argued that wartime policies designed to stabilize labor relations and "control rank-and-file militancy" would be "transferred to the peacetime era without any serious questioning of the wisdom of the application of policies originally designed for a quite different time." And in her classic *Yale Law Journal* essay of 1981, Katherine Van Wezel Stone argued that the ideology of "industrial pluralism," which projected a false equality between the power of labor and management, "serves as a vehicle for the manipulation of employee discontent and for the legitimization of existing inequalities of power in the workplace." The elaborate system of grievance handling and arbitration put in place by WLB experts and the postwar courts that followed their lead functioned largely as a therapeutic apparatus of control, not a mechanism designed to achieve industrial justice.[16]

But not all historians have agreed with this doleful perspective. Indeed, if the industrial relations system put in place during the 1940s was so hostile to working-class interests, then why have almost all employers resisted it? Why did company executives see union contracts, seniority systems, and grievance procedures as such a threat to their managerial prerogatives, to the flexibility of their enterprise, to their "right to manage"? And this managerial antiunionism has been even more the case in the years since 1980, when one has had to search far and wide for any pocket of militant shop floor unionism.

What seems so clear now, in an era of union defeat and retreat, is that almost any system of "industrial jurisprudence," which was the phrase used by labor economist Sumner Slichter at the time, or "workplace contractualism," a term later coined by historian David Brody, represents a terrain of struggle that is advantageous to most workers in most places. As Steven Tolliday and Jonathan Zeitlin argued shortly after the appearance of *Labor's War at Home*, and in opposition to the perspective put forward in that book, "The contractual system of collective bargaining which emerged from the Second World War placed substantial constraints on management's freedom to deploy labor and to impose arbitrary discipline."[17] This was a judgment that was certainly sustained by those studying the struggle of unions to secure a foothold in the textile industry of the American South, or in industries where women or people of color represented a substantial proportion of the workforce. In his story of two North Carolina textile plants unionized during the war, Daniel Clark hails the grievance procedures and arbitration system as "liberating forces" in the lives of these mill workers.[18] African Americans became staunch unionists, as well as firm proponents of the grievance procedure, even in unions and workplaces where the seniority system was structured to defend the interests of the white majority. This is because they understood that for those at the bottom of the workplace hierarchy, to those who had long been subjected to the capricious exercise of power by petty elites or to an ethnically coded set of discriminations, the very bureaucratization of labor relations had an impact that was liberating in the world of work. Unionism forced the company to pay "the job, not the man," asserted a black Birmingham steelworker. "CIO came along and said, well, if you get on a job, from the day you're hired, your seniority starts," remembered a wartime packinghouse worker. "And whoever comes behind you, gets behind you. Color has nothing to do with it."[19]

Some working-class militants may have found this war-era corporatism a poor bargain, but business executives, Southern bourbons, and most of the GOP hated the New Dealism of the 1940s even more. In their important studies, Alan Brinkley and Steven Fraser have sustained my view that the New Deal was very much on the defensive after 1938. The New Deal order did remain intact, but at the policy level, labor-liberals fought a defensive, rearguard battle. In his biography of Sidney Hillman, Fraser titles his chapter on Hillman's sojourn as a high-level government official "The Fall to Power." New Deal liberals and Keynesian planners who sought to use the defense-era mobilization crisis to advance a social-democratic perspective found that de facto control of the corporate economy's commanding heights was almost entirely beyond their influence.[20] "The military services were insulated from popular pressures and were not part of the New Deal coalition," writes political scientist Brian Waddell. "They had no agenda for displacing corporate prerogatives through their management of mobilization, as did the New Dealers." FDR's secretary of war, Henry Stimson, reflected the military–corporate Wall Street mind-set in a 1941 entry in his diary: "If you are going to try to go to war, or prepare for war, in a capitalist country, you have got to let business make money out of the process or business won't work."[21]

Despite much wishful historiography, no "corporate liberal" bloc ever emerged in the United States, even at the height of union strength and New Deal political hegemony. Howell Harris has demonstrated that even the most "realistic" U.S.

firms, like General Motors, U.S. Rubber, and General Electric, were determined to contain, constrain, and marginalize trade unionism. Sanford Jacoby sustains Harris's doleful perspective in his *Modern Manors: Welfare Capitalism since the New Deal* by rediscovering a cohort of powerful "progressive" firms that successfully stymied the union impulse, even when this required outright violation of National Labor Relations Board and WLB directives. Historians of Southern labor and industrialization have never detected much managerial interest there in a postwar accord with the unions. Moreover, Jefferson Cowie's superb *Capital Moves: RCA's 70-Year Quest for Cheap Labor* demonstrates that even when companies avoided an outright confrontation with labor, corporate liberal firms like RCA systematically relocated production to North American sites that were previously thought inhospitable to effective unionism.[22]

Andrew Workman's detailed study of the National Association of Manufacturers (NAM) further sustains the view that most American corporations found war-era corporatism intolerable. The participation of NAM leaders in FDR's 1941 labor-management conference setting up the WLB soon generated a backlash that put a new, aggressive set of antiunion, anti–New Deal leaders in charge of the business group. This hardening of management outlook was best exemplified by the famous 1944 photograph of two fully armed soldiers carrying Montgomery Ward's reactionary chairman, Sewell Avery, out of the corporation's Chicago headquarters. Because Avery had defied a WLB order to sign a collective bargaining agreement with his unionized employees, Roosevelt had the government seize Montgomery Ward. But Avery thereby became a hero to the anti–New Deal right. Thus, by 1945, when the Truman administration tried to orchestrate a postwar compact between labor and capital, the NAM skillfully and determinedly sabotaged the high-profile labor-management conference held in November of that year. Above all, NAM wanted to eliminate the role of the state in establishing an industry-wide incomes policy, and it sought to discipline union strength at the shop floor level. This aggressive stance made unavoidable a massive postwar strike wave and thus helped precipitate the antilabor backlash that saturated American political culture in the years immediately following.[23]

This drift to the right in corporate policy and wartime administrative governance was framed by the consolidation, in Congress and in the national political discourse, of a generation-spanning alliance between Republicans and Southern Democrats. After a careful assessment, Ira Katznelson and his associates have determined that the key element cementing this conservative coalition was the hostility of both factions to the rise of a powerful trade union movement. Until the late 1930s, Southern Democrats supported most New Deal social legislation, albeit with the proviso that such initiatives would protect the Southern racial order and the regional advantages of New South agriculture and manufacturing. But this Southern allegiance to the New Deal collapsed after 1938 when organized labor became a more assertive component within the Democratic Party. Southern pro-labor voting stopped, and in the war-era Congresses an antilabor conservative coalition became dominant. The war cemented the Dixiecrat alliance with the Republicans, because a labor-backed reform of the South now posed a real threat to the racial oligarchy of the region. Wartime labor shortages and military conscription facilitated union organizing and civil rights agitation. Writes Katznelson: "In this more uncertain moment of rapid economic and central state expansion, the South redrew the line between those aspects of the New Deal it would tolerate and those it could not."[24]

But conservative elites did not get everything they wanted in World War II. Even as they increased their influence within the state's labor-relations apparatus, their social and economic power was challenged by a countermobilization from below that sought to take advantage of the unprecedented demand for labor while at the same time actualizing the social patriotic ethos that was the quasi-official ideology of the World War II home front. Indeed this increasingly contentious juxtaposition, between a rightward drifting state apparatus and an increasingly organized and self-mobilized working class, represents the great paradox of the war, a dichotomy that would be resolved in the postwar years by a rapid, politically brutal divorce of popular aspirations from the state policies needed to fulfill them.

In a shrewd critique of *Labor's War at Home*, Gary Gerstle has argued that the working class of World War II "did not just go to work. It went to war." By this he means that war workers took their patriotism seriously, and their war-era cultural standing and social value to the nation perhaps even more so. In 1940 a majority of industrial workers in the North and West were still immigrants or the sons and daughters of immigrants. The coercive Americanization crusades of World War I had been directed at these Poles, Hungarians, Jews, Slavs, and Italians, but the ideological thrust of World War II was far more pluralist. In what FDR called the "arsenal of democracy," the workers became the soldiers of production, and it was now patriotic, not socially demeaning, to take a factory job. Every foxhole movie and war bond campaign celebrated the ethnic heterogeneity of plebian America. Likewise, the new industrial unions were vehicles not only for gaining economic power but also for overcoming cultural discrimination. CIO electoral propaganda in 1944 proclaimed, "All of us in America are foreigners or the children of foreigners . . . They built the railroads, they built the highways, they built the factories . . . They all have equal rights to share in America."[25] Working-class agency during the war therefore represented a culmination of the pluralist impulse inaugurated by the New Deal itself. To Gerstle, rising wages and full employment "in conjunction with the wartime celebration of the nation's multicultural character allowed European ethnics to believe that the American dream had finally been placed within their grasp."[26]

All true, yet in the first edition of *Labor's War at Home*, I devalued the social patriotism of the wartime working class, in part because it was difficult to do otherwise in an era when "hard hat" hyper-patriotism was so crassly manipulated by the Nixon White House.[27] But during World War II, social integration—a belief in the American dream—did not spell social quiescence. Indeed the very sense of Americanism that Gerstle so effectively evokes laid the basis for the claims upon their employers and the state that working-class Americans made with such frequency during World War II and after. Although the character of their aspirations would differ according to their gender, race, age, and occupation, the social-patriotic ethos generated by antifascist propaganda and war-era mobilization politicized new aspects of working-class life.

Take the wage issue, for example. While wartime pay was higher than ever, wages represented more than money to most workers. The level of reimbursement symbolized a worker's social worth, and in years past the pay packet had often been an explicit social marker ranking the status of men and women, black and white, Slav and German. Thus, in a war in which patriotic egalitarianism was a pervasive home-front rationale, and in which workers' pay was a product of governmental fiat, inequalities of all sorts—in pay, promotions, seniority, and general respect—proved to be among the most vexing and persistent causes of shop floor discontent.[28] In his study of the "politics of sacrifice" during the war, Mark Leff finds that the War Advertising Council and other business interests feared such a political construction. They therefore worked strenuously to manipulate and constrain an ideology of equal sacrifice, "to curb its subversive potential."[29]

Indeed, a patriotic subversion of the old order took many forms. Ethnic hierarchies lost much of their potency during World War II, although we also understand that one overripe fruit of the war era's social patriotism, even of its more liberal brand of cultural pluralism, was the transformation of ethnicity into a sense of entitled whiteness. The white working class became more unified, more militant, and more determined to police its own boundaries, both at work, where seniority rights and skill definitions were highly racialized, and even more so in the working-class neighborhoods where the defense of racial exclusivity consistently trumped laborite liberalism. As Tom Sugrue, Kenneth Durr, John T. McGreevy, and Bruce Nelson have shown in such graphic detail, this white defensive militancy became the submerged rock upon which postwar liberalism would splinter, first at the municipal level and later on a larger political stage. The degree to which New Deal pluralism and wartime social patriotism had reconstructed white ethnic America remained somewhat veiled for nearly two decades, until the rise of an antistate, Wallacite discourse in the 1960s gave to this insular racism a political legitimacy it had never before enjoyed, at least outside the South.[30]

By contrast, the legitimacy and visibility of the African American freedom struggle, and that of the Mexican American civil rights movement in the West, took a quantum leap forward during World War II itself. There is not much on this in *Labor's War at Home*, but there should have been, because, with some notable exceptions, most labor historians have postulated that mass industrial unionism has more often than not put the citizenship rights of its members and their families high on the sociopolitical agenda. And this was certainly true during World War II, even taking into account the violent racism of so many in the white rank and file and the hate strikes that periodically exploded in Detroit, Mobile, Los Angeles, and other industrial cities.[31]

There were two reasons for the giant leap forward in civil rights consciousness. First, the war inaugurated a quarter century of African American migration from farm to city and from the South to the North and West. Compared to the Great Migration of World War I, the African American proletarianization experience during the era from 1941 to 1946 (and extended in a continuous fashion until the deep recession of 1957–1958) was broader, longer, and more massive. Second, this process of class recomposition was accompanied by an ideological transformation that pushed the issue of African American political and economic rights to near the top of American liberalism's immediate postwar agenda. Just as the New Deal had offered a new kind of pluralist citizenship to immigrant America, so too did World War II engender a vibrant rights-conscious sense of entitlement among African Americans. This was not because the army or the mobilization agencies or even the newly established Fair Employment Practices Commission (FEPC) were staunch friends of civil rights liberalism. They were not, but the patriotic egalitarianism of the war effort, combined with the creation of a set of state institutions open to grievance and redress, laid the basis for a dialectically powerful relationship—not unlike that of the early 1960s—between social mobilization at the bottom and state building from above. Thus, at the start of the war a reporter for the NAACP's official publication, *The Crisis,* labeled the CIO a "lamp of democracy" throughout the old Confederate states. The NAACP recruited tens of thousands of unionized workers, increasing its membership ninefold during World War II, even as it became a foundational pillar of the emergent labor-liberal coalition.[32]

The flagship agency was the FEPC, established by the Roosevelt liberals to fend off A. Philip Randolph's 1941 March on Washington. The FEPC had little institutional power, but its symbolic import was hardly less than that of the Freedman's Bureau in the early Reconstruction era. "It legitimatized black demands and emboldened protest," writes historian Eileen Boris. FEPC hearings, investigations, and grievance procedures gave African Americans a point of leverage with the federal government that proved corrosive to the old racial order. Despite its embattled status within the state apparat—a Southern filibuster would finally kill it early in 1946—the FEPC's energetic, union-connected, interracial staff served as one of the late New Deal's great mobilizing bureaucracies. As the *Atlanta Journal* sourly put it in 1944, "So adroit are its maneuvers that it is usually out of the picture when any trouble it has started is full-blown. It calls on other government agencies to enforce its decrees and whip dissenters into line."[33]

This kind of mobilization from below, legitimated by government policy from above, also generated a powerful dialectic in the gendered world of consumption politics.[34] Here we find another front in the crucial battle over the relationship between wages and prices that had been so thoroughly politicized during World War II. Indeed, UAW president Walter Reuther would inaugurate the great postwar strike wave with the slogan "Purchasing Power for Prosperity." The key agency in this battle was the Office of Price Administration (OPA). Like the National Labor Relations Board (NLRB) and the FEPC, the OPA's effectiveness depended upon the organized activism of huge numbers of once voiceless individuals. In 1945 OPA employed nearly seventy-five thousand and enlisted the voluntary participation of another three hundred thousand, mainly urban housewives and union activists, who checked the prices and quality of the consumer goods regulated by the government. OPA chief Chester Bowles, a spirited New Deal liberal, called the volunteer price checkers "as American as baseball." Many merchants denounced them as a "kitchen gestapo," but the polls found that more than 80 percent of all citizens backed OPA price-control regulations. In response, the National Association of Manufacturers poured as much money into anti-OPA propaganda as it would later spend on agitation for the 1947 Taft-Hartley Act. NAM called OPA an agency leading to "regimented chaos," an oxymoronic phrase that nevertheless captured business' fear of a powerful state whose regulatory purposes were implemented by an organized activist citizenry.[35]

In recent years many historians, policy makers, and labor partisans have argued for both the existence of and virtue of a "labor-management accord" that governed industrial relations in a generation-long era following World War II. Writing in the early 1980s, economists Samuel Bowles, David Gordon, and Thomas Weisskopf were among the first scholars to identify a "tacit agreement between corporate capitalists and the organized labor movement." Fifteen years later AFL-CIO president John Sweeney himself called for the restoration of the "unwritten social compact" between capital and labor; while Robert Reich, President Clinton's first secretary of labor, jawboned corporations to restore their side of the accord.[36]

Although *Labor's War at Home* emphasized the routinization of conflict in postwar labor-management relations, the book saw this postwar settlement as something quite fragile and hardly a victory for ordinary workers. Indeed, phrases like "social compact" and "social contract" were first deployed in the early 1980s by liberals and laborites who were anxious to condemn wage cuts, denounce corporate union busting, and define what they seemed to be losing in Reagan's America. But such language was altogether absent in the first decades after the end of World War II. Most unionists would have thought the very idea of a consensual accord between themselves and their corporate adversaries a clever piece of management propaganda. Unionists were well aware that no sector of American capital had agreed, even under wartime conditions, to an "accord" with labor or the New Deal state. There was no corporatist settlement, either of the hard variety embodied in tripartite mechanisms of economic regulation, nor in the soft bargaining patterns whereby the unions sought to regulate wages and working conditions—and even company pricing policies—in a single industry. A kind of meso-corporatism did structure a few otherwise highly competitive industries, such as trucking, airlines, railroads, and municipal transport. In those industries the extraordinarily high level of unionization reached during the war—above 90 percent—persisted for three decades afterwards. But such corporatist arrangements came flying apart where management in these competitive industries went on the postwar offensive: first in textiles, where War Labor Board orders were routinely violated in 1944 and 1945, and then in retail trade, electrical products, and all along unionism's white-collar frontier.[37]

Though the destruction of trade unionism in the core midcentury industries—auto, steel, rubber, and construction—was not on the corporate agenda, the depoliticization of collective bargaining was an almost universal goal of these industries' corporate managers. All across the business spectrum, from brass-hat conservatives on the right to corporate liberal statesmen on the left, postwar executives sought to privatize and ghettoize bargaining relationships and economic conflict. The abolition or devaluation of the war era's mobilizing bureaucracies—the War Labor Board, NLRB, OPA, and FEPC—stood near the top of the postwar Republican business agenda. Conflict over the degree to which the unions could still enlist the state in recalibrating the relationship between capital and labor constituted the heart of so many of the celebrated struggles of the postwar era: the 1946 strike wave, the subsequent fight over OPA, enactment of the Taft-Hartley Act in 1947, and the battle over company-paid health insurance and pensions during the 1949–1950 collective bargaining round.[38] By the 1950s the divorce between the system of collective bargaining and American politics was far more complete than in any other industrial democracy. Although midcentury strike levels remained comparatively high, the industrial relations system of that era was so "free" that liberal Democratic political victories in 1948, 1958, and 1964 had virtually no impact upon this increasingly insular collective bargaining regime.

So were there any alternative structures that might have emerged from the labor politics of World War II? In *Labor's War at Home* I saw the wildcat strikers and the militant shop stewards as heroic figures, a vibrant, combative opposition not only to the warfare state but also to management and union bureaucracy alike. But their allure has faded over the years. Labor historians studying midcentury America have fragmented point-of-production militancy into a set of competing impulses, not all admirable from a contemporary standpoint. Meanwhile, almost all historians have become more attuned either to formal political and policy initiatives or to the cultural, racial, and gender substructures that have framed the working-class experience. And in recent years trade union leadership, conservative as well as radical, has won a certain appreciation, if only because of its embattled role in American political life.[39]

Yet the demise of these warfare state rebels remains crucial to understanding the fate of unionism and working-class power in the postwar era. Although the wildcat strikers of World War II never developed the kind of political program or the kind of leadership that could make their perspective fully legitimate, their unpredictable militancy did embody a syndicalist current that kept the old "labor question" a focus of unresolved contention. By standing outside the corporatist structures of the wartime state, these industrial radicals brought into question a whole set of policy and political arrangements: WLB wage ceilings, labor's alliance with the Democratic Party, even the meaning of patriotism in an era of endemic international tensions. They politicized the emergent system of industrial relations by adding a contingent, ideological dimension to issues that state managers, corporate executives, and not a few union officials sought to routinize and consolidate. Their exit from the postwar stage therefore made the union movement a more insular, depoliticized entity, and therefore one of far less potency and promise.

CHAPTER 2

Supply-Chain Tourist;
or, How Globalization Has
Transformed the Labor Question

I'm not much of a tourist, but I'm proud to think that I have visited what are, arguably, the three most important nodes of capitalist production during the last hundred years. When I toured the huge Ford production complex at River Rouge during the winter of 1978, "Detroit," as both organizational metaphor and industrial city, was already well past its prime. But the world of classical Fordism still cast an impressive shadow across the economic landscape and the social imagination. The Rouge then employed some thirty thousand workers in a highly integrated complex of seventeen buildings that sucked in iron ore, silica, and coal at one end and transformed them into steel, glass, axles, fenders, and engine blocks before assembling all of those parts into a set of cars and pickups that were the visible marker of U.S. manufacturing prowess and working-class well-being. You could almost touch it: the giant parking lots, the smokestacks belching hot white vapor from the giant Rouge power plant, the modernist glass-and-steel Ford World Headquarters a couple of miles away, and the suburban swath of single-family, working-class houses that stretched for miles from Dearborn to Ypsilanti. Visit the Detroit Institute of the Arts and you could find the still stunning set of Diego Rivera murals that captured this Fordist world in all its romance and brutality.[1]

Twenty-seven years later I flew into Bentonville, Arkansas, to tour a second node of the capitalist world. It is easy to get there because there are so many direct flights—from Denver, Chicago, La Guardia, and Los Angeles—to this once remote Arkansas town. It is still not very big. Between Fayetteville and the Missouri line there are hardly more than two hundred thousand people. But it is one of the fastest-growing metropolitan regions in the country. In Bentonville, where Wal-Mart maintains its world headquarters in an unimpressive, low-slung building next to the original company warehouse, the parking lots are full, the streets are crowded, and new construction can be found everywhere.

Most important, Bentonville is home to at least five hundred, perhaps a thousand, branch offices of the largest Wal-Mart "vendors," who have planted their corporate flag in northwest Arkansas in the hope that they can maintain or increase their sales to the world's largest buyer of consumer products. Procter and Gamble, which in 1987 may well have been the first company to put an office near Wal-Mart's headquarters, now has a staff of nearly two hundred in Fayetteville; likewise Sanyo, Levi Strauss, Nestlé, Johnson and Johnson, Eastman Kodak, Mattel, and Kraft Foods maintain large offices in what the locals sometimes call "Vendorville." Walt Disney's large retail business has its headquarters, not in Los Angeles, but in nearby Rogers, Arkansas. These Wal-Mart suppliers are a Who's Who of American and international business, staffed by ambitious young executives who have come to see a posting to once-remote Bentonville as the crucial step that can make or break a corporate career.[2] If they can meet Wal-Mart's exacting price and performance standards, their products will be literally sucked into the huge stream of commodities that flow through the world's largest and most efficient supply chain. For any manufacturer it is the brass ring of American salesmanship, which explains why all those sophisticates from New York, Hong Kong, and Los Angeles are eating so many surprisingly good meals in northwest Arkansas.[3]

The final stop on my recent tour of the capitalist world was Guangdong Province in coastal South China. With more than 40 million migrant workers, thousands of factories, and new cities like Shenzhen, which has mushroomed to more than seven million people in just a quarter century, Guangdong lays an arguable claim to being the contemporary "workshop of the world," following in the footsteps of nineteenth-century Manchester and early twentieth-century Detroit. This was my thought when we taxied across Dongguan, a gritty, smoggy, sprawling landscape located on the north side of the Pearl River between Guangzhou (the old Canton) and skyscraper-etched Shenzhen. We drove for more than an hour late one Sunday afternoon, along broad but heavily trafficked streets, continuously bordered by bustling stores, welding shops, warehouses, small manufacturers, and the occasional large factory complex. This is what Michigan Avenue or West Grand Boulevard must have felt like in 1925 or even 1950, before recession and deindustrialization had shuttered the shops, denuded the factories, and silenced the sidewalks.

Because of its proximity to Hong Kong and Macao, as well as its remoteness from the capital, the Chinese government in Beijing chose Shenzhen as a special economic zone in 1979. A few years later the entire Pearl River delta became a virtual free market, with low corporate taxes, few environmental or urban planning regulations, and, most importantly, the free movement of capital and profits in and out of the region. The results were spectacular. Gross domestic product in the Pearl River region leaped from $8 billion in 1980 to $351 billion in 2006. Shenzhen's population rose twentyfold. Guangdong Province itself, which covers most of the Pearl River delta, produces a third of China's total exports. And 10 percent of all that finds its way to Wal-Mart's U.S. shelves.[4]

Although Wal-Mart owns no factories outright, its presence is unmistakable. Its world buying headquarters is in Shenzhen, and it has already built several big stores in the province, with more to come. Wal-Mart is feared and respected by everyone involved with any aspect of the export trade, which is why the executives at the Yantian International Container Terminal in Shenzhen, now the fourth-largest port in the world, give Wal-Mart-bound cargoes top priority. "Wal-Mart is king," a port official told us. Indeed, when we visited there, two of their top executives were on their way to Bentonville. On the same trip managers at the huge Nike–Yue Yuen factory complex in Dongguan bragged that they could fill an order from the States in just two months. Modern highways and bridges speed cargo to the container port, where ships are loaded in half the time it takes California longshoremen to accomplish the same task.[5]

The Rouge, Bentonville, Guangdong: these places represent the past and present of capitalist production, global trade, and management technique. They also signify a new configuration for a "labor question" that once again vexes all of those who work within or comment upon the global pathways that move so much of the world's commerce from one continent to another. Indeed, these regimes of production and distribution, from the Rouge to Guangdong, pretty well mark the arc traveled by my own historical and political imagination. I was part of the New Left generation that "industrialized" in about 1970, following in the footsteps of David Montgomery, Stan Weir, and Archie Green, who were part of the college-educated generation of people who spent a decade or more on the shop floor during and after World War II. I never actually got my hands dirty in this fashion, but for nearly two decades my intellect and my inspiration were shaped by rust belt factories, mills, and mines and the women and men who made them hum—or, better yet, brought them to a silent halt during a work stoppage.

My interest in studying the auto industry and its workers in the 1970s arose from the same motivation that propelled a goodly number of comrades and colleagues to actually get a job at the Rouge, Chevy Gear and Axle, or Chrysler's storied Jefferson Avenue assembly plant. These were the companies, the production facilities, and the workers who occupied the "commanding heights" of the American economy. As management theorist Peter Drucker put it in 1946, when near-continuous warfare between shop militants in the auto factories and their management adversaries seemed to be the fulcrum for an even larger set of class politics: "The automobile industry stands for modern industry all over the globe. It is to the twentieth century what the Lancashire cotton mills were to the nineteenth century: the industry of industries."[6] The production of motor vehicles then held a cultural and ideological importance that made an understanding of this economic sector central to figuring out how twentieth-century society worked.

Henry Ford had once celebrated the machinery of mass production as the "new Messiah," a viewpoint with which the Soviets could find much in common. So if Engels had studied the condition of the working class in Manchester to seek a revolutionary solution to the labor question of his day, my generation would have a similar motivation for its investigation of the social politics of Detroit and the world historic industry with which it was near synonymous.

Of course, the American automobile industry, which had seemed so solid and stolid during the middle decades of the twentieth century, was already beginning to crumble, putting into question the model of corporate governance and working-class organization that went with it. That was too bad, because both academic mandarins as well as left-wing labor historians found a certain tidy logic to the market-making, price-setting supremacy of General Motors, U.S. Steel, and General Electric. These were all vertically integrated manufacturing firms that truly occupied the commanding heights of the U.S. economy and whose organizational template was being reproduced throughout the world. Harvard's Alfred Chandler argued that the visible hand of management had replaced the unpredictable anarchy of the free market when it came to actually running these giant bureaucracies; likewise Peter Drucker had greatly irritated top executives at General Motors when he described their company as an essentially political organization, not unlike that of a state planning bureaucracy, when he published *The Concept of the Corporation* in 1946.

All of this greatly pleased left-wing labor historians of my generation. If the market was indeed a myth, and if a business elite set prices, cartelized markets, determined wage levels, and influenced government regulatory policy, then a politically sophisticated countermobilization—working-class at its core, but also including a popular front of consumers, liberal intellectuals, and partisans of the newly proletarianized immigrants and African Americans—might well shift American politics to the left. The unions and a farsighted labor leadership were obviously central to this project. C. Wright Mills captured the hopes and fears of this labor metaphysic in his 1948 study of the that leadership strata, *The New Men of Power*:

> To have an American labor movement capable of carrying out the program of the left, making allies among the middle class, and moving upstream against the main drift, there must be a rank and file of vigorous workers, a brace of labor intellectuals, and a set of politically alert labor leaders. There must be the power and there must be the intellect. Yet neither the intellectuals nor the workers at large are in a position to take up an alliance and fight against the great trend. The unions are the organizational key to the matter.[7]

It would not be an exaggeration to say that the entire first half of my academic career has been at attempt to figure out why the unions failed to do what Mills and his generation had once hoped they might accomplish. One reason for that failure is that the structure of American capitalism has been transformed during the last third of a century, and with it the agenda of a good slice of the academic left. The rise of Wal-Mart embodies this transformation, but today it is by no means a unique business enterprise. Rather, it symbolizes the power, at home and abroad, of a set of corporations whose structure and outlook differ quite radically from the midcentury manufacturing titans that once seemed so potent and permanent. Today more people are employed in the retail sector of the economy than in all of manufacturing and construction combined. Wal-Mart, with 2.2 million employees worldwide, is by far the largest private sector company on earth, and in terms of the proportion of gross national product that it commands, rivals that of General Motors and U.S. Steel in their heyday. But Wal-Mart owns no factories either in the United States or East Asia; it does not even own or operate the container ships or the four-million-square-foot San Bernardino distribution center that is so crucial to the transshipment of the billions of dollars in consumer products that leave Hong Kong and Shenzhen each month, destined for sale on a million Wal-Mart shelves in more than four thousand North American discount stores. Wal-Mart is not General Motors; there are no unions, most employees are women, and the company manufacturers nothing. But just as GM once set the pattern for wages, working conditions, pensions, and health benefits for a huge slice of the American economy, so too Wal-Mart and its retail rivals do much to construct the nation's employment template today. With the possible exception of the big Wall Street banks, these retailers are by far the most influential enterprises in American business today.

All of this caught us by surprise, and by "us" I don't just mean labor historians. For decades neither economists nor politicians gave retailing the respect it deserved. Shopping was what we did once all the heavy lifting had been sweated out of us: after the steel had been poured, the automobiles assembled, the skyscrapers built, and the crops harvested.

But the new and innovative set of great retailers that emerged by the 1990s were not just huge employers with an enormous stream of revenue; their connections with a global manufacturing network were practically incestuous. They might not own the Asian or Central American factories from which they sourced all those big-box consumables, but their "vendors" were linked to them by a "supply chain" that evoked the iron shackles subordinating slave to master.

Wal-Mart and the other retailers are global companies, but globalization is hardly a new phenomenon. Ford had begun to sell cars abroad as early as 1913, and after 1919 it was truly a worldwide corporation, having rubber plantations in Brazil, dealerships in Great Britain, and assembly plants in Australia and South Africa. Early in the twentieth century, U.S. world trade as a percentage of gross national product was double the proportional size it would achieve in the 1950s and 1960s and not all that lower than it is today. But there is a huge difference between the globalization of Ford and that of Wal-Mart. In the Fordist era, that

Dearborn-headquartered manufacturing enterprise turned the central gear of a supply chain that extended all the way from Brazilian rubber plantations and the Minnesota Iron Range to your neighborhood auto dealer. The manufacturing enterprise—above all, that vast assortment of buildings, machinery, and men that constituted the great River Rouge complex—stood at the center of Ford's purchasing/production/distribution nexus. Indeed, for roughly a century, from 1880 until 1980, during the heyday of domestic, oligopolistic mass production, U.S. manufacturers reigned supreme, often "administering" prices in order to achieve healthy profits and cartel-like control of markets. Even the manufacturers of food items and light consumer goods, like Hartz Mountain, Gillette, 3M, Hershey, Kraft, and Coca-Cola, conducted themselves in an imperious manner when they stocked the shelves of the regional grocery and drug chains that sold their wares.

Today, however, the retailers stand at the apex of the world's supply chains; they use their enormous buying power and highly sophisticated telecommunication links to dominate all aspects of the production/distribution/sales nexus. At least one-half of all global trade revolves around and is driven by the supply chains that have their nerve centers in places like Bentonville, Atlanta (Home Depot); Minneapolis (Target); Troy, Michigan (K-Mart); Paris (Carrefour); Stockholm (Ikea); and Issaquah, Washington (Costco). Using a wide variety of new information technologies, these retailers collect point-of-sale (POS) data and relay it electronically through their supply chain to initiate replenishment orders almost instantaneously. Thus, when Wal-Mart sells a tube of toothpaste in Memphis, that information passes straight through the P & G headquarters office in Cincinnati, flashing directly to the toothpaste factory in Mexico, which adjusts its production schedule accordingly.[8]

Wal-Mart is therefore not simply a huge retailer, but increasingly it has become a manufacturing giant in all but name. The retailer tracks consumer behavior with meticulous care and then transmits consumer preferences down the supply chain. Replenishment is put in motion almost immediately, with the supplier required to make more frequent deliveries of smaller lots. This is just in time for retailers, or "lean retailing." To make it all work, the supply firms and the discount retailers have to be functionally linked, even if they retain a separate legal and administrative existence. The giant retailers of our day, Wal-Mart first among them, "pull" production out of their far-flung network of vendors. The manufacturers no longer "push" it onto the retailer or the consumer. Or to extend the metaphor, the nearly continuous stream of container ships that move between Shenzhen and the Long Beach/Los Angeles port complex are "pulled" across the Pacific, not "pushed" by the Chinese manufacturers who stuff their product into nearly half a million forty-foot containers each year. Moreover "pull" production requires speed, predictability, and accuracy in the delivery of goods. "Supply chain management"—the new business school buzz phrase—is the "science" of getting this to happen in the most efficient and cost-effective way.[9]

All of this has made life increasingly difficult for workers both at home and abroad. The rise of a system of global supply chains, with their multilayered set of factories, vendors, and transport links, has created a world system in which legal ownership of the forces of production have been divorced from operational control. This shift has generated a system in which accountability for labor conditions is legally diffused and knowledge of the actual producers is far from transparent. In effect, we are building a universal sweatshop in which we have unleashed the same unregulated competitive pressures that once made life so miserable in London's East End or on the Lower East Side of Manhattan. The globally dispersed system of production that exists today means if workers fight for their rights in one factory, the manufacturer might well shift its production to another, "friendlier" one—often in another country. Just as tenement sweatshops opened and closed in rapid succession a century ago, so too are contemporary factories readily moved around the globe, even from China, which has reportedly lost manufacturing to other Asian countries (such as Vietnam) as a result of rising wages and the implementation of a new contract-labor law.[10]

"Globalization" is too sweeping a word to describe this new regime or the new labor question it has engendered. I prefer the historically resonant term "merchant capitalism." The retail-dominated supply chains that now organize such a large proportion of international trade herald the return to prominence and power of a particular organizational form in the history of world capitalism that we once thought was long past. Merchant capitalism was and is a form of market exchange, primarily in commodities, in which traders, shippers, merchants, and financiers play key roles over and above the commodity producers and manufacturing enterprises of our time. The last time such a system reigned supreme came in the century before the American Civil War, when the sale and distribution of cotton, tobacco, sugar, and wheat was controlled by the great trading companies and financial institutions of New York, Liverpool, and London. Like the global retailers of our time, they favored free trade, a weak regulatory state, transnational production, and cheap, if not unfree, labor. They were often partisans of the Southern cause, not unlike contemporary retailers who find that authoritarian regimes in Asia, Central America, and parts of Africa are most hospitable to the kind of sweated labor that lies at the base of their giant supply chains.[11]

And it is an economic structure whose global reach, political agenda, and labor relations bulwark the conservative, neoliberal turn that has shifted politics and economic policy to the right throughout those North Atlantic nation-states that once seemed so firmly on the road to social democratic regulation of the market. Contemporary merchant capitalists, like their antebellum ancestors, favor a weak state and an unregulated market, thus limiting the capacity of any polity to regulate and structure labor and employment standards. Needless to say, this thinning of state capacity is not what Karl Marx had in mind when he predicted the withering away of the state.

Nevertheless, the decline of the regulatory state and the manufacturing-based trade unions that once sustained it is having a large impact on the way scholars and activists conceive of the modern labor question and its remedies, making some of the ideas and movements that came to the fore in the nineteenth century relevant once again. Although the socialist idea is certainly in eclipse, the definition, measurement, and advocacy of human rights now constitutes a pervasive way we define the extent to which individuals hold and exercise citizenship, both civic and industrial. Indeed it was in precisely such circumstances that the world's first human rights nongovernmental organization (NGO), Britain's Anti-Slavery Society, came to play an outsized role in curbing the excesses that flowed from the merchant capital regime. And like today's NGOs, it deployed the weapons of the weak: investigation, exposure, moral suasion, and boycott. Similar groups on both sides of the Atlantic, including the Congo Reform Association, the Consumer's League, and the NAACP, would later utilize many of these same approaches in their efforts to resolve that bundle of social pathologies that constituted the labor question of their era.[12]

Today many NGOs exist that monitor, expose, berate, and measure the working conditions and environmental standards that are present in the factories from which Wal-Mart and other retailers source their product. Human Rights Watch, the Fair Labor Association, the Worker Rights Consortium, and the numerous Hong King–based groups keep the pressure on Wal-Mart, Nike, Disney, and Target. In response, Wal-Mart and all the other retailers have developed their own sometimes quite elaborate codes of social responsibility. The effectiveness of these internal monitoring arrangements is subject to considerable debate. In general they have some impact at the margins, but they make no fundamental transformations in how Wal-Mart goes about purchasing its goods or how its contractors go about producing them.[13]

It is revealing, of course, that so much international attention now attaches to the development and implementation of these codes of conduct. In the heyday of American Fordism, most critiques of the social impact of industrial capitalism were directed toward the key manufacturing enterprises, largely by trade unions and the government, but sometimes by organized consumers as well. It is a tribute to and indication of the shift in the structure of world capitalism that we now direct our concern toward the brands and retailers that today stand at the apex of their global supply chains. That is because the essence of the twenty-first-century labor question, as well as its resolution, no longer resides at the point of production in a struggle between workers and the owners of the factories in which they labor. Instead the site of value production in the contemporary world is found at every link along a set of global supply chains, in which the manufacturer and the warehouse operator, the ports and the shipping companies, the retailers and their branded vendors jockey for power and profit. To tame this system we'll need ideas and institutions, social movements and new legal structures that are truly global in their ambition and effectiveness.

But at this point in the early twenty-first century, no set of voluntary organizations, worker alliances, governmental organizations, or rival economic institutions has generated either the will or the wherewithal to transform these retail-driven supply chains. And that is why Wal-Mart and its clones occupy so much terrain along the heights of our world economy and why, for this historian as well as so many other scholars, these companies have become such a source of fascination and disdain, not unlike that once commanded by the great automobile enterprises headquartered in or near Detroit.

CHAPTER 3

Historians as Public Intellectuals

What's great about writing history is that everyone likes a good story, that academic jargon can often be kept to a minimum, and that a big readership, of a book or a blog, is rarely sniffed at as pandering to the crowd. Many historians find an audience far larger than that of their own professional discipline. Fulfilling such ambitions may be far easier today than two or three decades ago, because even if newspapers and journals of opinion are struggling, the Web, the blogosphere, and all the other social media have opened the door for just about anyone to be a pundit or a professor with worldwide reach. Editors and other gatekeepers have lost a lot of their veto power, their journalistic prestige, and their financial clout. With a little moxie, just about anyone can get thousands of people to read their stuff on virtually any conceivable subject—and sometimes make a living at it.

Does this make for an abundance of "public intellectuals"? Ever since Russell Jacoby published *The Last Intellectuals* in 1987, academics of my generation have aspired to fill the vacuum Jacoby so provocatively identified.[1] Unlike an earlier generation of intellectuals—Dwight Macdonald, Mary McCarthy, Daniel Bell, and I. F. Stone are prime examples—who wrote for the educated public, often without an academic pedigree, today's thinkers, so ran the Jacoby indictment, have flocked to the universities, where the politics of tenure loom larger than the culture of politics. Too many intellectuals wrote only for each other in an increasingly narrow disciplinary vein, thus abdicating moral responsibility and cultural influence. In their place came a "public sphere" filled with facile journalists, think-tank policy mavens, and celebrity authors. As one might expect, conservative writers and publicists thrived in this atmosphere, if only because they generally had far fewer qualms than those on the left when it came to partisan policy analysis and culture-war polemics.

Jacoby's charge was overstated. True, the public intellectuals who seemed so prominent in the 1930s and 1940s had not originally come out of the academy. But in the postwar years, the universities, including the humanities, proliferated; offered more posts to aspiring scholars; and for the most part dropped the genteel anti-Semitism and anti-Catholicism, as well as the overt racism and institutional sexism, that had barred the gate to so many of the wrong sort. History departments all across the country were now home to men and women who had migrated to academia and to historical work precisely because it seemed the discipline most subversive of existing pieties and, if done right, a form of literature that might actually inspire others to action. Many in my New Left generation had a dusty copy of Edmund Wilson's *To the Finland Station* stashed somewhere on their back shelves. More relevant yet was C. Vann Woodward's *The Strange Career of Jim Crow*, which, when first published in 1955, put at the service of the civil rights movement and its vision of a desegregated South the authority and expertise of the nation's most distinguished historian of that same region. And if C. Wright Mills had been abandoned by most mainstream sociologists, he remained an icon among historians like myself who sought to move beyond postwar pluralism in our quest for an understanding of where power and prestige lay within the American body politic.[2]

But it was not just that Mills, Woodward, and Wilson enjoyed a large audience. Rather, their oeuvre carried a moral weight that they projected onto everything they wrote, even when their expertise did not extend quite so far. Their voices enjoyed respect in part because they spoke at a time when lay Americans, including those on the left, took for granted a kind of cultural hierarchy that venerated the voice and work of those who wrote for *Partisan Review,* who taught at Columbia and other elite schools, or whose books appeared on the *New York Times* best-seller list. There are still writers and academics who enjoy such prestige: the late Tony Judt and Christopher Hitchens come to mind; likewise Garry Wills and Paul Krugman, and among historians Eric Foner, Gordon Wood, Robert Darnton, and perhaps Michael Kazin, now co-editor of *Dissent.* Among the younger historical set, Jill Lepore writes insightful essays for the *New Yorker,* while Timothy Snyder's morally fraught commentaries on the multiple tragedies that engulfed Eastern Europe in the 1930s and 1940s now appear regularly in the *New York Review of Books.*

But most historians are still specialists whose public voices are directly dependent upon the expertise their books, articles, and talks have exhibited. I never write about the latest novel, art exhibit, or Middle East entanglement. For the lay audience I opine on pretty much the same topics to which I devote my scholarly energies: the history and status of the labor movement; how American capitalism is changing its shape; and what writers, activists, and intellectuals have had to say about all that. When I write an opinion piece in the *Los Angeles Times* or, more rarely, the *New York Times*, or when I give an interview to National Public Radio (NPR) or a print reporter, the topic is almost always one of the above. So for people like myself, I think the phrase "public intellectual" is often a pretentious one; more accurate and appropriate would be something like "activist intellectual," "labor intellectual," or a descriptor that actually reflects my institutional authority, which is why I normally identify myself as "Director of the Center for the Study of Work, Labor, and Democracy" at the University of California, Santa Barbara.

In one of his early books, C. Wright Mills made the point that writers and intellectuals do not seek to sway "public opinion" in some undifferentiated fashion. They are not like executives at a soap company who make a large media buy in order to shift the purchasing habits of millions. Instead the body politic is composed of a series of quite distinct "political publics." These are self-conscious and politically alert slices of the population, "communities either of ideology or interest that bring to bear a particular sensibility to the issues of the day." They in turn formulate the ideas and programs that operate in the consciousness of what Mills called "the passive atomized mass." In his day Mills identified five such publics, ranging from small groups on the radical left to a large and excitable liberal center and on to the sophisticated conservatives on the right, the elite Eastern bankers, lawyers, and politicians—the architects of the Cold War—who, Mills asserted, know what they want, want it all the time, and work patiently and effectively for its realization.[3]

Mills thought intellectuals were efficacious when they spoke to and for such "publics." And that is still true. With a very few exceptions, almost everyone who writes for the public is actually writing for one of these "publics," albeit a rather different set from those existing in Mills's time. The Web, with its plethora of well-focused blogs and online magazines, has made this much easier, but so too has the polarization and fragmentation of the political culture, probably greater today than in the past. *Life* magazine, with its five million weekly subscribers, is long gone, likewise the hegemony of the three major networks, and when it comes to our "newspaper of record," I think those on the right are correct to see the *New York Times* as standing for cultural pluralism, political liberalism, and a cosmopolitan worldview.

So what is my public? It might best be thought of as those who think of themselves in some self-conscious way as social progressives, those who are partisans, not of the labor movement as it now exists, but of one they hope can be reformed and rebuilt, as well as those in and around the academy who are interested in such questions. They read *Dissent*, *New Labor Forum*, the *Nation*, and *Talking Points Memo*. I therefore find it enormously gratifying when I hear a union staffer say that my book *State of the Union: A Century of American Labor* is one of the assigned texts in the union's educational program, or when I am invited to speak before a community group, including the local chamber of commerce or Rotary Club, or to talk on a show like NPR's *Marketplace*. In all of these appearances I am leveraging the status and expertise that comes with being a professor to advance a set of historical understandings upon which a set of progressive politics and policies can be built.

I first realized how this could work in the mid-1990s when I joined with some historian friends to use the credibility and visibility of an academic perch to make a few waves in the political culture. In 1995 John Sweeney, then president of the Service Employees International Union, led an insurgency within the AFL-CIO that ousted an old guard whose lineage went back to Lane Kirkland, George Meany, and the stand-pat unionists who had denounced the New Left, ridiculed feminists and gays, and supported the war in Vietnam. Many on the left greeted this changing of the guard with something less than enthusiasm. They had either written off the labor movement as an agent of social change or had noted, correctly, that Sweeney's ascension was closer to a palace coup than a broadly based social insurgency. But there was more at stake here than a mere rotation of chairs at the top. For decades the liberal academy had been at odds with the unions. The last iron curtain to fall was the one that divided New Left historians from those union leaders who sat around the huge oak conference table on the sixth floor of the AFL-CIO's marble headquarters, located right across from the White House.

Steve Fraser and I were then in a good position to set some ideas in motion. Steve, who worked in publishing, had just written a remarkably illuminating biography of Sidney Hillman, the CIO founder, who was also the longtime president of the Amalgamated Clothing Workers union. And I had just published a well-received biography of Walter Reuther, the unionist whose relationship to the left has always generated so much argument and debate, which is more than one could have said about George Meany and his circle. These biographies therefore made us "experts" on labor leadership, with credibility in the union movement and in the press, if not always among our comrades and friends on the left, including the academic left, who always had their own take on the relationship between formal union leadership and the social currents that had to be set in motion to transform the polity. Steve and I had few illusions about Sweeney and company, but we hoped that if left-leaning academics might once again orient some of their political aspirations toward a revitalization of the labor movement, then the unions themselves could be nudged toward a more open and activist social and cultural outlook.

So in early 1996 we organized a letter to the *New York Review of Books* that in carefully modulated terms hailed the accession of a new generation of labor leaders to the top offices at the AFL-CIO. A star-studded cluster of academics, ranging from old-time liberals like Arthur Schlesinger Jr. to the distinguished philosopher Richard Rorty, signed on, and after the letter appeared in the *NYRB*, it quickly spread throughout the known email universe.[4] This told us our ideas had legs, so we put together a committee of academics, including people like Joshua Freeman, Manning Marable, and Eric Foner, to organize a "Teach-in with the Labor Movement" at Columbia University. Held in October 1996, this was a spectacularly successful event, which put on the same podium John Sweeney, Betty Friedan, Cornel West, and Richard Rorty.[5] Thereafter, some dozen or more lesser labor teach-ins were held across the country, forging, for the moment at least, a kind of popular front between the new union leadership and the left academy. For the historically minded among us—and we were all historically minded—it recalled the days of the CIO/National Citizens Political Action Committee (1943–1947). The wall that had once so clearly divided the academic left from the nation's union leadership had been breached. Thereafter, we were "labor intellectuals," called upon by reporters at the *New York Times, Los Angles Times,* and NPR to comment on the labor movement in particular and the whole movement of the political economy in general.

A word may be in order here about the relationship between journalists and the academic experts that they consult and quote in their reportage. I fear that my chief claim to fame as a labor intellectual has been as a sound-bite provider for these reporters. Why do they call us up: people like Harley Shaiken at UC Berkeley; Ruth Milkman, Josh Freeman, and Stanley Aronowitz at CUNY Graduate Center; Michael Kazin at Georgetown; Kate Bronfenbrenner at Cornell; and Richard Freedman at Harvard? From some of these people, reporters really do get important, fresh social science research: Freedman, Bronfenbrenner, and Milkman have conducted important investigations into the ills that plague contemporary unions and the world of work, and there are many others who do similar investigations.

But for the historians, our function is somewhat different. The reporters who cover the labor beat want a broader viewpoint by individuals whose attachment to the university cloaks them with an ostensible objectivity. Sometimes they want a historical analogy, imperfect as that might invariably be. At other times reporters just want to ratify a point that they have already begun to develop, but they need an "expert" to drive it home.

For example, there was a labor/business reporter at the now defunct print edition of the *Seattle Post Intelligencer* who called me up on occasion for my opinion about the latest twist in the chronic warfare taking place between the Boeing Company and its unionized machinists. Of course, I knew nothing about those complex collective-bargaining negotiations, which came as no surprise to the reporter. So he filled me in on the details and, as he hoped, I then offered him a quote reflecting the perspective of the trade unionists. The latter were either unwilling to make the same kind of statement, or the reporter feared that their views might be discounted too easily. But to avoid charges of journalistic bias, the reporter in question then immediately made another call, this to a business school professor or similar management-oriented expert, to get a statement reflecting the corporate viewpoint. Why all of this phoning around? The reporter was the expert here, and we academics, left or right, were just kibitzers. But in our contemporary journalistic culture, the reporters needed a legitimized source to make the points they already knew must go into their reportage. And that is one of the functions, perhaps the most common, performed by academic authorities.

My involvement with the contemporary debate that now swirls around Wal-Mart business practices represents a somewhat more authentic intervention by an academic functioning as an engaged intellectual. This commitment began in 2003 and 2004 during a long, painful grocery strike in Southern California when seventy thousand workers struck or were locked out of area stores in a dispute triggered by Wal-Mart's imminent penetration of the California supermarket industry. The unions had considerable support on the picket line and among many shoppers, but they were notably inept at explaining the larger issues that made the strike such an important national conflict. At one moment they told reporters Wal-Mart was irrelevant because it still had only a small footprint in the California grocery industry; at another they denounced the Arkansas company as the "Beast of Bentonville." So I was once again on the phone to a lot of local reporters, who educated me about the specific issues in the strike. In turn, I rummaged through my understanding of labor and business history for analogies that would put the current conflict in some larger context.

At one point the director of the UC Santa Barbara Interdisciplinary Humanities Center, with which I was associated, asked if I could put together a debate with a Wal-Mart spokesperson. This struck me as improbable, but the idea of a public event considering the importance of that big company was now in motion. A lot of others were interested too, so after about a month of emails and phone calls, I had put together a pretty good conference, which I titled "Wal-Mart: Template for Twenty-First-Century Capitalism?" Held on April 12, 2004, the timing of the conference could not have been better. The strike finally ended in February, a major defeat for the unions, but on April 7 the citizens of Inglewood, California, rejected a Wal-Mart-sponsored referendum that would have put a huge Supercenter in their community. And the *Los Angeles Times* had just won a Pulitzer Prize for a series of articles on the "Wal-Mart Effect."

The power of the *New York Times* cannot be underestimated, at least in academe. When labor reporter Steven Greenhouse gave our conference a big play on the front page of the now defunct "Arts and Ideas" section, I was once again crowned an "expert" on a contemporary social issue.[6] I tried to use this platform to argue that Wal-Mart now occupies the same strategic high ground in the world capitalist system that manufacturing companies like General Motors or U.S. Steel commanded half a century and more ago. And if Wal-Mart was so powerful, as a de facto "legislator" of contemporary American social policy, then it must necessarily become subject to governmental regulation and the countervailing power generated by trade unions and local governments. This argument must have struck a nerve, even among the Wal-Mart brass, because in February 2005 then Wal-Mart CEO H. Lee Scott delivered a speech titled "Wal-Mart and California: A Key Moment in Time for American Capitalism" to a Los Angeles business audience. The speech was a point-by-point refutation of the ideas put forward at our conference and in a *New York Review of Books* essay by the British journalist Simon Head, who had participated in the Santa Barbara event.[7]

Conferences of this sort, which mobilize historians, sociologists, legal scholars, and others to explore the larger meaning of a contemporary historical controversy, political issue, or social phenomena, have been among the most rewarding and successful ventures I have undertaken as an academic activist. We have explored the way intellectuals have thought about twentieth-century capitalism; probed the politics and ideas that motivated the young New Leftists who wrote the 1962 Port Huron Statement; analyzed the ideological and legal structure of right-wing antiunionism during the last century; and examined the success and failures of the International Labor Organization in establishing a set of enforceable labor standards.[8] By bringing together twenty or thirty like-minded scholars and activists, one can begin to identify common problems, set a realistic agenda, and tilt the larger conversation, within the academy and without, in a fruitful direction.

That has also been the aim of the series of op-ed writing workshops that my Center for the Study of Work, Labor, and Democracy has hosted. I've always thought that as a matter of course, all scholars should write for a larger lay public. The ability to translate one's academic expertise into an invitingly readable eight-hundred-word package is a skill, the essence of which can be taught by those journalists and writers who have themselves mastered the art. So from across the country we have periodically assembled historians and other academics for such workshops. Among the teachers have been Ruth Rosen, the noted historian of American women who for many years was a *San Francisco Chronicle* columnist; Rick Perlstein, the biographer of Barry Goldwater, Richard Nixon, and Ronald Reagan; and Harold Meyerson, a public intellectual in his own right as well as an editor at the *American Prospect* and columnist for the *Washington Post*.

Every historian should be a public intellectual. Such work not only makes use of their academic talents but also marks them as engaged citizens in a world where one's voice is just as important as the vote in the maintenance of a vibrant democracy.

PART II

Capital, Labor, and the State

In order to reform capitalism it is necessary to know where the power to reshape it lies, from the commanding heights of Wall Street and Washington to the gritty combat over authority and pay in thousands of factories, offices, and stores. This seems obvious, but too often social historians have ignored any serious probe into the changing character of U.S. enterprise, especially when they studied the structure of the firm in the years after the great merger movement at the turn of the twentieth century. Thus I have long been appreciative of the work of Gardiner Means and Adolf Berle, who published *The American Corporation and Private Property* in 1932. In keeping with the larger ethos of the New Deal, they argued that the subordination of the mass of shareholders, the lawful owners of the enterprise, to an autonomous and self-interested management cadre provided the reformist rationale for the exercise of power by other stakeholders, including government regulators and organized labor.

This idea reached its fruition in the World War II years and immediately thereafter when a species of corporatism gave voice to New Dealers and their labor allies in the construction of an American social contract. For almost two decades key decisions involving wages, prices, and the relative power of labor and capital would be the product of a set of political conflicts and bargains, many resolved in the Oval Office itself. That form of governance, which I discuss in this section's "From Corporatism to Collective Bargaining," collapsed within a few years after the end of the war when the corporations successfully put in place an increasingly privatized system of collective bargaining.

To the extent that the legitimacy and authority of management had been weakened during this era of corporatist experimentation, the distribution of power was up for grabs in much of shop floor America. I explore this conflict by looking first at the emergence of a distinctive supervisory interest within the corporation, given voice and clout by the brief but brilliant mid-twentieth-century trajectory of independent foreman unionism in the automobile, coal, and other industries. These "men in the middle" were responsible for labor discipline, so their failure to identify with the larger managerial ideology proved a significant threat to traditional lines of corporate authority. Passage of the Taft-Hartley Act in 1947 stripped foremen of the protections of the American labor law, but maintaining the loyalty of this strata has often remained problematic even at resolutely anti-union companies like Wal-Mart. The defection of the first-line supervisors was but one cause and consequence of the remarkable burst of trade union militancy that engulfed many factories in the 1940s and early 1950s. To what extent did this phenomenon coincide with Communist influence and leadership of those same unions? I explore this relationship in the last essay in this section, concluding that whatever the virtues of Communist militancy when it came to racial and gender equality, as well as the distribution of authority within the workplace, the fatal linkage between such salutary activism and the larger Stalinist politics of those same militants did much to make that kind of shop floor power anathema within American political culture.

CHAPTER 4

Tribunes of the Shareholder Class

It is surely a coincidence that the tragic destruction of the World Trade Center, located just a few blocks from the New York Stock Exchange, and home to so many stock, bond, and currency traders, was followed within the same decade by two other events that had significant impact on America's financial industry: (1) the self-destruction of Enron and WorldCom, and (2) the 2008 world financial crisis, which did even more damage. These calamities are of vastly different meanings, but they do serve to illustrate just how naturalized, normalized, and pervasive giant corporations and their financial handmaidens have become in contemporary American life. The Enron implosion was dramatic, the largest bankruptcy to that time in history, and the 2008 meltdown was truly cataclysmic, but neither disaster seems to have had much of a ripple effect in either our politics or business culture. In the contemporary United States, corporate capitalism is truly hegemonic.

This was not always so. In the post–Civil War history of American capitalism, the New Deal represented the most powerful, sustained, and culturally resonant effort to transform the corporation and accommodate it to an ethos that was far more democratic and pluralistic. The New Deal now seems radical to us, but only because we have become so complicit with the idea that the great American corporations are resistant to any fundamental reform. Indeed the ideological impulse behind the New Deal effort was neither socialist, anticapitalist, or authoritarian, but it was a radical experiment nevertheless, certainly when measured against the tepid reforms of recent years. The Great Depression was the occasion, the opportunity, the event that generated the ideological vacuum into which new ideas about corporate governance could pour. But those ideas had been germinating for more than a generation.

The key text for this effort, the book that a contemporary described as "the law, the logic and the philosophy of the New Deal," was *The Modern Corporation and Private Property*, published in August 1932 by Adolf Berle and Gardiner Means. Berle was a lawyer and Means an economist. Both were the offspring of

Congregational ministers, and both were familiar with the practical operation of the American corporation. Their collaboration began before the financial crash; indeed, when the book appeared three years later, they hardly took note of the Great Depression, because their argument hardly depended upon the existence of an immediate economic crisis.

But the book, which instantly became a controversial classic, provided an ideological rationale for New Deal planning, consumer activism, labor organizing, and financial regulation of the large corporation and by extension of all American capitalism. Berle and Means argued that America's two hundred largest corporations, which then controlled one-third of the national wealth, had themselves abridged the fundamentals of a liberal capitalist order. Berle and Means were not Brandeisian "small is beautiful" trustbusters. The giant corporation was "the flower of our industrial organization." Concentration was a problem, but not for its own sake. Something more fundamental was wrong in that the immense power of those who ran America's largest corporations was essentially unfettered, not only by the state but also by those who were their ostensible masters: the shareholder themselves. This is why Adolf Berle was happy to think of himself as the Karl Marx of the shareholder class.[1]

Wrote Berle and Means: "It has often been said that the owner of a horse is responsible. If the horse lives he must feed it. If the horse dies he must bury it. No such responsibility attaches to a share of stock. The owner is practically powerless . . . The spiritual values that formerly went with ownership have been separated from it . . . the responsibility and the substance which have been an integral part of ownership in the past are being transferred to a separate group in whose hands lies control."[2]

Not only had oligarchy replaced competition, but also, and of even more consequence, management usurped the prerogatives of traditional ownership. If the shareholders had therefore lost control of the corporation to a set of unelected, self-perpetuating managers, then the modern corporation could best be understood not in terms of "the traditional logic of property and profits . . . not in terms of business enterprise but in terms of social organization." And like the church, the military, and the state, such power had to be either regulated or democratized if a republican government were to exist. The rise of these illegitimate controlling elements, with their potential for abuse, have now "placed the community in a position to demand that the modern corporation serve not alone the owners or the control but all society."[3]

Over and over again they wrote, the American corporation has "ceased to be a private business device" and has become "a major social institution." This critique exemplified a turn toward the "socioeconomic" mode of reformist thought identified by Howard Brick in his *Transcending Capitalism: Visions of a New Society in Modern American Thought*. With Thorstein Veblen, who denounced the "make-believe" property rights of modern shareholders, and Rudolf Hilferding, who postulated a new era of "organized capitalism," Berle and Means rejected the vocabulary of Adam Smith.[4] Private property, private enterprise, individual initiative, the profit motive, wealth, and competition have simply "ceased to be accurate" ways of naming the most important features of modern business.[5] The financial manipulations that had become such a scandal during the 1920s, and that have reemerged in the years since the decay of the New Deal order in the 1970s, have disrupted, distorted, and delegitimized the whole system of private capitalism. Thus did Charles Beard applaud the book as the most important work bearing on American statecraft "since the federalist papers," while fifty years later the conservative economist George Stigler remarked ruefully, "There was no better date in modern history to launch an attack on the large corporations than 1932, and no better place than New York City."[6]

Indeed, Berle and Means wrote during an era when the shareholder-owned "public corporation" seemed to be the indispensible locomotive of capitalism. This was the era, as Julia Ott reminds us, when the New York Stock Exchange and big, investor-owned corporations such as American Telephone & Telegraph declared themselves the harbingers of a new era of shareholder democracy.[7] Such institutions had been invented in the mid-nineteenth century, and by the 1930s this ownership model, whatever its flaws, seemed destined for an exceedingly long life. Hence came the importance of the Berle and Means defense of the stockholders, the public, and the employees over and against an elite and self-serving managerial caste. But it is important to recognize that the public corporation was and is a historically rooted phenomenon that flourished during a particular moment in the history of capitalism. By the end of the twentieth century, it had grown fragile and had acquired potent competitors. The average life expectancy of public companies shrank from sixty-five years in the 1920s to less than ten in the 1990s. There were many more bankruptcies than in earlier decades. In the West private equity firms and tight-knit partnerships have flourished in finance and high tech, while in Asia family-owned conglomerates and state-owned enterprises have driven economic expansion. All of these competitors to the public corporation have done away with shareholders and, through subcontracting and outsourcing, huge numbers of directly employed workers as well.[8]

So the New Deal of Berle and Means came at a propitious moment in the history of the corporation. Adolf Berle was a sometime speechwriter for President Roosevelt, but his ideas were so potent and so resonant that just one year after its publication, *Time* magazine labeled *The Modern Corporation and Private Property* "the economic Bible of the Roosevelt administration."[9] By the time FDR accepted his party's nomination for a second term at the 1936 Philadelphia convention, the president's denunciation of the "money changers" and "economic royalists" skillfully combined an appeal to long-entrenched populist sentiment with some of the analytical outlook of Berle and Means.

> Out of our modern civilization economic royalists carved new dynasties. New kingdoms were built upon concentration of control over material things.

Through new uses of corporations, banks and securities—all undreamed of by the fathers—the whole structure of modern life was impressed into this royal service . . .

The privileged princes of these new economic dynasties, thirsting for power, reached out for control over government itself. They created a new despotism and wrapped it in the robes of legal sanction. In its service new mercenaries sought to regiment the people, their labor, and their property.

The hours men and women worked, the wages they received, the conditions of their labor—these had passed beyond the control of the people, and were imposed by this new industrial dictatorship. The savings of the average family, the capital of the small businessman, the investments set aside for old age—other people's money—these were tools which the new economic royalty used to dig itself in.[10]

So if those who control these giant public corporations had demonstrated the illegitimacy of their power, what could be done about it? As a Roosevelt brains truster, Adolf Berle and other like-minded reformers played a large role in writing some of the key regulatory laws of the early New Deal, laws designed to correct the specific abuses illuminated by *The Modern Corporation and Private Property* and the many books, investigations, and congressional hearings that followed. Three pieces of legislation in particular—the Securities Act of 1933, the Securities Exchange Act of 1934, and the Public Utility Holding Company Act of 1935—addressed the issues Berle and Means raised in their book: the transparency of financial activities, equal treatment between corporate insiders and outside shareholders, and some limitation on the concentration of control in basic infrastructure industries.[11] We know something about the importance of such regulation, and the resistance offered by those who will be regulated, simply by recalling how difficult it has become to regulate contemporary finance, even in the wake of such huge scandals as Enron, WorldCom, and the 2008 banking meltdown.

But of far more importance than these pieces of regulatory control, whose efficacy would become attenuated in the long run, was the early New Deal impulse to get inside the black box of the corporation and transform it in some democratic and pluralist fashion. Berle and Means and other Depression-era reformers wanted to make American capitalism more legitimate by creating a set of countervailing forces that could challenge and restrain the control deployed by managers and financiers, whose unaccountable power had so deeply eroded the whole edifice of American democracy. Between the revolution and unconstrained capitalism lay a middle way. New Dealers like Berle and Means thought that if capitalism were to survive, "the control of the great corporations should develop into a purely neutral technocracy, balancing a variety of claims by various groups in the community and assigning to each a portion of the income stream on the basis of public policy rather than private cupidity."[12] What the New Deal promised, according to Berle, was to serve as a "counterbalance [to] the effects of organization gone wrong." The New Deal acted by "mobilizing industry and requiring it to meet the responsibilities of an income-distributing group."[13]

New Deal regulation required the mobilization of new groups and new elements of the body politic. By far the most important such countervailing force was a reinvigorated labor movement whose voice and clout was essential if incomes were to be raised and if a highly regulated capitalism was to function in an equitable fashion. Labor's voice was crucial to New Deal capitalism because the trade unions themselves possessed an intimate understanding of business practice, conditions, and outcome. Only they could "enforce" government-mandated minimum-wage standards and maximum-hour regulations. As retailer Edward Filene noted wryly in 1933, "Our labor unions have a better understanding of what is good for business today than our chambers of commerce have."[14] Self-organization was essential, argued Robert Wagner, to ensure that "the fruits of industry must be distributed more bounteously among the masses of wage-earners who create the bulk of consumer demand."[15]

Historians today recognize that New Deal advocacy of a bountiful consumption—what labor leaders like Walter Reuther would later call "purchasing power for prosperity"—did not generate an insular or depoliticized privatization of family or community life. A century before, when the "producing classes" bulwarked a virtuous republic, the designation "consumer" seemed not far removed from that of the dysfunctional "parasite." But the New Deal worked an imaginative revolution: mass consumption now stood shoulder to shoulder with mass production as a foundational component of both a humane capitalism and a reinvigorated democracy. The New Deal and the new labor movement took the nascent consumer culture of the twentieth century and made of it a political project. An "American" standard of living was becoming a right of citizenship, and if the achievement of that new entitlement required a radical transformation of the American political economy, so be it. Roosevelt's secretary of labor, Frances Perkins, put it this way in 1933: "If . . . the wages of mill workers in the South should be raised to the point where workers could buy shoes, that would be a social revolution."[16]

Far from generating a sense of passive dependency, New Deal relief programs, especially those involving work and wages, generated an active sense of citizenship. Indeed, against fear and dependency the New Deal counterposed "security," precisely in order to generate that participatory democracy desired by the founders. So universal was this security consciousness that even opponents of the New Deal sought to champion that aspiration. At the 1939 New York World's Fair, the Equitable Insurance Company sponsored a "Garden of Security." Nine years later the militantly conservative National Association of Manufacturers admitted, "The employee's urge for security is stronger than ever, and every company has responsibility to make maximum provision . . . to cushion employees against the economic hazards."[17] And of course every post–World War II president has borrowed moral capital from the New Deal when they invoke "national security."

Berle and Means's book on corporate governance struck a chord because most reformers and radicals believed a great contradiction lay at the heart of American capitalism. Outside the walls of the private enterprise, American political culture celebrated a Jeffersonian world of free speech, democratic participation, and masterless autonomy. But within the corporate world and the nearby industrial municipalities, autocracy, obedience, and social deference were the order of the day, bolstered by a century of legal precedent and business practice. When confronting their employers, American workers had no statutory right to free speech, assembly, or petition. In the reactionary era right after World War I, thousands of unionists were fired, blacklisted, and literally forced out of town. The judiciary stubbornly adhered to an imaginary world of "free labor" in which individual workers freely and equitably negotiated their pay and perks with those who hired them at the great corporations that now bestrode the land. Pro-union workers called the town of Aliquippa, Pennsylvania, "Little Siberia" because of the czar-like rule of the Jones & Laughlin Steel Company. The company's president, Tom Girdler, was a paternalist who paid good wages and boasted that his door was always open. But "we couldn't call our souls our own," reported a fearful steelworker. "We couldn't think unionism."[18]

The remedy was "industrial democracy" predicated upon a thoroughly republican sense of democratic governance. New Deal–era advocates of "industrial democracy" were Whiggist evolutionaries who viewed the new system as simply the next stage in the flowering of American freedom. It encompassed collective bargaining, of course, but it evoked a far more ambitious social agenda. On the shop floor industrial democrats envisioned an "industrial jurisprudence," a constitutionalization of factory governance, and the growth of a two-party system that put unions and managers on an equal footing.[19] An "American standard of living" for employed workers would be bulwarked by an entitled social "security" enfolding the rest of the population. "Industrial tyranny," asserted Senator Robert Wagner, was "incompatible with a republican form of government."[20] The bourgeois norms celebrated in U.S. courts and civil society—due process, free speech, the right of assembly and petition—would now find their place in factories, mills, and offices. This was a radical prospect indeed and a frightful threat to property and its prerogatives.

The counterattack would not be long in coming and it was manifest on two fronts. The first has been related to the growth in the ideological and moral authority of the managerial strata that was the object of such scorn by Berle and Means. The second involves the very structure of the firm so as to make its regulation or democratization far more difficult.

The re-legitimization of corporate management began during World War II when "dollar-a-year men" and other corporate executives linked the government-funded production success to a sense of renewed prestige for corporate America. That era of militarized Keynesianism also proved remarkably seductive to many erstwhile critics of corporate power. Instead of worrying that the separation of ownership from control would lead to the hegemony of an overweening and self-interested executive strata, many students of postwar management saluted that same division between shareholders and executives as an entirely salutatory, even an anticapitalist or postcapitalist, development. "We now know that management is a generic function of all organizations, whatever their specific mission," wrote Peter Drucker in *Post-Capitalist Society.* "It is the generic organ of the knowledge society."[21] Corporate managers, now freed from their subordination to those who legally owned the corporation, could pursue goals other than profits, including sales, growth, and the prestige that came from producing high-quality products of advanced technology. "Progress Is Our Most Important Product," asserted General Electric in one of its midcentury advertising campaigns. And as Ralph Dahrendorf put it, "Never has the imputation of a profit motive been further from the real motives of men than it is for modern bureaucratic managers."[22]

All of this seemed antiquated by the end of the 1970s, a decade characterized by a chronic profit squeeze and stock market slump. The rise of foreign competition began to put major U.S. firms under enormous pressure while at the same time depriving reformers of the idea—and perhaps the reality—that the top two hundred corporations monopolized so much of the market. In any one country that might still be true, but now the playing field was truly global. There were no longer three car companies with an oligopolistic grip on one continental market, but nearly a dozen global competitors in this key industry, thus for the first time in decades subjecting the once insular managers at Ford and General Motors to real competitive pressures and an insecure hold on power. When the GM board, frustrated by the Japanese competitors who had stolen market share, actually fired CEO Robert Stempel in 1992, the shock waves spread far and wide.

Indeed, many firms now seemed ripe for a takeover by another set of managers who could, in the parlance of the time, boost "shareholder value," now increasingly seen as the essential raison d'être of the firm. By the end of the 1980s, nearly one-third of all companies on the *Fortune* 500 had received takeover bids during the previous decade.[23] Through mutual funds and pension funds, stockholders finally seemed to hold real power and could on occasion directly influence corporate policies. Today a new economic theory of the firm has shifted the focus of corporate law and analysis from questions of social and economic power to the maximization of value for investors—from collective concepts to individualist ones, thus sharply devaluing the message Berle and Means offered three-quarters of a century ago. As Dalia Tsuk put it in a recent history of the rise and fall of their influence, the law and economics scholars of the 1970s and 1980s turned the corporation—a social, economic, and political organization—into a "contractual arrangement, a tool of making profits for investors."[24] So powerful has been their impact that even after the dramatic collapse of the banking system in 2008, the "too big to fail" financial institutions have proven remarkably successful in staving off, in the name of market efficiency and economic recovery, any effort to impose regulations of the sort that emerged with such power during the Depression decade.

The second development that has marginalized the work of Berle and Means has arisen from how new technologies and organizational strategies have transformed the legal and moral burden under which corporate managers now function. In the late 1920s, when Ronald Coase, then a young British socialist, first spent time in the United States, he visited Detroit and came up with a puzzle: how could economists say that Lenin was wrong in thinking that the Russian economy could be run like one big factory when Ford, General Motors, and other vertically integrated firms seemed to be doing very well indeed? They were privately owned planning bureaucracies, a point Peter Drucker would later make in his own far more extensive study of GM management. But not all corporations were gigantic. Some were small, highly competitive, and limited to just one part of the value production chain. In his seminal essay of 1937, "The Nature of the Firm," Coase answered his own query with an insight about why firms exist in the first place. They do function like centrally planned economies, he wrote, but unlike in the Soviet Union, where coercive methods are the norm, in a capitalist economy differential market or transaction costs determine the degree of vertical integration of any given firm in any given market. If markets were costless to use, firms would not exist. Instead, people would make arm's-length transactions. But because markets are costly to use, which is a function of transport and communication expense, the most efficient production processes often take place in a firm, which requires a managerial strata necessary for non-market coordination. Alfred Chandler would later historicize this insight in his masterwork *The Visible Hand: The Managerial Revolution in American Business*, published in 1977.[25]

The last few decades have seen technological and organizational developments which, in effect, have stood Coase and Chandler on their heads. The vertically integrated firm is in the process of disaggregation. All the big automakers have either spun off or kept commercially separate the parts production infrastructure that remains essential to their business. Apple makes no computer products, but purchases them from Foxconn and other Asian vendors. Likewise, the rapid growth of subcontracting, outsourcing, and independent contracting among workers who used to be directly employed by a large firm has become endemic within the service and transport sectors of the economy.

All of this is most dramatically apparent in the rise of the big-box retailers who command a set of global supply chains, made possible by the telecommunications revolution, innovations in container shipping, and the growth of low-cost East Asian manufacturing. These supply chains are functionally well integrated and utterly dominated by big-box retailers like Wal-Mart and Home Depot. Managers in Bentonville, Atlanta, and elsewhere exercise the kind of organizational control that once so alarmed Berle and Means. Deployment of checkout scanners and product bar codes creates a flow of data so great and potent that it has given retailers the upper hand over manufacturers and wholesalers when it comes to an intimate knowledge of sales, customers, and pricing. Retailers therefore have the capacity to contract, even for time-sensitive products, where labor is cheap and manufacturers eager to do their bidding.

However, this tight coordination takes place not by formally integrating the supply chain into one legal corporate entity, but by making the market itself a hyperefficient mechanism whereby management exercises its will and power. Therefore, the great retailers of Europe and the United States have no legal responsibility, or even much moral responsibility, for those who labor along many of the links in their supply chain. In China and elsewhere millions of workers supply the products that end up on the shelves of all the big-box retailers. But none of these people work directly for Wal-Mart, Target, or the other big retailers who require the production of such a continuous stream of consumer durables. Most firms have established "corporate social responsibility" staffs, but such initiatives are but a pale substitute for the absolute legal and administrative responsibility that reformers once thought a core function of management.[26] Today the argument of Berle and Means—that corporate power requires a measure of outside control and internal democratization—holds little purchase. This is not because the market itself fulfills these tasks, but because the ideology of the efficient and self-correcting market holds such a grip on the imagination of so many.

CHAPTER 5

"The Man in the Middle"

A Social History of Automobile Industry Foremen

The study of frontline supervisors—in the factory, office, hospital ward, and academic workplace—is once again making waves. The quest for a more efficient, and perhaps more humane, workplace all too often begins with advice and admonition directed toward those who are charged with supervising the daily work lives of the dozen or so individuals who fall under their direct authority. Many of the management handbooks for sale in this nation's airport bookshops purport to explain how one can either get along with an irascible boss or, conversely, offer tips on making the staff work productively and harmoniously with their immediate supervisor. Such advice manuals echo an even older set of studies that bemoan foremen and forewomen as "men in the middle" of the workplace hierarchy. They were the "marginal men of industry" whose jobs were in desperate need of reform.[1]

Not unexpectedly the National Labor Relations Board (NLRB) and the federal jurists have periodically recalibrated their definition of what constitutes the managerial strata in a wide variety of industries and worksites. Since the passage of the Taft-Hartley Act in 1947 virtually all of this redefinition has moved in a direction that is pleasing to corporate ownership. They have happily "promoted" millions of workers into the ranks of management, not to actually enhance their paycheck or their privileges, but to forcefully ensure their "loyalty" by making it legally impossible for them to join a trade union or exercise other democratic rights.[2] In an expansive study of this phenomenon, historian Jean-Christian Vinel rightly observes that corporate insistence upon the "undivided loyalty of its management" has become the "bulwark protecting the hegemony of the business world against the encroachment of freedom of association."[3]

Unfortunately, much of this discussion, especially that in even the most sophisticated business journals as well as in the sociological and industrial relations literature, has had an ahistorical quality that assumes that the traditional role played by foremen and other frontline supervisors has been determined exclusively by either the technology of production or the structures of management.

These have been important, but they cannot be divorced from either the larger politics of production or the changing consciousness of foremen and supervisors in the first half of the twentieth century.

Foremen in the Mass Production Factory

This essay seeks to uncover a slice of this complex history by emphasizing how cultural and political forces, as well as structural changes in the organization of work, shaped the role foremen played in the factory hierarchy. During the late 1930s and early 1940s, the changing collective identity of this stratum not only sustained a brief experiment in foreman unionism but also challenged the structure of authority inside the production facilities of the nation's premier industry. In the process foremen began to explore and expand the definition of what constituted a self-conscious working-class identity at midcentury.

In their studies of the early twentieth-century factory, historians Daniel Nelson and Stephen Meyer have demonstrated that the deployment of Frederick Taylor's ideas on management was only possible with the virtual destruction of the shop floor "empire" commanded by many nineteenth-century foremen. The power, autonomy, and prestige of both "inside contractors" and skilled mechanics could not survive where both the technology and organization of production were geared to scientifically managed mass production facilities. As factories became larger and work more compartmentalized, and as production became standardized and coordinated, the foreman-contractor—who bid on a job, hired the workers, and then determined the pace, layout, and methods of work—vanished from the factory. Likewise, the skilled worker, who at one time might have employed a couple of helpers out of his own pay, became a toolmaker or repairman who served a vital though auxiliary role in the mass production facility.[4]

Much of the skilled work was taken over and systematized by a burgeoning managerial stratum, including a growing corps of engineers, accountants, clerks, inspectors, and personnel managers. In those industries that began to approach the ideal of mass production—rubber, meatpacking, oil, chemicals, automobiles—production line foremen had little say in scheduling or engineering and only a slight voice in the maintenance of the production facility or the control of product quality. Foremen did have some responsibility for cost control, and they sometimes kept rudimentary production and personnel records, but these tasks were often taken over by specially trained clerks in the larger factories.

With technical production decisions centralized, the foreman's role in recruiting, promoting, and firing his workers also underwent a dramatic transformation. Managerial awareness of the large cost of worker turnover, especially during World War I, led many firms to set up personnel departments that did much of the recruiting, testing, and assignment of the workforce.[5] By the end of the 1920s about 65 percent of some 224 large factories surveyed by the U.S. Department of Labor had a central employment office handling hiring for the plant. All the major automobile companies recruited through a central office in 1930, and more than 80 percent of the surveyed firms in the iron and steel, petroleum, refining, and food processing industries did as well. Centralized hiring enabled large firms to more easily maintain age and health standards, establish more uniform wage rates, and screen unionists and other undesirables. Foremen still had the right to reject a recruit in their department, and they could use their influence to facilitate the hiring of a friend or relative, but such action was the exception, not the norm, in the core firms of the auto industry.[6]

"Getting Out Production"

Despite these genuine limitations on their power, foremen retained one essential function: they were responsible for labor discipline, for "getting out production" on time and up to standard. Style and technique might vary, but this would remain the first-line supervisor's basic responsibility decade after decade. In 1912 an *Iron Age* correspondent noted that under Ford's new production setup "the foreman in each department is purely a production man." His "particular duty" was "to see to it that the men under him turn out so many pieces per day and personally work to correct whatever may prevent it."[7] Forty years later foremen in a unionized auto plant told Yale University researchers virtually the identical story. "Ninety percent of my job is knowing how to break in and handle men," reported one foreman on the final assembly line. "It is very easy for the men to rebel, and then things go to hell before you know it."[8]

To maintain labor discipline production foremen held several social and organization weapons. First, the sheer number of foremen increased dramatically in the first two decades of the twentieth century. In auto plants and other continuous-flow production facilities, the sequential and integrated character of production made the careless or recalcitrant worker a costly threat to overall efficiency, far greater than when small batch production was the norm. Close supervision was therefore essential. At Ford's Highland Park factory the ratio of foremen to production workers increased at a phenomenal rate. In 1914 one foreman directed an average of fifty-three workers; in 1917 each supervisor oversaw the work of only fifteen. In manufacturing industry as a whole, the number of foremen increased more than 300 percent in an era when total employment did not quite double.[9]

Second, production foremen still held almost unlimited authority over the work lives of the men and women they supervised. Foremen had the unfettered right to assign jobs of varying levels of pay, difficulty, and pleasantness, and their voices went far beyond their jurisdiction in determining promotions or transfers. While establishment of central personnel offices had deprived foremen of their ability to hire workers off the street, managers were still extremely reluctant to deprive first-line supervisors of the right to discharge employees. As one manager put it in 1926, the "foreman in the last analysis cannot help being a personnel man."[10] In the auto industry, employment managers and higher officials retained the sole right to discharge a worker in almost three-quarters of all firms surveyed in 1930, but this formal authority was rarely used to countermand a foreman's disciplinary action for fear of "demoralizing" the workers in his department. In this industry, reported economist W. Ellison Chalmers in 1932, "a strong position in favor of keeping the authority in the hands of the foremen" meant that employment managers "very seldom straighten the case out for the worker unless the foremen and superintendent agree on giving the man another chance." Most large auto firms declared a commitment to "adjust difficulties" between worker and foreman, but in few cases did higher-level management make a foreman work with an employee he sought to discharge. At Ford workers had the right to petition a discharge to the company's employment office, but even if they were vindicated there, such workers were always transferred to another department.[11]

When it came to layoffs, foremen had even greater unilateral power. In theory, some combination of efficiency, seniority, and family responsibility determined the layoff order during slack times, but in practice foremen had enormous discretion in making the individual selections. During the brief recession in 1927, for example, the National Industrial Conference Board, a business group, found that 90 percent of the firms it surveyed allowed their foremen to make the initial evaluation of who would be laid off; 60 percent left the layoff decision entirely up to the foremen.[12] Autoworker Clayton W. Fountain recalled in later years how the application of this power looked to the average worker:

> The annual layoff during the model change was always a menace . . . The bosses would pick the men off a few at a time, telling them to stay home until they were notified to come back . . . The foremen had the say. If he happened to like you, or if you sucked around him and did him favors—or if you were one of the bastards who worked like hell and turned out more than production—you might be picked to work a few weeks longer than the next guy.[13]

On the assembly line, and in closely related departments where semiskilled labor predominated, a foreman's authority was further advanced through the mediators he chose among the workforce itself. These were the variously named petty functionaries—crew chief, lead man, pusher, setup man, gang boss, and straw boss—who, in contrast to the foreman, spent most of their time in actual production. Foremen selected these workers to see that their orders were actually carried out and the pace of production maintained. Setup men were generally experienced or clever workers who made the initial adjustment when a machine was installed or its workload altered. Paid a nickel or so more than production workers, setup men were also responsible for determining, in consultation with the foreman, the pace or quota of the new machine operation. Pushers and lead men, also paid a few cents an hour above the norm, were selected because of their loyalty and propensity to hard work. They were placed in those strategic locations in the production process, such as the first man on a subassembly crew, where their own work rhythm could automatically set the pace for the rest of the working gang.[14]

Finally, the straw boss played a key role. Straw bosses, sometimes called working leaders or speed bosses, were combination pusher, relief man, spy, and all-around foreman substitute. "What we call a straw boss," reported the Communist militant Bill McKie in 1934, "is a man who is not officially recognized as a foreman in the Ford plant, but is usually appointed by the foreman himself to look after particular gangs."[15] They were often chosen because they were of the same ethnic or language group as their work crew, thus enabling them to more effectively transmit the foreman's orders. Unlike lead men, straw bosses might not be continually engaged in production, but their responsibility for hurrying the work was still at the core of their duties. When the Ford Motor Company was struggling out of the postwar recession in 1922, management doubled the number of straw bosses to intensify the work pace.[16] Indeed, straw bosses could be difficult taskmasters, as Frank Marquart remembered from his stint at Chevy Gear and Axle: "One night I had machine trouble and fell behind in production. The straw boss, a sub-human pusher who had the authority to hire and fire, bellowed like a bull. When I tried to explain that I had machine trouble, he roared: 'I don't give a damn what you had, you get out production or you get fired—That's the rule around here, and no goddamn excuses.'"[17]

Interwar Cultural Values

A foreman's power and his sense of social identity were also sustained by a set of social and cultural expectations that were largely intact until the 1940s. Most auto industry foremen took home wages about 25 percent higher than the men they supervised. More important, their paycheck was a good deal more predictable because managers sought to keep a core of experienced men employed even during large layoffs. Such employment stability enabled foremen to purchase solid houses in the better working-class neighborhoods and maintain a standard of living that approached that of the lower middle class. The overwhelming majority were married, and their children had good prospects of completing high school. Compared with the average production worker, who frequently changed jobs and firms during layoffs and recessions, foremen stayed put and amassed some of the greatest seniority of any group in the midcentury industrial plant. In one survey conducted in the 1940s, foremen were found to be about fifteen years older than even the average member of the white-collar staff and had a turnover rate about one-third as high.[18]

A Protestant, lower-middle-class outlook was one of the most distinctive elements of the foreman's worldview in this era. In the prosperous 1920s, when ethnic cleavages were most manifest, first-line supervisors easily maintained a set of values that, on the surface at least, emphasized self-improvement, organizational loyalty, and unhyphenated Americanism. This outlook served to distance this overwhelmingly Anglo-Saxon and German group from the heavily Catholic, immigrant working class and linked them, if somewhat tenuously, to the white-collar workers and the bureaucratic culture of corporate America. Advancing this orientation were the popular foremanship training classes offered by the YMCA in the first four decades of the twentieth century, and the company and community foremen's clubs that proliferated throughout many of the middle-sized industrial cities of the Midwest. Part social club and part business association, the management-dominated National Association of Foremen emphasized education, self-advancement, and social intercourse between foremen in different industries and between foremen and top management.[19]

As both ideology and social network, Freemasonry played a particularly influential role in sustaining this supervisory work culture. Reaching its greatest popular influence in the 1920s, Freemasonry stood for brotherhood and respectability and propagated a creed of sober self-improvement, conventional morality, and class harmony. Lower-middle-class white-collar workers composed about half its membership, and skilled craftsmen accounted for another 15 percent. Masons maintained an elaborate ritual, reinforcing a sense of social selectivity, but the quasi-religious elements that had infused nineteenth-century Freemasonry gave way to a more secular content that easily accommodated itself to the commercial culture and respectable evangelicalism of urban white-collar workers and small businessmen. It is not surprising therefore that many foremen joined the order: Masonry's anti-Catholic, Americanist flavor strengthened the lines that divided them from much of the factory workforce; moreover, its emphasis on the social and moral links between men of divergent occupations and class standings gave credence to top management's insistence that once promoted out of the workforce, foremen were now part of the company's "management team."[20]

Aside from its ideological message, Masonry served as a factory social network that partially overlapped the formal hierarchy of management's power and authority. At the Ford Motor Company, Protestant workmen proudly wore their Masonic rings with the expectation that membership in the organization would win them a promotion to foreman or at least protect them from the sometimes capricious discipline meted out by the company's infamous service department. Since Ford boss Harry Bennett was an active Mason, there was indeed some validity to the anti-Masonic charge that it was "not what you know, but who you know" that won advancement in the Ford organization. As foundry foreman Roy Campbell remembered the mid-1930s, "If you wanted to get anyplace or hold a job with any responsibility you better be a Mason." Almost all general foremen there were Masons, and although some particularly bright and ambitious Catholic workmen were promoted to the supervisory ranks, these foremen remained under considerable pressure to join the order. Masonic influence was also pervasive among supervisory employees at Kelsey-Hayes, Packard Motor Company, and Cadillac in Detroit and at General Motors–controlled North American Aviation in California.[21]

The Wrong Side of the Collar Line

By the end of the 1920s automobile industry foremen seemed to have found their place as tough, loyal sergeants in the management hierarchy. Yet auto industry foremen would soon demonstrate that despite their formal role in management they were in fact an integral part of the working class itself. This was true in two ways. First, foremen were subject to a wide set of social and organizational influences that brought their interests into a parallel relationship with that of their subordinate workmates. Foremen had higher wages and more authority, but, as we shall see, their factory role was far closer to that of a semiautonomous skilled worker than a management official. Second, their consciousness was never a simple reflection of their place in the factory hierarchy. When a mobilization of rank-and-file workers broke open the social mold of the traditional factory in the late 1930s, foremen became subject to a dynamic set of pressures propelling them into a de facto alliance with the brand of militant industrial unionism that was then sweeping the auto industry.

Foremen stood on the wrong side of the collar line; they got their hands dirty, they were recruited directly out of the workforce, were rarely salaried, and wore work clothes that were almost indistinguishable from those of the average worker. At Ford foremen wore the same numbered badge as did other workers in the plant; the great social dividing line there was drawn between those who were on salary—they had a star imprinted on their metal badge—and the vast majority of hourly workers. At the Rouge foremen had neither desks nor telephones; they kept their few records at little stand-up "pulpits" close to the department they supervised. They were not often skilled craftsmen, but their work values had much in common with such workers. They took enormous pride in the efficient, autonomous operation of their department. At Ford and Chrysler foremen were routinely expected to know how to set up and run the machines of all the workers they supervised, and they were proud of their ability to solve production problems without assistance or interference from higher levels of plant supervision.[22]

The production-oriented outlook of such foremen had a Veblenite flavor when they came into conflict with higher management, especially the college-educated, and sometimes condescending, white-collar staff. These staff specialists were frequently resented, not only by foremen but also by general foremen and plant superintendents. Sociologist Melvin Dalton found that such line personnel shared a blue-collar production culture. They referred to their white-collar superiors as "college punks," "slide-rules," and "chair-warmers." "First-line foremen were inclined to feel that top management had brought in the production planning, industrial relations and engineering staffs as clubs with which to control the lower line," concluded Dalton. "Hence they frequently regarded the projects of staff personnel as manipulative devices and reacted by cooperating with production workers . . . to defeat insistent and uncompromising members of the staff."[23]

Although foremen were responsible for labor discipline, even this task was full of ambiguity. They themselves were the objects of a managerial effort to rationalize and intensify production, but first-line supervisors were also subject to the intimate and unremitting social and psychological pressure generated by the workers under them. In the 1940s it became a passionately held axiom of corporate spokesmen that foremen were part of management, but executives as early as 1926 recognized that "the foreman stands on the middle ground between management and employee." He had a "dual personality: to the company he represents the workman, to the workman he is the company."[24] This tension made foremen both the "master and victim of doubletalk," concluded the famous industrial psychologist Fritz J. Roethlisberger. "The foreman is management's contribution to the social pathology of American culture."[25]

The pressures generated by the daily world of work drew foremen into a degree of informal accommodation with their subordinates. Foremen spent the bulk of their workday not with higher-level management or other foremen, but with a production crew upon whose efforts the foreman's own success depended. A measure of friendly cooperation was therefore essential to efficient production, and a degree of psychological accommodation was vital if foremen were to avoid the isolation and ostracism of which even a nonunion work crew was capable. Thus, foremen often shared many of the same attitudes toward their job as did ordinary production workers. They wanted predictable work quotas, stable piece rates, and steady work. They wanted a smoothly running department, which meant they wanted to avoid conflict with both management above and workers below.

When Stanley Mathewson took his working tour of industrial America in 1930, he found numerous instances in which foremen or straw bosses "conspired" with their workers to thwart the will of the managerial staff. "They don't want the rate cut any more than we do," one worker told Mathewson. "It just makes the men sore and causes a lot of trouble."[26] Fifteen years later sociologist Donald Roy found foremen just as hostile to time-study people, "the true hatchet men of upper management." In the Chicago machine shop he studied, Roy found that foremen tolerated the elaborate stratagems workers devised to bend the piecework rules. "You've got to chisel a little around here to make money," one foreman asserted.[27] And in the more authoritarian setting of GM's Framingham, Massachusetts, assembly plant, a postwar foreman defined one of his prime duties as that of social "shock absorber," with the "ability to take pressure from above, but not pass it on."[28]

A region of chronic conflict between foremen and their supervisors came in the realm of manpower management. Unforeseen equipment breakdowns, schedule changes, and absenteeism always seemed to keep foremen on the short end of the manpower stick—or so it appeared to them. This made the foremen's job much more difficult; sometimes they had to do the production work themselves, but more often it forced them to drive the men harder or to scurry around in search of stray workers in other departments to fill the gaps. Thus, foremen were often reluctant to grant workers adequate relief time on the job, and they could be harsh disciplinarians when it came to unauthorized absences. But by the same token, foremen sought to maintain a certain "fat" in their manpower roster, ready for use when the inevitable emergency arose. In the early 1930s W. Ellison Chalmers was surprised to find that many Ford workers considered themselves in alliance with their straw bosses or foremen against the plant superintendent and the company's notorious service department. Foremen penalized obvious idleness, he reported in 1934, but they also told workers that any loafing should be done by leaning against the inside of a car body, where they would not be spotted by the service personnel. This subterranean conflict between foremen and managers was more systematically confirmed after World War II.[29] Charles Walker and his team of researchers from Yale found that absenteeism, along with quality control, was the most vexing problem faced by foremen at GM's Framingham plant. "It seems to me that if I can't be trusted to judge how many men I need, I shouldn't be a foreman," reported one first-line supervisor in final assembly. "We just get treated as if we can't be trusted."[30]

The Impact of the New Industrial Unionism

Given the conflicting pressures under which foremen functioned during the interwar era, the organization of strong industrial unions in the late 1930s was bound to precipitate a major crisis for first-line supervisors. The empowerment of workers at the shop floor level proved the central thrust of the union movement in its early years. Almost by definition, therefore, the success of this effort required the diminution or elimination of the power traditionally exercised by foremen. "With the coming of the Union, the foreman finds his whole world turned upside down," asserted a United Automobile Workers (UAW) stewards manual. "His small-time dictatorship has been overthrown and he must be adjusted to a democratic system of shop government."[31] The transformation in power relationships could be dramatic. "First we had to cut down the size of those hard-boiled foremen," recalled a Dodge worker. "Sometimes foremen would jerk up the automatic conveyor a couple of notches and speed up the line. We cured them of that practice: we simply let jobs go by half finished."[32]

A more subtle but hardly less important erosion of foreman power took place as the new unions developed a set of uniform regulations to govern shop floor working conditions. Seniority rules, job bidding, and grievance procedures gave workers an elementary sense of job security, because these contractual devices sharply limited the foreman's ability to either reward or punish his subordinates. In the early years union shop stewards often patrolled their department to police the contract and maintain informal contact with their men. When grievances arose, most contracts insisted that stewards first take them up with the foremen for immediate resolution. But in a situation where the union's shop floor strength was clearly manifest, stewards often "short-circuited" the foremen, taking their grievances directly to plant management, where the real power lay. Executives and superintendents frequently cooperated in this operation; either they doubted the loyalty of the foremen, or they considered union problems far too important to be left to the lowly foremen.[33] "Sometimes the employer stands behind the foreman," complained a Murray Corporation supervisor in 1943, "but more frequently the foreman is thrown to the wolves."[34]

Unionism in the automobile industry also had the effect of stripping foremen of the lead men, pushers, and straw bosses who projected their authority in the shop. Most workers hated these petty tyrants, and the new UAW insisted that any individual who worked on production had to be a union member; therefore, these intermediate categories were either upgraded to full foreman status, eliminated, or refined. Setup men became "special operators," while straw bosses lost their disciplinary and production control function, becoming instead the slightly higher paid "relief" or "utility" workers who rotated jobs as members of the work crew took their breaks. At the Rouge foundry the very second grievance handled by committeeman Shelton Tappes involved the status of some ninety straw bosses there. Forty-two were upgraded to foremen, but the rest lost their quasi-supervisory status and were returned to production worker roles. Working leaders were also eliminated in most production departments or made part of the union, where they still played a functional role, as in tool and die work.[35]

As shop stewards exhibited their power and foremen lost their departmental corporals, managers compensated for the changing equation of shop floor power by substantially increasing the number of first-line supervisors. For example, in the railroad operations of the River Rouge plant, unionized yardmasters assigned switch orders to the crews and oversaw their execution. By 1945 Ford management had concluded that supervision needed to be tightened up. The existing foremen, spread over three shifts, were inadequate for the job. So Ford eliminated the yardmaster job and assigned twelve additional foremen to the yard.[36] In like manner, the ratios of foremen to production workers, which had ranged as high as 50:1 on line operations, were now sharply reduced. At the Rouge 2,226 foremen supervised 67,360 workers in July 1935; eleven years later 3,020 supervised a workforce that had shrunk by 3,853. Thus, Ford's foremen-to-worker ratio increased about 50 percent.[37]

Indeed, the 1940s was an era of large increases in both the absolute numbers and in the proportion of American manufacturing foremen. While the ratio of foremen to production workers had remained static between 1920 and 1940, the next decade saw a 70 percent increase in the number of foremen and a 21 percent increase in the ratio of first-line supervisors to the production workforce.[38] This phenomenon was not merely a product of the conversion and reconversion of U.S. industry to war production, for the foreman-to-worker ratio continued to increase in the next few decades as well.[39]

Foreman Unionism

Although rank-and-file militancy eroded the power enjoyed by manufacturing foremen, the union idea also promised fundamental changes in the role foremen would play in the twentieth-century factory. During the next decade many foremen sought to win for themselves some of the same protections against managerial authority that the unionized rank and file had already begun to secure. This meant that foremen would enjoy the protections of a seniority system, a grievance procedure, and a rationalized wage structure. But beyond this, foreman unionization also held out the vision of a more radical transformation as to how work and authority would be organized in the midcentury factory. Foremen, after all, were the linchpins of a hierarchical, bureaucratic work process, and any fundamental change in their status necessarily reverberated throughout the factory social structure.

Foreman unionism arose in those places where the new Congress of Industrial Organizations (CIO) unions had proven most disruptive to the old order. At the Kelsey-Hayes Wheel Company, a labor-intensive parts plant, shop conditions were revolutionized by UAW Local 174, a militant union led by a coalition of radicals that included the famous Reuther brothers. Within a few weeks of the organization of the five-thousand-worker plant in late 1936, wages almost doubled and a strong steward system was installed. Swept up in this movement, Clarence Bolds, a veteran foreman with an older brother active in the International Typographical Union (which had long organized pressroom foremen), began urging foremen to join Local 174. Bolds's efforts were encouraged by the UAW—he spoke at the local's joint council meetings—but his work first bore fruit during the recession of 1938 when Kelsey-Hayes forced foremen to take a 10–15 percent salary reduction and a two-week stretch of work at half pay. Since the wages of the company's production workers were protected by a contract, the benefits of unionism seemed manifest.

In December 1938 Bolds and a group of Kelsey-Hayes foremen won a charter from the CIO as United Foremen and Supervisors, Local Industrial Union 918. Although Bolds had lobbied for direct affiliation with the UAW, auto union activists in Local 174 were not entirely convinced that the foremen might not be or become corporate pawns. In any event, the independent union expanded rapidly, recruiting almost 100 percent of the Kelsey-Hayes supervisory workforce in a couple of weeks and then winning a cancellation of the wage cut. Local 918 won few written contracts but nevertheless soon expanded to at least sixteen other Detroit plants and enrolled more than nine hundred foremen.[40]

In practice Local 918 functioned in a close alliance with the UAW. For example, at the Universal Cooler Corporation, the local negotiated a contract (really a supplement to the UAW agreement there) that provided foremen with grievance adjustment, seniority protection, and a two-week vacation. But the clause that foremen pointed to with at least equal satisfaction read: "It is mutually agreed and understood that the Universal Cooler Corporation will not demand or request any act or action whatever of its supervisory employees which would tend to strain or break the existing harmonious and fraternal relationship between United Foremen and Supervisors and the UAW and Local 174." To one foreman, this simply meant: "No longer are we to be forced to treat employees like heels."[41] Bolds himself cast the cordial relationship he expected to build with the production workers union in a radical light. "With the organization of foremen and supervisors into a bona fide labor union," Bolds asserted in the *Michigan CIO News*, "management loses its last outpost in the plants, and organized labor gains a valuable ally." He went on to say: "Management loses its cat's paw, the one it always used to pull its chestnuts from the fire . . . It loses the group it used as a union busting, union baiting force and through which it spread false rumors to cause internal dissention in labor's ranks . . . The threat of strikebreakers becomes less than nothing, for without supervision to show them how and what to do, they are helpless."[42]

An early conflict involving CIO foremen occurred at Chrysler during the UAW's long, bitter strike in the fall of 1939. The central issue in this work stoppage was the union's effort to win joint control of production standards at the corporation's Dodge Main, Dodge Truck, and Jefferson Avenue plants. After the UAW swept Chrysler's NLRB elections in the spring, Chrysler locals had orchestrated a series of slowdowns and stoppages to demonstrate union strength. With some 500 "white button" stewards at Dodge Main alone, the UAW maintained a powerful shop floor presence to neutralize the power of management's lower-level officials and spread union influence throughout all phases of the production process. Chrysler replied by firing some 150 union activists in August, which in turn precipitated a corporation-wide lockout strike two months later.[43] "Production schedules are the management's function," declared a Chrysler spokesman. "You may as well know now that we do not intend to give you union control of production."[44]

Foremen were caught squarely in the middle of this battle. Local 918 had a substantial but unrecognized organization in the Chrysler plants, and top management there suspected, with some justification, that these foremen were unreliable sergeants in the struggle against the union. In mid-November, therefore, Chrysler fired forty-eight Dodge Truck foremen, all members of Local 918. Bolds shortly thereafter petitioned Chrysler for a formal bargaining session so that upon the corporation's refusal Local 918 could file an unfair labor practices charge with the NLRB. But Chrysler now used the foremen's petition to assert that the CIO "wanted to sit on both sides of the bargaining table." Widely publicizing the incident, Chrysler called off negotiations with the UAW, threatened a back-to-work movement, and demanded that the CIO repudiate the foremen's group.[45] CIO officials did little to resist Chrysler's new demands. The long strike, over issues not readily comprehensible to the public, was proving an embarrassment; furthermore, the status of foremen under the Wagner Act was a subject of much controversy. Thus, in the final strike settlement the CIO agreed to disband Local 918 in all Chrysler plants and in effect repudiated any immediate effort to organize foremen in heavy industry.[46]

The Chrysler fight had a threefold legacy. First, managers in large corporations were sensitized to the potential defection of their first-line supervisors, especially to any organizational links they might forge with unions of production workers. At the same time, the CIO, increasingly attuned to the growing conservative backlash of the late 1930s, sought to avoid opening a new battlefront with management, and quite possibly with the government, by taking a hands-off attitude toward foreman unionization. And, finally, foremen themselves seemingly recognized that direct affiliation with the industrial union might carry an unexpectedly heavy public relations and organizational burden. Thus, when the next round of auto industry supervisory unionism began in late 1941, its institutional form would be independent of the union that was composed of the production workers themselves.

The Foreman's Association of America

World War II economic mobilization increased supervisory disenchantment with existing factory arrangements. In the new full-employment economy, the foremen's tradition of employment security was of much less value, yet supervisors found that many economic benefits of the wartime boom were passing them by. With their pay constrained by the government's wage and salary controls, but without the plentiful overtime pay enjoyed by production workers, many foremen found their wartime wage hovering little above that of the men and women they supervised.[47]

Furthermore, the ranks of supervision were greatly diluted by the rapid upgrading of production workers, who were given crash courses in basic foremanship by individual companies and the federal Training Within Industry organization. At General Motors 42 percent of its nineteen thousand foremen had been on the job less than one year in 1943. At Chrysler's De Soto Wyoming Avenue plant, the number of foremen tripled in the three and a half years after mobilization began in early 1941. Fully 85 percent of the new foremen had been recruited from the ranks of the plant's unionized workforce.[48] Wartime foremen were thus likely to have had a direct personal experience with the industrial unions during their most aggressive phase, although it would prove to be the old-time foremen, not the new recruits, who would spearhead the efforts toward foremen organization. Regardless of their tenure, many wartime foremen could expect to return to the ranks once the war ended, the veterans returned, and industry's manpower needs shrank. As a result, they were preoccupied with job security and naturally considered unionism the way to get it. "They have not been properly trained or instructed in order to function efficiently," complained a middle-level manager at Packard, "nor have they the proper viewpoint of management toward their jobs."[49]

The Foreman's Association of America built its spectacular wartime growth upon this disenchantment. The new organization took much of its character from its place of origin and largest organizational base: the four-thousand-member supervisory force employed at Ford's giant River Rouge complex. Although pre-war supervisors at Ford were noted for their hard-driving manner, these same foremen also inhabited a world of insecurity and fear. Under Harry Bennett the company was notorious for its administrative disorder and brutality. Service department personnel harassed foremen and their subordinates, lines of authority were indistinct, and employment records were often incomplete. Supervisory pay varied considerably between the nineteen separate buildings at the Rouge; for example, when a seniority and classification system was later established, many foremen found that for several years they had been assigned supervisory tasks but were listed on the employment roll as mere working leaders.[50]

The union breakthrough at the Rouge struck this archaic supervisory structure like a whirlwind. During the summer and fall of 1941 production standards everywhere were cut back and petty shop rules ignored. In many buildings UAW committeemen won the de facto right to veto supervisory decisions. "We noticed a very definite change in attitude of the working man," recalled one supervisor some years later. "They got very independent. It was terrible for a while, just awful . . . The bosses were just people to look down on after the union came in. We were just dirt after that."[51] Many foremen sought to join Local 600 immediately after it won recognition in May 1941, but the union rejected their affiliation after it signed a contract with Ford that limited its membership to nonsupervisory blue-collar workers.

Rouge foremen would have to undertake their own organization; it began soon in Ford's newly built Pratt & Whitney Aircraft Building. In this massive but still incomplete facility, the technical landscape was as chaotic as the shop floor social relationships were explosive. To staff the new facility, Ford managers had recruited five hundred foremen from throughout the Rouge complex itself. These men were the pick of the supervisory staff: experienced but still ambitious, technically competent, many with skilled trades backgrounds. But in the summer of 1941 they found no roof over much of the new building, machine tools scattered everywhere, and layout plans that required clever modification before actual production of the complicated, precision-tooled Pratt & Whitney engines could begin. To get their newly hired workforce into shape, most foremen were working seven days a week, ten hours a day. Their pay, they soon found, varied not according to their work responsibility but remained linked to their prewar assignments.[52]

All this put foremen working in the aircraft building under enormous pressure; it deeply offended their sense of order and efficiency and sparked the first informal group meetings. Led by twenty-eight-year-old Robert Keys, a few aircraft unit foremen met as a "social club" in August and September, but in October they held a joint meeting with the foundry unit foremen, attended by about 350. By this time Keys and the other foremen activists were being swamped by inquiries about the new organization; they found it easy to pull together a plant-wide meeting of 1,200 at Fordson High School the next month, formally establishing the Foreman's Association of America (FAA) and electing a set of officers. By the end of the year the FAA had 4,020 members in six Ford chapters.[53]

Early efforts to communicate with Ford management were unsuccessful until May 1942 when Ford discharged an FAA building chairman who sought to represent another foreman on a grievance. After 169 fellow foremen in the upset building stopped work to protest the discharge, Ford dismissed them all. At this point the FAA, then representing more than 3,700 members at the Rouge, threatened a strike, which finally forced Ford's top management to take notice of the new organization. All foremen were reinstated and a joint committee was established to negotiate a new wage scale and grievance procedure. In November the FAA concluded a fairly elaborate agreement with Ford that boosted wages 15 percent and began a process that would rationalize supervisory job classifications. At the same time Ford created a foremen's personnel office to handle supervisory grievances and administer the reclassification scheme.[54]

During 1942 the FAA spread to Packard, Chrysler, Briggs, Hudson, and Kelsey-Hayes, where the CIO had once enrolled foremen, and then to other plants in the Detroit area. By the end of the year the association had eight chapters in thirty-two different plants for a total membership of some nine thousand. When a chapter was organized, it took in not only the foremen but also most of the general foremen above them. Among the production line supervisory staff there was extremely little opposition to the new organization; thus, when the NLRB began to hold certification elections in 1944 and 1945, pro-FAA votes usually ran about nine to one, higher even than that of the CIO unions in their most dynamic phase.[55] With no paid staff or organizing department, the FAA came "as close to being a spontaneous development as anything that requires organization can be," admitted *Business Week* in late 1942. The next year the FAA doubled its membership and began to spread beyond the Detroit area, enrolling supervisors in the rubber, steel, and aircraft industries. By early 1945 the FAA had enlisted thirty-three thousand foremen in 152 chapters, largely in the Midwest and almost always in mills or factories first organized by the new industrial unions.[56]

The Foreman's Association: Ideology and Politics

The early FAA activists shared several important social characteristics. Almost all were veteran foremen. Youthful Robert Keys, the FAA founder and first president, had been a Rouge foreman since 1935, and his father had almost thirty years of supervisory experience at Ford. Carl Brown, the FAA'S first paid organizer, had made foreman at Ford's Highland Park factory in 1924, and Ford activist Bertram Fenwick was promoted to foreman in 1927 and general foreman in 1929. At Packard FAA chapter chairman Prosper Traen had been promoted to foreman in 1932 and later made general foreman, and Chrysler leader Frank Elliott had almost as many years supervisory experience. DeSoto FAA activist Roger Erickson had been a foreman since 1937. Production workers who had recently upgraded to the position of foreman undoubtedly made up a substantial portion of the FAA rank and file, but the association cadre was almost universally prewar foremen with several years' experience.[57]

FAA leaders were proud of their technical proficiency and appalled at what they viewed as managerial confusion and inefficiency. Few association leaders seem to have won their posts through Masonic or other "inside" connections; the activists in the organization were typically ambitious and highly competent Catholics who had been promoted from the production worker rank and file despite their religious background. Keys and Theodore Bonaventura, another aircraft building FAA pioneer, had graduated from the Ford Trade School, the rigorous high school located in the Rouge itself. Bonaventura, an instructor there for several years until he was put in charge of sixteen other foremen in the aircraft building, was disgusted with wartime cost-plus waste and saw the FAA as, among other things, a vehicle for putting some "backbone" into the Ford organization. Fred Temple, another FAA sparkplug, had moved rapidly from a skilled-trades apprenticeship to foundry foreman at age nineteen, with responsibility for the production of technically difficult castings. Fenwick had not taken apprenticeship training, but he was an effective and resourceful supervisor of more than twelve hundred workers in the stamping plant, and on at least one occasion he had assisted Henry Ford in experimental work on an early V-8 engine. He was contemptuous of those plant superintendents and managers who had won their posts through the connections they enjoyed with Harry Bennett and other high Ford officials. Keys spoke for many of these production-minded foremen when he later told a congressional committee, "We are trying to establish a program in the plants where we work that the employers themselves have failed to establish—a program of harmony, cooperation and efficiency."[58]

The social ideology put forward by the Foreman's Association was one of inherent ambiguity. Unlike the CIO supervisory union, the FAA sought to maintain an institutional distance between itself and the UAW, but its independence was continually undermined by the growing hostility of the employers and by the everyday alliances that association members forged with rank-and-file workers. As the FAA constitution's preamble announced: "The foreman fits between two enormous powers: ownership and management on top; and labor unions, with enormous numbers, on the bottom . . . in the ceaseless struggle between ownership and wage labor the foreman will become a victim unless all foremen are organized."[59] The FAA's effort to carve out a separate identity for itself was in part a calculated effort to assuage the fears of employers like Ford, Packard, and Chrysler, who suspected, rightly as it turned out, that no supervisory union could exist for long without the tacit support and cooperation of the industrial workers themselves. But the FAA's adoption of the view that its members were the "men in the middle" also reflected a certain resentment that foremen felt toward the newly empowered rank-and-file workers. Foremen were genuinely upset when even a small minority of their subordinates earned more than they did, for such a discrepancy seemed to mirror in a highly visible form the changing power relationship in the factory. As the veteran Packard foreman Alfred Bounim put it in 1944: "We want to be honored men among honored people. This is why we are fighting . . . The rank and file gets [pay] increases all the time. All the CIO has to do is to make a serious complaint and they get it; they are even successful in getting foremen removed."[60]

But as much as individual foremen might feel a personal sense of anxiety, the actual process of building a union drove the FAA, despite its formal ideology, into an increasingly intimate collaboration with the CIO as an institution and with rank-and-file workers as individuals. Because executive management fiercely resisted the organization of foremen, the FAA had to define itself as an opponent of top management and search for other allies in its battle for survival. With public opinion generally hostile to foreman unionization and with the government labor relations agencies unreliable, the FAA turned to the UAW and other industrial unions for aid and encouragement. On one level this informal alliance represented a practical recognition that the new trade unions were the only force that was powerful enough to enable the FAA to survive in its struggle with the corporations. However, on a deeper social and psychological level, the foremen's union orientation proved a tribute to the ability of a newly mobilized working class to sweep into its orbit whole social strata that in more socially quiescent times might have opposed it.

In the 1940s unionizing foremen increasingly rejected the role of labor disciplinarian. This attitude reflected the social pressures generated by a militant stewards organization, but it was also part of the changing consciousness of foremen themselves. "Let the employer quit issuing troublemaking orders through foremen to the rank and file with the purpose of testing out how far he can push labor around without backwash," complained FAA president Keys in 1944.[61] Instead, argued FAA membership director Harold M. Kelley, the association sought "harmony and good fellowship . . . making working conditions much more pleasant for all."[62] At Ford, where a collective bargaining contract was eventually worked out with the corporation, the association demanded strict adherence to seniority in all promotions and demotions, not simply as an equitable way to handle the postwar layoffs but also as a shield against management's ability to select and assign new jobs to the "red apple boys" and "company men" within the supervisory ranks themselves. Foremen saw their work as production, not general labor discipline, and they resisted those traditional policing functions expected of first-line supervisors, such as searching the washrooms for loafers and penalizing workers who left work early or punched each others' time cards. Foremen also refused to discipline UAW committeemen who did union business on company time, because FAA officials sought to exercise this right as well.[63]

Organizational necessity along with shop floor social pressures forced the association to develop close ties with the unions representing production workers. Most individual foremen were New Deal Democrats, and the FAA generally endorsed the CIO's social and economic agenda. The association considered itself part of the "labor movement as a whole," and the CIO in turn welcomed the organization of first-line supervisors.[64] Despite repeated public protestations of their mutual independence, foremen and production workers were drawn into an increasingly intimate alliance. As even Chrysler attorney Theodore Iserman admitted, "'Solidarity of labor' is not an empty phrase, but a strong and active force."[65] Many UAW locals helped the FAA organize their plants: foremen at Murray and Briggs met in the UAW local halls near these factories; at out-of-state plants—such as North American Aviation in Inglewood, California; Glen L. Martin in Omaha, Nebraska; and John Deere in East Moline, Illinois—UAW officials helped spark FAA organizational activity.[66]

The collaboration between organized foremen and the UAW proved most apparent in a series of strikes called by the FAA in 1943 and 1944. These work stoppages—first at Ford and then at Chrysler, Briggs, Packard, Hudson, Murray, and other Detroit-area firms—were designed to demonstrate the strength of organized foremen and to force government labor relations agencies to adopt a less hostile view of foreman unionization. In particular, the FAA sought to reverse the NLRB's 1943 Maryland Drydock decision that denied foremen the protection of the Wagner Act. In May 1943 Keys won from CIO leaders the assurance that although rank-and-file workers would pass through FAA picket lines, they would refuse to take foremen's jobs once inside the factory. As things turned out, foremen received much more than this support, and their strikes, especially the multiday walkouts called in May 1944, proved exceptionally effective. Rank-and-file workers let production slide, refused to cooperate with working foremen, and in some instances, as at Packard and Briggs, joined the FAA picket lines.[67]

Many businessmen had hoped that the end of the war would ease the pressure for organization of supervisory personnel; they thought that unreliable temporary foremen would now revert to production line jobs and that the end of wartime wage and salary controls would rebalance take-home earnings of first-line supervisors and production workers. As war plants closed, FAA membership did decline, but the vitality of the association was actually enhanced as seniority protections and grievance procedures became more important to foremen threatened by postwar factory reorganization. As *Business Week* put it in May 1946, "It seems clear that a few dollars more or less in the pay envelope will not determine the success or failure of efforts to build unions of foremen." The FAA had chapters at more than one hundred worksites, bargained informally with an increasingly large number of companies, held annual conventions, and leased a country club for its members' exclusive use.[68]

Foreman unionization seemed to be making headway on the legal-political front as well. The strikes the FAA had waged in 1943 and 1944 had forced the National War Labor Board to hold a series of well-publicized hearings substantiating foremen's claims that their power and status had fallen in recent decades. More importantly, the NLRB, also reading the newspaper headlines, first modified and then reversed its 1943 Maryland Drydock decision, which had consigned foremen to a nonunion managerial realm. In its March 1945 Packard case, the board used the same criterion advanced by the Foreman's Association in distinguishing first-line supervisors from top management: they were employees under the Wagner Act because they did not set policy. The next year the board went further and ruled in a case involving coal mine supervisors at the Jones and Laughlin Steel Company: foremen could not be barred from membership in a rank-and-file union if the employees' freedom of choice under the Wagner Act were not to be abridged. The FAA won NLRB elections at Hudson, Chrysler, and Packard and secured a ballot slot at twenty-five additional factories. Encouraged by the Packard and Jones and Laughlin decisions, both the CIO and the AFL became more active as organizers of first-line supervisors, usually in separately chartered locals. By the early postwar years, an estimated one hundred thousand foremen were organized into some sort of collective bargaining unit.[69]

The Managerial Vision

Corporate management never reconciled itself to the unionization of first-line supervisors. Because most American managers defined the structure of industrial enterprise as one that was necessarily hierarchical and authoritarian, the independent organization of foremen seemed to deprive them of the essential instruments by which they confronted and controlled the newly empowered but still "undisciplined" rank-and-file workers. By the end of the war most managers in the auto industry had concluded that "containment" was the most realistic policy to adopt toward the new industrial unions, especially on issues involving power relationships and management prerogatives at the shop floor level. There management would fight to retain or regain control of work standards, manpower allocation, and discipline, but to conduct this struggle with any chance of success managers would require loyal first-line supervisors in numbers sufficient to compete with union stewards and committeemen.[70] "We must rely upon the foremen to try and keep down those emotional surges of the men in the plants and urge them to rely on the grievance procedure," argued a Ford Motor Company spokesman. "If we do not have the foreman to do that, who is going to do it?"[71]

Management feared industrial anarchy. Seniority rights, grievance procedures, and union representation by foremen were subversive, because if supervisors themselves felt less threatened by orders from above, then the immense social and psychological pressures generated from below would surely turn them into unreliable agents. Hence corporate rhetoric often used the military analogy. For example, a Detroit machine shop executive in 1943 asserted, "Picture if you can the confusion of an army in the field if the non-commissioned officers were forced to listen to the commands of the men in their ranks as well as those of their superior officers." Similarly a Hudson manager insisted that foreman unionization would force industrial corporations to downgrade first-line supervisors because "no army can risk granting a commission to one who holds partial allegiance to another country."[72] If foremen were organized, decried the president of the Automobile Manufacturers Association, "mass production" would go "into just sheer mob production."[73]

These alarming predictions were surely exaggerated. Foreman unionization had existed for decades in the printing and building trades and in many shipyards and machine shops. And as the Foreman's Association and other organized supervisory groups repeatedly pointed out, production did not collapse in those newly organized factories and mills where management recognized unions of foremen. For the most part, first-line supervisors still obeyed orders from above, disciplined production workers when necessary, and produced the work in reasonable time. In fact, many FAA foremen argued that factory efficiency rose when foremen unionized, because work could now proceed in an "atmosphere cleared of treachery and political intrigue."[74]

Yet the stakes were high in the battle over foreman unionization, because this fight was central to the larger conflict over the legitimacy and limits of corporate power in the 1940s. Foreman organization did not just threaten to weaken management authority at the point of production; rather, it eroded the vitality of corporate ideology in society at large by shattering the unitary façade of management and opening the door to a much larger definition of what constituted a self-conscious working-class identity. Thus, General Motors president Charles E. Wilson viewed foreman unionization as "one more step toward participation in management by labor organizations, one more serious encroachment upon management."[75]

The loyalty of a whole middle stratum of white- and gray-collar workers seemed at issue in the wake of the powerful social currents set in motion by the rise of supervisory unionism. "The Foreman Abdicates" ran a *Fortune* headline in 1945, but the larger issue was whether or not the lower-middle class—clerical workers, salesmen, store managers, bank tellers, engineers, and draftsmen—would also abandon their identification with the corporate order. "Where will unionization end?" asked Wilson. "With the vice presidents?" As almost all managers recognized, a militant breakthrough by organized foremen promised to accelerate this mutiny.[76]

Demise of the Foreman's Association

The decisive battle over foreman unionization came at the Ford Motor Company in the late spring of 1947. Ford had bargained with the Foreman's Association since mid-1942 and actually signed a contract with the association in May 1944. Although the new management team that took over at Ford in 1945 and 1946 was among the most liberal and progressive in heavy industry, Ford Motor Company, like its more conservative and intransigent competitors, was determined to win back foremen to the "management team." Between 1945 and 1948 the corporation undertook administrative and organizational reforms designed to differentiate foremen from rank-and-file workers and bring them into a closer psychological and organizational relationship with top management. The corporation inaugurated a series of supervisory bulletins; gave foremen separate locker facilities, parking spaces, and cafeterias; and insisted they wear white shirts and ties on the factory floor. For the first time foremen were given name badges distinguishing them from rank-and-file workers. In early 1946 foremen at Ford were put on salary and given a 15 percent wage increase. A pay differential of at least 25 percent was mandated between foremen and the average pay of their top five subordinates. More frequent meetings were held with top management, and foreman training courses, emphasizing the human relations and leadership skills then popular among industrial psychologists, became mandatory. Even the leaders of the FAA admitted that Ford's personnel changes, and similar reforms undertaken at other manufacturing firms, had materially improved the conditions of first-line supervisors without really altering the basic relationship to top management.[77]

In the contract negotiations that began in early 1947, Ford did not initially seek the destruction of the FAA, but it was nevertheless determined to bring its foremen "closer to other groups in management." The probable enactment of the Taft-Hartley Act, whose section 2(3) included a redefinition of the term "employee" so as to specifically exclude all first-line supervisors, greatly encouraged the company program. This section represented an important victory for those in management who had fought to deprive foremen of any protections of the Wagner Act so recently interpreted by the NLRB and the courts. Although Ford had not been active in this campaign, company negotiators used the more favorable legal and political climate to demand that general foremen be excluded from the FAA bargaining unit and that merit rather than seniority be more heavily weighed in promotions and demotions. In turn, the FAA insisted upon a union shop: first, it feared that the Ford reforms might in fact undermine the loyalty of the union foremen; and second, the association sought assurance that the corporation would not use Taft-Hartley as a club to break the FAA.[78]

With negotiations fruitless and FAA leaders feeling increasingly desperate, the association struck Ford on May 21, successfully pulling a large majority of the four-thousand-man supervisory force out of the plant. The strike was not ineffective: FAA picket lines were spirited, rank-and-file workers entered the plant but refused to take over supervisory work (more than a thousand workers were laid off for laxity in the performance of their jobs), and production declined dramatically in several departments. But the strike was probably a tactical blunder. Not only did it give Ford the opportunity to use formal passage of the Taft-Hartley Act on June 23 as an occasion to simply cancel its recognition of the FAA and fire its leading activists, but also the association had done little to coordinate its activities with the UAW.[79] Any hope that the foremen might survive their strike floundered when the UAW denied the FAA request that rank-and-file workers respect the supervisory picket lines. UAW leaders recognized that if the FAA collapsed, foremen would again become "stooges" for management. But the faction-ridden UAW was then in the midst of its own negotiations with the company, out of which leaders of the UAW's Ford department hoped to bring a precedent-setting pension plan to boost their fortunes in the scramble for power within the union. Although active UAW support of the FAA would, of course, sidetrack this effort, in the larger sense UAW abandonment of the FAA was part of a general shift by a new industrial union leadership away from a contest with management over control of the shop floor work environment and toward a greater focus on wage and fringe benefits for their members. Ford management easily accommodated this shift; the contract signed with the UAW in August 1947 not only opened the door to a pension plan but also included a clause in which the union promised it would "not organize, or attempt to assist in the organization of supervisory employees."[80]

Defeat at Ford and passage of the Taft-Hartley Act effectively smashed the FAA in the auto industry. By the end of 1947 the association lost most of its other contracts; the NLRB dismissed some sixty-six cases the FAA had brought before the board; and important chapters like those at DeSoto, Packard, and Chrysler, which maintained shadow existences for some years, withdrew from the association. The FAA staggered on, sometimes negotiating "secret" agreements with supplier firms fearful of Big Three retaliation, but by the end of the 1950s little of the association remained in the industry.[81]

Still the "Man in the Middle"

The shifting social terrain of most postwar auto factories helped reopen the social distance that had once existed between the supervisory strata and rank-and-file workers. In the quarter century after the end of World War II the gradual atrophy of the shop steward system made it again possible for auto industry foremen to perform the disciplinary functions they had found so difficult in the 1940s. Thus, at Chrysler the strong tradition of shop floor activism that persisted until the managerial onslaught of 1957–1958 had forced supervisors into an accommodating, often cooperative relationship with rank-and-file work groups, while at the same time the tradition distanced foremen from top management. Thereafter, the Chrysler effort to recast its labor relations policy in the GM mold increased tensions on the shop floor and reduced the informal bargaining latitude enjoyed by first-line supervisors. After that "we were puppets on a string," recalled one Chrysler supervisor.[82]

The cultural distance between foremen and workers also widened, especially in the 1960s and early 1970s. Although most foremen were still recruited from the ranks of the workforce, Ford and GM made an effort to hire college-educated foremen, making this job the first rung on the advancement ladder for about a quarter of the managerial workforce.[83] The new recruitment pattern increased social distance between workers and supervisors and dramatically reinforced the growing racial antagonism that was manifest in many auto plants in the 1960s. In most urban factories a cohort of older white foremen found themselves in command of a predominantly black and Hispanic workforce. Until top management began a forced draft effort to recruit minority supervisors, the ethnic cleavage between workers and their foremen could be stark, a distant reflection of the cultural polarization that had once divided pre–World War II auto plants along Protestant-Masonic and immigrant-Catholic lines. In the high-employment years between 1967 and 1973, these tensions were quite literally explosive.[84]

But despite these social polarities, the structures of work and authority that gave rise to supervisory unionism have remained remarkably unchanged. Thus, management consultant John Patton could echo FAA complaints in 1973 when he argued that the first-line supervisor was "still being held responsible for functions over which he no longer has any real authority or control."[85] Although auto management intensified training programs, expanded career ladders, and increased status-building minor privileges, repeated surveys have found that a majority of supervisors continue to resist full identification with higher-level management. Given the social and psychological tensions inherent in the job, almost half of all rank-and-file workers promoted to supervisory ranks voluntarily return to the shop floor. "One might say that supervisors are still back where they started," concluded a Harvard Business School study, "walking the tightrope between management and workers."[86]

CHAPTER 6

From Corporatism to Collective Bargaining

Organized Labor and the Eclipse
of Social Democracy in the Postwar Era

In recent years the decline of the trade union movement and the eclipse of the liberal ideology it long sustained has thrown into question the political assumptions and organizational structures upon which the New Deal system of social regulation has rested. While the postwar generation of economists and social scientists once found the social and political "settlement" of the 1940s a bulwark of pluralist democracy and progressive economic advance, contemporary observers have been far more critical. Because of its very stability, the "labor-capital accord" that emerged after World War II may well have foreclosed the possibility of a more progressive approach to American capitalism's chronic difficulties, made manifest in the Great Depression itself, and then, more than a generation later, in the social tensions that accompanied the latter-day erosion of American industry's world hegemony. In this process the peculiarly American system of interclass accommodation that jelled in the 1940s—a decentralized system characterized by extremely detailed, firm-centered collective bargaining contracts; a relatively low level of social welfare spending; and a labor market segmented by race, gender, region, and industry—stood counterpoised to the once hopeful effort to expand the welfare state and refashion American politics along more "European," explicitly social democratic lines.[1]

The turning point came between 1946 and 1948 when a still powerful trade union movement found its efforts to bargain over the shape of the postwar political economy decisively blocked by a powerful remobilization of business and conservative forces. Labor's ambitions were thereafter sharply curbed, and its economic program was reduced to a sort of militant-interest-group politics, in which a Keynesian emphasis on sustained growth and productivity gain sharing replaced labor's earlier commitment to economic planning and social solidarity. This forced retreat narrowed the political appeal of labor-liberalism and contributed both to the demobilization and division of those social forces that had long sustained it.

Union Power

The dramatic growth of the organized working class put the American system of industrial relations at a crossroads in 1945. In the years since 1933 the number of unionized workers had increased more than fivefold to more than fourteen million. About 30 percent of all American workers were organized, a density greater than at any time before and a level that for the first time equaled that of northern Europe. Unions seemed to be on the verge of recruiting millions of new workers in the service trades, in white-collar occupations, across great stretches of the South and Southwest, and even among the lower ranks of management.[2] "Your success has been one of the most surprising products of American politics in several generations," Interior Secretary Harold Ickes told a cheering Congress of Industrial Organizations (CIO) convention just after Roosevelt's 1944 reelection. "You are on your way and you must let no one stop you or even slow up your march." Three years later the sober-minded Harvard economist Sumner Slichter still considered U.S. trade unions "the most powerful economic organizations which the country has ever seen."[3]

It was not size alone that contributed to this assessment. The élan so noticeable in many sections of the labor movement rested upon a degree of union consciousness, in some cases amounting to working-class loyalty, that today would seem quite extraordinary. The mid-1940s were no period of social quiescence, for the war itself had had a complex and dichotomous impact on working Americans. It had provided them with a taste of postwar affluence and had attuned them to the daily influence of large bureaucratic institutions like the military and the government mobilization agencies. But the labor shortages of that era and the social patriotic ideology advanced by government and union alike also engendered a self-confident mood that quickly translated itself into a remarkable burst of rank-and-file activism. Led by shop stewards and local union officers, hundreds of thousands of workers had taken part in a wildcat strike movement that had focused on a militant defense of union power in the workplace itself. And the now forgotten series of postwar general strikes called by central labor councils in Oakland, California; Lancaster, Pennsylvania; Stamford, Connecticut; and Akron, Ohio, are indicative of the extent to which working-class activity still retained an occasionally explosive character even in the later half of the 1940s.[4]

The economic power wielded by American trade unions was by its very nature political power, for the New Deal had thoroughly politicized all relations between the union movement, the business community, and the state. The New Deal differed from previous state-building eras not only because of the relatively more favorable political and legislative environment it created for organized labor but also, and perhaps even more important, because the New Deal provided a set of semipermanent political structures in which key issues of vital concern to the trade union movement might be accommodated. Although the industry codes negotiated under the National Recovery Administration were declared unconstitutional in 1935, the Fair Labor Standards Act established new wage and hour standards three years later. The National Labor Relations Board established the legal basis of union power and provided the arena in which jurisdictional disputes between the unions might be resolved, while the National War Labor Board had provided a tripartite institution that both set national wage policy and contributed to the rapid wartime growth of the new trade unions. The successive appearances of these agencies seemed to signal the fact that in the future as in the past, the fortunes of organized labor would be determined as much by a process of politicized bargaining in Washington as by the give-and-take of contract collective bargaining.[5]

As a result of the wartime mobilization, the United States seemed to advance toward the kind of labor-backed corporatism that would later characterize social policy in northern Europe and Scandinavia. Corporatism of this sort called for government agencies composed of capital, labor, and "public" representatives to substitute rational, democratic planning for the chaos and inequities of the market. The premier examples of such corporatist institutions in 1940s America were the War Labor Board (WLB) and its wartime companion, the Office of Price Administration—administrative regimes that began to reorder wage and price relations within and between industries. Although union officials often denounced both agencies for their accommodation of politically resourceful business and producer groups, the maintenance of institutions such as these were nevertheless seen by most liberal and labor spokesmen as the kernel of a postwar incomes policy. That policy would continue the rationalization of the labor market begun during the war, set profit and price guidelines, and redistribute income into worker and consumer hands. These agencies were usually staffed by individuals who were somewhat sympathetic to their consumer and trade union constituencies and headed by New Dealers like Chester Bowles and William H. Davis who recognized the legitimacy of labor's corporate interests.[6]

The War Labor Board, for example, socialized much of the trade union movement's prewar agenda, thus making seniority and grievance systems, vacation pay and night-shift supplements, and sick leave and paid mealtimes standard "entitlements" mandated for an increasingly large section of the working class. Likewise, the WLB's effort to limit wartime pay, known as the Little Steel wage formula, was bitterly resisted by the more highly paid and better-organized sections of the working class, but this wage-setting mechanism nevertheless had enough loopholes and special dispensations to enable low-paid workers in labor-short industries to bring their wages closer to the national average. Thus wages among black workers rose twice as rapidly as among white workers, and weekly earnings in cotton textiles and in retail trade increased about 50 percent faster than in high-wage industries like steel and auto production.[7] By the onset of postwar reconversion, WLB wage policy was explicitly egalitarian. "It is not desirable to increase hourly earnings in each industry in accordance with the rise of productivity in that industry," declared a July 1945 memorandum. "The proper goal of policy is to increase hourly earning generally in proportion to the average increase of productivity in the economy *as a whole*."[8]

Labor's Vision

Since contemporary trade unions have often been equated with "special interest politics," it is important to recognize that the American trade union movement of the immediate postwar era, especially its industrial union wing, adopted a social agenda that was broad, ambitious, and not without prospects for success. The unions thought the welfare of the working class would be advanced not only, or even primarily, by periodic wage bargaining but also by a political realignment of the major parties that would give them a powerful voice in the management of industry, expansion of the welfare state, and planning the overall shape of the nation's political economy. The union agenda was never an entirely consistent one, but its thrust meshed well with the corporatist strain that characterized late New Deal social policy.

This perspective was most graphically manifest in the demand for tripartite industry governance, embodied in the Industry Council Plan put forward by CIO president Philip Murray early in the war. The industry council idea represented an admixture of Catholic social reformism and New Deal–era faith in business-labor-government cooperation. Under the general guidance of a friendly government, the Industry Council Plan contemplated the fusion of economic and political bargaining at the very highest levels of industry governance. Here was the essence of the CIO's corporatist vision: organized labor would have a voice in the production goals, investment decisions, and employment patterns of the nation's core industries. "The Industry Council Plan," wrote Philip Murray, "is a program for democratic economic planning and for participation by the people in the key decisions of the big corporations." Such important elements of the union movement's wartime agenda as the guaranteed annual wage, industry-wide bargaining, and rationalization of the wage structure could be won only through this initiative.[9]

If the CIO plan had something of an abstract air about it, the proposals put forward by the young autoworker leader Walter Reuther had a good deal more political bite. Reuther rose to national prominence in 1940 and 1941 with a widely publicized "500 planes a day" plan to resolve the military aviation bottleneck through a state-sponsored rationalization of the entire auto/aircraft industry. Reuther proposed a tripartite Aircraft Production Board that would have the power to reorganize production facilities without regard for corporate boundaries, markets, or personnel. It would conscript labor and work space where and when needed and secure for the United Auto Workers (UAW) at least a veto over a wide range of managerial functions. Winning wide support among those New Dealers who still retained a commitment to social planning, the Reuther plan was ultimately delayed and then defeated by an automobile industry that was both hostile to social experimentation and increasingly well represented within the government's wartime production agencies.[10]

The Reuther plan nevertheless cast a long shadow, for it contained hallmarks of the strategic approach that was so characteristic of labor-liberalism in the 1940s: an assault on management's traditional power made in the name of economic efficiency and the public interest, and an effort to shift power relations within the structure of industry and politics, usually by means of a tripartite governmental entity empowered to plan for whole sections of the economy. Thus auto executive George Romney declared, "Walter Reuther is the most dangerous man in Detroit because no one is more skillful in bringing about the revolution without seeming to disturb the existing forms of society."[11]

Indeed, the union movement defined the left wing of what was possible in the political affairs of the day. Its vision and its power attracted a species of political animal that is hardly existent today: the "labor-liberal," who saw organized labor as absolutely central to the successful pursuit of his or her political agenda. After 1943 the CIO's new Political Action Committee put organizational backbone into the northern Democratic party, and the next year its "People's Program for 1944" codified many of the central themes that would define liberalism in the immediate postwar years: big-power cooperation, full employment, cultural pluralism, and economic planning.[12] "Labor's role in our national progress is unique and paramount," affirmed Supreme Court Justice William O. Douglas as late as 1948. "It is labor, organized and independent labor, that can supply much of the leadership, energy and motive power which we need today."[13]

But labor-liberalism was never a coherent or static doctrine, and in the mid-decade years its opinion-molding, policy-oriented adherents had made a subtle shift in their thinking about how the political economy could be made both efficient and just. New Dealers who had once entertained "underconsumptionist" assumptions of U.S. economic maturity and stagnation had been startled by the remarkable success of the American mobilization effort. Structural changes in the distribution of economic power, such as those envisioned by the CIO's various schemes for tripartite governance of industry, now seemed less necessary to ensure economic growth and full employment. "Our phenomenal economic success in the forties is a tribute to the resiliency of the system," declared economist Seymour E. Harris in the introduction to a 1948 collection of essays by Leon Keyserling, Alvin Hansen, Chester Bowles, and other New Dealers. *Saving American Capitalism: A Liberal Economic Program* saw a Keynesian program of demand stimulation, social welfare expenditure, and economic planning for specific industry sectors and geographic regions as the "blueprint for a second new deal," designed to assure that "capitalism is not but a passing phase in the historical process from feudalism to socialism."[14] High on this liberal agenda was a long-overdue expansion of Social Security and unemployment insurance, elaboration of a system of national health insurance, and a commitment to full employment. Union wage demands were of particular social usefulness, for now the labor movement's traditional demand for higher income meshed easily with the emerging Keynesian view that aggregate demand must be sustained and income redistributed to avoid a new slump.

During World War II many liberals had seen the regulatory apparatus of the federal government as the key arena in which such plans for postwar reconstruction might be generated. But their failure to prevent corporate domination of the reconversion process, combined with their disappointment that the long-sought Employment Act of 1946 eschewed real economic planning, forced those economists and administrators who had championed a progressive reconversion program to look elsewhere, primarily to the union movement, where the economic muscle and voting strength of labor's battalions might yet advance their agenda. Thus Donald Montgomery, the former Agriculture Department consumer counsel who resigned when that department undermined wartime price controls, took over the UAW's Washington office, and in 1945 emerged as the author of "Purchasing Power for Prosperity," the UAW's left-Keynesian manifesto in the 1945–1946 GM strike. Likewise, Robert Nathan, who had played a central role in shaping the abortive reconversion schemes of the Office of War Mobilization and Reconversion, reemerged in 1947 as the author of the CIO's "Nathan Report," which advocated a class-wide wage increase as a way of repairing the damage done by the collapse of price controls and fulfilling the redistributive economic program that the Truman administration was unwilling to inaugurate.[15]

Labor and the Search for a Reconversion Wage Program

The CIO hoped to take the tripartite, corporatist model of wage-price bargaining that had emerged during the war and use it to bridge the uncertain political currents of the reconversion era. The industrial union federation wanted a National Production Board that would preside over the reconversion of defense plants to civilian production, maintain a semblance of price control, and establish a set of wage guidelines designed to defend working-class incomes. As CIO president Philip Murray told a 1944 labor meeting, "Only chaos and destruction of our industrial life will result if employers look to the war's end as an opportunity for a union-breaking, wage cutting, open-shop drive, and if labor unions have to resort to widespread strikes to defend their very existence and the living standards of their members."[16] To forestall such a prospect, the CIO in March 1945 sponsored a "Labor-Management Charter" with William Green of the American Federation of Labor (AFL) and Eric Johnston, the corporate liberal president of the U.S. Chamber of Commerce. Consisting of a list of often irreconcilable platitudes hailing the virtues of unfettered free enterprise and the rights of labor, the charter nevertheless symbolized the CIO's hope for cooperation with the liberal wing of American capitalism in stabilizing postwar industrial relations along roughly the lines established during the war. "It's Industrial Peace for the Postwar Period," headlined the *CIO News*. In return for management support for the unamended Wagner Act and a high-wage, high-employment postwar strategy, the unions pledged to defend "a system of private competitive capitalism" including "the inherent right and responsibility of management to direct the operations of an enterprise."[17]

The businessmen with whom the CIO hoped to work were collective bargaining progressives and moderate Keynesians who favored a countercyclical fiscal policy and a degree of structural reform as the minimum program necessary to stabilize postwar capitalism. Often influenced by the Committee for Economic Development and the Twentieth Century Fund, they also supported the 1946 Full Employment Act in something like its original, liberal form. Among these progressive industrialists with whom the CIO sought an alliance, in addition to the Chamber of Commerce's Eric Johnston, who called for a "people's capitalism" in the postwar era, was Paul Hoffman of the Studebaker Corporation, who took pride in his company's harmonious relationship with organized labor. But the most famous of these progressives was undoubtedly Henry J. Kaiser, the maverick West Coast industrialist who had built his empire on New Deal construction projects and wartime contracts. Hardly an opponent of government planning or public works spending, Kaiser's good relations with the unions and the pioneering health-care facilities at his shipyards and mills added to his reputation as a social liberal. In 1945 he won strong UAW cooperation for a well-publicized effort to convert the giant Willow Run bomber plant to civilian car production.[18]

Implementation of a new wage-price policy was one of the key elements in such an accord with the liberal wing of the business community, so state action was essential. The CIO wanted a 20 or 30 percent increase in real wages to make up for the elimination of overtime pay at the end of the war, and many New Dealers like Commerce Secretary Henry Wallace and William Davis, now head of the Office of Economic Stabilization, considered such a wage boost essential to maintain living standards and avoid the long-feared postwar downturn.[19]

Such forecasts were music to CIO ears, but the political and social base for such a liberal postwar prospect had already been eroded. Since 1938 labor-liberalism had been on the defensive, stymied by the defection of Southern agriculture from the New Deal coalition, by the political rejuvenation of a conservative manufacturing interest during World War II, and by the reemergence of long-standing ethnic and social tensions within the urban Democratic Party. Certainly emblematic of this stalemate was Harry Truman's selection as vice president in 1944, replacing Henry Wallace, the labor-liberal favorite. FDR's successor was not a New Dealer, but a border-state Democrat, a party centrist whose political skill would lie in successfully presiding over an increasingly factionalized party coalition.[20]

Truman certainly recognized that in order to govern, the unions and their liberal allies had to be accommodated—this was the lesson that Clark Clifford would drill home in his famous strategy memorandum on the 1948 campaign—but even before the Cold War came to dominate its outlook, the personnel of his administration took on a particularly parochial outlook. Within a year virtually all of FDR's cabinet resigned, to be replaced by men like John Snyder, a Missouri banker now at the Office of War Mobilization and Reconversion (OWMR) who would come to have an "ideological fear" of Walter Reuther. California oilman Edwin Pauley, then serving in the Navy Department, sought industry exploitation of the government's rich oil reserves.[21] Moreover, Truman had none of the patrician equanimity with which FDR faced the leaders of the labor movement. Although the president prided himself on his humble origins, he found emotionally jarring and somehow illegitimate the power and resources now commanded by trade union leaders. Thus Clark Clifford remembered a bitter 1946 showdown with the United Mine Workers' John L. Lewis as "the moment when Truman finally and irrevocably stepped out from the shadow of FDR to become President in his own right."[22]

Truman's inadequacies aside, the CIO had profoundly misjudged the tenor of the postwar business community. The progressive industrialists with whom the industrial union federation hoped to achieve an accord were in fact a relatively non-influential minority. Key business spokesmen were those practical conservatives who presided over the core manufacturing firms in the unionized steel, electrical, auto, rubber, and transport industries. Led by men such as John A. Stephens of U.S. Steel, Ira Mosher of the National Association of Manufacturers, and Charles E. Wilson of General Motors, these industrialists had emerged from the war with enormous sophistication and self-confidence. Unlike their counterparts in continental Europe, or even in the British Isles, who had been tarred with the brush of collaboration or appeasement, American business leaders found the wartime experience one of both commercial success and political advance. They felt little need for the kind of state-sponsored labor-management collaboration that helped legitimize a mixed capitalist economy in Germany, France, and Italy in the immediate postwar era.

These industrialists recognized the potential usefulness of the new industrial unions as stabilizers of the labor force and moderators of industrial conflict, but they also sought the restoration of managerial prerogatives that wartime conditions had eroded in the areas of product pricing, market allocation, and shop floor work environment. They were intensely suspicious of the kind of New Deal social engineering favored by labor, and only with some reluctance did they accommodate themselves to the modest degree of economic stimulation that would later go by the name "commercial Keynesianism." Looking forward to a postwar boom, they wanted to be free of government or union interference in determining the wage-price relationship in each industry.[23] Thus the long-awaited National Labor-Management Conference that President Truman convened in November 1945 was doomed to failure. No accord proved possible on either the prerogatives of management or the scope of legitimate union demands, and on the crucial issue of a general wage policy, the CIO got nowhere. Philip Murray offered industry a de facto policy of labor peace in return for a pattern wage increase, which Truman had endorsed in a speech of October 30, but the opposition was so great that the issue never secured a place on the formal conference agenda.[24]

The CIO faced resistance not only from industry but also from within the labor movement itself. The AFL unions had never been as committed as the CIO to the tripartite bargaining arrangements of the war era, and these unions demanded a return to free and unrestricted collective bargaining. In part this stemmed from the AFL's tradition of Gompersarian voluntarism, but it also reflected the contrasting organizational base of the two labor federations. The CIO unions were overwhelmingly concentrated in the manufacturing sector of the economy, where they faced oligopolistically organized employers who were themselves capable of imposing a new wage pattern. But only 35 percent of AFL membership lay in this heavy industrial sector, while construction, transportation, and service trades proved the federation's most important centers of strength. These decentralized, and now booming, sectors of the economy were less subject to the pattern-setting guidelines established by core firms like General Motors and U.S. Steel. With almost seven million members in 1945, the AFL was not only 30 percent larger than the CIO but actually growing more rapidly, in part because its flexible model of mixed craft and industrial unionism seemed to fit more closely the actual contours of the postwar economy than did the CIO brand of mass organization. This meant that although CIO unions like the United Steelworkers and the UAW remained innovative and powerful institutions, their political and organizational weight was often less impressive than it seemed.[25]

Although he was an industrial unionist, John L. Lewis spoke most forthrightly for the AFL viewpoint. Repeated clashes between the United Mine Workers (UMW) and the Roosevelt administration during the war had soured the mine leader on the kind of state-sponsored industrial planning arrangements he had once advocated as the CIO's first president. Lewis was now determined to exercise his union's power unfettered by a new set of federal regulations. "What Murray and the CIO are asking for," declared Lewis at the Labor-Management conference, "is a corporate state, wherein the activities of the people are regulated and constrained by a dictatorial government. We are opposed to the corporate state."[26]

The GM Strike and American Liberalism

This stalemate led directly to the General Motors strike, actually begun while the conference remained in session, and then to the general strike wave that spread throughout basic industry in the winter of 1946. Like Walter Reuther's other wartime "plans," the GM strike program made a strong appeal to the national interest—this time not so much in terms of rationalized production and democratic control, but as part of the emerging Keynesian consensus that a substantial boost in mass purchasing power would be necessary to avoid a postwar depression. The UAW's demand that industry pacesetter GM raise wages by some 30 percent without increasing the price of its product seemed adventuresome in a collective bargaining negotiation; even more so was its demand that GM "open the books" to demonstrate its ability to pay. The company quickly denounced these UAW demands as European-style socialism, but in fact they were little more than standard Office of Price Administration (OPA) price-setting procedures now translated into the language of collective bargaining.[27]

While this program was formally directed against the giant automaker, it was in practice a union demand against the state as well, for its ultimate success rested upon the ability of an increasingly embattled OPA to resist industry pressure and enforce price guidelines well into the postwar era. This program won Reuther a wave of support, both within the UAW, where it prepared the way for his election as union president, and among influential liberals who identified with the union effort. A union-sponsored "National Citizens Committee on the GM-UAW Dispute" lauded the UAW's determination to lift "collective bargaining to a new high level by insisting that the advancement of Labor's interest shall not be made at the expense of the public." And a strike support committee, headquartered at NAACP offices in New York, quickly enrolled such luminaries as Eleanor Roosevelt, Wayne Morse, Reinhold Niebuhr, Walter White, and Leon Henderson.[28]

Reuther and the rest of the CIO won an 18.5-cent wage increase during the postwar round of strikes and negotiations that ended in the late winter of 1946. But the effort to turn this struggle into a downward redistribution of real income was decisively repulsed, first by the adamant opposition of industrial management, second by Truman administration vacillation (OWMR director John Snyder played the key role here), and finally by division and timidity within trade union ranks, especially after Philip Murray made it clear that the steelworkers union would not turn its midwinter strike into a political conflict with the Truman administration over the maintenance of price controls.

The 1946 strike settlement ended left-liberal hopes that organized labor could play a direct role in reshaping class relations for the society as a whole. Thereafter Reutherite social unionism gradually tied its fate more closely to that of industry and moved away from a strategy that sought to use union power to demand structural changes in the political economy. Instead the UAW worked toward negotiation of an increasingly privatized welfare program that eventually succeeded in providing economic security for employed autoworkers. But just as postwar liberalism gradually reduced its commitment to national planning and eschewed issues of social and economic control, so too did the UAW abandon the quest for labor participation in running the automobile industry. And just as liberalism increasingly came to define itself as largely concerned with the maintenance of economic growth and an expansion of the welfare state, so too would the UAW and the rest of the labor movement define its mission in these terms.[29]

Taft-Hartley and American Politics

Although the immediate postwar strike wave had proven the largest since 1919, the pattern wage increases won by the UAW and other major unions soon evaporated under the galloping inflation that was let loose when government price controls were cut back during the summer. In the fall, therefore, all the major unions had to return to the bargaining table to demand another round of wage increases. Unions that sought to improve on postwar wage patterns, such as the Railway Brotherhoods and the UMW, now found that "free" collective bargaining of the sort advocated by John L. Lewis brought them into bitter confrontations with the government. The frequent strikes and annual pay boosts of this era, which industry used to raise prices, were at least partially responsible for creating the conservative, antilabor political climate that gave Republicans their large victory in the 1946 elections and then culminated in the passage of the Taft-Hartley Act in 1947.[30]

Passage of the Taft-Hartley Act over President Truman's veto proved a milestone, not only for the actual legal restrictions the new law imposed on the trade unions but also as a symbol of the shifting relationship between the unions and the state during the late 1940s. The law sought to curb the practice of interunion solidarity, eliminate the radical cadre who still held influence within trade union ranks, and contain the labor movement to roughly its existing geographic and demographic terrain. The anti-Communist affidavits, the prohibition against secondary boycotts, the enactment of Section 14b allowing states to prohibit the union shop, the ban on foreman unionism—all these sections of the law had been on the agenda of the National Association of Manufacturers and other conservative groups since 1938. Of course, Taft-Hartley was not the fascist-like "slave labor law" denounced by the AFL and CIO alike. In later years, unions like the Teamsters prospered even in right-to-work states, while the bargaining relationship between employers and most big industrial unions was relatively unaffected by the new law.[31] But if Taft-Hartley did not destroy the union movement, it did impose upon it a legal/administrative straitjacket that encouraged contractual parochialism and penalized any serious attempt to project a class-wide political-economic strategy.

This explains the union movement's enormous hostility to Taft-Hartley. As CIO counsel Lee Pressman put it in 1947, "When you think of it merely as a combination of individual provisions, you are losing entirely the full impact of the program, the sinister conspiracy that has been hatched." Union leaders correctly recognized that the act represented the definitive end of the brief era when the state served as an arena in which the trade unions could bargain for the kind of tripartite accommodation with industry that had been so characteristic of the New Deal years. At the very highest levels a trust had been broken, which is why Philip Murray declared the law "conceived in sin."[32] Taft-Hartley had altered the whole texture of the sociopolitical environment, and the failure of the congressional Democrats to repeal the law in 1949 proved the final blow for many unionists. As Arthur Goldberg, who replaced Lee Pressman as CIO lawyer, sadly put it in late 1949, the law had "in its most fundamental aspect created great changes in our industrial *mores* with incalculable effects."[33]

The Search for Political Realignment

If the tide of public sentiment, congressional votes, and administration policy all seemed to be shifting against the unions, these organizations were not without the resources to mount a counterattack. There were two elements in this strategy: the first, Operation Dixie, the CIO campaign to organize the South, was carefully planned and well funded; the second, labor's search for a political alternative to Truman, and quite possibly to the Democratic Party, represented more of an unfocused mood than a program of action. Nevertheless, both of these efforts were not without the prospect of some real impact on the body politic; but in both cases failure became almost inevitable when the Communist issue and the Cold War became a central focus of domestic politics in postwar America.

In the mid-1940s the fate of the trade unions and of the movement for black freedom were more closely linked than at any other time in American history. American blacks were overwhelmingly proletarian, and after almost two million had been enrolled in labor's ranks, the fight for civil rights entered a much larger and more dynamic phase, putting it near the top of the national political agenda. In cities like Detroit and Pittsburgh, and even in Birmingham and Memphis, the trade unions played a vanguard role during the 1940s. This was hardly because of the racial egalitarianism of their rank and file (white working-class racism was probably on the rise after 1943); rather, unionists with any sort of strategic vision recognized the simple organizational necessity of forging a union movement with at least a minimal degree of interracial solidarity.[34] Thus, after his multistate tour of the old Confederacy in mid-1941, the NAACP'S Harold Preece concluded that the CIO had become a "lamp of democracy" and said, "The South has not known such a force since the historic Union Leagues in the great days of the Reconstruction era."[35]

Of course, this link between CIO-style unionism and the mobilization of an increasingly self-confident black movement was instantly appreciated by the political leadership of the white South, whose militant opposition to even the most attenuated New Deal reforms can be dated from the birth of this interracial alliance in the late 1930s. The CIO therefore sought to break the political power of the Bourbon South, both at home and in Congress, by striking at its heart: the bastions of racial segregation and low-wage labor in the Deep South. During the war both labor federations had made substantial inroads in that region, organizing more than eight hundred thousand new workers.[36] In 1944 the CIO's new Political Action Committee (CIO-PAC) had mobilized war workers in Alabama and Texas shipyards to defeat such well-known labor baiters as Martin Dies and Joe Starnes. And in Winston-Salem, wartime organization of the heavily black R. J. Reynolds Tobacco Company overnight transformed that city's NAACP chapter into the largest and most vital in the seaboard South, which in turn opened local politics to black participation for the first time since the Populist era.[37]

Beginning in mid-1946, Operation Dixie sought to replay these local breakthroughs on an even larger scale, in the process mobilizing an interracial electorate that could realign the very shape of Southern politics. "When Georgia is organized . . .," predicted Van Bittner, CIO Southern organizing director, "you will find our old friend Gene Talmadge trying to break into the doors of the CIO conventions and tell our people that he has always been misunderstood."[38]

But Operation Dixie was a thorough failure. The CIO put up a million dollars, recruited some two hundred organizers, and opened scores of offices throughout the South. Not to be outflanked, the AFL almost immediately opened its own rival campaign to bring authentic "American" unionism to the region. While some inroads were made in 1946 and 1947, the resistance from the political and industrial leadership of the white South proved overwhelming, and the proportion of union nonfarm labor in the South declined from just above 20 percent in 1945 to something under 18 percent ten years later. Meanwhile, white supremacists made the CIO-PAC a whipping boy in each election season, and with the rise of the Dixiecrats and the defeat of such pro-union racial moderates as Claude Pepper and Frank Graham later in the decade, the Southern congressional delegation was even more monolithically reactionary in 1950 than it had been five years before.[39]

Operation Dixie's failure was cause and consequence of the stalemate in domestic politics that characterized the early postwar years. To have organized the South in the late 1940s would have required a massive, socially disruptive interracial campaign reminiscent of the CIO at its most militant moment in the late 1930s—indeed, it was a campaign not dissimilar from that which the modern civil rights movement would wage in the 1960s. Moreover, it would have required the kind of federal backing, both legal and ideological, offered by the Wagner Act in the 1930s and the Supreme Court's *Brown v. Board of Education* decision twenty years later.

Although many of the political ingredients for such a symbiosis were available, such a campaign never jelled in 1946 and 1947. First, the white South was economically and politically stronger in 1946 than it had been ten or twelve years earlier. The New Deal's massive intervention in the agricultural economy of that region had revived cotton and tobacco cultivation and begun a process of financial subsidy and farm mechanization that tilted the balance of power in the rural South still further to the political and social interests of large landowners. In the long run, New Deal agricultural policies would proletarianize millions of rural blacks and set the stage for the transformation of the Democratic Party and the civil rights movement in the 1960s, but in the late 1940s such displacement merely generated a labor surplus that depopulated the countryside and intensified racial competition at the bottom of the labor market.[40] Moreover, direct federal pressure upon the white South would remain quite timid in the postwar years, notwithstanding the celebrated bolt of the Dixiecrats at the 1948 Democratic National Convention. Reluctant to fragment the crumbling Democratic coalition, Truman tried long and hard to accommodate both civil rights liberals and Southern white supremacists. "The strategy," an assistant later explained, "was to start with a bold measure and then temporize to pick up the right-wing forces."[41]

The government's timidity was matched by that of organized labor and its liberal allies. Red-baiting and race-baiting had long been staples of Southern anti-unionism, but instead of directly confronting these attacks, CIO leaders sought to deflect Southern xenophobia by excluding Communists and other radicals from participation in Operation Dixie. Thus resources of the Communist-led trade unions and of Popular Front institutions like the Southern Conference for Human Welfare and the Highlander Folk School were shunted aside.[42] Of course, CIO anti-Communism was not alone responsible for the defeat of Operation Dixie; the decisive battles in the key textile mill towns were over by the end of 1946, before this issue became all-consuming. But the labor movement's internal conflict may well have turned a tactical defeat into a disorganized rout. For example, two of the most dynamic unions in the postwar South, the Mine, Mill, and Smelter Workers (known as Mine, Mill) and the Food and Tobacco Workers, were heavily black organizations that were hospitable to the Communists. By 1949 locals of these unions were being systematically raided by anti-Communist CIO unions. The crisis came to a head in Alabama when Murray's own United Steelworkers (USW) broke the Mine, Mill local that represented militant black iron miners around Birmingham. Recruiting their cadre from elements close to the Ku Klux Klan, USW locals in northern Alabama blended anti-Communism with overt racism to raid the Mine, Mill union and destroy one of the black community's most progressive institutions. The legacy of this fratricidal conflict extended well into the 1960s when Birmingham became synonymous with brutal white resistance to the civil rights movement.[43]

The Cold War's chilling effect on domestic politics also sealed the fate of labor-liberal efforts to find an effective vehicle that could stem the rightward drift in national politics. Until the spring of 1948, labor-liberals almost uniformly repudiated Truman as their presidential candidate and proposed replacing him with men as different as Dwight D. Eisenhower and William O. Douglas. More significant, the structure of the Democratic Party also came under scrutiny. The CIO, the new Americans for Democratic Action, and the AFL favored its "realignment," either by liberalization of the South or, if that failed, the expulsion of the Dixie-crats. Moreover, there was still enough interest in the formation of a third party to create at least a serious debate within some of the major unions—notably the UAW—and within sections of the liberal community. Mainstream union leaders had always held a dichotomous view of this subject. In the short run (that is, before the next election), unionists rejected the third-party idea on the grounds that it would "divide progressive forces." But when unionists looked further down the line, the labor party idea seemed more attractive. In 1946 C. Wright Mills found that among CIO national officers, 65 percent favored such a new political initiative in ten years' time.[44]

Yet as the Democratic Party declined in both its liberalism and its electability, the union determination to preserve the unity of "progressive" forces seemed increasingly tenuous. Thus in the spring of 1946, John Dewey, Norman Thomas, and Walter Reuther, all identified with the anti-Communist wing of American liberalism, issued a call for a National Educational Committee for a New Party. A year later the UAW's secretary-treasurer, the socialist Emil Mazey, told local union presidents to take "concrete action in building an independent labor party of workers and farmers." So unsure was Reuther of Truman's reelection that he scheduled a union-wide third-party political education meeting for January 21, 1949, the day after Thomas Dewey's presidential inauguration.[45]

Ironically, it was the actual formation of a third party—the Progressive Party, which ran Henry Wallace for president—that put a decisive end to such political experimentation and brought the industrial union wing of the labor movement even closer to the Democratic Party. For nearly a decade Wallace had enjoyed remarkable support in labor-liberal circles; as late as 1947 his vision of a global New Deal and great-power collaboration coincided with that of many liberals and the entire CIO wing of the labor movement. But his candidacy brought into sharp relief two issues that would prove crucial to the political reformulation of postwar labor-liberalism. The first was the Marshall Plan, and more generally the effort to integrate into an American-dominated world order the shattered economies of the industrialized West and commodity-producing South. Although initially greeted with some skepticism even by anti-Communist union leaders like Walter Reuther, the Marshall Plan won strong endorsement from most liberals as their hopes for the construction of a purely domestic full-employment welfare state declined, and as the Truman administration advanced the European Recovery Program as a key to international trade and North Atlantic prosperity.[46]

The second issue raised by the Wallace candidacy was the legitimacy of the Communists in American political life, and more broadly the possibility that Popular Front politics might have a continuing relevance in postwar America. Wallace refused to accept the postwar settlement that was emerging abroad and at home. He wanted détente with the Soviet Union (accepting its control of

Eastern Europe) and saw the Marshall Plan as little more than an effort to drive Western Europe into the straitjacket constructed by a newly hegemonic American capitalism. At home he denounced Taft-Hartley, defended those unions that defied its sanctions, and tried to ally himself with the most advanced forms of civil rights militancy.[47]

By 1948 the Wallace candidacy was therefore anathema, for it represented a break with what was becoming fundamental in postwar America: alignment with the government in the battalions of the new Cold War and exclusion of the Communists from the political arena. This was made explicit in a January 1948 CIO Executive Council resolution rejecting the Progressive Party and endorsing the Marshall Plan. A powerful Wallace movement threatened to taint the CIO with the badge of disloyalty. "The real issue," asserted the ever cautious Philip Murray, "is the jeopardy in which you place your Unions."[48] Truman's well-crafted opening to the labor-liberals—his Taft-Hartley veto message in June 1947, his accommodation of the urban coalition's pressure for federal civil rights action in the summer of 1948, and his pseudo-populist "Give 'em Hell, Harry" presidential campaign in the fall—solidified labor-liberal ties with the Democratic Party. Although the trade unions might still differ privately on bargaining goals or even their approach to Taft-Hartley, any divergence from the CIO election strategy was tantamount to organizational treason, which was in fact one of the charges leveled against several unions expelled from the CIO in 1949.[49]

Organized labor's failure to build its own political party may well have been overdetermined, even in an era when its organizational strength reached a twentieth-century apogee. The peculiarities of the American electoral system, the concentration of union strength in a relative handful of states, the ideological pressures generated by the Cold War, and the continuing ethnic and racial divisions within the working class are only the most obvious factors that sealed labor's alliance with the Democratic Party. But the costs of this political marriage still require calculation. Even in the urban North the Democratic Party rarely offered the representatives of organized labor more than a subordinate role in the development of its political program. The CIO bargained with the Democratic Party "much as it would with an employer," admitted PAC head Jack Kroll in the early 1950s.[50]

Two important consequences flowed from this dilemma. At the level of national policy formation, organized labor had no effective vehicle through which it could exert systematic pressure upon either the Democratic Party or the state apparatus. The trade unions maintained an extensive lobbying operation in Washington and in most state capitals, but on any given issue of interest to their membership, they were forced to rebuild the labor-liberal coalition all over again. Thus labor took justifiable credit for the reelection of Truman in 1948, but it proved incapable of translating this vote into a coherent congressional majority after Congress convened three months later. In turn, this radical disjunction between the relative solidity of the working-class vote and the weakness of its political representation contributed to the demobilization and depoliticization of a large part of the American working class in these years. Denied access to a political leadership that could articulate their specific class-oriented interests, workers found their consciousness shaped either by the parochial interests of their union or, more likely, by the vaguely populist rhetoric of mainstream Democrats.[51]

Privatization of the Welfare State

After 1947 the defensive political posture adopted by even the most liberal of the CIO unions enhanced the apparent appeal of a narrowly focused brand of private-sector collective bargaining. For example, the conservative victory in the 1946 congressional elections had a dramatic impact on Walter Reuther's own thinking. In a radio debate of May 1946, well before the elections, Reuther told his audience that rhetoric about a "government controlled economy" was a big-business scare tactic. The real question, he said, is "how much government control and for whose benefit." But in the wake of the massive Republican victory of November 1946, Reuther made a rhetorical about-face, now urging "free labor" and "free management" to join in solving their problems, or a "superstate will arise to do it for us."[52] Or as Reuther put it in another context, "I'd rather bargain with General Motors than with the government . . . General Motors has no army."[53]

General Motors and other big companies also sought a long-range accommodation with their own unions. GM wanted to contain unionism within what it considered its "proper sphere"; otherwise, declared Charles Wilson, the "border area of collective bargaining will be a constant battleground between unions and management."[54] To executives like Wilson this fear was exacerbated by the realization that inflationary pressures generated by Cold War military spending would be a permanent feature of the postwar scene. The UAW effort to link company pricing policy to a negotiated wage package in 1946 had been staved off by GM, but the company realized that disruptive strikes and contentious annual wage negotiations, especially if couched as part of a broader offensive against corporate power, merely served to embitter labor relations on the shop floor and hamper the company's long-range planning.

Therefore in the spring of 1948—just after the Czech coup and during the months when Congress debated an administration request for a $3.3 billion military procurement package—GM offered the UAW a contract that seemed to promise social peace even in an era of continuous inflation. Two features were central to the new social order: first, an automatic cost-of-living adjustment (COLA) keyed to the general price index; second, a 2 percent "annual improvement factor" (AIF) wage increase designed to reflect, if only partially, the still larger annual rise in GM productivity. To GM, such permanently escalating labor costs would prove tolerable because this industrial giant faced little effective competition, either foreign or domestic, so it could easily "administer" any price increases made necessary by the new labor contract.[55]

The agreement was a dramatic, even radical, departure from past union practice. Reuther himself had rejected wage escalation until early 1948, and a Twentieth Century Fund survey of union leaders taken later the same year revealed that more than 90 percent opposed COLA clauses in their contracts. With the general wage declines of 1921, 1930–1932, and 1938 still a living memory, most union leaders instinctively rejected the premise upon which the GM-UAW contract was based: the emergence of a new era of inflationary prosperity and relative social peace. Labor leaders thought such schemes foreclosed the possibility of a large increase in the real standard of living, and they continued to fear that such a wage formula would become a downhill escalator when the inevitable postwar depression finally arrived. The UAW, for example, described the 1948 GM pact as only a "holding action" that protected GM workers until the labor-liberal coalition could replace it with more comprehensive sociopolitical guidelines.[56]

But when the 1949 recession turned out to be less than the depression many had expected, the gateway was open to the further elaboration of such an accommodation between the big unions and the major corporations. Again the UAW pioneered the way, with a new agreement: a five-year "Treaty of Detroit" that provided an improved COLA and AIF and a $125-a-month pension. *Fortune* magazine hailed the 1950 UAW-GM contract as "the first that unmistakably accepts the existing distribution of income between wages and profits as 'normal' if not as 'fair.' . . . It is the first major union contract that explicitly accepts objective economic facts—cost of living and productivity—as determining wages, thus throwing overboard all theories of wages as determined by political power and of profits as 'surplus value.'" By the early 1960s the COLA principle had been incorporated in more than 50 percent of all major union contracts, and in the inflationary 1960s and 1970s it spread even wider: to Social Security, to some welfare programs, and to wage determination in some units of the government and nonunion sector.[57]

Just as the negotiation of COLA agreements came in the wake of the union movement's forced retreat from the effort to reshape the Truman administration's early economic policy, so too did the new interest in pension and health and welfare plans represent a parallel privatization of the labor movement's commitment to an expanded welfare state. Initially, American trade unionists overwhelmingly favored a public, federal system for financing social benefits like pensions, health care, and unemployment insurance. Both the CIO and AFL worked for the passage of the Wagner-Murray-Dingell Bill, a 1945 proposal that would have liberalized and federalized the American social welfare system in a fashion not dissimilar to that envisioned by the British government's pathbreaking Beveridge Report of 1942, which laid the basis for the welfare state constructed by the postwar Labour government.[58]

But the same forces that gutted the Full Employment Act of 1946 also destroyed labor-backed efforts to raise the social wage in these same postwar years. "Nothing more clearly distinguishes the post-war political climate of the USA from that of Great Britain than the almost unqualified refusal of its legislature to respond to proposals for social reform," wrote the British political scientist Vivian Vale. The United States devoted about 4.4 percent of its GNP to Social Security in 1949, a proportion less than half that of even the austere economies of war-torn Western Europe.[59]

Organized labor still found company-funded pension and health schemes distasteful—their coverage was incomplete, their financing was mistrusted, and they smacked of old-fashioned paternalism—but the political impasse faced by postwar unionists seemed to offer no alternatives.[60] The UMW made the first important postwar commitment in this area when John L. Lewis fought for an employer-funded health and welfare system in the spring of 1946. His several wartime years of conflict with the government had soured Lewis on the whole idea of the liberal administrative state. He found, for example, that when federal authorities seized actual control of the coal mines in 1943 and 1946, little changed in terms of the safety or health of those workers represented by the UMW. Lewis would feel confident only if the UMW itself played the decisive role in providing safety, health, and retirement benefits in the mines. His struggle over this issue entailed a series of strikes and legal confrontations with the administration, but the UMW's ultimate success proved crucial in reducing labor's support of a federal effort in this area. Thus in 1948, after Lewis had finally established the UMW health and welfare program, he told the embattled advocates of Truman's national health insurance scheme that the UMW would no longer stand in support of this initiative.[61]

Unlike Lewis, mainstream union leaders never abandoned their formal commitment to an expanded welfare state, but at the same time they retreated, if more subtly, to a more parochial outlook. Immediately after the disastrous midterm elections of 1946, CIO leaders announced that they were not going to wait "for perhaps another ten years until the Social Security laws are amended adequately." Instead they would press for pensions and health benefits in their next collective bargaining round. Some unionists of a more explicitly social democratic outlook, like Walter Reuther and William Pollock of the Textile Workers Union, theorized that if employers were saddled with large pension and health insurance costs, they would join "shoulder to shoulder" with labor-liberal forces to demand higher federal payments to relieve them of this burden.[62] But such assumptions proved naïve. The big unions themselves no longer saw an increase in federal welfare expenditures as an urgent task. And after the steel and auto unions established the heavy-industry pension and health benefit pattern in 1949, employers were more than ready to fold these additional costs into their product prices. Moreover, managers recognized that company-specific benefits built employee loyalty, and at some level they understood that a social wage of minimal proportions was advantageous to their class interest, even if their own firm had to bear additional costs as a consequence.[63]

Despite these limitations, it looked as if the key wage and benefit bargains negotiated by the big unions would generate the kind of class-wide settlement in the United States that was characteristic of industry-labor relationships in northern Europe. Beginning in 1946 there were four distinct collective bargaining rounds in which the wage pattern hammered out in the steel or auto industry became the standard applied in rubber, meatpacking, electrical products, and other core industries. Similarly, pensions, health benefits, and supplemental unemployment payments were also copied by many large employers, both union and nonunion, private and public.[64]

But this sort of pattern bargaining had a remarkably anemic life. It never spread much beyond the oligopolistically structured core industries, and even there it required a strong union that could take labor costs out of competition to make the pattern stick. Where unions were weak, as in electrical products and textiles, or where competition was fierce, as in automotive parts and food processing, wage and benefit guidelines established in Detroit or Pittsburgh were reproduced only imperfectly. For example, in the Detroit-area auto parts industry only about a quarter of all companies, employing 40 percent of the workforce, followed the pattern of the Big Three.[65] Similarly, cost-of-living adjustments were rarely extended to workers in those segments of the labor market outside the core industrial/governmental sector. As a result, wage disparities increased dramatically within the postwar working class. The relatively egalitarian wage patterns of the mid-1940s began to erode even in the high employment years of the Korean War, but they underwent a truly radical deterioration in the inflationary era after 1965 when workers outside of the primary labor market found themselves defenseless against renewed inflation and labor-cost competition.[66]

The Postwar Legacy

The weakness of the postwar welfare state and the extreme fragmentation inherent in the American system of industrial relations did much to redivide the American working class into a unionized segment that until the 1980s enjoyed an almost Western European level of social welfare protection, and a still larger stratum, predominantly young, minority, and female, that was left out in the cold. Because so much of the postwar social struggle has taken place at the level of the firm rather than within a broader political arena, this American system has reinforced the postwar economy's tendency to construct segmented and unequal labor markets. This multitiered system of industrial relations has served to erode solidarity within the working class and has made it difficult to counter claims that welfare spending and social equity are harmful to economic growth. The classic resentment felt by many blue-collar workers toward those on state-supported welfare is partly rooted in the system of double taxation that the organized working class has borne in the postwar era. Union workers pay to support two welfare systems: their own, funded by a "tax" on their total pay periodically renegotiated in their contract, and that of the government, paid for by a tax system that grew increasingly regressive as the postwar years advanced. In turn, organized labor has come to be perceived (and all too often perceives itself) as a special-interest group, in which its advocacy of welfare state measures that would raise the social wage for all workers has taken on an increasingly mechanical quality.[67]

Among other consequences, these divisions within the working class and between labor and its erstwhile allies have progressively weakened political support for the structures of the welfare state erected in the New Deal era. American unions remain supporters of Social Security, national health insurance, and minority-targeted welfare programs, but their ability to mobilize either their own members or a broader constituency on these issues declined during most of the postwar era. A militant civil rights movement, not the unions, put these issues back on the national agenda for a time in the 1960s. Moreover, labor's postwar abdication from any sustained struggle over the structure of the political economy has had its own debilitating consequences. As older industries decline, it has both sapped the loyalty of the labor movement's original blue-collar constituency and, at the same time, deprived the unions of any effective voice in recent debates over the patterning of work and wages in the largely non-union service and retail sectors of the economy, the revival of American manufacturing, or the reform of the nation's health-care system.

CHAPTER 7

Communism On the Shop Floor and Off

Communism, of the capital "C" variety, hardly exists in the world today, and in the United States it is an idea and a movement that is increasingly part of a distant past, more contemporary than Populism or Prohibition, but of seemingly less twenty-first-century relevance than evangelical Protestantism or environmental activism. And yet this is a phenomenon that still generates the same kind of debates that divided the left, and the left from the right, more than half a century ago. In some instances, documents flowing out of the Moscow archives have helped shed new light on the politics and affiliations of an Alger Hiss or a Harry Bridges, but such revelations are hardly needed to keep this pot boiling, because the real issue involves the fate, character, and legitimacy of the American radical tradition, especially during that moment in the middle decades of the twentieth century when the Communists were at their influential apogee within a dynamic new trade union movement, as well as in almost every other area of progressive U.S. politics. For example, the founders of *New Politics*, where this essay first appeared, have been unwilling to concede that the Communists, both those who were in the unions and those who were out, actually constituted a part of the indigenous American left. And more recently it has become commonplace for some, within the academy and without, to once again mount an aggressive effort to reduce all Communist activity in the United States to a species of Soviet spy craft.[1]

Sociologists Judith Stepan-Norris (University of California, Irvine) and Maurice Zeitlin (University of California, Los Angeles) have thrown into this debate a massively researched excavation of the Communist-led trade unions titled *Left Out: Reds and America's Industrial Unions*.[2] They did not visit the Moscow state archives, but they did take the freeway to the California Institute of Technology, where they found a unique documentary resource: a large and representative set of collective bargaining contracts (collected by Cal Tech to help business fight the new unions) that they have analyzed to compare "Red" American trade unionism with those labor organizations led by unionists whose ideology was less politically well defined or with those of an outright anti-Communist orientation. Their thesis is straightforward: American Communist apologies "for the crimes of the Soviet regime should not be allowed to distort or obscure Communist unionists' real, radical, and democratic, achievements—whether these unionists were officers of CIO internationals, local officers, or worker activists in the shops."[3]

To make this case the authors take aim at a species of anti-Communist argumentation that began in the 1930s and 1940s chiefly among Socialist and Trotskyist intellectuals who were at war with the rise of American Stalinism. This attack proved potent because it broke so sharply from that of a much older antiradical tradition. From 1886, when the Haymarket bombs in Chicago first mobilized conservatives against radical labor, until the early 1930s, anti-Communists accused the revolutionary left of being just that: revolutionaries who sought the destruction of the existing trade unions ("dual unionism"); violence on the picket line; and the subversion of family, church, and ethnic hierarchy. Although much was made of Communist allegiance to the Soviet Union in the 1920s, conservatives made few distinctions between the Industrial Workers of the World, the antiwar Socialists, and post–World War I Communists, all of whom seemed to be impractical, impatient, destructive agitators. To unsympathetic observers, Communist strikes and Communist unions—in New York City garment shops, Gastonia textile mills, New Mexico coal mines—all collapsed because their ideological leadership did not know how to make the kind of deals and compromises necessary to maintain stable trade unionism.

But this critique of the Communist-line union leadership was transformed during the next third of a century, and largely along lines advanced by liberals, ex-Socialists, and those influenced by the Trotskyist analysis of Stalinism, both in the Soviet Union and at home. There were still conservatives who attacked the Communists for race mixing, treasonous un-Americanism, and the subversion of a paternalistic plant community, but of far more consequence during the era of World War II and the Cold War that followed was the charge that Communist union leaders failed at their primary duty: representing the rank and file, fighting for racial and gender equality, advancing a progressive version of trade unionism within the workplace and the larger polity. Because their main allegiance lay with the ruling strata of the Soviet Union, Communist-line unionists subordinated the interests of their own membership to the foreign-policy needs of an alien, authoritarian state. This made for increasing moderation during the years after the sit-down strikes, when the Soviets sought to convince President Roosevelt and the New Dealers that they were suitable partners in an antifascist alliance, but it made for strike militancy during the era of the Stalin-Hitler nonaggression pact, when American Communists insisted that "the Yanks are not coming."[4]

World War II has always been Exhibit A in this bill of charges. With the Soviet Union fighting for its life, Communist trade unionists were "the great reactionaries," opined liberal columnists Joseph and Stewart Alsop. They were "counterfeit revolutionaries," in the words of the labor radical Sidney Lens.[5] Communists in the unions defended the no-strike pledge; denounced the mine strikes led by John L. Lewis; abandoned the March on Washington movement led by A. Philip Randolph;

and favored incentive pay, a crackdown on wildcat strikes, and labor-management cooperation in the factories. And even during the Cold War this line of attack did not cease: liberals and those on the anti-Communist left claimed that unions like the United Electrical Workers, fearful of raids from the CIO and under constant attack by the government, signed sweetheart contracts with General Electric and Westinghouse in order to make themselves more acceptable to big business than their anti-Communist rivals. They were now "Red Company Unions." And of course the Communists were not trade union democrats. Writing in 1948, C. Wright Mills endorsed the liberal-left charge that when they are in control, the Communist intrigue "prefers wrecking a union to losing control of it."[6]

Maurice Zeitlin and Judith Stepan-Norris are not the first scholars to take issue with this line of analysis. A generation of New Left and post–New Left historians of labor, feminism, civil rights, music, film, fiction, journalism, and the law have uncovered a world of complexity beneath the hyper-political schema advanced by observers like Theodore Draper, Irving Howe, and Max Kampelman, the latter a Hubert Humphrey staffer who wrote *The Communist Party vs. the CIO* in the 1950s.[7] More than a million people probably passed through the Communist Party (CP) during the midcentury decades, and not all of them took lock-step orders from party headquarters in Union Square. Robin Kelley's celebrated study of black Alabama Communists makes that abundantly clear. As an anonymous black Communist told a CP functionary from the North, "Ain't no foreign country in the world foreign as Alabama to a New Yorker. They know all about England, maybe, France, never met one who knew 'Bama."[8] Indeed, when it came to the labor movement, party discipline was loose, and the farther one got into the field, the more autonomy unionists enjoyed, especially on those day-to-day issues that were specific to each firm, workforce, and industry. Thus Michael Honey has demonstrated the extent to which Memphis union Communists advanced the civil rights frontier even during World War II;[9] Ron Schatz has shown how the United Electrical Workers (UE) turned industry incentive-pay schemes to rank-and-file advantage;[10] Toni Gilpin has reminded us that locals of the Farm Equipment Workers of America built a powerful shop steward system that was in many instances superior to that of the UAW in its agriculture equipment locals;[11] and Joshua Freeman has explained how the legacy of New York City's extensive network of Communist and ex-Communist trade union leaders gave to the municipal labor movement in the 1950s and 1960s a remarkably aggressive and politicized profile.[12]

Stepan-Norris and Zeitlin take such historical studies and personal memoirs and combine them with as much large-N statistical evidence as they can muster to demonstrate that the most significant achievement of the Communists was "the building of a combative, class-conscious industrial union movement." As we shall see, the authors are frequently fetishistic about the virtues of CP leadership, but there can no longer be much doubt that when it came to actual trade union practice, the sixteen or eighteen CIO unions that fell within the Communist orbit were effective, militant labor organizations that were at least as internally democratic as other affiliates, negotiating contracts equal or superior to those of the unions led by non-Communist officials.

The authors demonstrate that mega-historical theories of trade union development—whether pluralist, Marxist, or based on some Weberian variant—fail if they do not take into account the politics and ideology of both union leaders and their corporate adversaries. Democracy is rooted in factions, insurgency, and counterpoised ideologies. Stepan-Norris and Zeitlin restore a contingent quality to labor history that is often missing in the grand theories generated by social scientists and not a few historians. Politics and policy, not an "iron law of oligarchy," subverted the progressive, democratic promise of the Depression-era labor movement. Bureaucratic practices were becoming manifest on both the left and right of the American union movement, but such an undemocratic drift was as much a function of the American labor law, government pressure, and, most importantly, corporate labor policies as it was any inter-logic of trade union development. Stepan-Norris and Zeitlin turn the epigram of Robert Michels upside down. Instead of "Who says 'organization' says 'oligarchy,'" the authors respond, "Who says 'the unrestricted power of capital' says 'oligarchy.'"[13]

Indeed, Stepan-Norris and Zeitlin confirm in rigorous fashion what historians and memoirists have been writing for some time. On a whole variety of issues that constituted the progressive midcentury social union agenda, the Communist unions were significantly better than non-Communist or anti-Communist unions. Why precisely this is the case remains a bit fuzzy, but there is no doubt that on many shop issues, on race and gender equality, those unions denominated as Communist were more democratic, militant, and organizationally progressive. For example, when the authors examined a sample of California contracts negotiated by the locals of the CIO big three unions, they found that over the years from 1938 to 1955, 6 percent of UE contracts contained a total no-strike provision, 53 percent of UAW contracts contained such a work-stoppage prohibition, and 68 percent of those covered by the United Steelworkers had such a provision. Likewise, 93 percent of all UE contracts specified that a shop steward had to be present at the grievance procedure's first step, 48 percent of UAW contracts had a similar provision, while only a quarter of those in steel assured this progressive union right. All of this remained true even during World War II, when Communist chief Earl Browder denounced shop militancy and hailed a new era of labor-management cooperation that reflected the larger alignment of American capital and Soviet power in the antifascist struggle. But Stepan-Norris and Zeitlin confirm, both through anecdote and statistical survey, the perspective long advanced by memoirists and historians alike: regardless of the directives from Moscow or Union Square, Communists in the trade unions remained militant opponents of shop management. "We conducted business as usual in the unions," California Communist Dorothy Healey told the authors. "We never stopped fighting on the shop floor, whatever the national leadership under Browder was saying . . . we never gave anything away. It was the tasks imposed by the day-to-day defense of workers that mattered. We never stopped to ask if what we did violated the no-strike pledge or Browder's incentive plans."[14]

This same impulse was hardly confined to Communist trade unionists. There was much "right-wing" militancy as well during the two decades that followed the labor upsurge of the 1930s. Regardless of the contract language or the politics of the union leadership, workers do seek a kind of shop control of the production process: craft and building-trades workers often declared their allegiance to an anti-Communist, socially conservative unionism, but during most of the twentieth century these skilled workers defended a set of job-protecting work rules with a ferocity that was virtually unmatched throughout North America. And in the factories, one did not have to be represented by a Communist-led local to battle for shop control of the production process. In his account of Chrysler unionism from the early sit-down strikes to the era of the Dodge Revolutionary Union Movement, Steve Jefferys has demonstrated that a dense phalanx of "blue button" shop stewards and a tradition of wildcat strikes kept management on the defensive for years. Likewise, at Ford's great River Rouge complex, where Stepan-Norris and Zeitlin overstate somewhat the degree of Communist influence, shop militancy had a multiplicity of sources, some of which were explicitly anti-Communist in their origins and orientation.[15]

Because of their relentless effort to celebrate Communist-led union militancy, Stepan-Norris and Zeitlin downplay the overall nature of the business community's hostility to CIO-style unionism. There was no labor-management accord or consensus in the postwar years. Corporate leaders and their political spokesmen believed that when it came to bargaining issues or shop floor militancy, the distinction between Communists and their more conventional trade union counterparts was rather slim. "Nothing is more dangerous than to assume that those who today attack 'Communists' within the union, and who are in consequence unthinkingly labeled 'right-wingers' are ipso facto believers in private enterprise or in our form of government," warned Stuart Ball, counsel for Montgomery Ward, late in 1946. "It is not necessary to pin the label of 'Marxist' upon a labor leader to prove that what he believes is incompatible with our basic political and economic beliefs." In textiles, retail trade, shoemaking, tobacco processing, and office employment, business played the anti-Communist card to keep its workplaces union free. But the issue was always unionism, not Communism.[16]

The authors are right to declare the purge of the Communists from the CIO and the main body of American labor "An American Tragedy." This is hardly controversial, because even the anti-Communists within the CIO came to realize that the 1949–1950 expulsion of unions representing more than a million workers had a devastating impact on all of American labor, both in terms of economic clout, political influence, and shop floor practice. Indeed, even in the late 1940s the justification for the purge came almost entirely in terms of real politic. Philip Murray, Walter Reuther, and Mike Quill of the Transport Workers

Union were happy to borrow the rhetoric of democracy and anti-Stalinism in their anti-Communist crusade, but the real issue was always U.S. government blackmail: unless the CIO got rid of this politically unorthodox faction, the industrial union federation would find itself under attack by both the Truman administration and the resurgent GOP right wing. This turned out to be the perspective of the Communists (the Union Square variety) themselves, who soon urged the expelled unions to rejoin the labor "mainstream" even if it meant the demise of their organizational independence. Stepan-Norris and Zeitlin think this was another New York/Moscow blunder, and they advance the somewhat fanciful idea—albeit based on the dogged perseverance of the Communists and their allies still in command of unions like the UE, the International Longshore and Warehouse Union (ILWU), and Mine, Mill—that the expelled CP unions might have formed a cohesive, organizationally aggressive alliance in the 1950s. The authors call this the "third labor federation" that never was.

How do the authors explain the virtues of Communist trade union practice? Clearly it was a question neither of centralized direction nor of ideology, because at numerous points Stepan-Norris and Zeitlin deride and denounce the hyper-political formulations put out by party headquarters. The Communists functioned best when they functioned as quasi-autonomous trade unionists. So what made them better than the Socialists, the Reutherites, or the Industrial Workers of the World (IWW) remnants? The authors don't say. Or rather they advance the somewhat nostalgic view that if organizers latched on to Communist politics in the 1920s and 1930s when the going was tough, then they were sure to advance a militant and democratic unionism despite the misbegotten advice from the CP politicos.

Actually, I think there is another dimension to this question. Like the Socialists, the Wobblies, and other left-wing formations, the Communists recruited from the same social strata: first- and second-generation immigrants, alienated urban workers, ex-populists, and a bit later, science-oriented academics, African Americans, Jews, and the creative intellectuals of Hollywood and New York. But if the party was not the internally Stalinist organization of which its critics complained (the American CP did not hold state power), how do we explain the coherence of the party even when its trade union element was in quasi-revolt against headquarters?

The answer is in the Soviet Union and the mystique it gave to party membership and party activism. The sense that the American Communist Party was part of a worldwide movement that took guidance from the successful revolutionaries (later antifascists) in Russia provided the emotive, cohesive glue that made the American Communists something other than another reform organization. It explains why the Communists, unlike the Depression-era Socialists, remained a disciplined force despite the party's rotating membership and infamous political zigzags. The Socialist Party, which started off the interwar period with a sizable proletarian base, disintegrated during the 1930s, because tactical political differences led to organizational splits, after which party members simply decamped into the CIO or other progressive organizations like the Union for Democratic Action, forerunner of the Americans for Democratic Action. This was the path taken by Walter Reuther, Reinhold Niebuhr, and Paul Douglas. For good—but chiefly ill—the Communists had the Soviet lodestar, which until 1956 gave even the most independent-operating Communists a collective élan shared by comrades in both nearby shops and old-world cities.

To understand union Communism's rise and demise, the ideological issue cannot be avoided. *Left Out* marginalizes CP politics through a relentless focus on the collective bargaining relationship, on measuring Communist effectiveness in the shop floor contest for power. There is much to be said for this perspective, because a militant, independent shop floor organization is the essence of trade unionism and an autonomous working-class political voice. But the CIO was not a syndicalist formation. Indeed it was the program of the right, not the left, to reduce all labor politics to collective bargaining, and once this was accomplished, the containment, retreat, and destruction of the labor movement was virtually foreordained. That was the essential logic of the Taft-Hartley Act passed in 1947. Thus to the extent that the authors measure union progressivism by a firm-centered collective bargaining standard, they are playing a game where shop militancy alone would have a self-defeating character.

The CIO's greatest triumphs came when its affiliates linked union power and a political program to push forward the New Deal and the coalition that sustained it. The CIO always had to move forward, to generate a political bloc that could influence elections, make the state an ally, and win over a large slice of the middle class. Otherwise union labor would become isolated and defensive, and ultimately transformed into the parochial interest group that its opponents were delighted to combat. And it is precisely in this way that the Red economism celebrated by Stepan-Norris and Zeitlin became dysfunctional. It was not that a more moderate program would have won over those layers of the lower middle class that were in fact being captured by the political right; rather, the labor left needed a transitional, social democratic program that would link shop militancy to the New Deal's larger political universe. By emphasizing the autonomy of the CP unionists from the meddlesome Union Square politicos (as in the CP union reluctance to endorse Henry Wallace's Progressive Party in 1948), Stepan-Norris and Zeitlin actually demonstrate how and why the Communist-led labor project failed to crystallize a set of politics that could appeal much beyond the world of traditional trade unionism. The Communists themselves were not unaware of the need for such a linked agenda, but the authors of *Left Out* downplay this ideological disjunction, and for good reason, because it was in the larger, liberal political world that Stalinism, trade union or otherwise, became such an obnoxious obstacle to the construction of a midcentury progressive bloc.

PART III

The Rights Revolution

These essays demonstrate how the rise of a civil rights consciousness during the middle decades of the twentieth century was both organically linked to the rise of the New Deal–era trade unions while at the same time this new rights consciousness provided a set of legal and ideological structures that helped weaken those same institutions. When in the mid-1980s Robert Korstad and I began to formulate the essay "Opportunities Found and Lost: Labor, Radicals, and the Early Civil Rights Movement," the idea of a long civil rights movement that had its origins in the upheavals of the late New Deal was but an obscure construction. It has gained a good deal of ground in subsequent years, as historians such as Jacqueline Hall, Patricia Sullivan, Eric Arnesen, and Glenda Gilmore have demonstrated. Indeed, the legal scholar Risa Goluboff, whose work I review in the second essay in this section, has demonstrated that in the 1940s the legal and political assault on the Jim Crow order was important not just in terms of its movement-building potential, which Korstad and I emphasized, but also as a way of conceptualizing a working-class-oriented definition of the very meaning of civil rights.

Whatever its character, the rights regime that did emerge in the second half of the twentieth century proved enormously liberating, not only in the United States but throughout the world as well, and especially in the less industrialized and democratic nations where the demand for human rights and civil liberties has sparked reform and revolution. But for both workers and citizens, an orientation that privileges individual rights above all else can also function as both a poor substitute for and a legal subversion of the institutions that once provided a collective voice for workers and other subaltern strata.

I explore this trade-off in the essay "A New Era of Global Human Rights: Good for the Workers?" Just as the British Anti-Slavery Society and the Congo Association sought to abolish or reform unfree labor in the nineteenth century, so too does the contemporary proliferation of nongovernmental organizations attempt to ameliorate the sweated work that is so commonly found among those who are employed in the manufacture, distribution, and sale of consumer goods in China, India, Bangladesh, Central America, and elsewhere. And in the United States itself, this new reform order has its own parallel: while the unions struggle for their very existence, fighting to preserve a fragment of the power and dignity they had once won for their own members, the rights regime fought for by the civil rights movement has weathered the neoliberal storms of recent decades in far better shape, even if a conservative Supreme Court is determined to limit the scope of a rights-based remedy for millions of workers.

CHAPTER 8

Opportunities Found and Lost

Labor, Radicals, and the Early Civil Rights Movement

WITH ROBERT KORSTAD

Most historians would agree that the modern civil rights movement did not begin with the Supreme Court's decision in *Brown v. Board of Education*. Yet all too often the movement's history has been written as if events before the mid-1950s constituted a kind of prehistory, important only insofar as they laid the legal and political foundation for the spectacular advances that came later. Those were the "forgotten years of the Negro Revolution," wrote one historian; they were the "seed time of racial and legal metamorphosis," according to another. But such a periodization profoundly underestimates the tempo and misjudges the social dynamic of the freedom struggle.[1]

The civil rights era began, dramatically and decisively, in the early 1940s when the social structure of black America took on an increasingly urban, proletarian character. A predominantly Southern rural and small-town population was soon transformed into one of the most urban of all major ethnic groups. More than two million blacks migrated to Northern and Western industrial areas during the 1940s, while another million moved from farm to city within the South. Northern black voters doubled their numbers between 1940 and 1948, and in the eleven states of the Old South black registration more than quadrupled, reaching over one million by 1952. Likewise, membership in the National Association for the Advancement of Colored People (NAACP) soared, growing from 50,000 in 355 branches in 1940 to almost 450,000 in 1,073 branches six years later.[2]

The half million black workers who joined unions affiliated with the Congress of Industrial Organizations (CIO) were in the vanguard of efforts to transform race relations. The NAACP and the Urban League had become friendlier toward labor in the Depression era, but their legal and social work orientation had not prepared them to act effectively in the workplaces and working-class neighborhoods where black Americans fought their most decisive struggles of the late 1930s and 1940s. By the early 1940s it was commonplace for sympathetic observers to assert the centrality of mass unionization in the civil rights struggle. A Rosenwald Fund study concluded, not without misgivings, that "the characteristic movements among Negroes are now for the first time becoming proletarian," while a *Crisis* reporter found the CIO a "lamp of democracy" throughout the old Confederate states. "The South has not known such a force since the historic Union Leagues in the great days of the Reconstruction era."[3]

This movement gained much of its dynamic character from the relationship that arose between unionized blacks and the federal government and proved somewhat similar to the creative tension that linked the church-based civil rights movement and the state almost two decades later. In the 1950s the *Brown* decision legitimated much of the subsequent social struggle, but it remained essentially a dead letter until given political force by a growing protest movement. In like manner, the rise of industrial unions and the evolution of late–New Deal labor legislation offered working-class blacks an economic and political standard by which they could legitimate their demands and stimulate a popular struggle. The "one man, one vote" policy implemented in thousands of National Labor Relations Board (NLRB) elections, the industrial "citizenship" that union contracts offered once-marginal elements of the working class, and the patriotic egalitarianism of the government's wartime propaganda—all generated a rights consciousness that gave working-class black militancy a moral justification in some ways as powerful as that evoked by the Baptist spirituality of Martin Luther King Jr. a generation later.[4] During the war the Fair Employment Practices Commission (FEPC) held little direct authority, but like the Civil Rights Commission of the late 1950s, it served to expose racist conditions and spur on black activism wherever it undertook its well-publicized investigations. And just as a disruptive and independent civil rights movement in the 1960s could pressure the federal government to enforce its own laws and move against local elites, so too did the mobilization of the black working class in the 1940s make civil rights an issue that could not be ignored by union officers, white executives, or government officials.[5]

This essay explores two examples of the workplace-oriented civil rights militancy that arose in the 1940s—one in the South and one in the North. It analyzes the unionization of predominantly black tobacco workers in Winston-Salem, North Carolina, and the ferment in the United Auto Workers in Detroit, Michigan, that made that city a center of black working-class activism in the North. Similar movements took root among newly organized workers in the cotton compress mills of Memphis, the tobacco factories of Richmond and Charleston, the steel mills of Pittsburgh and Birmingham, the stockyards and farm equipment factories of Chicago and Louisville, and the shipyards of Baltimore and Oakland.[6]

Winston-Salem in the War

Winston-Salem had been a center of tobacco processing since the 1880s, and the R. J. Reynolds Tobacco Company dominated the life of the city's eighty thousand citizens. By the 1940s whites held most of the higher-paying machine-tending

jobs, but blacks formed the majority of the workforce, concentrated in the prepa-
ration departments where they cleaned, stemmed, and conditioned the tobacco.[7]
The jobs were physically demanding, the air was hot and dusty, and in departments with machinery, the noise was deafening. Most black workers made only
a few cents above minimum wage, and benefits were few. Black women workers
experienced frequent verbal and occasional sexual abuse. Reynolds maintained
a determined opposition to trade unionism, and two unsuccessful American
Federation of Labor (AFL) efforts to organize segregated locals had soured most
black workers on trade unionism.

But in 1943 a CIO organizing effort succeeded. Led by the United Cannery,
Agricultural, Packing and Allied Workers of America (UCAPAWA), a new union
drive championed black dignity and self-organization, employing several young
black organizers who had gotten their start in the interracial Southern Tenant
Farmers Union. Their discreet two-year organizing campaign made a dramatic
breakthrough when black women in one of the stemmeries stopped work on June
17. A severe labor shortage, chronic wage grievances, and a recent speedup gave
the women both the resources and the incentive to transform a departmental
sit-down into a festive, plant-wide strike. The UCAPAWA quickly signed up
about eight thousand black workers, organized a committee to negotiate with
the company, and asked the NLRB to hold an election.[8]

The effort to win union recognition at Reynolds sparked a spirited debate
about who constituted the legitimate leadership of the black community in
Winston-Salem. Midway through the campaign, six local black business and
professional men—a college professor, an undertaker, a dentist, a store owner,
and two ministers—dubbed "colored leaders" by the *Winston-Salem Journal*,
wrote a long letter to the editor urging workers to reject the "followers of John
L. Lewis and William Green" and to remain loyal to Reynolds. In the absence of
any formal leadership, elected or otherwise, representatives of Winston-Salem's
small black middle class had served as spokesmen, brokering with the white
elite for small concessions in a tightly segregated society. The fight for collective bargaining, they argued, had to remain secondary to the more important
goal of racial betterment, which could only be achieved by "good will, friendly
understanding, and mutual respect and co-operation between the races." Partly
because of their own vulnerability to economic pressure, such traditional black
leaders judged unions, like other institutions, by their ability to deliver jobs and
maintain a precarious racial equilibrium.[9]

The union campaign at Reynolds transformed the expectations tobacco workers held of the old community leadership. Reynolds workers responded to calls
for moderation from "college-trained people" with indignation. "Our leaders,"
complained Mabel Jessup, "always look clean and refreshed at the end of the
hottest day, because they work in very pleasant environments . . . All I ask of our
leaders is that they obtain a job in one of the factories as a laborer and work two

weeks. Then write what they think." W. L. Griffin felt betrayed. "I have attended church regularly for the past thirty years," he wrote, "and unity and co-operation have been taught and preached from the pulpits of the various Negro churches. Now that the laboring class of people are about to unite and co-operate on a wholesale scale for the purpose of collective bargaining, these same leaders seem to disagree with that which they have taught their people." Others rejected the influence of people who "have always told us what the white people want, but somehow or other are particularly silent on what we want." "We feel we are the leaders instead of you," asserted a group of union members.[10]

Reynolds, the only major tobacco manufacturer in the country not under a union contract, followed tried-and-true methods to break the union. Management used lower-level supervisors to intimidate unionists and supported a "no union" movement among white workers, whose organizers were given freedom to roam the company's workshops and warehouses. That group, the R. J. Reynolds Employees Association, sought a place on the NLRB ballot in order to delay the increasingly certain CIO victory. Meanwhile the white business community organized an Emergency Citizens Committee to help defeat the CIO. In a well-publicized resolution, the committee blamed the recent strikes on "self-seeking representatives of the CIO" and warned that continued subversion of existing race relations would "likely lead to riots and bloodshed."[11]

In earlier times this combination of antiunion forces would probably have derailed the organizing effort. But during World War II, black workers had allies who helped shift the balance of power. The NLRB closely supervised each stage of the election process and denied the company's request to divide the workforce into two bargaining units, which would have weakened the position of black workers. When local judges sought to delay the election, government attorneys removed the case to federal court. In December 1943 an NLRB election gave the CIO a resounding victory. But continued federal assistance, from the United States Conciliation Service and the National War Labor Board, was still needed to secure Reynolds workers a union contract in 1944.[12]

That first agreement resembled hundreds of other wartime labor-management contracts, but in the context of Winston-Salem's traditional system of race relations it had radical implications, because it generated a new set of shop floor rights embodied in the seniority, grievance, and wage adjustment procedures. The contract did not attack factory segregation—for the most part white workers continued to control the better-paying jobs—but it did call forth a new corps of black leaders to defend the rights Reynolds workers had recently won. The one hundred or so elected shop stewards were the "most important people in the plant," remembered union activist Velma Hopkins. They were the "natural leaders," people who had "taken up money for flowers if someone died or would talk to the foreman [even] before the union." Now the union structure reinforced the capabilities of such workers: "We had training classes for the shop stewards: What to do, how to do it. We went over the contract thoroughly." The shop stewards transformed the traditional paternalism of Reynolds management into an explicit system of benefits and responsibilities. They made the collective bargaining agreement a bill of rights.[13]

The growing self-confidence of black women, who constituted roughly half of the total workforce, proved particularly subversive of existing social relations. To the white men who ran the Reynolds plants, nothing could have been more disturbing than the demand that they negotiate on a basis of equality with people whom they regarded as deeply inferior—by virtue of their sex as well as their class and race. When union leaders like Theodosia Simpson, Velma Hopkins, and Moranda Smith sat down at the bargaining table with company executives, social stereotypes naturally came under assault, but the challenge proved equally dramatic on the shop floor. For example, Ruby Jones, the daughter of a railway fireman, became one of the most outspoken shop stewards. Perplexed by her newfound aggressiveness, a foreman demanded, "Ruby, what do you want?" "I want your respect," she replied, "that's all I ask."[14]

By the summer of 1944, Local 22 of the reorganized and renamed Food, Tobacco, Agricultural and Allied Workers (FTA) had become the center of an alternative social world that linked black workers together regardless of job, neighborhood, or church affiliation. The union hall, only a few blocks from the Reynolds Building, housed a constant round of meetings, plays, and musical entertainments, as well as classes in labor history, black history, and current events. Local 22 sponsored softball teams, checker tournaments, sewing circles, and swimming clubs. Its vigorous educational program and well-stocked library introduced many black workers (and a few whites) to a larger radical culture few had glimpsed before. "You know, at that little library they [the city of Winston-Salem] had for us, you couldn't find any books on Negro history," remembered Viola Brown. "They didn't have books by Aptheker, Dubois, or Frederick Douglass. But we had them at *our* library."[15]

The Communist Party was the key political grouping in FTA and in Local 22. FTA president Donald Henderson had long been associated with the party, and many organizers who passed through Winston-Salem shared his political sympathies. By 1947 party organizers had recruited about 150 Winston-Salem blacks, almost all tobacco workers. Most of these workers saw the party as both a militant civil rights organization, which in the 1930s had defended such black victims of white Southern racism as the Scottsboro boys and Angelo Herndon, and as a cosmopolitan group, introducing members to the larger world of politics and ideas. The white North Carolina Communist leader Junius Scales recalled that the "top leaders [of Local 22] . . . just soaked up all the educational efforts that were directed at them. The Party's program had an explanation of events locally, nationally, and worldwide which substantiated everything they had felt instinctively . . . It really meant business on racism." The party was an integrated institution in which the social conventions of the segregated South were self-consciously violated, but it also accommodated itself to the culture of the black community. In Winston-Salem, therefore, the party met regularly in a black church and started the meetings with a hymn and a prayer.[16]

The Communist Party's relative success in Winston-Salem was replicated in other black industrial districts. In the South a clear majority of the party's new recruits were black, and in Northern states like Illinois and Michigan the proportion ranged from 25 to 40 percent. The party's relative success among American blacks was not based on its programmatic consistency; during the late 1940s the NAACP and other critics pointed out that the wartime party had denounced civil rights struggles when they challenged the Roosevelt administration or its conduct of the war effort, but that the party grew more militant once Soviet-American relations cooled.[17] However, the party never abandoned its assault on Jim Crow, and, unlike the NAACP, which directed much of its energy toward the courts and Congress, the Communists or their front groups more often organized around social or political issues subject to locally initiated protests, petitions, and pickets. Moreover, the party adopted what today would be called an affirmative action policy that recognized the special disabilities under which black workers functioned, in the party as well as in the larger community. Although there were elements of tokenism and manipulation in the implementation of that policy, the party's unique effort to develop black leaders gave the Communists a special standing among politically active blacks.[18]

Tobacco industry trade unionism revitalized black political activism in Winston-Salem. Until the coming of the CIO, NAACP attacks on racial discrimination seemed radical, and few blacks risked associating with the organization. A 1942 membership drive did increase branch size from 11 to 100, but most new members came from the traditional black middle class, mainly teachers and municipal bus drivers. The Winston-Salem NAACP became a mass organization only after Local 22 conducted its own campaign for the city branch. As tobacco workers poured in, the local NAACP reached a membership of 1,991 by 1946, making it the largest unit in North Carolina.[19]

Unionists also attacked the policies that had disenfranchised Winston-Salem blacks for more than two generations. As part of the CIO Political Action Committee's voter registration and mobilization drive, Local 22 inaugurated citizenship classes, political rallies, and citywide mass meetings. Union activists challenged the power of registrars to judge the qualifications of black applicants and insisted that black veterans vote without further tests. The activists encouraged the city's blacks to participate in electoral politics. "Politics IS food, clothes, and housing," declared the committee that registered some seven hundred new black voters in the months before the 1944 elections.[20] After a visit to Winston-Salem in 1944, a *Pittsburgh Courier* correspondent wrote: "I was aware of a growing solidarity and intelligent mass action that will mean the dawn of a New Day in the South. One cannot visit Winston-Salem and mingle with the thousands of workers without sensing a revolution in thought and action. If there is a 'New' Negro, he is to be found in the ranks of the labor movement."[21] Organization and political power gave the black community greater leverage at city hall and at the county court-house. NAACP and union officials regularly took part in municipal government debate on social services for the black community, minority representation in the police and fire departments, and low-cost public housing. In 1944 and 1946 newly enfranchised blacks helped reelect Congressman John Folger, a New Deal supporter, against strong conservative opposition. In 1947, after black registration had increased some tenfold in the previous three years, a minister, Kenneth Williams, won a seat on the board of aldermen, becoming the first black city official in the twentieth-century South to be elected against a white opponent.[22]

Civil Rights Militancy in Detroit

The social dynamic that had begun to revolutionize Winston-Salem played it-self out on a far larger scale in Detroit, making that city a center of civil rights militancy in the war years. Newly organized black autoworkers pushed forward the frontier of racial equality on the shop floor, in the political arena, and within the powerful, million-member United Auto Workers (UAW). Despite increasing racism among white workers, union goals and civil rights aims largely paralleled each other in the 1940s. In 1940 about 4 percent of all autoworkers were black; the proportion more than doubled during the war and rose to about one-fifth of the auto workforce in 1960. Although proportionally less numerous than in Winston-Salem, blacks were nevertheless central to the labor process in many of Detroit's key manufacturing facilities. Excluded from assembly operations and skilled work, blacks dominated the difficult and unhealthy, but absolutely essential, work in foundry, paint shop, and wet sanding operations.[23]

Ford Motor Company's great River Rouge complex contained the largest concentration of black workers in the country. More than half of its nine thousand black workers labored in the foundry, but Henry Ford's peculiar brand of inter-war paternalism had enabled blacks to secure some jobs in virtually every Ford department. The company therefore proved a mecca for black workers. Those who worked there proudly announced, "I work for Henry Ford," and wore their plant badges on the lapels of their Sunday coats. Ford reinforced his hold on the loyalty of Detroit's black working class by establishing what amounted to a separate personnel department that recruited new workers on the recommendation of an influential black minister. That policy, which continued until the early 1940s, strengthened the pro-company, antiunion attitude of most churchmen and reinforced the hostility shown the early CIO by leaders of the Detroit Urban League and the local NAACP branch.[24]

UAW leaders recognized that unless black workers were recruited to the union they might undermine efforts to consolidate UAW power in key manufacturing facilities. The danger became clear during the racially divisive 1939 Chrysler Corporation strike, when management tried to start a back-to-work movement spearheaded by black workers; it proved even more apparent during the 1940–1941 Ford organizing drive, when black workers hesitated to join the union. During the April 1941 Ford strike, several hundred workers scabbed inside the plant. In response, UAW leaders made a concerted effort to win over elements of the local black bourgeoisie who were not directly dependent on Ford's patronage network. The ensuing conflict within the Detroit NAACP chapter was resolved in favor of the UAW only after Ford's unionization. Thereafter black workers, whose participation in union activities had lagged well behind those of most whites, became among the most steadfast UAW members. The UAW itself provided an alternative focus of power, both cooperating with and challenging the black church and the NAACP as the most effective and legitimate representative of the black community.[25]

Many talented, politically sophisticated black officers and staffers emerged in the UAW during the mid-1940s, although never in numbers approaching their proportion of union membership. Blacks were a majority in almost every foundry and in most paint shops, so locals that represented manufacturing facilities usually adopted the United Mine Workers formula of including a black on the election slate as one of the top four officers. Locals with a large black membership also elected blacks to the annual UAW convention, where the 150–200 black delegates in attendance represented about 7 or 8 percent of the total voting roll. And almost a score of blacks also secured appointment as highly visible UAW international representatives during the early 1940s.[26]

Ford's River Rouge complex overshadowed all other Detroit-area production facilities as a center of black political power. Although most blacks had probably voted against the UAW in the NLRB elections of May 1941, the unionization process, particularly radical in its reorganization of shop floor social relations at the Rouge, helped transform the consciousness of these industrial workers. With several hundred shop committeemen in the vanguard, workers intimidated many foremen, challenged top management, and broke the company spy system. "We noticed a very definite change in attitude of the working man," recalled one supervisor. "It was terrible for a while . . . the bosses were just people to look down on after the union came in." For the next decade, Rouge Local 600 proved to be a center of civil rights militancy and a training ground for black leaders. The Rouge foundry sent more than a score of black delegates to every UAW convention, provided at least half of all black staffers hired by the UAW, and customarily supplied Local 600 with one of its top officers. Foundryman Shelton Tappes, a 1936 migrant from Alabama, helped negotiate a then unique antidiscrimination clause into the first UAW-Ford contract and went on to serve as recording secretary of the sixty-thousand-member local in the mid-1940s.[27]

The Rouge was also a center of Communist Party strength in Detroit. The radical tradition there had remained unbroken since World War I, when the Industrial Workers of the World and other radical union groups had briefly flourished. Skilled workers from northern Europe had provided most members during the difficult interwar years, but after 1941 the party recruited heavily among blacks, and at its peak in the late 1940s it enrolled 450 workers, almost half from the foundry. The Rouge was one of the few workplaces in the country where Communists, black or white, could proclaim their political allegiance without immediate persecution. As late as 1948 Nelson Davis, a black Communist who was elected vice president of the nine-thousand-man Rouge foundry unit within Local 600, sold several hundred subscriptions to the *Daily Worker* every year. But even here, Communist influence among black workers rested on the party's identification with civil rights issues; indeed many blacks saw the party's foundry department "club" as little more than a militant race organization.[28]

With almost one hundred thousand black workers organized in the Detroit area, black union activists played a central role in the civil rights struggle. They demanded the hiring and promotion of black workers in metropolitan war plants, poured into the Detroit NAACP chapter, and mobilized thousands to defend black occupancy of the Sojourner Truth Homes, a federally funded project that became a violent center of conflict between white neighborhood groups and the housing-starved black community. In those efforts black activists encountered enormous resistance not only from plant management and the Detroit political elite but also from white workers, mid-level union leaders under direct pressure from white constituents, and conservatives in the black community. But as in the civil rights movement of the early 1960s, black militants held the political initiative, so powerful white elites—the top officeholders in the UAW, company personnel officers, and the government officials who staffed the War Labor Board and War Manpower Commission—had to yield before this new wave of civil rights militancy.[29]

As in Winston-Salem, mass unionization transformed the character of the black community's traditional race advancement organizations. Under pressure from Local 600 leaders like Tappes, Horace Sheffield (his rival for leadership of the foundry), and the pro-union minister Charles Hill, the NAACP and the Urban League became more militant and activist. Black community leadership still came largely from traditional strata—lawyers, ministers, doctors, and teachers—but the union upsurge reshaped the protest agenda and opened the door to new forms of mass struggle. The NAACP itself underwent a remarkable transformation. In a successful effort to fight white neighborhood groups and keep the Sojourner Truth housing project open to blacks, NAACP officials had worked closely with UAW militants for the first time to organize demonstrations and protests. That mobilization in turn energized the local NAACP, as almost twenty thousand new members joined, making the Detroit branch by far the largest in the nation. Black workers poured in from the region's recently unionized foundries, tire plants, and war production facilities, and from city government, streetcar lines, restaurants, and retail stores.[30]

By 1943 the Detroit NAACP was one of the most working-class-dominated chapters in the country. Its new labor committee, the largest and most active group in the branch, served as a forum for black workers to air their grievances and as a pressure group, urging companies and the government to advance black job rights. With UAW support, the labor committee sponsored an April 1943 march and rally that brought ten thousand to Cadillac Square to demand that managers open war industry jobs to thousands of still unemployed black women in the region. Although the NAACP old guard repulsed a direct electoral challenge from UAW members and their sympathizers, the chapter added two unionists to its executive board and backed protest campaigns largely shaped by black UAW militants: mass rallies, picket lines, and big lobbying delegations to city hall, Lansing, and Washington. By the end of the war the ministerial leadership of the black community was in eclipse. Horace White, a Congregational minister, admitted, "The CIO has usurped moral leadership in the [Negro] community."[31]

On the shop floor, black workers sought to break out of traditional job ghettos in the foundry and janitorial service, precipitating a series of explosive "hate" strikes as white workers walked off the job to stop the integration of black workers into formerly all-white departments. The strikes were almost always failures, however, not only because federal officials and UAW leaders quickly mobilized to cut them off but also because they failed to intimidate most black workers. During the war there were probably as many demonstrations and protest strikes led by African Americans as racially inspired white walkouts.[32] For example, at Packard, scene of one of the most infamous hate strikes of the war, black workers eventually triumphed over white recalcitrance. A racialist personnel manager, a divided union leadership, and a heavily Southern workforce heightened racial tensions and precipitated several white stoppages that culminated in June 1943 when more than twenty-five thousand whites quit work to prevent the transfer of three blacks into an all-white department. But black workers were also active. Under the leadership of foundryman Christopher Alston, a Young Communist League member, they had shut down the foundry earlier to demand that union leaders take more forceful action against recalcitrant whites; and in the months after the big wildcat hate strike, those same blacks conducted strikes and protests that kept the attention of federal officials and local union leaders focused on their problems. Their militancy paid off; by the end of 1943 about five hundred African Americans had moved out of the Packard foundry and into previously all-white production jobs.[33]

Although newly assertive second-generation Poles and Hungarians had come to see their jobs and neighborhoods as under attack from the equally militant black community, top UAW officials championed civil rights during the war. In the aftermath of the great Detroit race riot of 1943, in which the police and roving bands of whites killed twenty-five blacks, the UAW stood out as the only predominantly white institution to defend the black community and denounce police brutality. During the hate strikes, UAW leaders often sought the protection of a War Labor Board back-to-work order in order to deflect white rank-and-file anger onto the government and away from themselves. But officials like UAW vice president Walter Reuther made it clear that "the UAW-CIO would tell any worker that refused to work with a colored worker that he could leave the plant because he did not belong there."[34]

Intra-union competition for black political support encouraged white UAW officials to put civil rights issues high on their agenda. During the 1940s black staffers and local union activists participated in an informal caucus that agitated for more black representatives in the union hierarchy and more effort to upgrade black workers in the auto shops. Initially chaired by Shelton Tappes of Local 600, the group was reorganized and strengthened by George Crockett, an FEPC lawyer the UAW hired to head its own Fair Employment Practices Committee in 1944. The overwhelming majority of UAW blacks, however, backed the caucus led by union secretary-treasurer George Addes and vice president Richard Frankensteen, in which Communists played an influential role. The Addes-Frankensteen caucus endorsed the symbolically crucial demand for a Negro seat on the UAW executive board and generally supported black-white slates in local union elections. The other major UAW faction was led by Walter Reuther and a coterie of ex-Socialists and Catholics, whose own internal union support came from workers in the General Motors plants (Flint and western Michigan), in the South, and in the aircraft-fabricating facilities of the East and Midwest. Support for Reuther's faction was particularly strong among the more assimilated Catholics and Appalachian whites in Northern industry. Reuther denounced proposals for a black executive board seat as "reverse Jim Crow," but his group also advocated civil rights, not so much because they expected to win black political support, but because the rapid growth of a quasi-autonomous black movement had made militancy on civil rights the sine qua non of serious political leadership in the UAW.[35]

A Moment of Opportunity

By the mid-1940s civil rights issues had reached a level of national political salience that they would not regain for another fifteen years. Once the domain of African American protest groups, leftist clergymen, and Communist-led unions and front organizations, civil rights advocacy was becoming a defining characteristic of urban liberalism. Thus ten states established fair employment practice commissions between 1945 and 1950, and four major cities—Chicago, Milwaukee, Minneapolis, and Philadelphia—enacted tough laws against job bias. Backed by the CIO, the Americans for Democratic Action spearheaded a successful effort to strengthen the Democratic Party's civil rights plank at the 1948 convention.[36]

In the South the labor movement seemed on the verge of a major breakthrough. *Fortune* magazine predicted that the CIO's "Operation Dixie" would soon organize key Southern industries like textiles. Black workers proved exceptionally responsive to such union campaigns, especially in industries like lumber, furniture, and tobacco, where they were sometimes a majority of the workforce. Between 1944 and 1946 the CIO's political action apparatus helped elect liberal congressmen and senators in a few Southern states, while organizations that promoted interracial cooperation, such as the Southern Conference for Human Welfare and Highlander Folk School, experienced their most rapid growth and greatest effectiveness in 1946 and 1947.[37]

The opportune moment soon passed. Thereafter, a decade-long decline in working-class black activism destroyed the organizational coherence and ideological élan of the labor-based civil rights movement. That defeat has been largely obscured by the brilliant legal victories won by civil rights lawyers in the 1940s and 1950s and by the reemergence of a new mass movement in the next decade. But in Winston-Salem, Detroit, and other industrial regions, the time had passed when unionized black labor was in the vanguard of the freedom struggle. Three elements contributed to the decline. First, the employer offensive of the late 1940s put all labor on the defensive. Conservatives used the Communist issue to attack New Deal and Fair Deal reforms, a strategy that isolated Communist-oriented black leaders and helped destroy what was left of the Popular Front. The employers' campaign proved particularly effective against many recently organized CIO locals with disproportionate numbers of black members. Meanwhile, mechanization and decentralization of the most labor-intensive and heavily black production facilities sapped the self-confidence of the black working class and contributed to high rates of urban unemployment in the years after the Korean War.

Second, the most characteristic institutions of American liberalism, including the unions, race advancement organizations, and liberal advocacy organizations, adopted a legal-administrative, if not bureaucratic, approach to winning citizenship rights for blacks. The major legislative goal of the union-backed Leadership Conference on Civil Rights in the 1950s was revision of Senate Rule 22, to limit the use of the filibuster that had long blocked passage of a national FEPC and other civil rights legislation. The UAW and other big unions cooperated with the NAACP in the effort, but the work was slow and frustrating and the struggle was far removed from the shop floor or the drugstore lunch counter.[38]

Finally, the routinization of the postwar industrial relations system precluded efforts by black workers to mobilize a constituency independent of the leadership. Focusing on incremental collective bargaining gains and committed to social change only if it were well controlled, the big unions became less responsive to the particular interests of their black members. By 1960 blacks had formed oppositional movements in several old CIO unions, but they now encountered resistance to their demands not only from much of the white rank and file but also from union leaders who presided over institutions that had accommodated themselves to much of the industrial status quo.[39]

Postwar Reaction: Winston-Salem

Like most labor-intensive Southern employers, R. J. Reynolds never reached an accommodation with union labor, although it signed contracts with Local 22 in 1945 and 1946. Minimum-wage laws and collective bargaining agreements had greatly increased costs of production, especially in the stemmeries, and the black women employed there were the heart and soul of the union. Soon after the war, the company began a mechanization campaign that eliminated several predominantly black departments. When the factories closed for Christmas in 1945, new stemming machines installed in one plant displaced more than seven hundred black women. The union proposed a "share the work" plan, but the company was determined to cut its workforce and change its racial composition by recruiting white workers from surrounding counties. The black proportion of the manufacturing labor force in Winston-Salem dropped from 44 to 36 percent between 1940 and 1960.[40]

The technological offensive undermined union strength, but by itself Reynolds could not destroy Local 22. When contract negotiations began in 1947, the company rejected union demands for a wage increase patterned after those won in steel, auto, and rubber earlier in the spring. Somewhat reluctantly, Local 22 called a strike on May 1. Black workers and virtually all of the Negro community solidly backed the union, which held out for thirty-eight days until a compromise settlement was reached. But in a pattern replicated throughout industrial America in those years, Communist influence within the union became the key issue around which management and its allies mounted their attack. The *Winston-Salem Journal* soon denounced Local 22 as "captured . . . lock, stock and barrel" by the Communist Party, warning readers that the strike would lead to "open rioting." This exposé brought Local 22 officers under the scrutiny of the House Committee on Un-American Activities (HUAC), which held a highly publicized hearing on the Winston-Salem situation in the summer of 1947.[41]

Communist Party members contributed to the volatility of the situation. In the late 1940s, Local 22 found itself politically vulnerable when foreign policy resolutions passed by the shop stewards' council followed Communist Party pronouncements. The party's insistence on the promotion of blacks to leadership positions sometimes put workers with little formal education into union jobs they could not handle. Moreover, the party's obsession with "white chauvinism" backfired. After the 1947 strike, Local 22 made a concerted effort to recruit white workers. Some young veterans joined the local, although the union allowed most to pay their dues secretly.[42] The party objected, remembered North Carolina leader Junius Scales, "'If they got any guts,' they would say, 'let them stand up and fight,' not realizing, as many black workers and union leaders realized, that for a white worker to just belong to a predominantly black union at that time was an act of great courage."[43]

With its workforce increasingly polarized along racial and political lines, Reynolds renewed its offensive in the spring of 1948. Black workers remained remarkably loyal to the union leadership, but the anti-Communist campaign had turned most white employees against the union and eroded support among blacks not directly involved in the conflict. The company refused to negotiate with Local 22 on the grounds that the union had not complied with the new Taft-Hartley Act. The law required union officers to sign an affidavit swearing they were not members of the Communist Party before a union could be certified as a bargaining agent by the NLRB. Initially, all the CIO internationals had refused to sign the affidavits, but by 1948 only Communist-oriented unions such as the FTA still held out. When Reynolds proved intransigent, there was little the union could do. The FTA had no standing with the NLRB, and it was too weak to win another strike.[44]

At the same time, Local 22 began to feel repercussions from the conflict within the CIO over the status of unions, like the FTA, that had rejected the Marshall Plan and endorsed Henry Wallace's Progressive Party presidential campaign in 1948. A rival CIO union, the United Transport Service Employees (UTSE), sent organizers into Winston-Salem to persuade black workers to abandon Local 22. In a March 1950 NLRB election, which the FTA requested after complying with the Taft-Hartley Act, the UTSE joined Local 22 on the ballot. The FTA local retained solid support among its black constituency, who faithfully paid dues to their stewards even after the contract had expired and in the face of condemnation of their union—from the company, the CIO, and HUAC. Even Alderman Williams, the black community leader, asked workers to vote against the union and "send the Communists away for good." Yet Local 22 captured a plurality of all the votes cast, and in a runoff two weeks later it won outright. But when the NLRB accepted the ballots of lower-level white supervisors, the scales again tipped against the local.[45]

Local 22 disappeared from Winston-Salem's political and economic life, and a far more accommodative black community leadership filled the void left by the union's defeat. Beginning in the mid-1940s, a coalition of middle-class blacks and white business moderates had sought to counter the growing union influence within the black community. They requested a study of local race relations by the National Urban League's Community Relations Project (CRP). Largely financed by Hanes Hosiery president James G. Hanes, the CRP study appeared in late 1947 and called for improved health, education, and recreational facilities, but it made no mention of workplace issues. The Urban League foresaw a cautious, "step by step approach" and proposed that an advisory committee drawn from the black middle class discuss community issues with their white counterparts and help city officials and white philanthropists channel welfare services to the black community. The *Winston-Salem Journal* called the CRP's recommendations a "blueprint for better community relations" but one that would not alter "the framework of race relations."[46]

The Urban League's program helped make Winston-Salem a model of racial moderation. Blacks continued to register and vote in relatively high numbers and to elect a single black alderman. The city high school was integrated without incident in 1957, while Winston-Salem desegregated its libraries, golf course, coliseum, and the police and fire departments. But the dynamic and democratic quality of the black struggle in Winston-Salem would never be recaptured. NAACP membership declined to less than five hundred in the early 1950s, and decision making once again moved behind closed doors. When a grievance arose from the black community, a group of ministers met quietly with Hanes; a few phone calls by the white industrialist led to desegregation in 1958 of the privately owned bus company that had long served Winston-Salem residents.[47]

A similar story unfolded in the plants of the R. J. Reynolds Tobacco Company. After the destruction of Local 22, the company blacklisted several leading union activists, yet Reynolds continued to abide by many of the wage standards, benefit provisions, and seniority policies negotiated during the union era. The company reorganized its personnel department; rationalized procedures for hiring, firing, and evaluating employees; and upgraded its supervisory force by weeding out old-timers and replacing them with college-educated foremen. To forestall union activity, Reynolds kept its wages slightly ahead of the rates paid by its unionized competitors.[48]

In February 1960, when sit-ins began at segregated Winston-Salem lunch counters, the voices of black protest were again heard in the city's streets. But the generation of blacks who had sustained Local 22 played little role in the new mobilization. College and high school students predominated on the picket lines and in the new protest organizations that confronted white paternalism and challenged the black community's ministerial leadership. NAACP membership rose once again; more radical blacks organized a chapter of the Congress of Racial Equality (CORE). Public segregation soon collapsed.[49]

The subsequent trajectory of the freedom struggle in Winston-Salem was typical of that in many black communities. Heightened racial tensions set the stage for a 1967 riot and a burst of radicalism, followed by the demobilization of the protest movement and years of trench warfare in the city council. The political career of Larry Little, the son of Reynolds workers who had been members of Local 22, highlighted the contrasts between the two generations of black activists. Little moved from leadership of the North Carolina Black Panther Party in 1969 to city alderman in 1977, but despite the radicalism of his rhetoric, crucial issues of economic security and workplace democracy were not restored to the political agenda in Winston-Salem. Because black activists of his generation confronted the city's white elite without the organized backing of a lively mass institution like Local 22, their challenge proved more episodic and less effective than that of the previous generation.[50]

The Limits of Liberalism in Postwar Detroit

A similar demobilization took place in Detroit after the war. There the union, as well as the companies, helped undermine the independent working-class base that black activists had built in the six years since UAW organization of the Ford Motor Company. Racial issues were not of primary importance in the factional conflict of 1946 and 1947 that brought Walter Reuther to the presidency of the UAW. The victory of his caucus was based both on rank-and-file endorsement of Reuther's bold social vision, especially as exemplified in the General Motors strike of 1945–1946, and in the Reuther group's anti-Communism, which struck an increasingly responsive chord after passage of the Taft-Hartley Act.[51] Nevertheless, the Reuther victory greatly diminished black influence and independence within the UAW and the labor-liberal community in which the union played such an important role. Reuther was as racially egalitarian as his opponents, but the political logic of his bitterly contested victory—he won less than 10 percent of black delegate votes in 1946—meant that Reuther owed no organizational debt to the growing proportion of union members who were African American.

When the Reuther group consolidated their control of the union in 1947, there was a large turnover in the Negro UAW staff. Blacks with ties to the opposition, such as John Conyers Sr. and William Hardin, two of the first black staffers, and the articulate lawyer George Crockett, the de facto leader of the UAW's black caucus, were ousted from their posts. The young dynamo Coleman Young lost his job with the Wayne County CIO council. Tappes was hired as a UAW international representative in the early 1950s, but only after he had broken with the Communists and lost his base of support in the Rouge plant.[52]

During the 1950s and 1960s the Reuther group understood that civil rights was a litmus test of labor-liberalism. Reuther sat on the board of directors of the NAACP, and the UAW probably contributed more funds to that organization than all other trade unions combined. The UAW also proved a ready source of emergency funds for the Montgomery Improvement Association, the Southern Christian Leadership Conference (SCLC), and Students for a Democratic Society's early community-organizing activities. Reuther was outraged that the AFL-CIO did not endorse the 1963 March on Washington; his union had provided much of the early funding, and he would be the most prominent white to speak at the interracial gathering.[53]

Reuther also maintained a high profile on civil rights issues within the UAW. As president he appointed himself co-director of the union's Fair Employment Practices Department and used his post to denounce racial discrimination and identify himself with postwar civil rights issues. Reuther pushed for a fair employment practices bill in Michigan and led the successful UAW effort to integrate the

American Bowling Congress. During the crucial months after he had won the UAW presidency, but before his caucus had consolidated control of the union, such activism helped defuse black opposition; when Reuther was reelected in 1947 he won about half of all black delegate votes.[54]

Despite this public, and well-publicized, appearance, the emergence of a more stable postwar brand of unionism undermined civil rights activism in the UAW. As in many unions, the Reuther regime sought to eliminate or to co-opt potentially dissident centers of political power. Local 600 was such a center of opposition, where black unionists still within the Communist orbit continued to play an influential, if somewhat muted, role well into the 1950s. Immediately after the 1952 HUAC hearings in Detroit, which publicized the continuing presence of Communists in Local 600, the UAW International Executive Board put the huge local under its direct administration. Six months later, tens of thousands of Rouge workers reelected their old officers, but the influence and independence of the giant local nevertheless waned in the next few years. Leaders of the UAW defused much of the local's oppositional character by appointing many of its key leaders, including Tappes and Sheffield, to the national union staff.

Equally important, Ford's postwar automation and decentralization slashed the Rouge workforce in half, eliminating the predominantly black production foundry. The same phenomenon was taking place in many of Detroit's other highly unionized production facilities, so that by the late 1960s a ring of relatively small and mainly white manufacturing facilities surrounded Detroit's million-plus black population. Meanwhile, high levels of black unemployment became a permanent feature of the urban landscape after the 1957–1958 recession. Not unexpectedly, the size and social influence of the unionized black working class ceased to grow, although this stagnation was masked by the militance of inner-city minority youth late in the 1960s.[55]

The UAW's Fair Employment Practices Department (FEPD) also defused civil rights activism in the union. After 1946 the department was led by William Oliver, a black foundryman from Ford's Highland Park factory. Unlike the politicized blacks from the Rouge, Oliver had no large reservoir of political support in the UAW, nor did he attempt to build one. During Oliver's tenure the FEPD had a dual role: it represented the UAW to the national civil rights community, the NAACP, the Urban League, and the more liberal federal agencies and congressmen; and it processed discrimination complaints as they percolated up from black workers in the locals. Rather than serving as an organizing center for UAW blacks, the FEPD bureaucratized the union's civil rights activities. "We are a fire station," admitted Tappes, who served in the department during the 1950s and 1960s, "and when the bell rings we run to put out the fire."[56]

A UAW retreat from civil rights militancy also became evident in politics. From 1937 to 1949 the UAW sought to reshape Detroit's formally "nonpartisan" electoral politics along interracial class lines. Thus in 1945 and 1949 Richard Frankensteen and George Edwards, both former UAW leaders, fought mayoral campaigns that helped move integrated housing and police brutality to the center of local political debate. Both were defeated by conservative candidates, but their labor-oriented campaigns nevertheless provided a focus around which civil rights forces could mobilize. However, after the CIO's "bitterest political defeat in the motor city," in 1949, the UAW ceased to expend its political capital in what many of its leaders now considered fruitless campaigns to take over city hall. The UAW continued to back Michigan's liberal governor G. Mennen Williams, but in the city proper the union made peace with conservatives like Albert Cobo and Louis Miriani, who had built much of their political base on segregationist homeowner movements.[57]

Neither the Communist Party nor the NAACP was able to fill the void opened up by the UAW default. In the early 1950s many erstwhile leaders of the union's black caucus joined the Detroit Negro Labor Council (NLC), a Communist front organization. But the NLC faced relentless pressure from the NAACP, HUAC, and the UAW, which denounced the council as a "Communist-dominated, dual unionist organization which has as its sole objective the disruption and wrecking of the American labor movement."[58] Both the UAW and the NAACP made exclusion of Communists from civil rights coalition work a high priority in the early 1950s, and the NLC dissolved in 1956. The NAACP, of course, maintained a cordial relationship with the UAW, but it also declined in postwar Detroit. After reaching a wartime peak of twenty-four thousand in 1944, membership dropped to six thousand in 1950 when there was much discussion of the need to "rehabilitate" what had once been the organization's largest unit. In the early 1950s national NAACP membership also fell to less than half its wartime level.[59]

When civil rights reemerged as a major issue in union and city politics in the late 1950s, the Reuther leadership often found its interests counterposed to the forces mobilized by the freedom movement of that era. By 1960 Detroit's population was about 30 percent black, and upward of a quarter of all autoworkers were Mexican or black. At the Rouge plant, between 50 and 60 percent of production workers were nonwhite.[60]

Reuther's mode of civil rights advocacy seemed increasingly inadequate as the fears and conflicts of the early Cold War era receded. Two issues seemed particularly egregious. First, black participation in UAW skilled trades apprenticeship programs stood at minuscule levels—1 percent or less. Second, no black sat on the UAW executive board, although blacks had been demanding that symbolically important post in UAW convention debates since the early 1940s. Failure to make progress on those problems genuinely embarrassed white UAW leaders, but Reuther and his colleagues were trapped by the regime over which they presided. Reuther hesitated to take on the militant and well-organized skilled trades, then in the midst of a long-simmering craft rebellion against the UAW's industrial unionism. Nor could a black be easily placed on the UAW executive board. In no UAW region did blacks command a majority of all workers; moreover, Reuther loyalists held all existing posts. Creating a new executive board slot seemed the only alternative, but that would dilute the power of existing board members and flatly repudiate Reuther's long-standing opposition to a specifically black seat on the executive board.[61]

In this context, and in the immediate aftermath of the Montgomery Bus Boycott, an independent black protest movement reemerged in Detroit politics with the founding of the Trade Union Leadership Council (TULC) in 1957. Initially TULC was little more than a caucus of UAW black staffers, but under the leadership of Horace Sheffield the organization challenged Reutherite hegemony. Despite the UAW's good reputation, Sheffield explained in 1960, a black-led organization was needed because "the liberal white trade unionists had long been 'mothballed,' . . . by the extensive growth of 'business unionism!'"[62] The TULC opened a new chapter in Detroit politics in the 1961 mayoralty race. The incumbent mayor, Louis Miriani, had the support of virtually all elements of the Detroit power structure, including the UAW, but he was hated by most blacks and not a few whites because of his defense of Detroit's increasingly brutal and racist police department. Sheffield used the mayoral campaign of Jerome Cavanagh, a young liberal lawyer, to establish his own network among Detroit's black trade union officials and make the TULC a mass organization of over seven thousand members in 1962 and 1963. Thereafter, a number of black activists whose political roots went back to the anti-Reuther forces of the 1940s won elective office, sometimes over bitter UAW protest. They included John Conyers Jr., who took Detroit's second black congressional seat in 1964; George Crockett, who won election as recorder's court judge in 1966 and later went on to Congress; and Coleman Young, who become the city's mayor in 1973.[63]

The TULC proved less successful in remolding UAW politics. The organization's mushroom growth, combined with the growth of the civil rights movement, forced the UAW to put a black on its executive board in 1962. However, for this position the Reuther leadership chose none of the blacks prominently associated with TULC militancy, but instead the relatively little known Nelson Jack Edwards, a black staff representative. Although black appointments to the UAW staff increased markedly in the 1960s, the TULC failed to generate a mass movement among rank-and-file black workers. The organization represented the generation of black activists who had been politicized in the 1940s, but many had spent the intervening years on union staffs or in local office, so they no longer enjoyed an organic link with the younger black militants who were flooding into Detroit's auto shops.[64]

When the Dodge Revolutionary Union Movement (DRUM) and other black insurgencies swept through the auto industry in the late 1960s, the new generation had come to see UAW liberalism as indistinguishable from corporate conservatism. They were mistaken, but in 1968, that year of great expectations and smashed hopes, such distinctions seemed beside the point. Many TULC veterans found DRUM's wholesale condemnation of the UAW irresponsible, while the young militants thought their elders merely a reformist wing of Reuther's union leadership. A reported exchange conveys DRUM members' impatience with TULC veterans' loyalty to the union. Shelton Tappes is said to have told a group of black Chrysler workers who had been fired for staging an outlaw strike and were picketing Solidarity House, the UAW's official home, "If the TULC had done what it was organized for there wouldn't be any such development as DRUM." And one of the young pickets reportedly answered, "And if Reuther and the other bureaucrats had done what the *union* was organized for, there wouldn't have been any need for TULC."[65]

Conclusion

E. P. Thompson once asserted that most social movements have a life cycle of about six years. And unless they make a decisive political impact in that time, that "window of opportunity," they will have little effect on the larger political structures they hope to transform.[66] For the black freedom struggle the mid-1940s offered such a time of opportunity, when a high-wage, high-employment economy; rapid unionization; and a pervasive federal presence gave the black working class remarkable self-confidence, which established the framework for the growth of an autonomous labor-oriented civil rights movement. The narrowing of public discourse in the early Cold War era contributed largely to the defeat and diffusion of that movement. The rise of anti-Communism shattered the Popular Front coalition on civil rights, while the retreat and containment of the union movement deprived black activists of the political and social space necessary to carry on an independent struggle. The disintegration of the black movement in the late 1940s ensured that when the civil rights struggle of the 1960s emerged it would have a different social character and an alternative political agenda, which eventually proved inadequate to the immense social problems that lay before it. Like the movement of the 1940s, the protests of the 1960s mobilized a black community that was overwhelmingly working-class. However, the key institutions of the new movement were not the trade unions, but the black church and independent protest organizations. Its community orientation and stirring championship of democratic values gave the modern civil rights movement a transcendent moral power that enabled a handful of organizers from groups like the Student Nonviolent Coordinating Committee, SCLC, and CORE to mobilize tens of thousands of Americans in a series of dramatic and crucial struggles. Yet even as this Second Reconstruction abolished legal segregation and discrimination, many movement activists, including Martin Luther King Jr., recognized the limits of their accomplishment. After 1965 they sought to raise issues of economic equality and working-class empowerment to the moral high ground earlier occupied by the assault against de jure segregation.[67] In retrospect, we can see how greatly they were handicapped by their inability to seize the opportunities that a very different sort of civil rights movement had found and lost twenty years before.

CHAPTER 9

The Lost Promise
of the Long Civil Rights Movement

In the fifteen decades since the demise of Reconstruction, the two most consequential political transformations that have taken place in U.S. history are those that arose first out of the New Deal impulse of the 1930s and then, just thirty years later, the new set of laws and mores that are identified with the triumph of the civil rights movement. Indeed, one might well argue that these two moments of remarkably inventive statecraft, so often put into separate historiographical boxes, are in fact part of the same mid-twentieth-century age of social reform, in which the dialectical interplay between social movements, political reform, and judicial innovations transformed the meaning of citizenship for tens of millions of Americans.

The Long Civil Rights Movement

The idea that the New Deal era of governmental activism and worker empowerment laid the groundwork for the civil rights movement and its judicial and legislative consequences is today the increasingly conventional wisdom. Few historians dissent from the idea that a long civil rights movement began at some point in the Depression decade. Jacquelyn Hall codified this idea in her 2004 presidential address at the Organization of American Historians. "The Long Civil Rights Movement: Contested Past, Contingent Future" argued that a reperiodization of the civil rights movement was essential to forestall neoconservative efforts to impose a color-blind, neoliberal interpretation on the very meaning of this great social reform.[1] Indeed, the idea of a long civil rights movement is not a metaphorical idea, of the sort that makes Denmark Vesey, Frederick Douglass, and Monroe Trotter progenitors of the civil rights impulse. Rather, this reperiodization requires a more concrete sense of immediate causation, in which the political and ideological transformations of the New Deal era created the conditions that led inextricably toward the mobilizations and legal/legislative victories of the late 1950s and early 1960s.

This is not an entirely new historiographical idea. As early as 1968, Richard Dalfiume published an essay on World War II, "Forgotten Years of the Negro Revolution," in the *Journal of American History*, and a decade later Harvard Sitkoff published *A New Deal for Blacks: The Emergence of Civil Rights as a National Issue*.[2] These efforts to demonstrate that something resembling a modern civil rights consciousness had entered the national political policy discourse were followed by a series of books, including those of Linda Reed, Patricia Sullivan, Timothy Tyson, Martha Biondi, Robert Korstad, and Glenda Gilmore, demonstrating that almost all of the players who would become prominent in the years after 1954 were actively engaged in a movement to transform racial mores and ideological constructs in the era of the New Deal and World War II.[3]

Some of these scholars, like Sullivan and Reed, emphasized the extent to which a coherent set of civil rights activists, working within well-defined organizations and campaigns, had been on the Southern scene during the years well before the Montgomery Bus Boycott in 1955. Others highlighted the role of key activists such as Ella Baker and Robert Williams, who were self-consciously radical in a fashion eschewed by the National Association for the Advancement of Colored People (NAACP) in the 1940s and 1950s, while scholars like Martha Biondi, Robert Korstad, and Glenda Gilmore made clear the extent to which the Communist Party, or individuals working within the fellow traveling political culture of that era, played key roles in the early years of the long civil rights movement. They waged vigorous campaigns to defend victims of discrimination, organized interracial trade unions, pushed for social and sexual equality between blacks and whites and men and women, and insisted upon the rights of African Americans not only to vote but also to run for office even in the most hostile political environments. These scholars published their books during the last couple of decades, often to counter the revisionist narrative so successfully promulgated by neoconservative intellectuals who emphasized a policy discourse that left little room for governmental efforts to regulate the labor market, unorthodox foreign policy views, or trade union militancy.[4] Thus, the historiographic construction of a long civil rights movement that embodied such social and political radicalism proved a boon to those liberals who sought to preserve for the progressive left, in the twenty-first century as well as in the twentieth, the ideas, ideologies, and social movements that they thought had long linked their cause to that of African American freedom.

Historical interest in the exploration of this longer, leftist, New Deal–oriented perspective on the civil rights movement has been spurred forward by the remarkable, widespread devaluation of the Supreme Court decision that once seemed to stand as a triumph of and inaugural marker for the entire civil rights impulse. For decades, the Court's 1954 decision in *Brown v. Board of Education* stood as both a culmination of the legal assault against segregation and as a warrant for Martin Luther King Jr. and others activists to expand the civil rights idea into a full-fledged movement, in the streets, in the legislatures, and in thousands of courtrooms, both North and South. But disillusionment with *Brown* has become near universal in scholarly circles, fostering the search for a more inspiring set of civil rights antecedents. *Brown* did not integrate the public schools, neither during the 1950s, when massive resistance in the South stymied the judicial edict, nor in the years after the civil rights breakthroughs of the 1960s, when patterns of housing segregation and income inequality subverted efforts to desegregate metropolitan school districts. As historian Charles M. Payne put it in a remarkably downbeat *Journal of American History* roundtable on the fiftieth anniversary of the Supreme Court decision, "*Brown v. Board of Education* is becoming a milestone in search of something to signify."[5] More than a mere media event, it was nevertheless "more hype than substance."[6]

Indeed, because the NAACP lawyers who litigated *Brown* were so determined to highlight the stigmatic social and psychological disabilities generated by the Jim Crow order, they simultaneously downplayed the economic structures that lay at the core of white supremacy and thus opened the door to a later generation of neoconservatives who would denounce affirmative action for perpetuating this same racial stigmatism. *Brown* was, therefore, the perfect Cold War ruling, argued legal scholar Mary Dudziak.[7] It was essentially a liberal, celebratory manifesto, highly useful in the ideological contest with the Soviets, but it was a ruling that did little to disturb the racial order in the South or the larger structures of economic inequality upon which Jim Crow had flourished for nearly a century.[8]

By sidelining the *Brown* decision, historians have thereby opened the door to a longer, more working-class-oriented definition of the civil rights impulse. Of course, it is not enough to demonstrate that the civil rights movement had its antecedents in the era of social reform that began during the 1930s. As Sundiata Keita Cha-Jua and Clarence Lang argue in a provocative critique of the "Long Movement" thesis, this historiographical turn "collapses periodization schemas, erases conceptual differences between waves of the black liberation movement and blurs regional distinctions in the African American experience."[9] Such a movement exists outside of time and history, they write, a perspective endorsed by Eric Arnesen, the prolific historian of African American labor, who argues that social movements rise and die in very specific social and ideological circumstances. An overlong schema "tends to reduce very different approaches and agendas to a too simple common denominator, minimizing the importance of chronology, precise periodization, and even conflicting agendas and demands."[10] To the extent that historians do flatten such chronological, conceptual, and political transformations, Cha-Jua, Lang, and Arnesen offer an important corrective, but their warning has actually been taken well into account among one important subset of scholars who have become advocates of the long civil rights movement thesis.

These are the labor historians who have not only extended the era of mass mobilization and political contestation back into the New Deal, but who have also argued, as Cha-Jua and Lang would have it, that the very meaning of civil rights has indeed been an ever changing concept, in some instances largely concerned with the legal and administrative desegregation of governmental institutions, in others emphasizing economic rights, and at still other times a near synonym for cultural self-expression and ethnic pride. Thus, it is not surprising that the idea of black liberation would take on a far more proletarian character in an era, the 1930s and 1940s, when trade unionism and industrial work stood for a progressive modernity and political power. W.E.B. DuBois put an African American "proletariat" at the center of the post–Civil War liberation movement when he provocatively titled one early chapter in his 1935 *Black Reconstruction in America*, "The General Strike."[11] Latter-day labor historians would be more subtle, but they nevertheless privileged the urbanization, proletarianization, and collective power of those African Americans who struggled to form or join unions, organize themselves politically, and extend the social protections of the New Deal state to those domestics, farmworkers, and public employees who had been so conspicuously left out in the cold.

The turn toward a laborite interpretation of the civil rights movement of the late 1930s and early 1940s began in the Reagan era when issues of school integration, residential desegregation, and public accommodations began to fade as sites of policy or judicial contestation, to be replaced by white-hot debates over employment policy, not just affirmative action but also trade union power, the minimum wage, and health and safety regulations, all of which had a dramatic impact on the economic status and political power of working-class African Americans, Latinos, and white women. So if contemporary civil rights discourse was largely about employment policy, then it seemed natural to recall a time when civil rights activists also saw their movement as a partial product of the era when economic fairness and union growth stood at the center of left-labor politics. Advancing this historiographic agenda was the turn toward the working class, which a generation of white New Leftists had made in the early 1970s. Initially this had little to do with a multiracialization of U.S. labor history: the notable early books of Sean Wilentz and Alan Dawley celebrated the nascent class-consciousness of white male artisans, as did the signature work of David Montgomery and even Herbert Gutman.[12]

But that historiographic moment proved a relatively brief one; after the publication of David Roediger's *Wages of Whiteness*,[13] it has been impossible for labor and social historians to think about either the history of trade unionism or the governmental regulations that determine other aspects of employment policy without taking into full consideration the racial—and gender—ideology of workers, managers, and policy entrepreneurs. Some historians, like Michelle Brattain, Bruce Nelson, Shelley Sallee, and Roediger himself, have emphasized the imitations that a discourse of "whiteness" has imposed on any sort of laborite social movement or the legal framework that has flowed from it.[14]

But most historians came to see the world of working-class politics as a venue in which a genuinely progressive, multiracial ethos had the best chance to realize itself. This was because the unions, for all their imperfections, were sites of racial empowerment, sometimes within a genuinely integrated context, but perhaps even more as political entities in which black caucuses and factions could emerge in an organic fashion, as they did in unions representing workers in the steel, packinghouse, auto, shipbuilding, and railroad industries in years that long preceded the 1960s. The most exemplary instance of all this was the smallish Brotherhood of Sleeping Car Porters, not a powerful union at all in traditional collective bargaining terms, but one whose autonomy, sense of racial self-identity, and determined leadership made it central to the civil rights impulse through the 1940s. Not unexpectedly, the career of A. Philip Randolph now stands second only to that of Martin Luther King Jr. as the subject of historical inquiry.

Labor historians were not just chroniclers of a social movement that made the union and the labor leader, rather than the church and preacher, key actors in mobilizing a mass movement for racial liberation. Beyond that, these historians have argued that the orientation toward work, unions, and left-wing politics gave to the New Deal–era civil rights movement a quite different definition than it would achieve under the tutelage of those who both litigated *Brown v. Board of Education* and later pressed for passage of the historic civil rights laws during liberalism's brief triumphal hour in the mid-1960s. As Robert Korstad and I put it in one of the earliest formulations positing a laborite agenda for the early civil rights movement, after 1965 civil rights leaders "sought to raise issues of economic equality and working-class empowerment to the moral high ground earlier occupied by the assault against de jure segregation. In retrospect, we can see how greatly they were handicapped by their inability to seize the opportunities a very different sort of civil rights movement found and lost twenty years before."[15]

In the more than twenty years since we first put forward that perspective, it is clear that while this formulation may be politically and culturally appealing to an academy of social democratic leanings, it lacks precision. With the rest of the historians who have celebrated the laborite character of the civil rights movement in the 1940s, such sentiments are just that, ideologically tinged sentiments that offer up little more than a kind of left-wing wistfulness that history had moved in another direction. What is needed to give this historical hypothesis some bite is the explication of a far more concrete set of policy, political, and legal/administrative alternatives that were available to civil rights partisans during that first laborite phase of the civil rights movement itself.

Goluboff's Laborite Perspective

Doing just that constitutes the signal achievement of Risa Goluboff's *The Lost Promise of Civil Rights*.[16] Her book incorporates the perspective of labor and social historians who have posited the importance and power of a working-class-oriented civil rights movement in the 1940s. She finds that an alternative set of legal strategies and organizing initiatives was available to civil rights litigators, indeed that these more economically radical strategies were successfully deployed, and, that if they had been consistently pursued would have given this plebian civil rights orientation an embedded character in law and social policy during the decades to come. In effect, Goluboff posits in the most precise fashion an alternative definition to the meaning of what we have come to think of as civil rights law and litigation and then asks why this more proletarian version was marginalized in the years after 1950.

Goluboff's book puts African American sharecroppers, tenant farmers, industrial workers, and those who became their advocates and attorneys at the center of the story. The judiciary and its decisions are not ignored, of course. With insight and intelligence Goluboff explores the implications of Lochner-era jurisprudence, but she puts the strategy pursued by the liberal attorneys housed in the Civil Rights Section of the Department of Justice and those in the NAACP front and center. Her book is therefore based not only on the archives of the main civil rights litigator of that era, the NAACP Legal Defense and Educational Fund (the Inc. Fund), but also the highly active NAACP branches, the files of the Department of Agriculture's Bureau of Agricultural Economics, the Department of Justice, the records of the Fair Employment Practices Commission, as well as a truly exhaustive reading of the judicial opinions and legal literature of the 1940s. And, of course, Goluboff's narrative has been greatly enhanced by the work of scores of historians exploring virtually every dimension of the long civil rights movement.

Goluboff is creatively revisionist when it comes to some long-cherished markers of the civil rights law. She downplays the importance of the famous "Footnote Four" in the Supreme Court's 1938 *United States v. Carolene Products* decision, because she does not find that the "strict scrutiny" enunciated therein actually established a new, post-1930s racially sensitive paradigm, guiding either civil rights litigation or judicial opinion writing.[17] There was no Whiggish road to *Brown v. Board of Education* laid out by *Carolene Products* or any other key decision. Rather the path toward a modern conception of civil rights would be forged by lawyers acting on cases of the workers who petitioned them for help.[18] Indeed, Goluboff puts the needs, frustrations, and oppressions of those who sought legal redress at the forefront of her narrative. She shows in poignant and textured detail how legal change begins with the injuries individuals experience in real life, as they complain to lawyers, neighbors, and public officials or to anyone else who would listen. "Law creation," she writes, "begins with complaints."[19]

Many of those pleas and complaints came out of the agricultural South. Here was a labor system of tenants, croppers, and day laborers whose subordination was ensured by a brutally oppressive regime of economic exploitation, by legally enforceable white supremacy, and by the studied abstention of the Roosevelt administration and the otherwise progressive reform measures enacted during the mid-1930s. Goluboff makes clear that this Jim Crow system, largely untouched by even the most liberal New Dealers, was not merely that of racial segregation and discrimination but, from the perspective of African Americans living in the South, represented a far more suffocating totality in which an insular labor market, the monopoly of economic power exercised by the plantation elite, and the legal regime that criminalized vagrancy and indebtedness consigned black agricultural laborers to something approaching involuntary servitude. In her examination and explication of scores of letters and court cases generated by the plight of these poor African Americans, Goluboff found that although race pervaded the complaints, "black workers were overwhelmingly preoccupied with the economic consequences of racial discrimination. The problem was not discrimination in the abstract, but discrimination that interfered with making a living."[20] Moreover, these black litigants made no distinction between state-mandated instances of discriminatory treatment and that meted out by employers or other private citizens. Indeed, no such distinction could be made in the rural South, where a system of coercive labor and slave-like debt peonage depended upon the most intimate and routine collaboration between sheriff, merchant, judge, and plantation owner. Goluboff argues that educational segregation was something of a special case in the South in that the schools were almost exclusively public and tax supported, whereas when it came to the world of work and property, it was impossible to make any distinction between de jure and de facto racial classification and discrimination.

This was the economic and racial context in which lynching and other gothic fruits of the Southland ripened, but, as Goluboff makes clear, the NAACP itself was not an active litigator on the peonage front. Rather, the assault on peonage and other forms of racially linked class oppression found its champions among the band of government-employed white lawyers who worked in the Department of Justice's little-known Civil Rights Section (CRS). This initiative flowed directly out of the famed investigative committee chaired by Senator Robert LaFollette of Wisconsin, which for four years, from 1936 to 1940, sought to "drain the industrial swamp" by investigating "violations of the rights of free speech and assembly and undue interference with the right of labor to organize and bargain collectively."[21] As Goluboff makes clear in her reading of this left-labor moment, terms like "civil rights," "civil liberties," and the "rights of labor" were virtually indistinguishable in the late 1930s. Thus, labor organizers and advocates supplied LaFollette with hundreds of stories and narratives of the illegal and autocratic resistance mounted by the nation's big corporations and big farms to the New Deal laws designed to protect working Americans. The investigative work was infused with passion. As a staff member wrote to a sympathetic congressman in 1940, "I really believe that today we are the most powerful agency in this country against Fascism."[22]

Equally important, the LaFollette staffers and the CRS lawyers reflected the left-liberal effort to incorporate into a progressive ideology not only the liberation of labor but also the deconstruction of the racial hierarchies that had once been almost invisible to white leftists. Gary Gerstle has argued that in the 1940s liberal ideology underwent a shift of "seismic proportions" from a concern with class-based economic reform to a focus on culture-based matters of race and ethnicity.[23] But this did not happen overnight, and while it was taking place a highly creative redefinition of what constituted a radical and racially pluralist democracy was on offer. This is the thrust of Dan Geary's important portrait of the California Popular Front radical Carey McWilliams, whose definition of antifascism, like that of so many other non-Communist progressives, became increasingly synonymous with one that advanced an activist ethno-racial democracy, not only in the nation's factories but in its fields, barrios, and ghettos as well.[24]

The Usefulness of the Thirteenth Amendment

Given this ideological move, the New Deal's Faustian bargain with the white South seemed increasingly intolerable. Indeed, as Goluboff makes clear, the CRS lawyers set out to subvert that bargain by bringing to bear upon the agricultural oligarchy of the Deep South what legal and administrative powers they could command. Of course, this was a politically sensitive task, so it helped that their main targets were the coercive and oppressive private practices that were deployed by white landowners to control their labor force. For this work, argues Goluboff, no legal warrant seemed better suited than the Thirteenth Amendment, because it required no state action to deploy. While it did not strike directly at the edifice of state-sanctioned segregation, it was nevertheless a highly capacious mandate that enabled CRS lawyers, backstopped by Attorney General Francis Biddle, to more easily and effectively get right inside the exploitative labor markets of the Deep South. For example, if a federal assault on lynching was anathema for the political class in the South, this was not the case when it came to a reform of agricultural labor relations in the rural districts. At one point, reports Goluboff, the Federal Bureau of Investigation, notorious a generation later for its collaboration with those Southern officials hostile to the civil rights movement, proved an efficient CRS partner when it deployed numerous agents to hunt down and interview scores of witnesses in a CRS prosecution of a Florida sugar cane operation. As Goluboff puts it, the Department of Justice attack on peonage "allowed the CRS to navigate safely between the prerogatives Southern whites most cherished and the rights claims African Americans most urgently pressed."[25]

With passion and conviction, Goluboff argues that the effort to deploy the Thirteenth Amendment in the twentieth-century South had momentous implications. It required an expansion of the idea of slavery, from the narrow, purely contractual definition the Lochner-era courts had offered to a conceptualization that brought within its ambit all of those "so far subjected to the will of another that he is held to labor or service against his will."[26] Thus, the CRS changed the name of the debt peonage cases to "involuntary servitude," which involved threats, physical and economic, against employees and croppers. The government attorneys sought to open up the Southern labor market by attacking vagrancy statutes, laws prohibiting recruitment of those who owed a debt to their employer, and even prohibitions against hitchhiking, which limited the mobility of African American laborers. CRS attorneys were not only demonstrating that their definition of involuntary servitude covered a wide array of heretofore customary labor management practices, but they were also simultaneously transforming the Lochner-era concept of "free labor" to mean that workers, industrial or agricultural, had the right to organize, bargain, and strike. And all this was on the basis of the long-neglected Thirteenth Amendment.

Goluboff has not been the first scholar to celebrate the liberating possibilities inherent in that amendment or to identify a set of historical actors who sought to deploy it for twentieth-century laborers. Before passage of the Wagner Act, argues James Gray Pope, the labor movement nurtured a vocal cadre of self-taught legal advocates who argued long and loud that the Thirteenth Amendment provided just the constitutional vehicle by which to challenge the labor injunction, the yellow-dog contract, and other restrictions on the right of labor to self-organization and to adequate remuneration.[27] None was more forceful or determined than Andrew Furuseth, the sailors' union leader from San Francisco, California, who argued that any restriction upon the right of man or woman to deploy or withhold their own labor power was an abridgement of the emancipation amendment.[28] Although the legal and legislative basis of the 1935 Wagner Act relied upon the Constitution's commerce clause (much to the regret of both Furuseth and his latter-day champion Jim Pope), the ideas and rhetoric that Senator Wagner and his supporters used to motivate the new law relied heavily upon the spirit animating the Thirteenth Amendment. Like Furuseth, Wagner himself situated his bill in the long sweep of history as "the next step in the logical unfolding of man's eternal quest for freedom."[29] He repeatedly likened the nonunion workplace to feudalism and slavery and promised that government enforcement of the right to organize would bestow upon workers "emancipation from economic slavery."[30] Argued a congressional ally of the senator in the debate over the law's enactment, "As Lincoln freed the blacks in the South, so the Wagner-Connery bill frees the industrial slaves of this country from the further tyranny and oppression of their overlords of wealth."[31]

Goluboff might well have linked her story more closely to this largely white trade union discourse, because it strengthens her revisionist framework and adds important context to the constitutional worldview of those she most closely studied. As the CRS lawyers must have been aware, such a mode of economic and social argumentation did not cease in the 1940s, even when US politics

moved sharply to the right. Thus, even conservative trade unionists declared
that the restrictions on union activity embodied in the 1947 Taft-Hartley Act
had made the new statute a "slave labor law,"[32] even if most observers at the time
thought such a phrase a demagogic exaggeration. But George Meany, that staunch
anti-Communist and later president of the American Federation of Labor and
Congress of Industrial Organizations (AFL-CIO), defended the proposition that
the new law was a step toward involuntary servitude. Taft-Hartley, he declared,
"completely demolishes the natural, organic development which is collective
bargaining, and substitutes, instead, what at best is paternalistic statism, and at
worst, out and out dictatorship."[33] The law's restrictions on the use of the boycott,
as well as its more general efforts to limit the spread of unionism, made more
difficult the equalization of wages and conditions among competing firms within
the same industry. This would eventually pit worker against worker, said Meany,
in a downward spiral that transformed human labor into a mere commodity and
workers into chattel. Quoting the great anti-injunction jurists Oliver Wendell
Holmes and Louis Brandeis, Meany argued that any government restrictions
upon the right to refuse work "reminds one of involuntary servitude."[34]

Although in the 1940s it would have been impossible to refound the main body
of National Labor Relations Act jurisprudence upon the Thirteenth Amendment, Goluboff finds that in the legal work undertaken by the wartime NAACP,
the deployment of that amendment or other legal tools that defended African
American work freedoms was increasingly attractive and efficacious. Of late, the
reputation of the NAACP as a mobilizing political institution, as distinct from
that of its legal strategy, has risen among historians of the civil rights movement.
Long gone are the days when Stokely Carmichael and Malcolm X derided it as
little more than an organization of well-dressed Uncle Toms. The very fact that
the NAACP still exists while all of its radical competitors have vanished from the
arena lends it a standing that cannot be gainsaid. Biographies of NAACP militants
like Robert F. Williams, Ella Baker, Medgar Evers, and Herbert Hill have made
clear that the organization consisted of a lot more than schoolteachers in the
South and high-profile litigators in New York.

The NAACP in Transition

But Goluboff remains a critic of the NAACP, even in the 1940s when Thurgood
Marshall and Charles Houston tilted their litigation strategy to the left, and when
the organization began to listen to the voices of a booming urban membership,
now increasingly working-class in composition. She celebrates these developments but nevertheless finds that the NAACP, and especially the now independent
Inc. Fund, was an organization whose legal strategy remained too often crippled
by the considerable weight of the black bourgeoisie within its ranks. This meant
that the NAACP put education rather than work at the forefront of its attack on

Jim Crow, that it targeted racial discrimination rather than racial inequality when its lawyers appeared in court, and that the organization gave far more emphasis to the psychological damage wrought by segregation than most members would have thought warranted. Such views are in accord with the historians and legal scholars whose fiftieth-anniversary evaluation of the *Brown* decision proved so doleful.

For example, Goluboff reports that the NAACP touchstone for its legal challenge to Jim Crow was the fact that whites singled out blacks for discriminatory treatment, not the fact that blacks lived in conditions of material inequality and insecurity.[35] Marshall, therefore, thought of the complaints that poured into the NAACP from agricultural workers in the South as "purely private" and not suitable for action by the NAACP.[36] And when the Inc. Fund did intervene in Southern disputes that sought to rectify economic inequalities, Marshall and other NAACP attorneys often tilted their meaning toward support of the NAACP's favored legal strategy. Thus, Marshall viewed litigation designed to equalize the salaries of African American teachers as part of the road toward an abolition of segregation in secondary school education, not a precedent that might be used to transform the labor market in the South. And Goluboff quotes Marshall directly to drive home the point that even in a set of horrendous Florida peonage cases, the NAACP was unwilling to directly attack the involuntary servitude and economic inequality that lay at the heart of Jim Crow. As Marshall himself put it, asserting the larger significance of the Florida litigation, "This is merely one more in a long line of cases which justify our continued action to secure the right to vote . . . in order to compel the law enforcement authorities in these state to give Negroes the equal protection of the laws to which they are entitled."[37]

But the NAACP could not ignore the wave of African American workers who were pouring into war industry factories, where they faced disabilities and discriminations in their work and within the unions to which they belonged. These workers, who were also swelling NAACP membership rolls in Detroit, Michigan; San Francisco and Oakland, California; and other production centers, represented a counterweight to the schoolteachers, dentists, and morticians who had long given the association its class coloration. So, as Goluboff explains, NAACP litigation strategy during World War II briefly tilted toward working-class concerns if only to accommodate the proletarianization of its own membership. Inc. Fund lawyers were not as fond of the Thirteenth Amendment as were the CRS litigators, but they also sought to break down the distinction between racial discriminations mandated by the state and those instigated by private employers. After all, in an economy when almost half of the GNP was now part of the war effort, such a division was increasingly spurious, whatever the constitutional precedents.

Goluboff celebrates the work of Charles Houston, the NAACP lawyer who most prominently embodied this shift toward working-class litigation and who bridged the gap between the work of the CRS and that of his organization. Although the Inc. Fund did not take peonage cases during World War II, Houston did see lawsuits against union discrimination as falling under the umbrella of the Thirteenth Amendment, because Houston saw obstacles to a person working at his or her chosen calling as an abridgement of free labor, a form of involuntary servitude. The NAACP was resolutely pro-union by the 1940s, but the pervasive discriminatory practices still present in many unions, especially those coming out of the old AFL job control tradition, such as the Boilermakers who controlled shipbuilding jobs in the Bay Area, pushed the Inc. Fund to demand that the government either ban segregation and discrimination in closed-shop unions or strip labor organizations of their power to determine who had the right to work at a given worksite.[38] Significantly, the argument here on behalf of African American workers was based not on the equal protection clause of the Four-teenth Amendment, but on a substantive reading of the due process rights in that same amendment. In effect, the NAACP attorneys were using the old Lochnerian free-labor ideology in order to secure for African American workers the right to make and enforce contracts, own property, and the "right to employment . . . on a par with the right to existence itself."[39] It was a social democratic reading of the law, akin to that deployed by the CRS attorneys when they used the Thirteenth Amendment to subvert peonage in the South.

The implications of this project were radical. Segregation itself would not be subject to frontal assault, but the economic and political disabilities of black workers and citizens would. The move toward an abolition of the distinction between public and private discrimination would continue, as *Shelley v. Kraemer*, the case that made racially restrictive housing covenants unenforceable, seemed to indicate. The distinction between de jure and de facto segregation, which so bedeviled civil rights litigators in the post-*Brown* years, especially when it came to housing, metropolitan area school desegregation, and employment patterns, would have taken a backseat to more direct and concrete efforts to advance the status and economic well-being of racial minorities.

But as Goluboff demonstrates, the NAACP chose another trajectory. Perhaps it was overdetermined, given the pressures generated by the Cold War, the de-mobilization of the black working class—Detroit NAACP membership dropped from nearly twenty-five thousand to just one-fifth of that number in the decade after the end of the war—and the slow but steady success that Inc. Fund lawyers were achieving in their assault on educational segregation. In any event, as the NAACP litigation strategy moved toward full confrontation with *Plessy v. Fer-guson*, the state-mandated separate but equal doctrine, the Inc. Fund abandoned most legal actions touching upon the private racial and economic hierarchies that also constituted Jim Crow. Indeed, the premise put forward in *Plessy* was that racial discrimination on its own, with no material inequality to accompany it, was harmful only if African Americans allowed it to be. So Marshall and the NAACP lawyers tried to find pure examples of segregation with no material in-equalities, thus constructing a fundamentally psychological theory of the harm generated by state-mandated segregation. Hence, the import of Kenneth Clark's (in)famous experiments, in 1939 and 1940, with white and colored dolls that purported to demonstrate feelings of racial inferiority among young African American children—a majority of the survey sample—who chose to identify with a white doll rather than one resembling their own race.[40] Given the enormous prestige of social psychology in popular and academic circles in the 1950s, it was not hard to develop a compelling argument that the essence of Jim Crow was not socioeconomic exploitation but sociological and psychological stigma.[41]

And who felt most keenly the stigma of racial discrimination? asks Goluboff. Why, of course, the elite black lawyers and other professionals who had become increasingly influential within NAACP and liberal circles in the postwar years. Indeed, in the years after *Brown*, NAACP lawyers themselves wondered why so many lawsuits to desegregate golf courses and clubhouses were instigated by African American dentists. Perhaps these lesser professionals sought a social status equivalent to doctors, white and black. Whatever the motivation, the Inc. Fund pursued the cases. As Inc. Fund lawyer Jack Greenberg later justified the expenditure of so much time and energy, "dentists had rights too, any defeat of segregation contributed to its ultimate destruction, and last but not least, these middle-class professionals were then the mainstay of the civil rights movement."[42]

Thus, Goluboff is in full agreement with Lani Guinier, Daryl Michael Scott, and other recent students of *Brown* who have "faulted the Court's dependence on psychological damage imagery to demonstrate the intangible costs of segregation."[43] Writes Goluboff: "Making *Plessy* the target—and interpreting *Plessy* as requiring the isolation of intangible harm—both compelled and liberated the NAACP to transform its class interests in integrating graduate schools, railroad dining cars, and middle-class neighborhoods into an apparently classless modern civil rights. This new civil rights would prove fundamentally unable to redress the economic hierarchies of Jim Crow America."[44]

So did the NAACP, in effect, abandon the African American working class in the years after *Brown*? Not all scholars agree with this dour assessment or with those historians of the long civil rights movement who share Goluboff's perspective. In a pointed rejoinder the legal scholar Sophia Lee makes a contrary claim. Despite the Cold War and the salience of the *Brown* decision, the NAACP itself "did not abandon economic rights and working-class issues."[45] While this may have been the trajectory pursued by the high-profile Inc. Fund, the NAACP used a combination of political pressure tactics and litigation within the National Labor Relations Board (NLRB) and other administrative agencies to advance a species of what Lee calls "workplace constitutionalism."[46] Well before passage of the 1964 Civil Rights Act, the NAACP had helped destroy the old state action barrier in corporate or union discrimination cases, fatally undermining the distinction between public and private in civil rights jurisprudence. Prodded forward by the organization's hyperactive labor secretary, Herbert Hill, as well as by a set of still vibrant working-class branches, the NAACP succeeded in establishing the principle that racial discrimination within the labor movement was an outright violation of the National Labor Relations Act.[47]

Goluboff does give relatively short shrift to the set of progressive developments that Sophia Lee has explicated, but I think she is right to devalue, in an ideological and political sense, this kind of successful litigation within the state's labor-relations apparatus. In contrast to the world of the late 1930s and the war years, labor and race issues were now compartmentalized in both the NAACP organization chart and, even more importantly, in the imagination of most liberals, laborites, and civil rights advocates. At one level, of course, the political alliance between the NAACP and the unions of the AFL and CIO was never stronger than in the late 1940s and early 1950s. From the perspective of the American labor leadership, support for racial equality was essential to their standing as progressives and liberals at mid-century. So Walter Reuther of the United Automobile, Aerospace and Agricultural Implement Workers of America (UAW), Philip Murray of the United Steelworkers, and David Dubinsky of the Ladies Garment Workers were eager to contribute to the NAACP, to serve on its national board, and to support its legislative and legal work. Of course, all this was in many ways a form of self-protection, because such trade unions were now shielded from much litigation charging internal discrimination. From the NAACP's perspective, this political alliance with official labor proved useful as the organization fought Cold War efforts to marginalize the civil rights group or keep labor contributions flowing. Conflicts with the labor movement over continued discrimination against minorities would be handled by agitators and organizers like Herbert Hill. By the early 1960s he would become a fierce critic of union discrimination against black workers, but his assaults remained tangential to the Inc. Fund strategy, both before and after *Brown*.[48]

Recasting and Constraining the Civil Rights Idea

Given this postwar shift in NAACP outlook, it is not surprising that the Justice Department lawyers also reconfigured their litigation strategy. As Goluboff makes clear, they were political creatures working within an increasingly conservative Washington agenda, which cast a skeptical Cold War eye on any governmental action designed to undermine existing economic arrangements at home. Overnight, litigation based on the Thirteenth Amendment vanished from the department's agenda, while labor and employment issues were now considered the province of the NLRB and the Labor Department, if they were considered at all in those years between the demise of the wartime Fair Employment Practices Commission and the passage of Title VII of the 1964 Civil Rights Act.

Goluboff points out that it was at just this time, in the post-*Brown* 1950s, when labor and civil rights issues had been cut asunder, that the otherwise obscure

Footnote Four in the *Carolene Products* decision finally came into judicial prominence. Since Marshall and other Inc. Fund lawyers had rejected grounding *Brown v. Board of Education* in the New Deal labor ethos, legal scholars and jurists now unearthed the *Carolene Products* ruling to provide *Brown* with a more secure doctrinal pedigree. For liberals in the academy and on the bench, Footnote Four justified much judicial review of those laws bearing on racial matters, but it put in a separate and lesser category those laws and rulings that constructed inequitable economic arrangements.

Ultimately this distinction would take on an ideological as well as a legal meaning, with far-reaching moral and political consequences for the character of liberalism, labor, and race in the post–World War II era. The recasting of the civil rights impulse so far away from its New Deal and laborite roots meant that even the 1963 March on Washington for Jobs and Freedom, the War on Poverty, and the inclusion of Title VII in the 1964 Civil Rights Act could not recreate the employment, labor, and civil rights agenda as it had been formulated in the late 1930s. And just as that agenda had defined Jim Crow as a totalizing system of economic inequality and legal disability, so too must we conclude, with Goluboff, that important elements of the Jim Crow order remain intact.

A visit to your local Wal-Mart, the largest private-sector employer of white women, African Americans, and Latinos in the United States, surely confirms this. While the company now takes moderately strenuous efforts to promote racial minorities and women, the structure of employment at this Arkansas-based company recalls elements of the old Jim Crow order that Andrew Furuseth, Senator Wagner, and the CRS attorneys would surely recognize: wages are low and inequitable; managers often flaunt federal wage and hour standards; and employment rights, aside from those covered by Title VII, are virtually nonexistent, so turnover is enormous. Most importantly, the company, like most other firms in the hotel, restaurant, and retail sectors of the economy, violates, ignores, and even ridicules the right of workers to organize a trade union.[49] Until all this is once again redefined as issues of civil rights, civil liberties, and economic freedom, the long civil rights movement will not be over.

CHAPTER 10

A New Era of Global Human Rights

Good for the Trade Unions?

A great paradox embodies the relationship between human rights and labor rights in the world today. Institutional trade unionism is not doing so well. This is most obvious in Anglo-America, where union density has declined dramatically during the last quarter century, and where unionism's influence, under both Labour and Democratic Party administrations, has been less than potent. With some notable exceptions—South Africa, South Korea, Brazil—one can say the same for union membership and power all over the world. According to the International Labor Organization's *World Labor Report*, trade union membership dropped sharply during the 1990s, falling to less than 20 percent of workers in forty-eight out of ninety-two countries. The decline was most serious in manufacturing, even though on a worldwide basis the manufacture of actual products in actual factories was a booming proposition.[1]

But in this globalized production system, the connections between employers and employees have become increasingly attenuated. Whereas employees used to work for an identifiable common employer, today they occupy an uncertain location on a global production and distribution chain. Indeed, globalization has shifted much production and employment beyond the reach of the labor law of any single country, and it has blurred the meaning of the employment relationship, both in the nation that hosts the corporate headquarters and in the country where supplier firms are located. World auto production today is near record levels, but the number of workers in the United States, Japan, and Europe who work directly for the great auto multinationals has been reduced by 50 percent over the last quarter century. In the United States the big domestic auto companies no longer care all that much about the wages they negotiate for currently employed union workers; the real issues are decentralization, outsourcing, and the flexibility of their supply chains.

This eclipse of trade unionism is not just one of declining numbers, bargaining leverage, and political clout. It has had a moral and ideological dimension as well. The effort to find some international mechanism that will defend trade unionism in a globalized economy has proven painfully slow and difficult, but this is not simply a question of capitalist power and prerogative. It reflects in addition a decline in the legitimacy and authority of unionism as an institution capable of defending the interests of ordinary people around the globe. Trade unions are too often considered defenders of the status quo; they are complicit in the maintenance of gender and racial hierarchies that are anathema in the global North. And in the global South those unions that actually do exist often seem to be an entrenched aristocracy. Thus in South Africa a showdown may well be in the offing between the unions, who represent a stratum of relatively well-off workers, and the African National Congress, which is desperate for export earnings and development funds.

All of this may well be contrasted, even causally related, to the remarkable growth that has taken place during the last quarter century in the moral authority and sheer political potency of the movement for international human rights. War criminals are being tried in The Hague, the rights of women have been put on the social and political agenda even in the Middle East, and the defense of minority ethnic rights has achieved a legitimacy not seen since Woodrow Wilson injected "self-determination" into the diplomatic lexicon at the end of World War I. At no time since 1948, when Eleanor Roosevelt presided over the negotiations that gave birth to the UN's Universal Declaration of Human Rights, has that document been held in higher regard. Even the most abusive governments pay lip service to its principles. All of the major industrial nations, except for the United States and China—admittedly big exceptions—have ratified the International Labor Organization (ILO) conventions that assert "freedom of assembly" as a fundamental human right. Even the U.S. government endorses the key ILO conventions, if not for itself, then for everyone else. So as a condition for lifting its trade embargo against Cuba, U.S. law requires that island nation to put in place a transition regime "allowing the establishment of independent trade unions as set forth in Conventions 87 and 98 of the ILO."[2]

This worldwide endorsement of the human rights idea has become the charter for a new kind of statecraft, even a new kind of globalized civil society. Thousands of nongovernmental organizations (NGOs) make it their business to expose human rights violations and push forward a social, economic, and legal framework to which sovereign states must accommodate themselves. There may well be as many as twenty-five thousand international NGOs in the world today; some twenty-five hundred are recognized by the United Nations. Not all are concerned with human rights, but many of the most important and highest profile take this portfolio as their primary mission. Amnesty International, for example, has more than a million members worldwide and has affiliates or networks in more than ninety countries and territories. Its London-based International Secretariat has a staff of over three hundred, which carries out research, coordinates worldwide lobbying, and maintains an impressive presence at many international conferences and institutions. Human Rights Watch went from a budget of $200,000 in 1979 to $20 million in 2001 and then published *Unfair Advantage: Workers' Freedom of Association in the United States under Human Rights Standards*, which is certainly one of the most devastating accounts of the hypocrisy and injustice under which trade unionists labor in one portion of North America. Like the world's first human rights NGO—the Anti-Slavery Society that helped abolish legal servitude within the British Empire—such international organizations command a legitimacy greater than that of many national governments. When he was UN secretary, Kofi Annan called these voluntary international organizations "the conscience of humanity."[3]

This new sensitivity to global human rights is undoubtedly a good thing for the cause of trade unionism, rights at work, and the democratic impulse. A symbiotic relationship clearly exists between a resolution of the two-century-old "labor question" and the advancement of democratic norms and human rights standards.

A manifestation of this relationship and of the legitimacy won by rights issues is found in the effort, largely motivated by activists in North America and Western Europe, to hold corporations directly accountable for their environmental, labor, and human rights conduct. This began in the 1970s when organizations like Greenpeace campaigned for ecologically sound whaling and fishing practices, but today it extends to the full range of corporate behavior, of which labor standards and labor rights are a prominent element. In the anti-sweatshop movement and in the worldwide fight against child labor, slavery, and the subjection of women, a de facto alliance now exists between numerous NGOs and several of the more progressive trade unions in North America and Europe, with some support from struggling worker organizations in Latin America, Africa, and Southeast Asia. Putting aside for a moment any consideration of the effectiveness of this alliance, or its impact on corporate policy, these movement-oriented advocacy groups have achieved a high-profile stature. Indeed, if hypocrisy is the tribute that vice pays to virtue, then we must nevertheless marvel at the corporate tribute that has been extracted.

By the early twenty-first century, some 182 labor and human rights codes of conduct had been put in place by transnational organizations, corporations, industry associations, and stakeholder groups. A variety of codes have entered the public policy marketplace. These are sponsored by nongovernmental organizations like the Fair Labor Association, the Worker Rights Consortium, the Ethical Trading Initiative, the Clean Clothes Campaign, the Rugmark Foundation, the Foulball Campaign, and Social Accountability 8000. At a time when most corporations and many politicians are rethinking and devaluing the idea of a society-wide labor-management social compact, or even of a more limited collective bargaining agreement, members of these workers rights consortia include company officials, trade unionists, human rights activists, religious leaders, student groups, and university administrators. Corporations have entered into these agreements because they fear adverse public relations and consumer boycotts, but we should not simply dismiss such a stratagem as risk avoidance. It says a lot when these multinationals recognize that human rights activists actually stand a chance of persuading millions of consumers that they should shun products produced under conditions where elementary labor standards and human rights are violated. Whatever their actual impact on third world labor rights, these corporate codes of conduct undermine, even contradict, the neoliberal globalizers who have heretofore conflated a free market in labor and goods with the capitalist utopianism that has flourished in the years since the end of the Cold War.[4]

Take Reebok International, for example. Reebok, which has positioned itself as the rights-conscious shoemaking multinational, first advertised this aspect of its corporate culture when in 1988 it underwrote an Amnesty International concert tour designed to bring awareness of human rights issues to young people. Reebok executives advertise their adherence to a corporate code of conduct "based on the core principles" expressed in the UN's Universal Declaration of Human Rights, and it markets soccer balls and other sporting goods with labels that assure consumers, "Guaranteed: Manufactured without Child Labor." The company even awards a "Reebok Human Rights Award" to activists who fight against child labor and repressive dictatorships.[5]

To gain some insight into the future of the relationship between human rights, workers rights, and the fate of trade unionism, one might be well served to look at the history of workers rights in the United States. In no other large country is rights consciousness of greater potency—in the law, in culture, in foreign policy, and in the subtleties of daily life and language. Since the 1960s a multicultural, gender-sensitive rights culture has been institutionalized, legitimized, and codified within the major corporations, inside the governmental bureaucracies, in academia, and all across the political spectrum. But during the same years that this rights culture became hegemonic, the labor movement, as idea, ideology, and institution, moved well into the imaginative shadows. In no other large nation, aside from those that are outright dictatorships, has unionism lost so many members and so much political and economic leverage. Despite the ascendance of progressive leaders at the AFL-CIO and in key unions, and despite the recruitment of thousands of energetic new organizers, the United States remains politically and legally hostile terrain for the revival of trade unionism, regardless of its structure, leadership, industry, or demographic composition. As the Human Rights Watch report *Unfair Advantage* pointed out in such graphic detail: "millions of workers are excluded from coverage by laws to protect rights of organizing, bargaining, and striking . . . recourse for labor rights violations is often delayed to a point where it ceases to provide redress. Remedies are weak and often ineffective. In a system replete with all the appearance of legality and due process, workers' exercise of rights to organize, to bargain, and to strike . . . has been frustrated by many employers who realize they have little to fear from labor law enforcement."[6]

The dichotomy between U.S. rights culture and trade unionism is graphically apparent when we consider the recent fate of two groups of low-wage service-economy workers engaged in conflict with their employer. Most were Hispanic or African American, and both groups of workers endured the kind of arduous, inequitable work lives that had once given moral urgency to the movements for both trade unionism and racial justice. During the 1980s Shoney's Restaurants still did business in the Jim Crow spirit that had shaped the racial mentality of founder Ray Danner when he opened his first Nashville Big Boy decades before. More than two-thirds of all African American workers were confined to the kitchen. When Danner found a restaurant where the dining room staff was too "dark," he ordered the managers to dismiss the blacks and "lighten" it up. All of this was embarrassing and increasingly unprofitable, so in 1992 the NAACP had little real difficulty in winning an extraordinary $132 million settlement against Shoney's. Danner was forced to pay nearly half out of his own pocket, and when Wall Street got wind that he might still control the company, its stock plunged and the Shoney's board kicked him out of the company. Thousands of African American workers took home sizable checks, while Shoney's instituted de facto hiring and promotion quotas designed to rectify the situation. "Our goal is to set human resource standards to which other companies aspire," boasted a company spokeswomen.[7]

But compare all this with the experience of the Latino women who worked for Sprint Corporation's La Conexion Familiar in San Francisco. In the low-wage world of telecommunications Taylorism, their dignity was under constant assault. By 1994 most had joined the Communications Workers of America (CWA), but just before the NLRB election Sprint shut down La Conexion and laid off all the employees. After CWA protest the NLRB slapped the company with more than fifty different labor law violations, including bribes, threats, and firing workers in direct response to the union organizing campaign. The government agency ordered Sprint to rehire the workers and pay them back wages, perhaps as much as $12 million.

But nothing happened. In contrast to the shaming and redemption through which Shoney's passed, Sprint executives felt no cause for alarm. They successfully lobbied the Clinton administration for various favors, reiterated their hard-line opposition to trade unions, and got a federal appeals court to throw out the adverse NLRB order. The company even codified its tactics in a "Union-Free Management Guide," declaring that of the "myriad of challenges" faced by Sprint, paramount "is the threat of union intervention in our business." Since neither Wall Street jitters, public approbation, nor government pressure held much of a threat, Sprint and most other U.S. firms were quite happy to skirt the law to get rid of union activists and intimidate workers.[8]

So how do we explain this combination: a powerful, pervasive culture of rights coexisting with a vicious antiunion praxis? We can win some perspective by looking at the first half of the twentieth century and reexamining the very different relationship that linked institutional trade unionism and the defense of individual rights, both on the job and off. The United States has never had a powerful socialist tradition, but core ideas of that impulse have often been carried forward by the union movement. This was especially true during the Great Depression, when two near-hegemonic ideas made the emergence of a mass labor movement resonate with many of the most embedded democratic aspirations of American republicanism.

First, in the depths of the Great Depression, trade unionism promised to police the anarchic competition of the market and push forward a Keynesian revival of an economy. For more than a third of a century, from about 1933 until the early 1970s, a highly politicized system of industry-wide collective bargaining generated something resembling the more formal corporatist frameworks that were reestablished in Europe after the end of World War II. In the United States, however, this macroeconomic function, the role played by unions as Keynesian stabilizer within an inherently unstable capitalism, was not enough to legitimize mass unionism among either political elites or the majority of American workers. Hence the second great rationale for the state-assisted rebirth of unionism during the Great Depression: "industrial democracy," or the formal, legal insertion of a rights regime within the world of work.

Arguing for the 1935 labor law that would bear his name, Senator Robert Wagner asserted, "industrial tyranny is incompatible with a Republican form of government." Unionism would bring to the shop and office floor those procedures and standards that had long been venerated in the courts, the legislatures, and at the ballot box. Collective bargaining, wrote Sumner Slichter, then the dean of American labor economists, is a method of "introducing civil rights into industry, that is, of requiring that management be conducted by rule rather than by arbitrary decision." And in 1941 a union handbook titled *How to Win for the Union?* confidentially asserted, "The contract is your constitution, and the settlements of grievances under it are the decisions of an industrial supreme court." On the shop floor industrial democrats envisioned an "industrial jurisprudence," a constitutionalization of factory government, and the growth of a two-party system that put unions and managers on an equal footing. The responsibilities and expectations of American citizenship—due process, free speech, the right of assembly and petition—would now find their place in factory, mill, and office. A civil society would be constructed within the very womb of the privately held enterprise. For millions of workers, a majority of them immigrants or the offspring of immigrants from Europe and the American South, trade unionism was the only road to civil rights, civil liberties, and real citizenship.[9]

But ideological and political support for this system collapsed even before union strength began its precipitous decline in the 1970s. Before the impact of global competition, before deindustrialization of the old mass-production sector, and even before the emergence of a militant brand of antiunionism within

large sections of the political establishment, the American trade union movement came under fierce ideological attack. The Cold War had made suspect the
whole discourse of "industrial democracy," but unionism's devaluation was not
merely a product of conservative assault or McCarthyite invective. By the end of
the 1950s many of America's most famous intellectuals, both radical and liberal,
were backing away from their allegiance to the unions, or even to the idea of a
working class organized to advance its own self-interest. Radicals like C. Wright
Mills touted the unions as "the most effective tool for the incorporation of the
working class in a system of oppression and imperialism." John Kenneth Galbraith
and other midcentury liberals thought unionism was a handmaiden to a benign,
corporate "technostructure."[10]

Most intellectuals and policy makers came to see the whole system of collective
bargaining as at best a pillar of the status quo, a system of incremental social advance that actually sustained a liberal variant of American capitalism. In the early
Cold War era this had seemed to be quite a virtue, which the Voice of America
celebrated in those nations where socialist ideals still dichotomized social conflict. Reinhold Niebuhr, America's foremost theologian and a minister who had
once denounced Henry Ford from a Detroit pulpit, summed up this conventional
wisdom at the end of the 1950s: "The equilibrium of power achieved between
management and labor . . . is one of the instruments used by a highly technical
society, with ever larger aggregates of power, to achieve that tolerable justice which
has rendered Western Civilization immune to the Communist virus."[11]

This was pretty thin gruel, especially in an era when the civil rights movement
and the New Left were measuring all social initiatives by a democratic standard
of far more robust character. Indeed, the rise of a dynamic, morally incisive
civil rights movement ratified a great shift in progressive American consciousness. During those dramatic years in the early 1960s, when demonstrations and
marches led by Martin Luther King and other militants pushed civil rights to
the top of the social agenda, the entire discourse of American liberalism shifted
decisively out of the New Deal–labor orbit and into a world in which the racial
divide colored all politics. From the early 1960s onward, the most legitimate,
and in many instances the most potent, defense of American job rights would
be found not through collective initiative, as codified in the Wagner Act and
advanced by the trade unions, but through an individual's claim to his or her
civil rights based on race, gender, age, or other attribute. If a new set of workers
rights were to be won, the decisive battles would take place not in the union hall
or across the bargaining table, but in the legislative chambers and in the courts.

The United States has been a worldwide pioneer in the promulgation of workplace rights encompassing the gender, sexual orientation, age, disability, and par-
enthood of employees. Title VII of the 1964 Civil Rights Act therefore stands with
the 1935 Wagner Act as a pillar upon which the world of work has been reshaped.
Indeed, while the American labor law has become increasingly dysfunctional,

Title VII, which bans workplace discrimination, opened the floodgates to a se-ries of new laws, labeled "civil rights," which proved central to the expansion of workers rights within the realm of factory, office, school, and salesroom. The list of such legislation is quite remarkable. In 1968 came the Age Discrimination in Employment Act, in 1969 the Mine Safety Act, in 1970 the Occupational Safety and Health Act, in 1973 the Rehabilitation Act, and in 1978 the Pregnancy Discrimina-tion Act. Indeed, in more recent years enactment of health care and insurance legislation has had a profound impact on the world of work. Congress passed the Americans with Disabilities Act in 1990 and the Family and Medical Leave Act three years later, and in the years after that the 2010 passage of "Obamacare" has begun to redefine the definition of full-time work for tens of millions of Ameri-cans. Meanwhile, legislation protecting people of differing sexual orientation has either been passed or is being debated in many states. A European trade unionist might observe that such social legislation merely enabled the United States to catch up with some of the welfare state safeguards that have long been present in Western Europe. That's true, because this recent advance in social legislation arises not out of the potency of the American labor left, which has been in retreat, but relies instead on the enormous political legitimacy amassed by the civil rights movement and its many rights-conscious heirs.

Organized labor stood on the winning side when this social legislation made it into the statute books, but in the years since 1970 American unions have been unable to make the rights revolution work for them. In health-care employment, in California agriculture, in the teaching professions, and in some service trades the civil rights impulse did merge with and advance the union cause. But for most of U.S. labor, especially that centered in the private sector, rights consciousness, which has revolutionized race and gender relations, has had little organizational payoff. Indeed, if one just looks at the timing and the numbers, an inverse re-lationship may well link the decline of unionism and rise of 1960s-1970s rights consciousness.

When we look at how the American labor law has functioned, the problems become clear. Rights are universal and individual, which means employers and individual members of management enjoy them just as much as workers. Under a regime of rights it becomes very difficult to privilege a trade union as an insti-tution that stands apart and above that of its membership. Take the issue of free speech, for example. Under the original Wagner Act there was no such thing as employer free speech. The existence of a trade union was entirely dependent upon employee choice, facilitated and protected by the federal government. But U.S. employers soon claimed that under any such regime their constitutional rights of free speech were being abridged. In the 1930s and 1940s unions and the National Labor Relations Board (created by the Wagner Act) tried to argue that employer speech in union election contests was tantamount to intimidation or coercion. However, this understanding of the social and psychological potency of employer speech was soon cast aside. Congress and the courts proved sympathetic to the management claim that in any union certification election their voice could not be silenced. The 1947 Taft-Hartley Act codified this claim, and American courts have proven highly sympathetic to the protection of this management "right." In the contemporary American workplace, employers use their free speech rights to hire psychologically sophisticated antiunion consultants, organize pro-company employee groups, hold mandatory captive audience meetings, tell workers that the factory will close or wages will decrease if they vote for a union, and spend millions of dollars on all sorts of antiunion propaganda.[12]

As deployed in American law and political culture, a discourse of rights has also subverted the very idea, and the institutional expression, of union solidarity. This is because solidarity is not just a song or a sentiment but requires a measure of coercion that can enforce the social bond when not all members of the organiza-tion—or the picket line—are in full agreement. Unions are combat organizations, and solidarity is not just another word for majority rule, especially when their existence is at stake. Thus, in recent decades, employer antiunionism has become increasingly oriented toward the ostensible protection of the individual rights of workers as against undemocratic unions and restrictive contracts that hamper the free choice of employees. A National Right to Work Committee, initially funded by Southern textile interests, specializes in making use of the new rights language—civil libertarian if not actually that of the civil rights movement—in order to perforate union solidarity and discredit the union idea. The Right to Work Committee has therefore declared the NAACP "prostituted" itself when that organization aligned itself with the AFL-CIO legislative agenda. Because of its "marriage of convenience to monopolistic labor unions," asserted a committee official, the NAACP's "first priority goes not to restricting union racial discrimi-nation, but to striking down all state laws against compulsory unionism."[13]

A further counter-position between the "rights" of workers and the potency of the union idea has arisen from a series of judicial decisions that privilege an extremely individualistic conception of workers rights. A distinction between the economic and political rights of an individual worker came to seem more natural in the United States with the devaluation of collective bargaining and the rise of civil rights and civil liberties consciousness in the 1950s and 1960s. As early as 1961, Hugo Black, one of the Supreme Court's most aggressive civil libertarians, argued that any attempt to make a dissenting unionist contribute to the political funds of his organization was "extortion" that the government had "no . . . power to enforce." Today right-wing antiunion forces take this species of rights liberalism and throw it back at labor in an effort to strip unions of any right to use employee dues money to endorse political candidates, mobilize their membership for a particular cause, or lobby Congress or the state legislatures. In California during the two decades before 2012 the unions have had to spend nearly $100 million during the course of three election cycles to defeat ballot propositions that would have virtually stripped unions of their capacity to mobilize membership dues on behalf of a unified political program.[14]

Given the evolution of the rights discourse in the United States, it is not surprising that the courts have begun to question the meaning of industrial solidarity itself, even in crucial strike situations. For example, the Supreme Court has held that workers have the right to resign their membership in the midst of a strike and then scab on their workmates free from the disciplinary penalties sought by their former union associates. "When there is a lawful dissolution of a union-member relation, the union has no more control over the former member than it has over the man in the street." Here the Supreme Court, once again led by its most liberal members, subverted the legal and ethical basis of collective solidarity, transforming this ancient union impulse into a coercive set of legal and administrative pressures that merely trampled on the workers rights of the individual ex-unionist, which was not far distant from the views promulgated by the antiunion right.[15]

Thus, the same species of rights-conscious liberalism that abolished racial segregation, ended McCarthyism, and legalized women's rights has also undermined the legal basis of union power and turned solidarity into a quaint and antique notion. One might respond to this eclipse of the American trade unions and to the devolution of collective bargaining by arguing that the protective functions these institutions once embodied are being taken over by an elaborate set of new agencies, new laws, and new advocates. If workers are protected against sexual harassment by a lawyer rather than their union shop steward, the employees' rights are protected nonetheless; and if the laws governing occupational safety and health regulate the work environment rather than a union contract clause, the factory air will smell just as sweet.

But acute problems arise, both in the United States and on a worldwide scale, in the substitution of a rights-based model of social regulation for one based on the collective advancement of mutual interests. The first is that of enforcement. The legal-regulatory system itself is simply not capable of enforcing by administrative order the inner life of millions of workplaces. As anti-sweatshop and human rights advocates are now rediscovering, no consistent regulation is really possible without hearing from the workers themselves, and their voices will remain silent unless they have some institution that protects them from the consequences of speaking up. Indeed the whole history of social regulation in the industrialized West has shown that no army of government inspectors can ensure management compliance without benefit of systematic, organized pressure at the work site itself.

Second, the spread of employee rights has suffered through its necessary dependence upon professional governmental expertise. No matter how well constructed, such regulation takes disputes out of the hands of those directly involved, furthers the influence of administrative professionals, sets up these experts as the target of everyone's resentment, and ends by increasing litigiousness and undermining government legitimacy. Rights consciousness therefore transfers authority into the hands of another body—a court, a panel, a government agency—to sort out the various claims and strike the approximate balance. Justice may be served for a particular individual, or even an entire class, but not always through a system of participatory debate and democratic decision making.

Third, the rights discourse has had virtually no impact on the structure of industry or employment, in either the United States or abroad. A rights-based approach to the democratization of the workplace fails to confront capital with demands that cannot be defined as a judicially protected mandate. In the United States workers have used the new workers rights that emerged out of the civil rights movement to democratize gender and racial hierarchies, only to see their real security and opportunities undermined by the dramatic transformation of a working environment over which they have had little control.

And, finally, the rights revolution has not generated conditions that produce strong unions, or tempered capital's prerogatives, despite the links that can be made between these worlds. In the American textile industry, for example, where civil rights laws smashed Jim Crow, the rights revolution did little to alter the character of managerial authority or to forestall massive deindustrialization and deunionization.

If global trade unionism is to avoid the fate that has befallen it in the United States, if it is to flourish in a world that privileges human rights, then two things are necessary. First, the unions must themselves champion the rights impulse so that it does not become the presumptive property of the corporations, the free marketers, or even the human rights NGOs. To flourish again trade unionism does require civil rights and human rights and their vigorous enforcement in every global workplace. We should not sneer at the ILO conventions, the Universal Declaration of Human Rights, or the work of Amnesty International and Human Rights Watch. But this is not enough, for as the U.S. example demonstrates, without a bold and society-shaping political and social program, human rights can devolve into something approximating libertarian individualism. Like the socialists of Europe and the industrial democrats of New Deal America, trade unionism requires a transformative vision to sustain its moral and institutional existence, to link individual rights and social purpose. Like the Congress of Industrial Organizations in 1930s America, like British Labour in 1945, like the South African unions in the epoch of apartheid, and like Polish Solidarity in the 1980s, a renewal of the labor movement becomes possible when the national project itself undergoes a democratic transformation.

PART IV

The Specter on the Right

Historians on the left now study the rise of the right. In this section I examine the origins of that conservative turn in politics, law, and culture that has so fascinated contemporary scholars. Here I not only explore the conservative triumph of the last three decades, but I also probe those weaknesses within the social democratic order, at home and abroad, that opened the door to the emergence of a potent conservatism during even the most liberal decades of the twentieth century. This was apparent during the Depression, and in the inaugural essay for this section I pose the query "Was the Fascist Door Open?" during that tumultuous decade. Then the American right refashioned and revitalized those conservative themes and tropes—denunciation of the welfare state as an overweening governmental bureaucracy, a culture war against all those who rejected the United States as a Christian nation, and the fear of home-grown social insurgencies—which have become highly successful in our own day. And that assault was given wide latitude in the 1950s and early 1960s by many of the most influential of America's liberal intellectuals. Their sanguine faith in social and political pluralism, economic modernization, and the amelioration of all the historic conflicts that were characteristic of nineteenth- and early twentieth-century capitalism made them a prominent but highly "wishful" cohort that found themselves subject to ideological ambush and marginalization when a dynamic conservative movement reemerged after 1973. In particular, this liberal wishfulness proved highly detrimental to the labor movement, which, even at the height of its size and power, faced an unrelenting ideological assault from the right that defined as corrupt and illegitimate virtually all efforts to tame the labor market, either by collective bargaining or state regulation.

The New Leftists of generation 1968 defined themselves against those Western liberals or the equally self-satisfied comrades who presided over an even more bureaucratic set of modernizing regimes in the East. But if the '68ers bravely and accurately deconstructed any number of liberal conceits, not to mention the very real repression that was characteristic of Eastern European Communism, they also failed to arm themselves for the looming war with the right. There the most decisive battles would take place not on a cultural terrain but within a world re-shaped by capitalism's propensity toward a creative destruction of so much that was once characteristic of business and politics during the middle decades of the twentieth century. In the essay "Did 1968 Change History?" I argue that when it came to the economy, New Leftists of that era thought capitalism was entirely too stable, a claustrophobic economic system that functioned with machine-like precision. If they wanted to overthrow that system, it was not because capitalism faced an imminent crisis, or even because it did not produce for the majority of the population, but because the existing economic order was such a sturdy, inhumane iron cage. And this was their greatest ideological failure, because it would be the right and not the left that would prove most successful in taking advantage of the radical shifts in the nature of world capitalism that were about to come.

The antistatist, neoliberal ideas that have accompanied the reconfiguration of American capitalism have generated a toxic environment for the trade unions, public as well as private. In "Bashing Public Employees and Their Unions" I consider the idea of governmental "sovereignty," as used by the right, to under-mine the rationale for collective bargaining in the public sector. From the Boston Police Strike of 1919 forward, conservatives have considered the organization of government workers to be incompatible with the sovereign status of those entities sustained by taxes and elected by the populace. Public employee unions subverted the will of elected officeholders and undermined state power. That antiunion ideology faded in the two decades after 1958 when public employee unionism grew by leaps and bounds, but in recent years it has returned, albeit in a distinctively neoliberal, antistate guise. Conservatives today charge that instead of challenging the power of the state, public sector unionism is illegitimate because these institutions support those governmental functions that regulate commerce, sustain public education, and provide other public goods now under attack from the neoliberal right.

CHAPTER 11

The United States in the Great Depression

Was the Fascist Door Open?

Was fascism a realistic possibility in the United States during the Great Depression? Certainly if one seeks to measure that possibility in terms of the depth and severity of the crisis, both in economic and political terms, the United States was in the same league with Germany and other European nations that were devastated by the Great Depression. Unemployment reached 25 percent, five thousand banks failed, and middle-class wealth evaporated almost as rapidly as in the Weimar inflation of 1923. From 1930 onward no year passed without a series of mass demonstrations by the unemployed or without violent confrontations between governmental authorities and working-class militants. In 1932 the famed Bonus March on Washington ended with the U.S. Army destroying the temporary living quarters of some twenty thousand unemployed, many world war veterans, who had gathered in the capital to demand relief.

Two celebrated novels, one published in 1935 and the other seventy years later, have framed and validated the fears and imaginings of the era. Both evoke the emergence of an American fascism, not by coup or putsch, but through the ordinary workings of presidential politics—familiar, messy, "American," yet in the rendering of these novelists all the more frightening. In *It Can't Happen Here* the Nobel Prize–winning novelist Sinclair Lewis stretches the political realities of the early New Deal years just enough to conjure up the possibility of an authoritarian presidency that, like the New Deal itself, denigrates old elites while at the same time celebrating the authority of a newly empowered federal government. In the novel the American electorate casts aside a too timid Franklin Roosevelt in 1936 and replaces him with a populist senator, modeled on the fiery Huey Long, who proceeds to nationalize banks and utilities; push women, blacks, and Jews back into their proper place; and organize a nationwide corps of paramilitary supporters. All the while, the newly empowered American president receives strong backing from an immensely popular radio preacher, clearly modeled after Father Charles Coughlin, a one-time supporter of FDR who became an increasingly shrill opponent as the Depression years wore on.[1]

It Can't Happen Here remained a curio piece during the long years of post–World War II prosperity, but the emergence of a more polarized brand of religiously inflected politics in recent years proved fertile ground for another dystopian novel, Philip Roth's *The Plot against America*, which appeared in the wake of George W. Bush's bitterly contested 2004 reelection. Roth imagines a United States where a lingering Depression and the prospect of war has generated a desperate search for extreme solutions, a context in which the popular but increasingly right-wing aviator Charles Lindbergh storms the deadlocked 1940 Republican National Convention, upsets Wendell Willkie for the nomination, and then barnstorms the nation to oust FDR from the White House. "Vote for Lindbergh or Vote for War" serves as his victorious campaign slogan. Under Lindbergh the United States becomes isolationist, anti-Semitic, and pro-German. Families are torn asunder as a late 1930s version of America's contemporary "culture wars" pervade daily life.[2]

These novels, and there are others offering up similar scenarios, make two things clear. First, if fascism ever did come to the United States, it would almost certainly come via the ordinary routines of American political life, often led by figures who had once thrived within that milieu. But, second, such novels also imagine that in Depression-era America, political and cultural life contained plenty of people and ideas that in central Europe would have been readily identified with fascist movements and ideologies. When it came to fascism, there was no such thing as an American exceptionalism.

The novels of Sinclair Lewis and Philip Roth ring with an element of truth because they highlight many of the cultural and ideological affinities that are common to both New Deal and European efforts to combat the Depression and reconstruct the nation. This is the comparative stance adopted by Wolfgang Schivelbusch, a cultural historian who divides his time between Berlin and New York. In his book *The Three New Deals: Reflections on Roosevelt's America, Mussolini's Italy, and Hitler's Germany*, Schivelbusch emphasizes the degree to which the American New Deal, rather than being a democratic alternative to Nazism or Italian fascism, looks like a successful and pioneering variant, especially when one examines the monumental architecture, veneration and celebration of the *Volk*, emphasis on mass propaganda in support of state activity, and even the rise in authority and prestige of the national police. Common to the leadership strata of the United States, Germany, and Italy was a modernizing, revitalizing impulse. Toward this end the repertoire of ideas and institutions available to reformist politicians in North America were not all that different from those on offer in central Europe. All were "new deals," post-liberal, state-capitalist systems, often with more in common among themselves than with classical Anglo-American liberalism that flourished before 1929. To many contemporary observers, Hitler, Mussolini, and Roosevelt were plebiscite-based leaders, autocrats who came to power through varying but thoroughly legal means.[3]

The inaugural address made by Franklin Roosevelt in the dark days of March 1933 exemplifies some of these themes. While that speech is famous for its reassuring assertion that "the only thing we have to fear is fear itself," Roosevelt also offered a call to arms that elevated the state and subordinated the individual in a manner that certainly could have been included in any speech offered by Hitler or Mussolini at that same time.

FDR announced on March 4, "If we are to go forward, we must move as a trained and loyal army willing to sacrifice for the good of a common discipline. We are, I know, ready and willing to submit our lives and property to such discipline, because it makes possible a leadership which aims at a larger good. I assume unhesitatingly the leadership of this great army of our people dedicated to a disciplined attack upon our common problems."[4] Soon after being sworn in, FDR asked Congress for "broad executive power to wage a war against the emergency, as great as the power that would be given to me if we were in fact invaded by a foreign foe." The National Socialist press caught the statist implications of FDR's rhetoric. Just as National Socialism superseded the decadent "bureaucratic age" of the Weimar Republic, the main Nazi newspaper, *Volkischer Beobachter* opined, so the New Deal had replaced "the uninhibited frenzy of market speculation" of the American 1920s. The paper stressed "Roosevelt's adoption of National Socialist strains of thought in his economic and social policies," praising especially his bold leadership. "If not always in the same words," the paper read, "Roosevelt, too, demands that collective good be put before individual self-interest . . . one can assume that he feels considerable affinity with the National Socialist philosophy."[5]

But rhetoric was hardly the only basis upon which historians have thought that a parallelism existed between the New Deal and fascist Europe. A similar approach to political economy played a key role as well. Although corporatism is oftentimes a muddy and ill-defined concept, there is no doubt that the National Industrial Recovery Act (NIRA) of 1933–1935 was by far the most corporatist experiment of the Roosevelt administration. As with Italian fascism, key economic and political decisions and arrangements were transposed from parliament to a set of governmental ministries—in the United States this was the National Recovery Administration (NRA)—which in turn delegated decisions involving prices, wages, market share, and worker organization to industry itself, whose leading figures, almost always representatives of the biggest firm, constructed a "code of fair competition." By 1935 there were more than seven hundred representatives, who legislated industrial conduct for the overwhelming bulk of the American economy. To enforce these codes the government sometimes went to court, but more often they sought to mobilize public opinion, with the symbol of the Blue Eagle and the catchphrase "We Do Our Part" standing at the center of a system of coercive voluntarism. Those who refused to display the Blue Eagle or adhere to the NRA codes were ostracized, penalized, and in some instances put out of business.[6]

FDR put General Hugh Johnson in charge of the NRA, assisted by Donald Richberg, a noted labor lawyer. Like many other American progressives, both were enthusiasts for Mussolini-style corporatism. Fascism's appeal to such liberals was found in its experimental nature, its antidogmatic temper, and its moral élan. Johnson, who had been a longtime aide to the industrialist Bernard Baruch, was a particularly close reader of the Italian propaganda pamphlet *The Structure of the Corporate State.* He and Richberg drafted the NIRA along corporatist lines. As in the reconstruction efforts of Germany and Italy, the NIRA entailed both massive public spending and cartel-like industrial planning, which was the province of the NRA. Although the NRA had a famous Section 7a, which provided that workers could exercise the right to form unions with "representatives of their own choosing," this right remained vague and unenforceable in 1933 and 1934. Indeed, this Section 7a might well have become its opposite, a kind of corporate labor front, because for most large corporations, especially those in steel, rubber, electrical products, and in many paternalistic family firms, Section 7a was interpreted as a warrant to establish company unions controlled by top executives. There would be much worker participation but no opportunity for independent unionism, a prospect endorsed by Richberg, who became an increasingly hostile, right-wing critic of the New Deal in later years and a particular opponent of trade unionism, regardless of the politics of its leadership.[7]

Indeed, the NRA gave the president enormous power, for the executive had the residual authority to override both labor and capital and impose such codes as the White House saw fit. Richberg later wrote that in drafting the NIRA, he and Johnson "called for a Man of Action, and we got one." Mussolini's own response to this was "*Ecco un ditatore!*"—"Behold a dictator!"[8]

Rexford Tugwell, one of the most left-wing and pro-planning members of the Roosevelt brains trust, made a trip to Italy in 1934 and was impressed with Mussolini's effort to overcome the economic crisis and modernize society. The Mussolini regime has "done many of the things which seem to me necessary," Tugwell wrote in his diary. "And at any rate [Italy] is being rebuilt physically in a systematic way. Mussolini certainly has the same people opposed to him as F.D.R. has. But he has the press controlled so they cannot scream lies at him daily. And he has a compact and disciplined nation although it lacks resources. On the surface, at least, he seems to have made enormous progress."[9]

Waldo Frank, the left-wing novelist and editor, mirrored the thoughts of Tugwell, but with a realistic sense of alarm:

> The NRA is the beginning of American Fascism. But unlike Italy and Germany, democratic parliamentarianism has for generations been strong in the Anglo-Saxon world; it is a tribal institution. Therefore, a Fascism that disposes of it, rather than sharpens and exploits it, is not to be expected in North America or Britain. Fascism may be so gradual in the United States that most voters will not

be aware of its existence. The true Fascist leaders will not be the present imita-
tors of German Führer and Italian condottieri, prancing in silver shirts. They
will be judicious, black-frocked gentlemen; graduates of the best universities.[10]

But the NRA did not lead to an American fascism. Despite its corporatist
ideology, and the affinity of some of its leaders for European-style estatism, the
NRA never turned into a blueprint for authoritarian governance in the United
States. There were three reasons for this. First, the whole point of the NRA was
not the elimination of conflict between capital and labor or even the suppression
of popular mobilizations, but rather the reduction and amelioration of conflict
between capitalists themselves. After three years of economic depression, the
early New Deal was determined to stamp out the hyper-competition that led to a
downward spiral of wages and prices. The architects of the NRA hated "cut throat
competition." General Johnson called it "savage wolfish competition without any
direction whatever." The real enemies of the NRA were neither the Communists
nor the more conservative trade unionists, although both labeled this corporatist
experiment fascist, but rather the medium and small-time manufacturers and
businesses that rebelled at the government-imposed codes of fair competition.
Indeed it was just such a legal challenge, in the famous Schechter poultry case, that
prompted a conservative Supreme Court to define the Constitution's commerce
clause in an exceedingly narrow fashion. By declaring that the government could
not regulate the wholesomeness of the poultry sold by a Brooklyn firm engaged
largely in intrastate commerce, the Court declared most provisions of the NIRA
unconstitutional.[11]

Second, the NRA was not antilabor, or rather it was not afraid of labor. Hostility to the presence of Communists and radicals in the ranks of labor and the
unemployed peaked in the years just before the victory of FDR in the 1932 presidential campaign. These were the months when local police beat up unemployed
demonstrators and when General Douglas MacArthur, ignoring the instructions
given him by President Herbert Hoover, sent troops and tanks against the Bonus
Army encamped within eyesight of the nation's capital. During 1933 and especially 1934, there was much labor activism and strife in the United States. In San
Francisco, Minneapolis, Toledo, and especially in the Carolina Piedmont, local
police, national guardsmen, and sheriff deputies were called out to battle strikers
and demonstrators.

But this conflict did not generate an antiradical call for a restoration of order.
It was not fodder for the extreme right, except in some locales such as plantation agriculture in the Deep South or on the huge cotton and vegetable farms of
central California. Indeed the 1934 elections generated another shift to the left in
the American body politic even as the emergence of Popular Front politics and
alliances tempered any overt challenge from either the left or labor. And the New
Deal skillfully accommodated its erstwhile opposition on the social democratic

left. While the marches of the unemployed on the nation's capital were met with tanks and gunfire in 1932, just three years later delegations of the unemployed were meeting in the Department of Labor auditorium. Likewise, the politician whose call for a restoration of industrial order rang most loudly was Robert Wagner, architect of the landmark labor law that bears his name. The 1935 Wagner Act did offer as its key rationale the establishment of industrial peace, but only after providing guarantees that genuinely independent trade unions had the power and solidarity to meet with their capitalist adversaries on a terrain that gave to labor the economic and political power necessary to cut a negotiated bargain.[12]

Ironically, Wagner got his chance to put forward one of the most radical pieces of legislation passed during the twentieth century, because even the crisis of the Great Depression had been insufficient to erode the essential features of American federalism and divided power. It was the Supreme Court, then a recalcitrant and conservative institution, that had put the final constitutional nail in the NIRA coffin, landing a one-two punch that coincided with the disaffection of much business opinion in 1934 and 1935. Wagner's new labor law was therefore a stopgap designed to repair the damage inflicted by the Court. And of course it had to work its way through Congress, often against the indifference or outright hostility of FDR, Johnson, and others who presided over the emergency reconstruction efforts. Had the NIRA been more powerful or more successful, the capacity of social democratic parliamentarians to put their impress upon politics would have been frustrated. In Europe corporatism was successfully anti-parliamentary; in the United States it coexisted with a still powerful legislature, which usefully and democratically jumped into the vacuum left by the collapse, both legal and economic, of FDR's corporatist experiment.[13]

But this is not the end of the story, in which a triumphant New Deal and revived labor movement slammed shut the door to U.S. fascism and other right-wing movements. Indeed, it was in the second half of the 1930s that we have to consider yet another moment when the door to American fascism began to squeak open, if only just a bit. By this point three things had happened that led to the emergence of a powerful brand of right-wing politics in the United States. I hesitate to call it fascist, because as Waldo Frank had observed, it worked largely through and not against the parliamentary and state-level organs of governance, but unlike the corporatist experimentation of the early New Deal, this post-1936 right-wing mobilization was clearly hostile to Roosevelt, to labor, to civil rights and civil liberties as well as isolationist when it came to foreign affairs. And in contrast to the parallels that were drawn between the NRA and Italian corporatism, the right-wing politics of the late 1930s, which extended into the next two decades, had far more of a Prussian flavor.[14]

The rise of a mass trade union movement generated enormous conflict, not just or primarily between capital and labor, but within the working class itself. By the 1930s a majority of all workers in the United States were immigrants, or the offspring of immigrants. They were Catholics, Jews, African Americans, and Latinos. White Protestants and northern Europeans constituted a minority of all workers, especially of the blue-collar workers organized into the new unions. Because American corporations had long commanded the loyalty of these more skilled, Protestant, native-born workers, many of the strikes and unionization campaigns of the early twentieth century took on the character of a kind of internal civil war, an ethnically tinged conflict exemplified by the great packinghouse and steel strikes of World War I and of the industrial conflict in automobiles and rubber and transport that reached its apogee between 1934 and 1937.

The emergence of the CIO therefore constituted the coming into citizenship of a generation of Eastern and southern European immigrants and their offspring. Conversely, the bitter resistance of the American Federation of Labor represented not so much an attachment of one wing of the union movement to craft organization per se as it did the defense of the petty privileges and power that native born and northern European workers still commanded within the factory hierarchy. At the great Ford Rouge complex, for example, the rise of the CIO ignited a multiethnic struggle for power in which the politics of central and southern Europe was often played out among the sixty thousand workers in Dearborn. The Protestant elite, many of whom were enrolled in the Masonic order, were pro-company, as were the African Americans who initially looked to Ford paternalism and were mistrustful of the Poles and Italians who constituted the backbone of the newly radical United Automobile Workers. The Anglo-Irish skilled tradesmen were often syndicalist militants on the one hand and company strivers on the other. Among the tool and die workers there was a pro-German element with Nazi sympathies, as well as a Communist grouping with roots among the Bohemians and Scots.[15]

This civil war within labor and the lower middle class provided the social energy out of which emerged a phalanx of right-wing populist movements that were hostile to the New Deal, to the new CIO, and to Jews, Communists, and African Americans. Among them was the Black Legion, active in the industrial Midwest, and the American Legion, a veterans organization, which became increasingly antilabor and anti-Communist in the 1930s. Meanwhile in California the predominantly Protestant, lower-middle-class followers of Upton Sinclair, who had run for governor on a quasi-socialist platform, shifted abruptly to the right in the late 1930s once it became obvious that New Deal social change in the Golden State would push radical longshoremen and Latino farmworkers to the fore.

Even more telling was the shift of the immensely popular radio priest Father Charles Coughlin from pro–New Deal to a virulent brand of anti-Communist, anti-Semitic isolationism. Coughlin had been the spokesperson for the American lower middle class and the Irish and Protestant skilled workers who aspired to join it. In Detroit, where Coughlin had played a key role in support of Chrysler unionists who were seeking to shift the company union there into the UAW, the clergyman recoiled in horror in 1935 and 1936 when it became clear that the leadership of the working class would not be Catholic corporatists, but rather a cosmopolitan cohort of secular radicals who saw the new unions as part and parcel of the New Deal coalition. From Coughlin's point of view, the Roosevel-tian welfare state threatened to decrease the prestige and moral authority of the church; while the culturally pluralist politics of the Popular Front promised to subvert the ethnic hierarchies and Christian ethos upon which Coughlin and other traditionalist clerics appealed, both on the radio and in their increasingly frequent revival meetings and convocations held in all the major industrial cities of the late Depression era. So Father Coughlin shifted to the right, campaigned for an anti–New Deal third party in 1936, and by the onset of the European war was highly critical of Britain, sympathetic to German aims, and determined to stop Roosevelt from abridging American neutrality.[16] Philip Roth's *The Plot against America* was therefore hardly a fantasy, but rather an alternate sociopo-litical universe running closely parallel to that which just happened to represent historical reality.

But ethnic tensions and resentments were insufficient to open the fascist door. Big capital also shifted to the right in the late 1930s, creating the alliance with an anxious lower middle class that has informed and structured right-wing U.S. populism in many a subsequent decade. The failure of the cartel-like NRA and the rise of a socialist-inflected labor movement after 1935 frightened many capi-talists who had earlier seen the NRA as either an opportunity to advance their interests or an essential stopgap to prevent total collapse of the economy. "The life preserver which is so necessary when the ship is sinking," observed a U.S. Chamber of Commerce official," becomes a heavy burden when man is back on dry land."[17] So now DuPont, GM, General Electric, Sears, the oil companies, and a whole cohort of proprietary capitalists moved hard against the New Deal. These businessmen formed the Liberty League, which bankrolled an effort to defeat FDR, stymie his program, and persuade the Supreme Court to declare invalid most New Deal legislation, including the Wagner Act. The "hate Roosevelt" quality of this bloc was greatly advanced by the explicitly social democratic, culturally pluralist character of the late-1930s New Deal. As historian Alan Brinkley has made clear, it was only in the years after 1936 that the term "New Dealer" came to stand for planning, government regulation, social experimentation, and labor power. The New Deal no longer represented an effort to revive a faltering capital-ism, but now proposed to regulate and tame it.[18]

Equally important was a shift in the target of right-wing politics in the late 1930s. President Roosevelt's court-packing plan of 1937 represented the decisive moment in the crystallization of an aggressively popular, if not populist, brand of antiunion, anti–New Deal sentiment. For more than half a century the Supreme Court had been the conservative defender of property against the government regulation from above and labor upheaval from below. When in early 1937 FDR offered the nation his plan to expand and thereby pack the Court with New Dealers, he opened the door to a world of antigovernment invective. Indeed, FDR's court-packing plan may be taken as the occasion at which modern conservatism achieved both a mass base and its ideological coherence. Until 1937 small producers, farmers, middle-class shop owners, as well as workers and consumers saw the large national business corporation as their enemy and nemesis. They hated the banks, utilities, and agricultural equipment makers. During the early Depression years, for example, chain stores had replaced the railroads, in the demonology of many Southerners as the latest embodiment of Yankee oppression and commercial seduction. The government loomed far smaller in their social imagination; it stood for the nearby post office, the useful agricultural extension service, and the maintenance of social order at home and abroad.

But FDR's court-packing plan, proffered in the very midst of the sit-down strikes, worked a symbolic revolution, for it seemed to embody all that was threatening in the social and political upheavals of the New Deal. There was the assault on property, the overreach of executive power, the subversion of a hallowed institution of American government, and the New Deal alliance with a radical social movement that threatened the status and power of the old middle class. Thereafter, the American right, no matter how radical, would seek to denounce, defame, and emasculate the power of the central government, but not to expand it except when it came to national security issues—a large exception, but nevertheless a delimited one. Thus the Supreme Court's eventual validation of the New Deal regulatory state set the stage for the rise of modern American conservatism, whose chief aim was less the conquest of state power than it was the continued fragmentation of American governmental authority.[19]

This becomes clear when we consider the history of the white South and its resistance to the reformism, of either class or race, that it confronted for two generations after the inauguration of the New Deal. In the 1930s the New Deal's offensive against the "colonial economy" of the South was unhappily endured by Southern politicos only as long as their immediate political and financial dependence on federal relief exceeded their longer-term determination to maintain Jim Crow and keep organized labor at bay. But after 1936 the rapprochement between Southern congressional Democrats and the Roosevelt administration crumbled, partly because the CIO had turned its attention to the mills, factories, and refineries of the industrial South and partly because, at the first hint of recovery, the benefits of federal relief paled beside the threat of federal intervention in Southern labor and race relations.

Extreme right-wing politics in the United States, especially in the South, thereafter barricaded itself behind the door of federalism, state's rights, and pure racism. The American South, which had last dominated the federal government in the years before the Civil War, was reasonably content to stave off New Deal reformism by deploying a threefold veto. In the Congress its representatives amended all welfare-state legislation to ensure that there were plenty of agricultural, racial, and regional exceptions. Second, all laws, whatever their content, were administered on a state and local basis, ensuring that good-ole-boy officials would take care to preserve class hierarchies and racial mores regardless of the edicts flowing from Washington. And, finally, the South remained essentially lawless when it came to any real effort to enforce a uniform set of social legislative norms. In a pattern that really did have a fascist character, Southern elites had long figured out how to mobilize a big slice of the white working class in the interest of a reactionary and violently oppressive racial order. Thus the bitter resistance to the civil rights movement and to the implementation of school desegregation, which reached its apogee in the 1950s, was just the most overt manifestation of the reactionary manipulation of popular white sentiment—a sentiment that had first become apparent when Southern elites confronted New Deal statutes covering crop allotments, minimum wages, welfare payments, worker rights, and voting procedures.[20]

So in the end the federal and regional character of the American state, and of the American right, saved the United States from the emergence of an authoritarian political movement that sought anything but veto power at the seat of national government. Had the American state had more of a Prussian character, opposition to the New Deal order might well have taken a more overtly anti-parliamentary, paramilitary character, as it briefly did in the racially tense 1950s and 1960s, when resistance to integration generated a revival of rhetoric celebrating "states' rights," accompanied by sometimes violent clashes with federal authorities. But despite all of its reactionary politics, this fascist road ended in a political cul-de-sac. The racial politics of the American South would eventually go national, but only after those politicians who championed that region's conservatism had learned to play the populist card and the parliamentary game.

CHAPTER 12

Market Triumphalism and the Wishful Liberals

In the decade that followed the end of the Cold War, a triumphalism of the free market seemed to characterize much social thought and commentary, mainly on the right and within the Republican Party, but among many erstwhile progressives as well. The idea that capitalist markets are essential to, or even define, the democratic idea has always been present in the West, but the idea achieved a near hegemonic power after the fall of the Berlin Wall. "Let us celebrate an American triumph," thundered Mort Zuckerman in *U.S. News & World Report* late in the 1990s, "a triumph" based on the rock of an unfettered capitalism: "privatize, deregulate, and do not interfere with the market."[1]

New Dealers and old-fashioned populists once held that laissez-faire capitalism presented the gravest danger to freedom, democracy, equality, and the material well-being of most citizens. But Americans were now told to believe that democracy and the free market are identical. Rather than distorting or subverting social harmony, capitalist markets would now prove themselves the key to the resolution of virtually all social and political problems, both at home and abroad. As Thomas Friedman of the *New York Times* put it: "International finance has turned the whole world into a parliamentary system" that allows people to "vote every hour, every day through their mutual funds, their pension funds, their brokers, and, more and more, from their own basements via the Internet." Thus markets are not just mediums of exchange, but mediums of consent.[2]

And in a maddening piece of ideological larceny, market triumphalists invoked that ultimate sanction—once the principal asset of the left—the stamp of historic inevitability. Francis Fukuyama put this most famously in his essay "The End of History," written just before the fall of the Berlin Wall: "Liberal democracy combined with open market economics has become the only model a state could follow." Shortly afterward futurist George Gilder offered a characteristic bit of eschatological certainty: "It is the entrepreneurs who know the rules of the world and the laws of God."[3] The 2002 "National Security Strategy of the United States of America," prepared under the authority of National

Security Advisor Condoleezza Rice, seemed to put the power of the American state behind the Fukuyama-Gilder thesis: "The great struggles of the twentieth century between liberty and totalitarianism ended with a decisive victory for the forces of freedom—and a single sustainable model for national success: freedom, democracy, and free enterprise."[4]

Even today, words like "reform" and "liberalization," and sometimes even "revolution," denote the process whereby an open market in labor and capital replaces the regulatory regimes, either social democratic or autocratic, that were erected earlier in the century. In effect, Woodrow Wilson, or a rather distorted version of Wilsonian liberalism, has won the great debate, not only with V. I. Lenin but also with Eduard Bernstein and John Strachy. "For years socialists used to argue among themselves about what kind of socialism they wanted," comments Denis MacShane, a former official of the International Metal Workers Federation, later a Labour Party MP. "But today, the choice of the left is no longer what kind of socialism it wants, but what kind of capitalism it can support."[5]

Of course, such market triumphalism is not just for foreign consumption. Although given much energy by the fall of Communism and the various "shock treatments" foisted upon Poland, Russia, Chile, Czechoslovakia, Indonesia, and other nations, the remedy was urged upon the United States itself. *Forbes* columnist Peter Huber argued that it was "market forces and the information age" that had beaten the Soviets and would soon force the dissolution of America's largest economic organizations. "If you have grown accustomed to a sheltered life inside a really large corporation," he advised, take care: "The next Kremlin to fall may be your own."[6]

Such sentiments were not appreciatively modified in the world that came to exist after September 11, 2001. "The sort of people who work in financial markets are not merely symbols but also practitioners of liberty," wrote Michael Lewis in the *New York Times Magazine*. "They do not suffer constraints on their private ambitions, and they work hard, if unintentionally, to free others from constraints . . . It tells you something about the worldview of the terrorists that they crashed half their arsenal into the World Trade Center. They believed that the bond traders are as critical as the U.S. generals and the politicians to extending liberty's influence in the world. They may be right. And that should make you feel proud."[7]

A decade later the financial crash that began in 2008, closely followed by the election of Barack Obama to the presidency, might well have been expected to temper such views. But critics of the new president's reforms, the Affordable Care Act above all, were quick to label his statecraft socialism or worse. In truth, Obama and his advisors shaped virtually every one of his initiatives, from health care to the bank and auto bailouts, along lines that privileged free market forces, constrained only by a set of regulations designed to make American capitalism work with more efficiency. "I believe that the free enterprise system is the greatest engine of prosperity the world's ever known," the president told more than 65 million viewers in an October 16, 2012, debate with Republican challenger Mitt Romney. "I believe in self-reliance and individual initiative and risk takers being rewarded."[8]

How to explain this market triumphalism? The most obvious explanation is that we live at a time when an American brand of political capitalism has proven itself the most internationally potent and economically successful on the planet. Despite the financial crisis, the American Century, first declared in 1941, has hardly run its course. As historian Michael Cox has pointed out, the U.S. model of global capitalism has proven supremely attractive because its gravitational pull is now almost entirely unimpeded by the attractive power of any other competing body. Not only did the Soviet Union collapse during the early 1990s, but so too did competition, both economic and ideological, from a Japan-centered Pacific Rim. From an ideological and model-building perspective, the collapse of the Soviet Union had been discounted long before it took place. Few critics of American capitalism looked east of the Elbe for inspiration or advice. Still, the demise of this empire, and the increasing marketization of the Chinese economy that preceded it, seemed to demonstrate that any organization of society that substituted economic planning for a market mechanism was bound to lead to a disaster of the first order, both political and social.[9] Indeed, the elimination of this world historic rival devalued the ideological role played by those Keynesian, social democratic programs and compacts that in the early Cold War years had been a vital component of the claim that in the world of "actually existing" capitalism the sharp elbows had been tucked and the market forces tamed. The collapse of the Soviet Union thus made possible the celebration of a globalized capitalism with nary a backward glance, especially when all this was accompanied by the eclipse of organized labor in the Atlantic world, the corrosive impact of America's uniquely bitter racial divide on social and economic policy, and the élan with which Ronald Reagan and Margaret Thatcher mobilized elements of the working class on behalf of laissez-faire principles.[10]

The demise of a Japanese-centered "Pacific Century" has been equally dramatic and perhaps even more potent in advancing the idea that there no longer exists any alternative to a distinctively American version of global markets and capitalist social mores. Japan had been the world's second-largest economy for more than thirty years, and in the 1970s and 1980s the entire East Asian model for advanced capitalism, with its quasi-planning from the top, its innovative and seemingly cooperative labor relations, and its technological prowess, represented the real challenge, both economic and ideological, to American theorists of a new laissez-faire. But the collapse of that nation's real estate, banking, and technology bubble in 1990 inaugurated more than a decade of stagnation and crisis. The stock market dropped 80 percent, economic growth evaporated, and American technology companies ran away from their once fearsome Japanese rivals. Despite the manipulation of every fiscal and monetary lever at its command, the Tokyo planning ministries and the highly politicized Japanese banks, which had once been given such credit for shaping the entire economic miracle, have found their recovery efforts repeatedly frustrated. To Paul Krugman, the Japanese experience has exemplified a deflationary, confidence-destroying "return of depression economics."[11]

The collapse of the Soviet Union, the stagnation of the Japanese economy, and the return of a modest degree of growth during the 1990s and after are the kind of facts that cannot be ignored. But they don't tell the whole story or explain the ease with which a triumphal mood had begun to ferment among an important slice of the American intelligentsia, even in the years before 1990. This is a story that Godfrey Hodgson has told so well in *The World Turned Right Side Up: A History of the Conservative Ascendancy in America*.[12] It is not necessary to repeat the story told in that book; instead this essay explores a question that has been almost invisible in the presumptive triumph of market economics and market morals. Why, at least until the 2008 financial collapse, was the success of such market populism, this species of capitalist utopianism, been so effortless, so uncontested, and so unexpected?

Well, of course it has not. Liberals and the left protested all the way, and there have been many others, both among the Keynesian liberals and the Burkian conservatives, who have entered a dissent. But since the 1970s market-oriented conservatives have been on the offensive while liberals have been living off the capital of the New Deal for more than two generations. That was and is a large reservoir of ideas, but it has not been enough to stem the right-wing tide when in the 1980s it became clear that capitalist markets, both petty and grand, foreign and domestic, did in fact undermine Eastern Europe's Communist regimes. At that point conservative intellectuals took this undeniable phenomenon and made of it a global, near meta-historical generalization, applying it not only to nations with command economies but also to every region and every regulation in the world.

The ideological success of the laissez-faire triumphalists has been eased because many of the most respected liberals and system-analyzing radicals have been so wrong about the trajectory of postwar capitalism, and well before the demise of the Soviet Union. Indeed, recent rhetoric declaring the global triumph of the market has obscured a salient fact of the postwar era: for most of those decades many liberal intellectuals, even some radical ones, chose not to focus debate on the virtues or faults of capitalism. They were silent on this question, not because they were themselves cheerleaders for corporate power, but because they felt the very phrase "market capitalism" no longer adequately described key traits of social life in the industrial West. They thought that capitalism itself was in the midst of a great transformation, one that gradually and inevitably substituted a socialized planning ethos for the outmoded anarchy of the market.

This was not only the perspective of the left, mind you, but of that once impressive species of liberal ideology that held hegemonic sway during the quarter century after the end of World War II. As historian Howard Brick has argued, left-liberal intellectuals were entrapped by a sort of "wishful thinking" in which an unheralded victory, a kind of "silent revolution," promised the effective suppression of the market and the subordination of economic affairs to social regulation. Through this prism the devaluation of economic institutions in the postwar liberal agenda represented an imaginative, even utopian, leap beyond the present toward a postcapitalist, or postindustrial order, where social needs might be addressed independently of pure economic forces. They hoped for and sought a progressive evolution of political society, in which purposeful planning and democratic decision making rendered market forces increasingly ineffectual.[13]

Both postwar liberals and those who stood on their left too readily assumed the hegemony of the New Deal order, the bureaucratization of industrial conflict, and the increasing interpenetration of political and economic structures. They postulated the existence of a postwar social compact, of a labor-management accord, of a corporate liberalism, of a military-industrial complex whose social and ideological consequence was one of claustrophobic inertia, not market fragmentation.[14] From Robert Taft, to Barry Goldwater, to Ronald Reagan, the left has rarely accorded conservative ideologues of the market the respect due a powerful adversary. John Kenneth Galbraith considered the right wing of the GOP "the stupid party," while a generation of postwar social scientists psychologized the right in order to marginalize it. In *The End of Ideology*, the urtext of postwar liberalism, Daniel Bell focused his considerable intellect exclusively upon the *left-wing* exhaustion of political ideas. He took no notice of the ideological revival on the *right*, which was about to launch the Goldwater insurgency.[15] Liberals and radicals alike were therefore left utterly unprepared for the social stress caused by the return of a capitalist economic crisis in the 1970s and the revival of a laissez-faire right wing in the 1980s and 1990s.[16]

Of course, it is important to understand that such unpreparedness was not simply a product of left-wing myopia or Cold War wishfulness. The crisis of transatlantic capitalism during the first half of the twentieth century had seemed to teach both policy liberals and social conservatives that free-market capitalism was an increasingly obsolete system at variance with the social, political, and psychological realities that structured economic life. Such was the worldview of Adolf Berle and Joseph Schumpeter, who were among the most influential theorists of capitalist transmutation during the first half of the twentieth century. Both were accomplished students of corporate finance and macroeconomic policy, both served at the highest levels of their respective governments during moments of acute crisis (post–World War I Austria, Depression-era America), and both wrote books of remarkable staying power, sustaining a coterie of academics and activist intellectuals well into the postwar era. Schumpeter, who came out of the great pre–World War I tradition of Austrian political economy, was undoubtedly the more profound intellectual, but his ideas about the trajectory of Western capitalism also sustained the more policy-oriented thinking generated by Adolf Berle, whose upper-class, Protestant progressive education gave him rapid entry to the highest New Deal/New Frontier circles.

With economist Gardiner Means, Adolf Berle wrote *The Modern Corporation and Private Property* in 1932. The book provided an ideological rationale for New Deal planning, consumer activism, labor organizing, and state regulation of the large corporation. America's huge corporations, which then controlled one-third of the national wealth, had themselves abridged the fundamentals of liberal capitalism. Not only had oligarchy replaced competition, but also, of even more consequence, management usurped the prerogatives of traditional ownership. If the shareholders had therefore lost control of the corporation to a set of unelected, self-perpetuating managers, then the modern corporation could best be understood not in terms of "the traditional logic of property and profits . . . not in terms of business enterprise but in terms of social organization." And like the church, the military, and the state, such power had to be either regulated or democratized if a republican government were to exist.[17] "Whatever the authors' original intent," wrote historian Richard Pells half a century later, "their ideas were continually cited as evidence that capitalism had to be replaced by a more collectivist economic system." Indeed, as late as 1982, Hoover Institution conservatives offered the book a backhanded compliment when they organized a conference largely designed to denounce its pernicious influence.[18]

Although Berle himself made his peace with a hawkish brand of postwar liberalism, he remained enough of an old Progressive to believe that corporate power and capitalist markets had to be self-consciously fought and tamed. By the 1950s and 1960s he was an opponent of the left, especially in Latin America, but Berle saw a vigorous brand of New Deal–style statecraft as essential to a well-regulated capitalism. As chair of the Twentieth Century Fund for two decades after 1950, Berle fully endorsed a mission statement that declared, "The Fund's approach is that of the social engineer who assembles and considers all the available information on a problem and then makes the best possible plan for action."[19] And as late as 1968 he retained much hope for social reform, arguing for the continuing growth of an American state, "partly as an administer of wealth distribution, partly as a direct distributor of certain products. In notable areas *production for use rather than production for profit* is emerging as the norm." This was a viewpoint that would soon lose its edge, and not only among liberals who had grown skeptical of such administrative hubris.[20]

Joseph Schumpeter was not a liberal. He was an Austrian conservative who venerated the values and lifestyle of the haute bourgeoisie from which he had sprung. Transplanted to the United States in the 1930s, he was instinctively hostile to the New Deal, to brains trust planning, and to left-wing intellectuals in general. Unlike Berle, he did not welcome the demise of the entrepreneur or the autonomous corporation, but in his famous *Capitalism, Socialism, and Democracy,* published in

1942, he forecast the inevitable decay and collectivist transmutation of laissez-faire into a rationalized and nationalized system, what he called "socialism."[21]

Like Berle, Schumpeter thought the entrepreneurial function was inevitably and necessarily becoming bureaucratized. But unlike the New Deal brains truster, whose big book was published at the very depth of the Depression, Schumpeter is important to our story because his highly influential theory of market demise depends not on a crisis of capitalism, but on the cultural contradictions inherent in capitalism's very success. Like Daniel Bell, who would write the *Cultural Contradictions of Capitalism* a quarter century on, Schumpeter saw a distinction between capitalism as an economic system, which he thought stable and successful, and the "civilization of capitalism," which he believed had been subverted by prosperity, inflation, and empowerment of the masses, in short by all those modern values that destroyed deference, loyalty, and tradition. "Capitalism," he argued at the onset of World War II, "creates a critical frame of mind which, after having destroyed the moral authority of so many other institutions, in the end turns against its own; the bourgeois finds to his amazement that the rationalist attitude does not stop at the credentials of kings and popes, but goes on to attack private property and the whole scheme of bourgeois values. The bourgeois fortress thus becomes politically defenseless."[22]

This sense of an inevitable, politicized transmutation of the market into something more systematic and more purposefully totalizing is very much a product of the early postwar years. The great collective effort put forth in World War II was in part responsible, but we can also see this kind of "big think" generalized and carried well into the early Cold War era, when ideological combat between two conflicting social systems had such a profound impact on Western social thought. It is important to remember that as late as 1960 the word "capitalism" had a distasteful odor in Europe, Asia, and even within the United States, where "free enterprise" was the preferred nomenclature. In Western Europe the State Department and the CIA supported the "Non-Communist Left," which enabled a generation of ex-socialist, but anti-Communist intellectuals the freedom to define the West in terms that marginalized existing market relationships and looked forward to a long era of progressive social reform.[23]

The management theorist Peter Drucker shared much of this same vision, even as he sought to put the idea of a planning order and a politicized capitalism at the service of corporate America. Like Schumpeter, Drucker was a theorist of capitalist stability. Indeed, he was the youngest member of an Austrian generation that also included Friedrich Hayek and Ludwig von Mises. But Drucker had a far more engaged, practical relationship to actually existing capitalism. After witnessing the Nazi rise to power, he emigrated to the United States, where he became one of the founding fathers of management science and one of the great tribunes of American capitalist civilization. Drucker was convinced that "nothing could induce the overwhelming majority of the American people to give up the belief in a free-enterprise economic system except a major catastrophe such as a new total war or a new total depression." But in 1946, when he wrote his pathbreaking *Concept of the Corporation,* he understood that such views were not universally endorsed. Thus he titled the first chapter of his study of General Motors "Capitalism in One Country."[24]

Like some twenty-first-century advocates of the universal market, Drucker often cast his mid-twentieth-century prescriptions in meta-historical terms. The modern corporation, he asserted, is the paradigmatic institution of the modern world, "the representative social actuality." Big business, he wrote in the *Concept of the Corporation*, is "the general condition of modern industrial society irrespective of the forms of social organization or the political beliefs adopted in particular countries . . . The emergence of Big Business as a social reality during the past fifty years is the most important event in the recent social history of the Western world."[25]

But if Drucker was a herald of corporate America, he was equally determined to divorce such views from any taint of the old laissez-faire. To Drucker and to a generation of societal savants who would follow, the corporation was essentially a planning mechanism, a Weberian rationalization of industrial society. "The problem of the political, social and economic organization of Big Business is not unique to one country but common to the entire western world. And this means that there is a wide area where it makes little difference whether we discuss conditions in the United States or in Russia, whether we assume a free-enterprise society, Communism or Nazism . . . the entire realm of social engineering is an objective realm."[26]

This effort to marginalize questions of economic organization and motivation is characteristic of the way Western intellectuals sought to wage the Cold War. In this schema, markets, profitability, and capitalism are but second-rate questions; the key issue is that of organization, planning, and technique. Management theorists like Drucker assumed that the primacy of market exchange had given way to new principles of corporate organization as social development came to depend on the encouragement of "social goods" like science and education. Since productivity gains now relied so heavily on such scientifically trained workers, public funding of research and education became the central motive force of economic development. In effect Max Weber would increasingly trump the economic forces identified either by Adam Smith or Karl Marx.[27]

On the left, liberals and radicals took the kind of thinking that went into Drucker's rather sanguine prognostication about the role that corporations and the state would play in a new regulatory planning regime and deployed it at the service of their social imagination. Unlike Drucker, Arthur Schlesinger Jr. was a liberal Democrat. When he published *The Vital Center* in 1949, Schlesinger declared himself a part of the "Non-Communist Left." He was a militant New Dealer who thought the pivot of American history turned upon the conflict between the business community, often in alliance with a not-so-democratic state, and the plebeian movements and their intellectual allies, who sought to rebalance the social scales. "Class conflict," wrote Schlesinger in *The Vital Center* "is essential if freedom is to be preserved, because it is the only barrier against class domination."[28]

But Schlesinger shared with Drucker a conviction that neither class nor economics stood at the fulcrum of social choice. Like so many others who had witnessed the rise of Stalinism and fascism and experienced the power of the warfare state, he was transfixed by the specter of an organizational revolution that transcended property relations and business interests. In the democratic West this augured well. "Britain has already submitted itself to social democracy," wrote Schlesinger in *The Vital Center*, and "the United States will very likely advance in that direction through a series of New Deals and the advance will be accelerated if the country fails to keep out of a depression." But Schlesinger expected no dramatic conflict, because in a post–New Deal America the differences among classes "are much less impassible than the differences between capitalist democracy and authoritarianism; and sometimes in the heat of battle the warring classes tend to forget their family relationship."[29]

We can see how some of these midcentury ideas were deployed at the service of a specific set of Cold War policy prescriptions, both foreign and domestic, when we consider the influential work of the first postwar generation of industrial relations scholar/activists. In 1951 when Clark Kerr, John Dunlop, Frederick Harbison, and Charles A. Myers proposed that the new and immensely rich Ford Foundation fund a worldwide study of "Labor Relations and Democratic Policy," echoes of a Depression-era set of radical, anticapitalist assumptions could still be found beneath the Cold War overlay that justified their ambitious research design. Drafted by Lloyd Fisher, a former Longshoremen's Union staffer who was now Kerr's aide-de-camp, the initial grant application argued that the "condition, character, and beliefs of the working classes will be among the decisive influences upon the political structure of modern nations . . . and world peace." But the Ford Foundation rejected the application, along with other international, labor-focused research proposals by such noted figures as Adolph Sturmthal, Sumner Slichter, and Margaret Catherwood.[30]

Paul Hoffman, the former head of the Marshall Plan in Europe, was then president of the Ford Foundation. Richard Bissell, who had also served with the European Cooperation Administration, was a key advisor, responsible for screening research proposals, among them that of Kerr and his associates. Bissell would soon move on to the Central Intelligence Agency, where he helped plan the coup in Guatemala, develop the U-2 spy plane, and organize the Bay of Pigs invasion. Indeed, even as he worked as a program officer at Ford in 1951 and 1952 Bissell was part of a high-level group of well-connected consultants who met regularly with director Alan Dulles and key CIA officers. Like the Ford Foundation itself,

Bissell thought of himself as an internationalist and a thoughtful liberal. He was a Keynesian economist, as well as an economic planner during World War II and in the postwar ECA. Bissell was opposed to the militarization of the Marshall Plan after 1950, because he was convinced that the essential ingredients to an effective anti-Communist foreign policy revolved around the encouragement of economic growth, social stability, high levels of education, and a culture of cosmopolitan exchange. He was therefore instrumental in funding MIT's Center for International Studies, where "modernization" studies under the direction of Walt W. Rostow proved so influential during the remainder of the 1950s.[31]

We don't know precisely what role Bissell played in the Ford Foundation's initial rejection of the Kerr-Fisher grant proposal, but it is clear that when Kerr resubmitted the application in early 1952 it had a very different character. Now titled "Utilization of Human Resources: A Comparative Analysis," the multi-university, multinational research design eliminated all mention of the phrase "working-class," and in its stead adopted in more explicit fashion the emerging discourse of modernization, industrialization, and human resources. This project fit in well with the Ford Foundation's funding priorities of the 1950s and 1960s: education, managerial expertise, economic development in the newly independent nations, and an orientation toward U.S. foreign policy that differed little from that of the Eisenhower Republicans. Indeed, throughout the 1950s the research project was guided through the Ford bureaucracy by Thomas Carroll, a Harvard Business School product, who encouraged Kerr and Dunlop to put the development of the managerial strata at the center of any theory of transnational industrialism.[32]

With a budget that eventually reached well into the millions, this remarkably influential, two-decade research effort funded at least ninety scholars (mainly at MIT, Berkeley, Harvard, and Princeton), and generated dozens of books, scores of articles, and numerous high-profile conferences. The "Inter-University Study," as it came to be called, was an engine of ideological reconfiguration in which an entire generation of left-of-center academic intellectuals became invested in a set of ideas that marginalized both class conflict and the business enterprise, capitalism and its ideological opponents. In their place the Kerr-Dunlop study put at the center of the postwar universe the inexorable growth of an increasingly hegemonic set of rule-making bureaucracies that structured labor, capital, and government in all industrial societies. A technically sophisticated, highly educated managerial strata was central to this process, both in the West and the East, and as the driving force behind economic development in Africa, Latin America, the Middle East, and the Indian subcontinent.[33]

By the time Clark Kerr, John Dunlop, and their associates published *Industrialism and Industrial Man* in 1960, they had reached the conclusion that the process of "industrialization" had replaced the dialectics of capitalism as a worldwide principle framing the evolution of society. As Kerr put with characteristic bravado, "In our times it is no longer the specter of Communism which is haunting

Europe, but rather emerging industrialization in many forms that is confronting the whole world. The giant of industrialization is stalking the earth, transforming almost all features of older and traditional societies." Classes would still exist in such a society, and unions would remain important institutions that represented the interests of lower-skilled manual workers. However, the resultant "conflict will take place in a system of pluralistic industrialism . . . it will take less the form of the open strife or the revolt and more the form of the bureaucratic contest. Persuasion, pressure, and manipulation will take the place of the face-to-face combat of an earlier age." But whatever the nature of the conflict, the stakes were far lower than those once imagined in earlier decades. Regardless of the form of industrialization—Soviet, Western, or in the underdeveloped world—a universal "web of rules" was intrinsic to industrialism's Weberian universe. These technocratic and rationalist constraints devalued collective action, marginalized the role of government, and heightened the centrality of the managerial elite as the "initiator" and "manipulator" of the industrial system.[34] So powerful was this bureaucratic, rule-making impulse that Kerr, who became president of the University of California in 1958, not only forecast a long-range convergence between the social structures of the Soviet Union and the United States, but even more famously, in his 1963 manifesto, *The Uses of the University*, he argued that in the growth of a knowledge economy, business would necessarily accommodate itself to the disinterested standards, the social mores, and the planning values characteristic of the nation's burgeoning set of institutions of higher education.[35]

The New Left had a far more critical vision of the United States than did Schlesinger, Kerr, and so many other organizational liberals. Berkeley radical Mario Savio would soon denounce Kerr's vision of business-university convergence, but Savio's generation shared this in common with the celebrated president of the University of California: both men believed that market capitalism had been bureaucratized in a society that had become increasingly subject to the rule of a managerial elite. If Kerr and Drucker saw this planning regime as one of progress, pluralism, and rationality, indeed if Kerr thought that the corporations themselves were taking on some of the characteristics of the science-driven university, then most on the left found Kerr's vision a nightmare, sometimes denoted by the phrase "garrison state."

On the emergent New Left, no figure was more influential in propagating this dark, claustrophobic vision than C. Wright Mills, who was, and remains, one of the most trenchant and popular critics of postwar American capitalism. At the core of Mills's analysis was a theory of capitalist development that foresaw economic instability leading not to radical reform, but to the rule of a new, statist power elite. In its twentieth-century form, capitalism was inherently unstable, prone to a recurrent cycle of depression, war, and hothouse boom. In the 1940s, when his amazingly prolific writing career began, Mills expected another slump in just a few short years, and according to his analysis, so too did the most sophisticated representatives of big business, who therefore backed an administratively guided political economy, a sort of postwar New Deal, but with a much more authoritarian, business-oriented elite firmly in command. Under this regime corporatist decision-making would replace parliamentary democracy, while the market would become merely a nostalgic small-town fiction under a regime of price, wage, and production controls. Mills called this "a corporate form of garrison state" or "a state capitalism with many corporate features," but whatever the nomenclature, it is "the main drift" that leads eventually to what Franz Neumann, that most influential student of fascism, had called "totalitarian-monopolistic-capitalism."[36]

As late as 1948, however, Mills's outlook was not one of despair, because he looked to the labor movement, "the chief social power upon which a genuine democracy can rest today," as the social formation that might well avert such a garrison state. He feared for organized labor, not because of its destruction at the hands of individual capitalists, even as the state looked on approvingly, but because Mills foresaw labor's claustrophobic incorporation into a suffocating, authoritarian, politically charged political/military regime, a devolution he sometimes labeled "the main drift." The *Power Elite*, his 1955 masterwork, elaborated upon this idea, and it became something of a bible for the early New Left, sharing shelf space with Herbert Marcuse's *One-Dimensional Man*, which also forecast a fat and sloppy working-class incorporation into the capitalist embrace.[37]

Mills was right about a lot, but this particular nightmare proved unfounded. Labor's fate was not incorporation, but fragmentation, marginalization, and a growing incapacity to make any sort of impress on the capitalist market, in either labor or goods. When Barry Goldwater began to denounce "monopoly unionism" in the late 1950s, he was not interested in construction of a regime that the New Left would later denote as "corporate liberalism." Representing a growing, self-confident ideological element that had never accepted either the New Deal or the managerial state, the Goldwater New Right wanted the market to reign supreme, in race relations as well as in business affairs and industrial relations. Goldwater and his growing list of allies in the middle rank of the Republican Party never bought into any version of a post–World War II labor-management accord. Nor did this new cohort of political activists countenance the growth of federal power over against that of the Southern oligarchy or individual units of business, which is why Goldwater's vote against the 1964 Civil Rights Act foreshadowed so accurately conservative priorities on race, market, and the constraint of state power.[38]

This was a trajectory that neither American liberals nor their left-wing critics understood. In the 1960s most thought that the Goldwaterite vision was a complete dead end. Instead, the United States was entering a world in which society would be organized according to some new, trans-economic principle. In "The Port Huron Statement," published by the Students for a Democratic

Society in 1962, one can find much criticism of American business, of social inequality, and especially of the "military-industrial complex." The latter phrase was taken from the farewell speech of President Dwight D. Eisenhower, who in effect now endorsed the dark analysis found in Mills's *The Power Elite*. Thus, if earlier generations of radicals had derided capitalism as an anarchic, irrational system, the New Left scorned American capitalism because it was too rational, based on a soul-destroying set of technological and bureaucratic imperatives that stifled individual expression.[39] "Do not fold, spindle, or mutilate." Thus did the New Leftists adopt as their individualistic credo the punch-card admonition of the early mainframes.

In the 1940s and 1950s liberal theorists of capitalist transmutation had thought that interest-group pluralism now constituted the only real basis for a well-constrained democracy. Schumpeter was an elitist who feared mass politics, and Berle thought "an equipoise of strong organizations" was necessary to balance managerial power with labor and consumer interests. Robert Dahl, the foremost theoretician of postwar political pluralism defined twentieth-century democracy as a "polyarchy,"[40] in which a kind of consensual democracy survives, but only as competing elites bargain, compromise, and govern. To all this the New Left counterposed participatory democracy and a new era of citizen activism. But the youthful SDSers who met at Port Huron could not figure out what to say about the shape of American capitalism. Indeed, after Paul Potter asked his New Left followers to "name the system" at a 1965 antiwar protest, he later reflected that "capitalism was for me and my generation an inadequate description of the evils of America."[41]

John Kenneth Galbraith, who was America's most celebrated and well-connected liberal economist in this era, codified such skittishness in his magnum opus of 1967, *The New Industrial State*. For liberals about to confront the 1970s and 1980s, no handbook could have been more disastrous. The corporations had once been regulated by the market and therefore independent of the state, argued Galbraith, following the lead of fellow New Dealer Adolf Berle. But under contemporary conditions,

> the mature corporation, as part of a comprehensive structure of planning, has no similar independence. It identifies itself with social goals, and adapts these to its needs . . . More specifically, if the state is effectively to manage demand, the public sector of the economy . . . must be relatively large. That means that the state is an important customer, and it is especially needed in developing advanced technology which would otherwise be beyond the scope of industrial planning. Under these circumstance the independence of the mature corporation is further circumscribed . . . There is no chance . . . of a solid front by mature corporations against the state.[42]

Market triumphalists have not let such views pass unnoticed. When President Clinton awarded Galbraith a Presidential Medal of Freedom in September 2000,

Virginia Postrel, author of *The Future and Its Enemies,* gave him the dustbin-of-history boot. "Galbraith has spent his career peddling nonsense," charged Postrel, a frequent contributor to the *Wall Street Journal* and to the libertarian magazine *Reason.* His argument for a planning technostructure, in both the United States and the old Soviet Union, she said, has been "utterly discredited by the experience of the past several decades."[43]

Indeed, those liberal intellectuals who devalued the pervasiveness and anarchic power of the capitalist market and instead projected a sociological convergence between the market-taming corporations of the industrial West and the planning bureaucracies of the statist East gave away much of the ideological ground that would soon be exploited by neoconservative intellectuals in the 1970s and 1980s. The latter preached a virtuous marriage between civil society, democracy, and untamed markets. As Seymour Martin Lipset put it in a 1978 symposium, "Capitalism, Socialism, and Democracy," sponsored by the neoconservative magazine *Commentary,* "The chief value of capitalism is not really its unequaled record of production and distribution of goods, but rather its guarantee of a private sector, a sector of society based upon property and income that is clearly distinguishable . . . from the power of the national state."[44]

Daniel Bell was as wishfully mistaken as Galbraith about the evolution of capitalist planning and the withering away of the market. But whereas no one today reads the *New Industrial State,* Bell's *The Coming of Post Industrial Society* (1973) is still widely respected. A new edition appeared in 1999, and, more importantly, Bell's concept of "post-industrialism," which one can also read as "post-market capitalism," is taken as a given by much of both left and right. To Bell, market exchange will atrophy in the new world of superabundant information and autonomous knowledge workers. This serves as useful camouflage for market triumphalists because it deflects attention from the unprecedented concentration and mobility of capital, devalues the autonomy and power of corporate managers, and ignores the very real growth of wage and wealth inequality. But Daniel Bell could make the idea of a postindustrial transformation wondrously seductive to left-of-center futurists. As he put it in *The Coming of Post Industrial Society:*

> It seems clear to me that, today, we in America are moving away from a society based on a private-enterprise market system toward one in which the most important economic decisions will be made at the political level, in terms of consciously defined "goals" and "priorities" . . . No social or economic order has a writ of immortality, and the consumer-oriented free-enterprise society no longer satisfies the citizenry, as once it did.
>
> This is a society that has rested on the premises of individualism and market rationality, in which the varied ends desired by individuals would be maximized by free exchange. We now move to a communal ethic, without the community being, as yet, wholly defined. In a sense, the movement away from governance by political economy to governance by political philosophy—for that is the

meaning of the shift—is a turn to non-capitalist modes of social thought. And this is the long-run historical tendency in Western society.[45]

In contrast to the pillorying taken by Galbraith, Daniel Bell received a warm embrace from those same triumphalist quarters. Francis Fukuyama declared that the appearance of a third edition of Bell's *The Coming of Post-Industrial Society* made him "realize just how right Bell was in his social forecasting." Fukuyama gave this old social democrat a pass, because he was willing to ignore chapters with headings such as "The Subordination of the Corporation" or "Social Choice and Social Planning." Bell's argument for a regulatory capitalism in a postindustrial world was simply shoved aside, out of mind and out of place. Instead, Fukuyama hailed what the post–Cold War conservatives found so affirming to their worldview: the breathless proclamation of a transformed techno-social era, the evisceration of all the industrial-age political and organizational categories, the demise of class antagonism, and even Bell's concern with the cultural tensions—especially the threat to bourgeois values—generated by such rapid social change.[46] And unlike Galbraith, who chose to ignore rather than argue with those to his left, Bell picked many a fight over the years, often against the New Left and its postmodern offspring.

But there is another reason why Reaganite conservatives from George Gilder to Newt Gingrich embraced Bell's idea of a postindustrial world. It devalues all that was or is characteristic of the old order, including the production of things in actual factories, various forms of routine service work, and the existence of a labor movement, either as a defender of a dying class of manual laborers or as an institution necessary to defend the interests of those who still worked for their bread in the postindustrial wonderland. Indeed, the failure of the trade unions to organize white-collar and professional workers, which was becoming well noted as the 1950s turned into the 1960s, seemed to confirm that these workers had an interest and outlook that was inherently hostile to the unions, the welfare state, and the planning impulse. House Speaker Newt Gingrich, for example, was a New South conservative whose ideological aversion to trade unionism and the welfare state came larded with a set of facile, techno-social imperatives derived from the most deterministic brand of postindustrial theory. He celebrated the writings of ex-leftists Alvin and Heidi Toffler, whose popular prognostications, including *Future Shock* (1970) and *The Third Wave* (1980), had much in common with the work of Daniel Bell and Peter Drucker. Indeed, Gingrich also had a theory of history that saw the technologically sophisticated corporation as the culmination of America's democratic heritage.[47]

This bundle of techno-social ideas actually began on the center left when a generation of hopeful savants sought to transform and devalue the meaning of work itself. In a burst of optimistic prognostication, public intellectuals of the 1950s, men like Norbert Wiener, William Foote Whyte, David Riesman, and Clark

Kerr, argued that, first, a new world of postwar consumption would replace work and production as the social and moral foci of life, and that, second, the decline in the hours of work and the growth in leisure-time activities would further marginalize the work experience. In their classic studies of midcentury blue-collar life, sociologists Eli Chinoy and Robert Dublin found that factory workers just wanted to get out of the factory, not make life there better. "If this finding holds generally," wrote Dublin, "the role and significance of work in American society has departed from its presumed historical position." Indeed, whatever the valuation of traditional work, the days of the factory were numbered. Just as tractors, reapers, and other forms of mechanization had slashed the farm population, so too would automation generate such an increase in factory productivity that blue-collar work would practically vanish. And as for the growing world of the salaried, white-collar employees emplaced within the bureaucratic corporation, both David Riesman and C. Wright Mills affirmed their alienation and psychological disengagement, a judgment available in the influential white-collar novels of that era, including Saul Bellow's *Adventures of Augie March* and Sloan Wilson's *The Man in the Grey Flannel Suit.*[48]

This mood was advanced in the late 1950s and early 1960s when a new era of factory "automation" seemed to burst upon the scene. There was a large trade in reports and conferences about how the working class would soon deal with all of its newfound leisure. A 1964 manifesto, "The Triple Revolution," signed by, among others, Robert Heilbroner, Irving Howe, Gunnar Myrdal, and Tom Hayden, foresaw in automation and cybernation "a new era of production" sparked by gains in productivity so large that one could cope with the disruptive effects only by severing the link between employment and income, a linchpin of the old capitalist industrial order. Trade unionists like Walter Reuther, who argued that such prognostications were rather premature, were thought to be unimaginative, if not somewhat conservative.[49]

The contemporary heirs to this kind of thinking have been those who have seen the late twentieth-century economy based on a "post-Fordist" production regime. In what they have called a "second industrial divide," MIT's Charles Sabel and Michael Piore held that cyber-world high technology, greater international competition, and a cultural differentiation of product markets had undermined Fordist mass production methods and the consumption patterns upon which it rested. Capital-intensive mass production, which both Henry Ford and Walter Reuther once thought key to a general abundance, has now become an economic albatross whose very rigidities have exacerbated periodic recessions and rendered U.S. products less competitive. The nineteenth-century victory of mass production over a supple, creative "craftism" was hardly inevitable, held Piore and Sable; it was in fact a "blind decision" whose techno-social debilities are only now becoming clear. Who wants to buy another Chevy when craftsmen at the Bavarian Motor Works can build a dozen different models that all feel custom-made?[50] And when millions of Americans hook up to thousands of Web-based narrowcasts, the mass consumer audience that used to watch *I Love Lucy* on Wednesday night has been forever fragmented.

Workers and corporations must therefore accommodate themselves to a new world of "flexible specialization" that requires a more highly educated workforce, rapid shifts in production technology, smaller firms serving specialized markets, and the creative deployment of skilled labor. In the 1970s and 1980s Germany, Austria, and northern Italy were held as the exemplars of this kind of productive system, while Japan's capacity to penetrate U.S. markets seemed to demonstrate the virtues of a non-adversarial, highly flexible work regime.[51]

Elements of this perspective have been present in the viewpoint of Robert Reich, Bill Clinton's first secretary of labor. Although Reich now staunchly defends the labor movement, the welfare state, and Keynesian economic planning, his earlier and more influential celebration of a powerful new class of "symbolic analysts" left little place for class politics within the body politic. "Symbolic analysis involves processes of thought and communication," wrote Reich, "rather than tangible production." According to his *The Next American Frontier,* a best seller of 1983: "This new organization of work necessarily will be more collaborative, participatory, and egalitarian than is high-volume, standardized production, for the simple reason that initiative, responsibility, and discretion must be so much more widely exercised within it. Since its success depends on quickly identifying and responding to opportunities in its rapidly changing environment, the flexible-system enterprise cannot afford rigidly hierarchical chains of authority."[52]

Such techno-social forecasting seemed to open up a new era of democratic "producerism," a hopeful, even inevitable world not altogether different from that once projected by Berle, Bell, and Galbraith. Indeed, in the *Second Industrial Divide* Piore and Sabel argued that computerized craftsmanship would propagate a new world production order amenable to a revitalized Jeffersonian democracy. Instead of acting as adjuncts to machines, post-Fordian skilled workers might become sturdy industrial yeomen. The computer, wrote Piore and Sabel, is a "machine that meets Marx's definition of an artisan's tool: it is an instrument that responds to and extends the productive capacities of the user."[53] In this schema, "post-Fordism" or "postindustrialism"—by the 1990s the two had merged into a somewhat gauzy construct—resolve the gritty conflicts of the old industrial order by simply leaving them behind. If a new era of technological innovation were empowering ordinary workers, then all of those issues of power, equality, and distribution that had once made the labor question so intractable had now been transcended.

But the stark fact is that in the twenty-first century more people on this planet work in factories than at any other moment in world history. There are more assembly line workers now than ever before, even if the production facilities are in Malaysia rather than Milwaukee, Sumatra rather than Saginaw. Likewise, the proletarianization of office and service work proceeds apace, even if the new telecommunication and call-processing centers are located in Bangalore rather than Boston, or North Dakota rather than Northern California. The goods and services thus produced still require bosses, banks, and bourses to commodify labor, turn a profit, and reproduce a capitalist social order. In its 1996 report even the World Bank took note of this phenomenon by appropriating *The Communist Manifesto* for its own free-trade purposes: "The need of a constantly expanding market for its products chases the bourgeoisie over the whole surface of the globe," wrote Karl Marx in 1848. "It must nestle everywhere, settle everywhere, establish connections everywhere."[54]

This understanding of capitalism's trajectory, in the twenty-first century as well as the nineteenth, returns us to the propositions advanced by the market triumphalists of our own time. Their conflation of the capitalist market with the democratic impulse has been highly influential, not only because it has been backed by the increasingly overt use of American power, but also because they have succeeded in returning us to a definition of liberal democracy that Marx himself would have recognized: a world of free trade, weak government, un-regulated wealth, and corporate cultural hegemony. The wishful intellectuals identified in this essay recognized the inequity and instability inherent in the world of nineteenth-century liberal capitalism, and to transform it they advanced a far more ambitious agenda, derived in large measure from the social demo-cratic aspirations that were so common on both sides of the Atlantic during the early twentieth century. Indeed, many of these theorists staked their optimistic prognostications upon the socializing dynamic that the Marxist tradition itself had understood to be a feature of capitalist development, especially in its late corporatist/militarist phase. They were anticapitalists insofar as they expected this system to transmute itself into a more harmonious and humane set of social and institutional arrangements. But these intellectuals forgot that capitalism is primarily a system not just of production but of power, of classes and not just culture. Without politics, ideology, and human agency, it will not transform itself into another system or another stage of history. If the end of the Cold War, and the wars that have followed, serves to remind us of this immutable circumstance, then the capitalist triumphalism of our time need not go unchallenged.

CHAPTER 13

Did 1968 Change History?

Before we can ask if 1968 changed history we must first define it. Of what are we speaking and remembering? What does it mean, these magical numbers, 1968? First, of course, it can stand for the entire 1960s, which accommodates quite a bit: the civil rights movement, of course, and the legislation that flowed from it, as well as the rise of African American radicalism and nationalism in the streets and factories of Detroit and points south. The term "1968" can stand in for the Great Society, too, although by that year that reform was clearly showing signs of fatigue. It can stand in for the second wave of American feminism and for the gay rights movement, which was already becoming a movement even before the Stonewall riots of 1969. And 1968 can mean all the tumultuous events in the political campaigns of that year: the Tet Offensive, the Eugene McCarthy and Robert Kennedy primary challenges to President Lyndon Johnson and to each other, the "abdication" of the president, the assassinations of Martin Luther King and Robert Kennedy, the Chicago Democratic Party convention, the emergence of George Wallace as a political and social phenomenon, and the presidential campaign that fall.

And that's just in the United States. In Europe and in Latin America events were equally tumultuous, with a general strike in Paris, huge demonstrations in London, and regime-shaking upheavals in Czechoslovakia, Mexico, Spain, Yugoslavia, and Poland. With customary thoroughness, scholars working with the German Historical Institute assembled for the fortieth anniversary of that notable year, historical narratives covering the tumult in some thirty-nine nations, ranging from Senegal and Egypt to Hungary and Denmark.[1]

However, in this offering 1968 means what most in the political culture think of as 1968: the largely student, mainly left-wing, predominantly male, Euro-American moment when a generation of radicals entertained what even at the time seemed to be utopian hopes and postures in the streets of Paris, Berlin, New York, and Mexico City. It was a New Left, which saw itself as distinct from both the Communists or Socialists, as well as being a left that stood against the mere social democratic reformism of many of the parties that had been in or near power in North America and Europe.

Indeed, one of the distinguishing features of the worldwide New Left in 1968 is that it arose not in the face of political reaction, but in a rebellion against a reformism grown stale and complacent. Thus in Britain and the United States the New Left flourished under Labour and the Democrats, and in West Germany the social democratic entry into a coalition government persuaded many young people of the need for a vigorous extra-parliamentary opposition. In France Charles de Gaulle presided over a conservative regime that nevertheless greatly accelerated the many social changes that were bringing French education, industry, and agriculture into a closer alignment with northern Europe. And even in Eastern Europe, Stalinist regimes had moved well beyond the institutionalized terror of the early 1950s.

It is easy to ridicule the student generation of 1968: the young, the privileged, the white and male. Revisited today, much of the Marxist, Trotskyist, Maoist, or anarcho-liberationist rhetoric of '68 does sounds ridiculous, even morally irresponsible. It was, as George Orwell put it in another context, a kind of playing with fire by people who don't even know that fire is hot. For any radical looking back from the early decades of the twenty-first century, the slogans of the year 1968 sound stale and absurd: "What do we want? Everything! When do we want it? Now!" This is narcissism with a red flag.

Nevertheless, the spirit was there, it was big, and it captured the imagination of millions. The worldwide character of the movement was noted at the time. The British anarchist publication *Black Dwarf* headlined, "We Shall Fight, We Shall Win—Paris, London, Rome, Berlin." Indeed, 1968 deserves to be compared to 1848 and 1919, also years of great collective, multinational hopes and failures. In France, perhaps the worldwide epicenter of 1968, the insurgents shook the system, with almost ten million workers on strike at the end of May. Workers and intellectuals assumed the role of heirs and custodians of an alternative France evoked by the memories of the Paris Commune of 1871 and the Popular Front factory occupations of 1936. But as David Caute wrote in his comprehensive survey *The Year of the Barricades*, "The strikers of May 1968 were playing Republicans against Kings on an historical board game that is not available . . . in the British or German cultures, and still less in the American."[2]

Indeed, the ebullient spirits that were released in 1968 could not transcend the political sociology of the various states in which the movement found itself imprisoned. In West Germany and Great Britain, student radicalism never sparked a large social movement, but, as in the United States, the university occupations and occasional violent clashes with police engendered a severe political backlash. While both Tito and de Gaulle had made dramatic and conciliatory television appearances at the height of the student rebellions in June 1968, government and educational leaders in North America and northern Europe found that the greatest political rewards were won by a defense of the existing order. Most Americans and most British applauded the use of police to clear student radicals from the university classrooms and the streets of Chicago and London.

In Eastern and Latin Europe, on the other hand, the ruling elites felt themselves on far more unfavorable terrain, largely because students and young intellectuals were able to forge links with wider strata of the population. The insurgencies there demonstrated how rapidly a transnational social movement could shake the symbiotic structures of power that had long held Europe in a Cold War embrace. These eruptions were also marked with some of the same avant-garde aspirations as those of Western youth, but here the attempt to liberate a region of autonomous cultural life meshed easily with the long-suppressed effort to end censorship and restore a measure of civic freedom. In Madrid students, academics, and workers rekindled something of the spirit of 1936 during their bitter yearlong struggle against Franco's repressive apparatus. In Warsaw students chanted, "Free art, free theater!" after government censors closed a nineteenth-century drama that contained anti-Russian references. Charles University students in Prague crowned the Beat poet Allen Ginsberg "King of the May" in 1965; thirty months later, a clash with police over a university power shortage set in motion the reform movement that came to be known as the Prague Spring. In many of these authoritarian states, opposition movements that were defeated in 1968 reemerged a decade or more later, providing the leadership and a good deal of the spirit for the "velvet revolutions" that brought down the Eastern European regimes in 1989.[3]

The year 1968 created or, at the very least, marked a generation. In every country, especially in Europe, there is the generation of 1968—far more decisively shaped than the generation of 1989 or even that of the World War II years. A good deal of this generational identification is highly negative, of course. David Horowitz has built a career denouncing the "destructive generation." Another contemporary critic asserts, "The distinguishing feature of the 68ers has continued to be their capacity for self-indulgence, and their blindness about the consequences of their actions for others."[4] But far more remember the generational experience with fondness, even if they have ceased to identify with the politics and culture expounded by the 1968ers. As Denis MacShane, a British Labour MP put it in a recent retrospective, "Before 1968 all was grey, conservative, male and old. After 1968, it got a lot better. I was 20 in 1968, and I cannot think of a better year in the last 200 to have been 20 in . . . Capitalism won as most 1968ers morphed into Richard Bransons with greater or lesser success, and 1968 produced no enduring reformist politics. But to be young in 1968 was very heaven, and today's Blimpish attacks prove just what a great moment in history it was."[5]

Timothy Garton Ash, who is of a younger generation, and whose greatest interests lie in recording the history of the events leading up to the genuine revolutions that transformed Eastern Europe in 1989, nevertheless pays his respects to the generational memory of 1968: "It's a general rule that the events we recall most intensely are those we experienced when young. The dawn you glimpsed when you were 20 may turn out to have been a false dawn; the one you witness at 50 may change the world for ever. But memory, that artful shyster, will always privilege the first. Moreover, while 1968 happened in both the western and the eastern halves of Europe, in Paris and in Prague, 1989 only really happened in the eastern half." And then Ash goes on: "The 68ers are a uniquely well-defined generation all across Europe—probably the best defined since what one might call the 39ers, those shaped for life by their youthful experience of the Second World War. Having been students in 1968, they now—at or around the age of 60—occupy the commanding heights of cultural production in most European countries. Think they're going to pass up a chance to talk about their youth? You must be joking. Not important, moi?"[6]

In the United States these generational remembrances are a good deal more muted, if only because the generation of '68 has been such a cultural and political punching bag for so many years. Moreover, in the United States the left-wing '68ers have a powerful set of conservative competitors, whose consciousness was also forged in the 1960s, albeit the year of Goldwater—1964—rather than the year of McCarthy, King, Mark Rudd, and Robert Kennedy.

In the United States the year 1968, or the 1960s more generally, should not be divorced from the long era of social reform that, with a few setbacks, extended all the way from 1932 until the early 1970s. Indeed one might well argue that the 1930s and the 1960s share a lot more in common than was once thought. From a policy level the 1960s were indeed the fulfillment, especially in terms of race and gender, of much that was implicit in the Rooseveltian project of thirty years before. And from a cultural perspective, we can now see, courtesy of Michael Denning, Alan Wald, Robin Kelley, and Gary Gerstle, that the 1930s had their own avant-garde, their own culture wars, their own ethnic and racial awakening. Likewise, the 1960s, even that defined by the generation that would become 1968, were not hostile to the project that we identify with militant unionism, the New Deal, and in Europe, the tradition of social democracy.[7]

Three issues define the extent to which the year 1968 did in fact change history. The first involves political party structures, the second considers international affairs, and the third, and some would say the most important, puts us at the juncture of culture, politics, and social transformation. One could find more, but these will be representative enough.

The Democratic Party was a mess in 1968. There were few state primaries in that era, so when the Democrats finally nominated Hubert Humphrey at their chaotic Chicago convention, it is probable that he was not the choice of a majority of active Democrats. Humphrey had not entered a single primary, and his muddled position on Vietnam satisfied neither the right nor the left in the Democratic Party. Reformers, associated mostly with antiwar candidate Eugene McCarthy, were outraged. They proposed a thorough revision of the delegate selection rules, a cause that seemed imperative after tens of thousands of young people battled the Chicago police in the streets and parks near the convention hotel. On August 27, the second night of the convention, delegates voted for a commission that would seek to ensure that "all Democratic voters have had full and timely opportunity to participate."

The McGovern-Fraser Commission, chaired first by Senator George McGovern and then Congressman Don Fraser of Minnesota, was stacked with party reformers, many of whom were deeply opposed to the war. It ended the old boss system of choosing presidential nominees and helped create the modern presidential primary system. Soft quotas were established for delegates. Women, young people, and blacks would have to be represented in numbers "in reasonable relationship" to their demographic presence in the party. And there would be an end to the practice of appointing ex officio delegates (i.e., the cronies of the bosses) to the convention. The influence of the big-city machines, of organized labor, and of the party apparatus itself declined. This led to a class shift in each party, because affluent liberals gained more power in the Democratic Party while middle class ideological conservatives won more say in the GOP.

No longer would party bosses have control over two-thirds to four-fifths of the delegates. Not only could they no longer appoint ex-officio delegates, but just as importantly—and against the desires of many on the commission—a number of state legislatures decided to institute new elections in order to comply with the jumble of new rules. Thus the modern presidential primary was born. In 1968 sixteen states held primaries. By 1972 twenty-eight did. By the twenty-first century, selection of a presidential candidate, at least for the party out of power, seemed to involve an existentially endless set of contests, with at least thirty-five state primaries and several more states holding caucuses.

The McGovern commission also changed the makeup of the party's followers. No longer would nonunionized working-class whites have the same influence in party affairs. As polls have consistently shown, they vote far less frequently in primary races than college-educated professionals. The latter are not only more civically engaged in general than their working-class counterparts, but they are also more knowledgeable about party affairs.

This reform within the Democratic Party soon produced its own conservative response. After the defeats of George McGovern and Jimmy Carter, elected officeholders believed that these changes had unduly diminished the role of party leaders and elected officials. The party appointed a commission chaired by Jim Hunt, then governor of North Carolina, to address this issue. The party abolished the midterm mini-conventions that had been a platform for influence by the Democratic left in 1974 and 1978. And the Hunt Commission created the super delegates, about 20 percent of all delegates, who at one point in the spring of 2008 seemed to hold the choice of party nominee in their hands. However thrilling the election of Barack Obama, the process by which he became the Democratic

Party nominee left much to be desired. Indeed we have the worst of both worlds: endless primaries that privilege media, upscale voters, and candidate charisma, combined with a set of "super delegates" whose influence remains sufficient to distort the nominating process in a crisis.[8]

But enough of this party politics and gamesmanship. When readers on the left think about 1968 they are interested in far larger structures and ideologies, including the Cold War and the era of détente that began right around that time. Historian Jeremi Suri argues that this purposefully constructed rapprochement was in fact a direct response by elites on both sides of the Iron Curtain to the youth-led social movements that had arisen in the late 1960s. As the CIA reported to Lyndon Johnson in summer of 1968, "dissidence, involving students and non-students alike, is a world-wide phenomenon." Organized militants were challenging leaders in France, Germany, Poland, Czechoslovakia, and Yugoslavia. One aide to Johnson remembered that the president "could not go anywhere . . . that was disastrous." LBJ's successor, Richard Nixon, labeled these conditions a "war at home."[9]

In his *Power and Protest: Global Revolution and the Rise of Détente*, Suri argues that détente flowed from chronic Cold War tensions that were brought to a head by the upheavals of 1968. There was an inherent irrationality to the nuclear Cold War, a chronic insecurity made more unacceptable by Vietnam. Détente, writes Suri, is a political response by ruling elites who seek to accommodate not just each other, but the populace at home who will no longer tolerate Cold War tensions and traumas.

Détente had its origins in Germany, the cockpit of the Cold War, where Willy Brandt inaugurated a policy of *Ostpolitik,* an economic and diplomatic opening toward the German Democratic Republic and other Communist states in the East. Soon Nixon also came to understand that with the Vietnam War sapping the legitimacy of his rule, a demobilization of Cold War rhetoric, even arms, was necessary. To the extent that Nixon had a plan to actually end the Vietnam War on favorable terms, it was to enlist China and Soviet Union in a deal to cool off Southeast Asia; this did not work, but the larger structure of détente would continue nonetheless. Thus Willy Brandt, Richard Nixon, and Leonid Brezhnev abandoned the muscular rhetoric and charismatic politics of their Cold War predecessors.

But none of this entailed an ideological truce at home. As Rick Perlstein shows in *Nixonland,* at the same moment that President Nixon was inaugurating détente with Soviets and opening the door to China, his administration mobilized its forces for a season of "positive polarization" against the "radical liberals," whom he sought to identify with the worst excesses of the generation of 1968. Nixon's second front, the home-front culture war, would long outlive his own presidency. As Suri puts it in *Power and Protest,* "The promise of détente became a stick with which to beat domestic critics."[10]

Détente, like the Democratic Party reforms, was but a temporary stopgap. It collapsed in less than a decade, but not before it had some remarkable long-range consequences. In the United States détente infuriated the Cold War right even more than it frustrated what remained of the New Left. Once this collaboration with the Communist regimes had served its purpose, the political immorality of the project became easy to see, giving a sense of élan to the neoconservatives and the Reaganites as they began their short march to power.

Meanwhile in Eastern Europe, especially in Poland, Hungary, Czechoslovakia, and East Germany, détente meant opening up to Western loans and standards of living, attempting a Goulash Communism to satisfy or thwart the spirits released in 1968. The indebtedness of the Eastern European states exploded. In Poland by 1980 annual debt service exceeded the total income generated from its exports to the West. This meant that the regime could sustain living standards only by juggling cutbacks and concessions in a series of legitimacy-draining crises that culminated in the Solidarity strikes of 1980–1981. Thus it was hardly the Reagan arms buildup, but rather the rumblings from below, perhaps infused by some of the still vibrant hopes of 1968, that prepared the way for the fall of Communism, in which so many veterans of the late 1960s played such prominent roles.[11]

Now let us finally turn to the culture wars, undoubtedly the greatest legacy of 1968 in the United States and, some would argue, the most important way 1968 changed history. Ironically, this claim comes as much or more from the conservative side of the political divide as from the old New Left. Indeed, American conservatives have been heavily invested in the cultural revolution of the 1960s, far more so than most on the left. It is the right, and not the left, that infuses culture change with the largest consequences, finding in an ill-defined set of ideas and values the cement that holds together civilization itself. The right has long turned Marx on his head, finding in a set of cultural tropes and ideological postures the foundational structures for the society they propose to maintain or build anew.

Conservatives, Mark Lilla has reminded us, do not speak much about the strictly political consequences of the 1960s, perhaps because these have proven ephemeral or indirect. President Nixon actually put in place many of the regulatory reforms that came out of the environmental movement. It was his Republican administration that finally integrated most Southern school systems and indexed social security to the Consumer Price Index. For a time the presidency became weaker while Congress and the courts became stronger. Reform of the seniority system took place in Congress, not always to the benefit of the liberals. However, that transformation was not really a product of the 1960s, but had its origins in the earnest liberal reformism of the 1950s.[12] Furthermore, conservatives are stumped when it comes to an explanation for the cultural revolution they detest so much. Instead they are content to endlessly recount its horrors, thereby inspiring the faithful, and putting themselves at the service of whatever questionable political forces might hold back the tide.[13]

The chief problem, said neoconservatives like Roger Kimball, who once wrote a book called *Tenured Radicals,* and Myron Magnet of the Manhattan Institute's *City Journal,* is that the events of 1968 and the generation that drew inspiration from that singular year generated a delegitimization of public authority in virtually every aspect of American life and letters. The nation's continuing difficulties arose not out of structural poverty or deindustrialization or even the social and cultural pathologies of the poor themselves, the "culture of poverty" or "ghetto culture." Rather the problem arose out of the "majority culture" itself, Magnet wrote in *The Dream and the Nightmare: The Sixties Legacy to the Underclass.* "Led by its elite institutions—the universities, the judiciary, the press, the great charitable foundations, even the mainstream churches—American culture underwent a revolution in the 1960s, which transformed some of its most basic beliefs and values, including its beliefs about the causes of poverty. When these new attitudes reached the poor, and particularly the urban, minority poor, the result was catastrophic: many of the new culture's beliefs downplayed the personal responsibility, self-control, and deferral of gratification that it takes to succeed."[14] The family had taken a particular blow, with birthrates down, illegitimacy up, and divorce more the rule than the exception.

But if the fruit of the 1960s was this decline in public and private morality, then why did it take place then and there? What were the ingredients that generated this phenomenon just two decades after the end of the Good War, even less since the onset of the moral and military conflict with the Communists. Once you define the 1960s as a cultural revolution, it becomes exceedingly difficult to explain it in something less than religious or meta-historical terms. After all, conservatives in the United States romanticize the affluent 1950s and are therefore reticent to seek the causes of the cultural revolution there. Likewise it would be taboo, albeit perhaps appropriate, to blame the civil rights movement itself for what conservatives saw as the decline in public morality, although that was in fact the view of a lot of white Southerners in the 1940s and 1950s who saw every reform leading to intermarriage and sexual promiscuity. That argument is off limits, which may be why a number of conservatives, starting with William Buckley in the 1950s and continuing long afterward, have set their sights not only on 1968 but on the entire Enlightenment tradition.

Then there is the accusation that a new class of intellectuals—teachers, reporters, and civil servants—have sprung up on American soil and captured our leading institutions. This is curious, because for decades before 1968 the politics of that new class was hardly left-wing, even in the eyes of the right. For every secular academic condemned by William Buckley in his 1951 *God and Man at Yale,* there were technocratic conservatives like Harvard president James Conant, theologians like Reinhold Niebuhr, or journalists like Walter Lippmann, all of whom were part of an influential class that commanded enormous respect from the conservative establishment.

The most sophisticated interpretation of the cultural radicalism that flowed out of the 1960s comes from the work of Daniel Bell, who distilled much of Joseph Schumpeter's dark forebodings about the trajectory of modern capitalism into his 1976 book, *The Cultural Contradictions of Capitalism*, originally begun as an essay that Bell started writing in the autumn of 1969. Bell argued that the eruptions of the late 1960s were not a deviation from the orderly bourgeois path marked out for modern capitalist society, but, as Schumpeter had warned years before, a working out of the logic inherent in capitalism itself. With Max Weber, Bell thought that capitalism developed and drew its strength from an ethic of sobriety, saving, and deferred gratification, but he added the observation that free-market capitalism itself worked powerfully to undermine those qualities and stimulate hedonism and the desire for self-realization and instant gratification. There was a tension between what capitalist society required of its citizens as producers and the habits it fostered in them as consumers. This contradiction, Bell wrote, would leave advanced capitalist societies without the moral basis they needed for continued prosperity and cohesion. Conservatives, who have always liked Daniel Bell for his condescension toward the left, have nevertheless been unable to stomach this argument. If capitalism generates 1968-style hedonism, then how can conservatives continue to celebrate the free market?[15]

Not all of those who see the cultural evanescence of 1968 as its most important legacy stand on the right. Virtually every textbook we use and every Democratic Party politician celebrates the new freedoms generated by that generation—those of racial minorities and women, first and foremost, but also the general transformation of mores found in education, journalism, clothing, literature, and so on. Michael Kazin has written a history of the American left, in both the nineteenth century and the twentieth, that makes this explicit. Most radical movements, he argues, from the abolitionists to the New Left, have failed to achieve their stated political goals, but they have nevertheless triumphed in the realm of culture and ideas. "Making values explicit" should be the central task of politics, declared the Port Huron Statement, the most important and long-lived manifesto of 1960s radicalism. "We regard men as infinitely precious and possessed of unfulfilled capacities for reason, freedom, and love." Thus the phrase "the personal is political" has become a cliché, but there are profound reasons that it has outlasted "Off the Pig" as a catchphrase from that era.

As Kazin put it:

> The long march of the post '68 left made its influence felt in many institutions. In the United States, it achieved something close to dominance in two particularly powerful ones: academia and Hollywood. That fact has long alarmed the American right, and with good reason. The anti-authoritarian, left-populist viewpoint taught in most history, literature, sociology, and government classes

shows up, in wittier form, in films and television programs by the likes of Michael Mann, Spike Lee, Michael Moore, Oliver Stone, etc. And such products of mass culture reinforce the reigning wisdom in colleges.[16]

Barack Obama could not exist except for the cultural and social transformations of 1968. Likewise in France, Nicholas Sarkozy, the divorced son of migrants, who entered office declaring himself at war with the legacy of 1968, maintained during his five-year presidential tenure a lifestyle of which many an aging cultural radical might well have approved.

But this species of left-wing cultural analysis, which offers an often triumphalist assessment of the transformation of social mores and personal values, can carry us only so far into an era of global markets, capitalist hegemony, and political reaction. Daniel Bell's notion that the individual self-expression promoted by 1960s radicals was itself a product of postwar capitalist success has been widely echoed in recent times. But the idea that an ethic of self-realization was inimical to the development of unconstrained markets and extreme inequality now looks highly problematic. This was not just a matter of those emblematic children of the 1960s, like Steve Jobs and Richard Branson, who went on to become billionaires. Rather, capitalism has found little in the cultural life of the 1960s that it has not been able to accommodate, absorb, and put to its own profitable uses. In creative industries anchored by Hollywood and Silicon Valley, and even in more prosaic businesses such as retail trade and manufacturing, values and styles that are seemingly characteristic of "The Sixties" have become well embedded, ranging all the way from casual Fridays to an assiduous effort to make the entire workplace hierarchy open to women, racial minorities, and gays. Individual self-expression and capitalist production have joined hands. The radical manifestos of forty years ago have become the business school clichés of today.

Tom Frank captured much of this phenomenon in his first book, *The Conquest of Cool*, a history of hip advertising in the 1960s. His second work, *One Market under God*, carried on this mode of analysis but noted its Christian inflection. In my own work on Wal-Mart I have found the same phenomenon—namely, the capacity of business management to adapt to and incorporate the innovations that first emerged on the left, sometimes giving to them a Protestant connotation.[17]

Take the idea of "servant leadership," for example. This is an idea, often popular in labor-intensive service and retail industries, that arose out of the late 1960s. Although we often think of it as biblical in origin, its author was actually Robert K. Greenleaf, a career personnel director at AT & T who rose to become head of that corporation's management research before he retired in 1964. Greenleaf was caught up in the intellectual ferment of the late 1960s, particularly the need of large organizations like the telephone company to find new sources of institutional legitimacy to win the allegiance of both customers and employees. Older motivational ideas emphasizing personal security, organizational efficiency, and career enhancement seemed to be losing their appeal as the spirit of the times seeped into even the most traditional enterprises. So Greenleaf founded a "Center for Applied Ethics" in his native Indiana and in 1970 wrote "The Servant as Leader." Servant leadership emphasized a holistic approach to work, a sense of community, and a sharing of power in decision making. The Lilly Endowment funded the early work of Greenleaf and his followers, but the servant leader concept has been popularized by a number of business writers, some with an explicitly evangelical orientation, like Ken Blanchard, Steven Covey, and Larry Spears.

It is precisely this kind of Christian teamwork that has become the functional ideology for those millions of mega-churchgoers, from the Carolinas to Orange County, that constitute the vast reservoir from which labor-intensive companies like Wal-Mart draw their managerial cadre and their hundreds of thousands of loyal employees. In an economy increasingly devoted to sales, service, and commoditization of the self, the "servant leader" idea rationalizes self-exploitation and lends a sacerdotal air to the corporate hierarchy. Thus in 2007 Wal-Mart announced that some 13,400 hourly workers with more than twenty years of service would take home an extra week's pay, a "Servant Leadership Bonus," perhaps designed to compensate them for the wage caps the company imposed on veteran employees just the year before.[18]

But when it comes to cultural transformations in general or the generation of 1968 in particular, I don't want to end on a note of cynicism. All revolutions, successful or not, link a transformation of the cultural and ideological terrain with a shift in power and governance. This was as true in the 1930s as it was in the late 1960s. Indeed, now that the New Deal is seventy-five years past and the year 1968 more than two score old, one can glimpse more clearly the similarities, both cultural and political, that existed between these two eras of reform, which often spanned the life of a single generation or linked together parents and offspring. The laborite New Deal had its own culturally radical flavor, far more than the partisans of 1968, right-wing or left, have been willing to credit. As Michael Denning has shown us, Popular Front culture had a lot to say about artistic and musical innovation as well as multiracial pluralism. There were culture wars in the 1930s as well as in later decades; one reason FDR was such a polarizing figure was that he embodied in his administration and in his persona the "class treason" that was so hateful to a generation of Yankee conservatives who had been the natural arbitrators of power and taste for so many decades. But unlike the generation of 1968, the New Dealers established a ruling order that lasted for two generations. Its cultural and social radicalism was backstopped by a transformation in the political economy that made it all seem highly naturalized. Thus while Barbara Bush could never stand Eleanor Roosevelt, Ronald Reagan, that lower-middle-class product of an alcoholic father, always held a candle for the New Deal president, even as he dismantled FDR's accomplishments.

And just as the 1930s are now seen as much more of a cultural revolt than was once thought likely, so too is the era of 1968 much more reformist than we once imagined. Despite all the talk of revolution, the economic program of the generation of 1968 was often rather incremental, in a New Dealish sort of fashion. The Port Huron Statement, which was written at an AFL-CIO summer education camp, is best remembered for its long prologue in which the phrase "participatory democracy" is made famous.

But the remaining sections of the historic document, detailing a series of programmatic reforms, might well have been passed at virtually any trade union convention of that era. There is much discussion of raising the minimum wage, empowering trade unionism in the white-collar world, rebuilding the cities, improving education, transforming the Democratic Party, and curbing the arms race. Indeed, the real problem faced by the generation of 1968, when it came to the economy, was that they thought capitalism was far too stable. It was not a crisis of capitalism that confronted these young radicals, but a claustrophobic economic system that seemed like a huge bureaucratic machine, well lubed and efficient. They wanted to overthrow capitalism not because it faced a crisis, or even because it did not produce for the majority of the population, but because it was such a sturdy iron cage. And this was their greatest ideological failure, because it would be the right, not the left, that would prove most successful in taking advantage of the radical shifts in the nature of world capitalism that were about to come.[19]

CHAPTER 14

Bashing Public Employees and Their Unions

When he was still President Obama's chief of staff, Rahm Emanuel, later mayor of Chicago, famously quipped, "Never allow a crisis to go to waste." Republican governors in Wisconsin, New Jersey, Ohio, and other states certainly took that advice to heart following the 2010 elections. By emphasizing, and in some cases manipulating, the red ink flowing through so many state budgets, they leveraged the crisis to strike a body blow at the public sector unions that represent so many teachers, professors, social workers, and other municipal employees. In Ohio, Indiana, Wisconsin, New Jersey, and Michigan, new laws curbed or ended collective bargaining by hundreds of thousands of public employees, eliminated dues check-off, and reduced wages and pensions. All this was accompanied by much ideologically pointed invective. Indiana governor Mitch Daniels called government workers "a new privileged class."[1] New Jersey governor Chris Christie labeled the public employee unions "special interests" who exploit the "overburdened taxpayers of New Jersey," thereby creating "two classes of citizens." He called leaders of the teachers' union "a group of political thugs," while Wisconsin's Scott Walker, who faced massive and sustained protests against his antiunion initiative, denounced "tone-deaf and out of touch union bosses."[2]

Unionists and Democrats denounced this as opportunism: by the second decade of the twenty-first century, public sector unions were the largest and most politically active segment of the labor movement. They made an inviting target, but it would be a mistake to see the GOP offensive against the unions as some kind of hasty and ill-planned gambit. The rhetoric and legislative program of politicians like Walker, who handily survived a liberal-labor recall effort in 2012, refracts a multi-decade effort by conservatives—in politics, academia, think tanks, and management—designed to eviscerate trade unionism so that it will, in effect, simply wither away. Their assault, both ideological and political, has depended neither upon the presence or absence of a fiscal crisis at the state level nor, for that matter, upon the profitability or competitiveness of those American companies threatened by global competition. The collective organization of workers, private or public, stands athwart their vision of how markets should work and the polity should function.

So opposition to public sector unionism has a long history. There have been three kinds of arguments, roughly chronological in their deployment, that have sought to delegitimize a collective voice for public employees and divorce their interest from that of the larger public good. The longest-standing argument against public sector unionism rests on the idea that such collective bargaining by workers in the public sector undercuts the sovereignty of government. The second idea is that public sector unionism makes government too expensive and sets a standard that private industry cannot meet. And the third conservative argument, which reflects the rise in recent years of an intense hostility to the very idea of a welfare state, asserts that public sector unions are bad not because they undermine the sovereignty of the state, but because they sustain it, especially insofar as the state, at either the local or national levels, creates a set of public goods, like education, infrastructure, health care, and even public safety, that conservatives seek to either abolish or privatize.[3]

The sovereignty argument had its first large play in August and September 1919 when Boston police joined the American Federation of Labor. Inflation had robbed their wages of half their value during the war, while a labor shortage had generated extraordinarily long hours for each officer on the beat. The argument put forward by the Boston elite against these Irish patrolmen would reverberate through the decades: a "police officer is not an employee but a State officer," and must be prevented "from coming under the direction and dictation of any organization which represents but one element or class of the community." Declaring that "no man can serve two masters," Boston's police commissioner suspended the entire union leadership, which precipitated a strike by more than a thousand police, and this during the early autumn of that most radical season, which saw the inauguration of strikes in steel, coal, and a dozen other major industries.[4]

When the cops failed to show up for work, crowds appeared in Scully Square, looting became widespread, and the specter of anarchy seemed to stalk the Hub City. President Woodrow Wilson famously called the strike an "intolerable crime against civilization." Governor Calvin Coolidge called in the state militia, denounced the striking police as deserters, and applauded Boston officials when they fired the entire workforce in the name of defending "the sovereignty of Massachusetts." Coolidge seemed to be standing between the Back Bay bourgeoisie and an onrushing Bolshevik tide, so by firing these otherwise conservative Irish cops the Massachusetts governor helped propel himself into the vice presidency and then to the White House itself.[5]

The police strike and other public employee strikes of the World War I era, including those of firemen and munitions workers in government arsenals, created a great divide in the American labor law. From this point onward, virtually everyone, including partisans of labor, envisioned one labor law for private sector employees and another for those who were employed by the state. This became clear during the New Deal when at the very height of the labor insurgency of that era, government workers, even those who wore blue collars and got their hands dirty, were a caste apart. President Roosevelt recognized that the "desire of Government employees for fair and adequate pay, reasonable hours of work, safe and suitable working conditions . . . is basically no different from that of employees in private industry." But when in 1938 Works Progress Administration laborers sought to emulate their brothers in the steel mills and auto factories by demanding collective bargaining with the government officials who administered that New Deal program, President Roosevelt, like Coolidge, relied on the sovereignty argument to assert that the "process of collective bargaining . . . cannot be transplanted into public service . . . The very nature and purposes of Government make it impossible for administrative officials to represent fully or bind the employer . . . the employer is the whole people, who speak by means of laws enacted by their representatives."[6]

The idea that the executive cannot "bargain away" essential legislative functions was strengthened in the 1940s as a more conservative mood became evident and as a rejection of public sector bargaining was given a thorough rendering in a series of state supreme court rulings during that decade. Typical was a 1947 Missouri Supreme Court ruling when some Springfield municipal employees sought to bargain with the city administration. "It is a familiar principle of constitutional law that the legislature cannot delegate its legislative powers and any attempted delegation thereof is void . . . If such powers cannot be delegated, they surely cannot be bargained or contracted away . . . Thus qualifications, tenure, compensation and working conditions of public officers and employees are wholly matters of lawmaking and cannot be the subject of bargaining or contract."[7]

But social reality made such arguments seem increasingly contradictory. In the quarter century after the end of World War II the permanent federal workforce doubled in size while state and municipal payrolls more than tripled. Such labor, wrote sociologist Stanley Aronowitz, has neither power nor aura, "only a kind of grudging indispensability." Thus teachers, social workers, hospital and mailroom clerks, garbage men, and street maintenance workers were in chronically short supply. Public employment became increasingly black and brown, not only because administrators sought out a low-wage workforce but also because racial minorities, still excluded from so many private-sector service jobs, valued the steady work and the ostensible protections embedded within even the most pro-management set of civil-service work rules.[8]

The sovereignty argument faded in the 1950s and was replaced by a doctrine scholars have labeled "industrial pluralism," a subset of the reigning doctrine that democracy consists of the pluralist interplay of powerful interest groups, which at the time were thought to govern labor and management in the private sector. Thus a committee of the American Bar Association declared in 1955, "The special legal [i.e., sovereign] status claimed for government as an employer which placed governmental employees in a less advantageous position than private employees ... is an apparent anachronism."[9] In the absence of a bargaining arrangement, wrote another study, "the sovereign employer has chosen coercion rather than conciliation." This was paternalism at best, wrote Wilson Hart, an Eisenhower-era personnel official in the Department of Defense, who asserted, "It is morally indefensible for the government to refuse to grant its own employees the same privileges which it compels private employers to grant to their own workers."[10]

Ironically, the spread of civil service merit systems to municipal government in the postwar era created conditions under which public employees were more rather than less likely to unionize. This is ironic because many opponents of public employee unionism, then and now, assert that such an institution is un-needed because of the widespread existence of civil service protections. But the unions themselves found no contradiction, with the American Federation of State County and Municipal Employees (AFSCME) declaring in the 1950s that one of its principal aims was "the extension of the merit system to all nonpolicy determining positions in all government jurisdictions."[11] And for good reason: civil service procedures helped make government a lifelong career; they protected workers who chose to speak up or organize; and they set a standard of fairness that the new public employee unions were determined to protect and police.

The civil rights movement merely heightened the demand for public sector representation, especially given the increasingly large proportion of jobs African Americans held in the post office, city hall, garbage collection, janitorial services, welfare offices, and other such pink-, gray-, and blue-collar government work. Following the example set in New York City and Philadelphia, in 1959 Wisconsin became the first state to enact legislation recognizing the rights of government workers to bargain collectively. Similar laws spread throughout the North and West, also inspired by Executive Order 10988, signed by President John F. Kennedy in 1962, which allowed federal workers to bargain over some aspects of their work, if not pay or benefits. Thirty-six states had enacted some kind of law governing public employee unionism by 1975. Strikes proliferated in the late 1960s and early 1970s, creating a situation where regardless of any antistrike provisions in the laws of individual states or any prohibitions against bargaining over pay or benefits, as in the federal sector, actual collective bargaining had come to public employees.[12]

This growth enjoyed much bipartisan support. On the left, the identification of public employee unionism with the civil rights impulse was codified by the world-famous Memphis Sanitation Strike of 1968, in whose service Martin Luther King was assassinated. Likewise, hospital unionism, largely in nonprofit chari-table institutions, was initially a product of Puerto Rican and African American activism on the East Coast. Those workers won labor law coverage for much of the health-care industry in 1974, the very last time that Congress expanded Wagner Act collective bargaining protections on a national scale. Meanwhile, a feminist consciousness filtered down to schoolteachers, nurses, clericals, and others in whose interests equal pay for comparable work became a rallying cry by the late 1970s. For many of these white women and people of color, the quest for union representation was inexorably linked to a demand for an upgrading of the public services in which they labored. This was especially true of overburdened and underfunded clinics, hospitals, welfare offices, and child-care centers whose budgets and level of service increased dramatically in the 1960s and 1970s as a new generation of government workers achieved workplace citizenship.

But equally important is the story on the political right, where Republicans saw the organization of police, firemen, and prison guards as a potent constituency, especially in an era when law and order politics gained much traction. The building trades had always been heavily Republican, and so too the Teamsters, which was actively organizing municipal workers in transport and sanitation. In 1980 Ronald Reagan won the endorsement of the Professional Air Traffic Controllers Organization (PATCO), composed mainly of ex-military personnel, because he promised, far more than did President Jimmy Carter, to upgrade the highly stressful system in which they worked. And Republicans of that era were class-struggle realists. Regardless of their own party allegiance, politicians from heavily industrialized locales with a strong union presence simply had no choice but to court labor's vote. As Richard Nixon once remarked, "No program works without labor cooperation."[13]

The entire era, 1965 to 1978, was one of a rising tide of public sector strikes, an enormous growth in government union size and power, and an increasing legitimization of such bargaining. The unions and the Democrats even sought a Wagner Act for public employees that would have extended collective bargaining to government workers in the Deep South. The fiscal crisis that engulfed so many American cities in the mid-1970s *did* stiffen governmental resistance at the bargaining table to any qualitative rise in public sector pay or benefits. But even in near-bankrupt New York City, whose travails are best remembered through the infamous *Daily News* headline "Ford to City: Drop Dead," the legitimacy of collective bargaining was not brought into question. And this was the case even when important elements of what we might think of as a neoliberal program targeting the postwar welfare state were put in place.

In New York, for example, the bankers and mavens who took charge of its finances when the city could not sell its revenue bonds were determined not just to curb union wages and benefits but also to trim the municipal welfare state and lower working-class expectations all around. They sought to balance the city budget with no increase in taxes on the FIRE—finance, insurance, and real estate—sector of the economy, which these elites saw as site for the future growth industries of urban America. And these elites wanted to put an end to New York City's vanguard role as a social democratic laboratory for a post–New Deal America. By the late 1970s public sector pay and benefits had finally caught up

with much of private industry, so instead of the UAW and the United Steelworkers setting the wage and benefit standard, now well-organized public employees
might do so. Business elites in both public and private sectors wanted to put an
end to this kind of pattern bargaining in which one powerful union copied the
wages and benefits won by another. And they wanted to roll back the "social
wages" that New Yorkers had long enjoyed. So a whole series of public goods
were put on the New York City chopping block: free tuition at City University of
New York, rent control, branch libraries and neighborhood clinics, subsidized
subway fares, even the city's Shakespeare in the Park program (which was saved).

But these financially oriented elites, who, for a time, practically destroyed
self-governance of America's largest city, did not use the crisis as the occasion
for an assault on the idea of public sector unionism and collective bargaining.
Indeed, the bankers and government officials were determined to co-opt the
unions and their leadership; to force the heads of the American Federation of
Teachers, AFSCME, and the other big unions to buy into the new austerity; and to
join a corporatist governing apparatus in which the unions staked their pension
funds on the success of a new round of state bond offerings, and in which union
leaders used their authority to win from an exceedingly skeptical membership
mass layoffs and a wage freeze. Such gun-to-the-head corporatist bargaining
worked, and even paid off, because when New York came roaring back in later
years, the unions cashed in their bonds and renewed routine bargaining with
the city and state.[14]

Even President Reagan's destruction of PATCO in August 1981 did not inaugurate an assault on public sector unionism. This was ironic because in his Rose
Garden statement at that time, demanding that the air traffic controllers return
to work, Reagan seemed to go out of his way to make a distinction, based on the
sovereignty argument, between public and private sector workers. "Let me make
one thing plain; I respect the right of workers in the private sector to strike,"
asserted the president in a final version of the statement that he edited himself.
"But we cannot compare labor management relations in the private sector with
government," Reagan continued. "Government cannot close down the assembly
line." Reagan's willingness to fire thousands of air traffic controllers did open the
floodgates to a long era in which corporate America slashed wages and benefits
and in which the union strike threat practically disappeared. But in the public
sector no such counteroffensive took place. Negotiations were tougher now, and
few government entities passed new collective bargaining laws for public employees in the 1980s. But wages and benefits were not cut, and union density in
the public sector held its own for the next three decades at about 35 percent of
all those on a governmental payroll.[15]

However, the sovereignty argument was being burnished once again on the
ideological right. A key figure here was the Wake Forest legal scholar Sylvester
Petro, who developed a critique of public sector unionism that amounted to

a modern-day abolitionism, startling and extreme in an era when municipal unionism was linked, as in Memphis and New York, to the rise of the civil rights movement. Drawing upon the same kind of libertarian analysis that Friedrich A. von Hayek had deployed in his *Road to Serfdom* (1944), Petro foresaw public sector unionism as "a fatal threat to popular sovereignty" and therefore a slippery slope that led to governmental tyranny. In the 1970s he warned that an effort by Democrats to pass a bill ensuring collective bargaining for all public employees would create a threat to the republic, forcing Americans "to take to the hills and the fields and the caves once more, as our ancestors have frequently had to do when integral—sovereign—government has broken down."[16]

Petro's ideas represented a challenge even to staunch antiunion conservatives who for three decades had staked their ideological and political fate on the "right-to-work" movement. Arising out of the South and Southwest in the Taft-Hartley era, right-to-work activists at the antiunion bar and in the legislature had sought to make the union shop illegal, which in the private sector and in face of hostile employers, meant the deunionization of many labor-intensive industries, especially in the South. But in the public sector, unions often represented only a fraction of the workforce—there was no tradition of the union shop—and here unionism was flourishing. So Petro had to convince conservatives that in the public sector, unionism itself was the problem: that the sovereignty argument, earlier voiced by Calvin Coolidge and even FDR, still proved persuasive.[17]

His ideas had traction. In 1975 Ralph de Toledano published *Let Our Cities Burn*, an attack on municipal unionism and a warning against passage of any further laws facilitating public sector collective bargaining. As Representative Philip Crane of Illinois put it, legislation encouraging public employee unionism was forcing a decisive question upon the nation: "Shall Government be sovereign or shall there be collective bargaining with Government?"[18] Note here that despite his mentorship by the likes of Hayek and Milton Friedman at the University of Chicago, Petro and others of like mind were offering a backhanded defense of government, which they saw as threatened by union power, a perspective that would soon metamorphose into something close to its opposite.

A step in that direction came when Petro and other conservatives denounced public sector unionism as inseparable from politics. Endorsing candidates, lobbying government employers—virtually all the things that government unions did—were inherently political acts. Public sector labor therefore "sat on both sides of the bargaining table." Thus even "agency fees," designed to pay for collective bargaining services by workers who chose not to join the union, were in effect the coerced support for union political activity that some workers might find objectionable. By the end of the 1990s it was standard operating procedure on the right to put forward legislation and referenda that stripped public sector unions of dues income in order to neuter their political leverage in state and local politics. In California the titanic 1998 battle over Proposition 226 was a case in point.

The conservative perspective contained a large grain of salt, if only because the demise of the strike and the evisceration of classic collective bargaining, in the public sector as well as the private, meant that for the unions political activism was proving itself to be just about the only efficacious way to organize new members and raise employment standards. Take, for example, the effort, partially successful, waged by public sector unions to create a new set of public goods that millions of ordinary Americans may well have to call upon. As Eileen Boris and Jennifer Klein have demonstrated in their book, *Caring for America: Home Health Care Workers in the Shadow of the Welfare State*, the provision of home health-care services in the United States has often been episodic, inadequate, underfunded, racially devalued, and largely channeled through an unsystematic array of private companies, hospitals, welfare agencies, and public entities. But the work is essential and growing for a rapidly expanding population of elderly and disabled people.

Beginning in the 1970s and 1980s, unions like the Service Employees International Union (SEIU) and AFSCME sought to organize some of these home health-care workers, increase their compensation, make universal the provision of such services, and fix an employer with whom they could actually bargain. In California, for example, the SEIU lobbied during the 1990s for the creation of a set of county-level public authorities as the official employer of tens of thousands of relatives and domestics who had been heretofore classified as "independent providers." When such a law did take effect in 1997, the rolls of workers formally on state and county payrolls grew by several hundred thousand, and the SEIU organized many of them—seventy-five thousand in Los Angeles County alone— after which the union sought to bargain for greater state funding, higher wages, and health coverage for these workers.[19] Not unexpectedly, many conservative state officials, in California and elsewhere, have fought against such an expansion. In Ohio, Michigan, and Wisconsin their exclusion from the governmental payroll was high on the Republican agenda. Indeed, right-wingers declare union efforts to elect and lobby state officials on behalf of these workers a form of corruption. As one critic interpreted the successful SEIU effort to bargain for more than ten thousand home health-care workers in Illinois, "[SEIU president Andrew] Stern cannily used political contributions and organizing to reroute welfare dollars into his union and create a whole new class of members."[20] The same critique was advanced by the Manhattan Institute's Steven Malanga in his antiunion book of 2010, *Shakedown: The Continuing Conspiracy against the American Taxpayer.*[21]

We have, therefore, a conjoining of two right-wing ideas in the recent assault on public sector unionism. First, wages and benefits that were once considered competitive with workers in the private sector now seem overly generous, especially during an era of fiscal crisis. This sentiment has been put on steroids by the virtual collapse of the private sector welfare state, generating right-wing resentment from workers who envy the steady wages and assured benefits of public workers. In 1980 the percentage of workers at medium and large companies who had a defined-benefit pension plan was 84, but by 2009 just 30 percent of workers in these larger companies were covered under such plans, a vexing circumstance during a long season when the investments upon which so many defined contribution plans turned sour in the stock market.

Right-wing populists therefore want the work life, health benefits, and retirement prospects of public employees to become just as miserable and insecure as those faced by the rest of the working population. This is accomplished through outsourcing, abolition of work rules, and an end to tenure and lifetime employment. Governor Scott Walker made the point this way: "My brother is a banquet manager and occasional bartender at a hotel. He pays nearly $800 a month for his family's health insurance and can put away only a little bit toward his 401k. He would love the plan I'm offering to public employees." The point, concluded Walker, is that "we can no longer live in a society where the public employees are the haves[,] and taxpayers who foot the bills are the have-nots."[22]

But perhaps even more important is the libertarian assault on government itself. The sovereignty argument has therefore been turned on its head. Unions are too powerful because they sustain a strong and intrusive state, not because they subvert it. They fund the Democratic Party, which supports the welfare state, and they lobby for more public service employment. The problem with government employee unions is not that they undermine the executive power, but that they are part of it. Indeed, libertarian-minded conservatives argue that unions unnecessarily increase the "demand" for government services. The blackmail threat of a strike and the political money and manpower that generates lobbyists and precinct walkers inexorably expands the public sector, bloating it with bodies, wages, services, and pensions that timid and intimated elected officials are powerless to resist. As *New York Times* columnist David Brooks put it in 2010: "Private sector mangers have to compete in the marketplace, so they have an incentive to push back against union requests . . . [But] Government managers possess a monopoly on their services and have little incentive to resist union demands. It would only make them unpopular . . . In states across the country, elected leaders raise state employee salaries in the fat years and then are careful to placate the unions by raising future pension benefits in the lean ones . . . The end result is sclerotic government."[23]

Have the public sector unions drained public funds and taken an outsized share of state and local expenditures? A careful study by the University of California, Berkeley Labor Center summarizes an enormous body of survey research on this very topic and confirms that the answer is a resounding no! First, the fiscal crisis of the several states is largely a product, not of bloated pensions, but of the housing bust, high unemployment, and the decline in tax revenues generated by the Great Recession that began in 2008. Revenue shortfalls at that time were more than twice as great as in the previous recession, that of 2001–2002, which followed the dot-com bust.

Moreover, public sector employment has been flat during the last thirty years. It has not increased as a consequence of the inexorable "demand" generated by collective bargaining. Between 1979 and 2009 state and local public sector employment has remained at just about 14.5 percent of the entire workforce. Indeed, state and local employment per each one thousand residents has also remained steady over the last twenty years, with public sector employment actually higher per one thousand residents in states with the least government union density. Likewise, compensation as a share of state budgets has actually declined over the last twenty years, with little evidence of a gap between unionized and nonunion states.[24]

And, finally, numerous studies have demonstrated that if education and tenure are held constant, public sector workers are not overcompensated for the work that they do. In California 55 percent of public employees hold a college degree, compared with just 35 percent of the state's private sector workers. Nor are pension contributions—which amount to about 3 percent of state budgets—blowing a hole in state finances. Such obligations are a problem, because, like all other investments, public and private, they have sunk with the stock market and with the decline in real interest rates.[25]

Although conservatives are wrong to think that in recent decades public sector unions have created a bloated and corrupt welfare state, their hostility is nevertheless well founded because these institutions do in fact stand athwart the increasingly libertarian, neoliberal agenda that so many on the right advocate. Trade unions oppose the fragmentation of the public school system, they fight the privatization of municipal services, they sustain the Democratic Party, and they politicize and mobilize voters who would otherwise remain alienated and voiceless. Imperfect and on the defensive, these institutions are nevertheless pillars of a state, both local and national, that still provides an essential set of public goods while at the same time maintaining a measure of popular sovereignty in the face of elite influence and corporate pressure.

PART V

Intellectuals and Their Ideas

Here the reader will find portraits of five activist intellectuals as well as some thoughts on why academics, as both a social group and as individuals, have become more important to the conflicts that engage the labor movement, public policy, and the political culture in our own day. C. Wright Mills was a university sociologist; Harvey Swados wanted to be a novelist when he could find the time and money; while Jay Lovestone, B. J. Widick, and Herbert Hill spent the most creative years of their work life within a set of highly partisan institutions. In their own contrasting ways, Lovestone and Widick were fierce warriors for the labor movement, while Hill became a take-no-prisoners advocate for the NAACP fight against racial discrimination. These figures are not uniformly admirable, and in many cases their ideas and activities proved simply disastrous, but they are nevertheless model intellectuals, and with the exception of Mills, almost entirely autodidactic. Their ideas were therefore "organic" to the causes and institutions with which they were identified, which sometimes limited their influence, even as it offered a certain gravitas to the political and ideological projects upon which they labored.

Most of these figures stood outside the academy, which in the 1950s and 1960s seemed to put them in closer touch with many of the political currents and conflicts of their time. Academic intellectuals had more freedom and security, but they were necessarily cloistered, as Russell Jacoby and other commentators on the demise of the public intellectual once argued. Ironically, that sense of academic isolation has largely vanished in recent years as the university comes under cultural and fiscal attack, as politics and public policy become more ideologically attenuated, and as academics are enlisted in contemporary policy battles, not only on Capitol Hill, but in the think tanks, trade unions, business lobbies, and through the proliferating set of blogs, websites, and the other social media of our time. Indeed, in the last two essays in this section, on graduate students and the trade union use of academic expertise, I explore why academics and teachers are today among the most politically active social strata in the nation as well as among the most heavily unionized. They cannot escape the contest of ideas and interest that is shaping the world in which we live.

CHAPTER 15

C. Wright Mills

The New Men of Power is a study of trade unions and their leaders, the American political scene, and the prospects for a radicalized democracy in the years just after World War II. When C. Wright Mills published the book in 1948, it identified a newly empowered set of strategic actors who led the nation's most important progressive institutions, "the only organizations capable of stopping the main drift towards war and slump." But unlike his politically acute, agenda-setting volumes published during the 1950s, of which *White Collar* and *The Power Elite* are the best known, Mills's equally expansive probe into the meaning and future of U.S. trade unionism quickly fell into the shadows. By the mid-1950s few observers would have called American unionists "a strategic elite," as Mills had once argued in a book whose very title now mocked the waning influence of a labor leadership firmly wedded to the Democratic Party, Cold War orthodoxy, and the collective bargaining routine. Organized labor seemed a stagnant force, largely defenseless against the political and economic hammer blows that befell the rank and file during the 1970s and 1980s.

But *The New Men of Power* bears rereading in the twenty-first century. This is not because the contemporary labor movement has regained the power held by union leaders in the 1940s, when Mills and his associates conducted the surveys and drafted the chapters that went into the book. Unions are far less powerful in terms of relative membership, raw economic power, and political influence than they were when *The New Men of Power* appeared. Nor does the American working class face an immediate, consciousness-changing crisis, such as a new war or a new depression, which Mills himself expected would put the unions at the center of the nation's political thought and action.

Enough has changed, however, to make the ideas and speculations put forward in *The New Men of Power* useful and exciting. Today, as in 1948, the unions stand on the left side of American politics and culture. They are under fierce attack, but they are also recruiting a new generation of young activists who seek to infuse the labor movement with a radical élan. New leaders have ascended to important posts in the trade union movement, and the old iron curtain that once divided official labor and the broad American left—academic, feminist, socialist, African American, Latino, and gay—has rusted away. Faced with a world of global production, a nearly useless labor law, and a corporate opposition that remains intransigently antiunion, many otherwise conventional union leaders have been forced to look for new allies and new ideas; likewise, social activists and intellectuals have come to see the revival of a powerful trade union movement as essential to their dreams for a better world. Living-wage campaigns, labor-backed immigration reform initiatives, and demonstrations against a corporate definition of globalism have helped labor throw off its parochial chains.

A similar sort of creative excitement infused the union movement in the mid-1940s when Mills began his study of the labor unions and their leadership. The labor movement had grown nearly fivefold in little more than a decade, and at fourteen million strong the unions then enrolled about one in three non-farmworkers. Politically, the trade unions defined the left wing of what seemed possible in American politics. Although the American Federation of Labor was larger than the decade-old Congress of Industrial Organizations, the latter was a more dynamic social formation, whose fractious leadership represented almost every left-of-center political tendency in the nation: FDR liberals, Catholic corporatists, old-line socialists, a handful of Trotskyists, and a far larger Communist bloc. Most important, the great industrial unions of that era contained a remarkable layer of alert, politically conscious militants who gave leadership to an industrial underclass—immigrants or the sons and daughters of immigrants, African Americans, Appalachian whites, the unskilled, and the uneducated—whose voice had long been muted.

Mills encountered this laborite universe by a circuitous path. He was born in Waco in 1916, and came of age in a Texas devoid of the political passions that others found so consuming during the Great Depression. "I did not personally experience 'the thirties,'" he once remarked. "At the time I just didn't get its mood." Mills became, according to the nomenclature of the 1940s, a radical "anti-Stalinist," but his politics, on topics both foreign and domestic, remained refreshingly unburdened by the trauma and disillusionment that had transfigured so many other left-wing thinkers at the end of the 1930s.

Mills earned a sociology PhD at the University of Wisconsin and quickly moved on to his first academic job at the University of Maryland. In Madison, Mills encountered two teachers who would have a large impact on the questions he would ask in *The New Men of Power*. The first was Hans Gerth, a left-wing German émigré who introduced Mills to the great European social theorists, especially Karl Marx, Max Weber, and Karl Mannheim. Mills considered Gerth "the only man worth listening to in this department." Later they would collaborate to translate and publish the writings of Weber, whose fruitful impress upon the Millsian worldview is evident in almost all of his work. Weber valued property, order, and individual liberty, but he nevertheless sought to trace out the multi-faceted process of bureaucratization and rationalization that was a characteristic feature of modern capitalism. Mills would not find it difficult to apply a Weberian analysis to the leadership strata of the American trade unions.

At Wisconsin, Mills also enrolled in Selig Perlman's well-attended classes on socialism and capitalism. Although Perlman disdained the left, or any sort of self-conscious intellectualism within the unions—his famous "job conscious" interpretation of the labor movement left little room for a visionary transformation of society—his brand of economistic institutionalism coexisted easily with a Weberian emphasis on functional role, legal constraint, and social status. As *The New Men of Power* demonstrates, Mills did not share Perlman's anti-Bolshevik hostility to intellectuals as an alien, corrupting presence within labor's body politic, but Mills did take from Perlman's lectures an appreciation of the history and institutional flavor of the American unions, especially as they served to mobilize and sell the labor power of their members, thus making unionism functional to the capitalist marketplace. Even as a pro-union radical, Mills remained acutely aware of the organizational logic and economic forces that made for conservatism and defensiveness within these institutions of the working class.

His real exposure to a radical understanding of labor's potential came at the otherwise provincial campus of the University of Maryland. Here Mills encountered a vigorous set of young historians: Kenneth Stampp, Frank Friedel, and Richard Hofstadter, whose brother-in-law, Harvey Swados, later a well-known novelist and journalist, would remain a lifelong friend. This circle soon put Mills in touch with an anti-Stalinist world of writers, intellectuals, and activists centered in New York. He wrote for *Partisan Review*, the *New Leader*, and the *New Republic*; and he collaborated with Dwight Macdonald in founding *politics*, the amazingly influential "little" magazine whose critique of the warfare state, advocacy of radical pacifism, and search for new forms of democratic participation prefigured much of the political sensibility of the New Left a generation later. By 1945 Mills was reading *Labor Action*, the revolutionary broadside published by the "third camp" Trotskyists in Max Shachtman's Workers Party.

Many of the key ideas that would later appear in *The New Men of Power* are found in the wartime essays and reviews Mills sent north from College Park. In a 1942 issue of *Partisan Review*, he hailed Franz Neumann's dissection of the Nazi regime, in which an imbricated set of political, industrial, and military elites created a system of state capitalism and eviscerated an independent working class. "If you read his book thoroughly," wrote Mills, "you see the harsh outlines of possible futures close around you." Like Shachtman, Macdonald, and Swados, Mills did not see World War II as a necessary defense against the fascist menace, but as a step toward an American version of the militarized, leviathan state. This is what Mills would call "the main drift." He would have served if the military's doctors had passed him through—high blood pressure and a weak heart would later kill him—but Mills still thought the war was "a god dammed blood bath to no end save misery and *mutual* death to *all* civilized values."

At the core of Mills's analysis was a crisis theory of capitalist development. The system was inherently unstable, prone to a recurrent cycle of depression, war, and hothouse boom. Mills expected another slump in just a few short years, And according to this analysis, so too did the most sophisticated representatives of big business, who backed an administratively guided political economy, a sort of postwar New Deal, but with a much more authoritarian, business-oriented elite firmly in command. At various points in *The New Men of Power*, Mills calls this "a corporate form of garrison state" or "a state capitalism with many corporate features," but whatever the nomenclature, it is "the main drift" that leads eventually to what Neumann called "totalitarian-monopolistic-capitalism."

Mills's outlook, however, was not one of despair. Increasingly he looked to the labor movement, "the chief social power upon which a genuine democracy can rest today." Influenced by the Shachtmanite Trotskyists, Mills saw within organized labor the potential for the emergence of a third camp that could resist both Stalinist and capitalist oppressions. He therefore applauded wartime union militancy, defending the otherwise unpopular set of coal strikes led by John L. Lewis in 1943.

Eager to get out of College Park, Mills leaped at the chance to take a research post at Columbia University early in 1945. There Mills juggled two or three projects at a time, supervised almost a dozen researchers, and spoke before both academic audiences and the unique New York world of labor intellectuals and radical activists. J.B.S. Hardman was one of the first people Mills looked up in New York, and he proved both a collaborator and a model for the kind of labor intellectual Mills thought so central to the future of the labor movement. Hardman (né Jacob Benjamin Salutsky) came out of the great tradition of Jewish radicalism under the czars. Exiled in 1908, Hardman sailed for New York, where he moved easily from radical, Yiddish-language journalism to editorship of the *Advance*, organ of Sidney Hillman's Amalgamated Clothing Workers. By 1944 Hardman, like Mills, had also come to see the need for the projection of a more programmatically radical agenda within the house of labor. To vitalize the unions and prepare them for the postwar battles, he founded the Inter-Union Institute for Labor and Democracy (IUI) and began editing a new monthly, *Labor and the Nation*, which began publication in 1945. Here Hardman sought to give voice and coherence to the work and ideas of the anti-Communist but socialist or social democratic staff of intellectuals, journalists, and academics, who still represented an important current within the unions and among labor's close allies.

Mills joined the Inter-Union Institute, wrote frequently for *Labor and the Nation*, and became friends with Hardman, who opened doors for Mills throughout the labor movement and gave him a feel for the social texture of the New York unions. In *The New Men of Power* much of the introduction, "What Are Labor

Leaders Like?" where Mills plays brilliantly with the contradictory character of union officials, reflects the inner history of Hardman's Amalgamated, from pre–World War I insurgency to late–New Deal statesmanship.

But Mills did not just use Hardman for insights into the structure of the unions. He thought that through the IUI he might have found the vehicle by which radicals like him could have an impact on the labor movement. "Many of the new research people," he wrote in 1946, probably indicating his own feelings, "are disaffected and morally unhappy: they will their minds to people they don't like for purposes they don't feel at one with . . . What some of them really want is to connect their skill and intelligence to a movement in which they can believe; they are ready to give a lot of energy to an organization that would harness these skills in the service of the left. And the left to most of them means labor." Thus the dedication in *The New Men of Power* reads "for J.B.S. Hardman, *Labor Intellectual*."

Taken as a whole, *The New Men of Power* reflects the dual nature of Mills's labor research project: an empirical set of core chapters that illuminates the character of modern unions and the state of mind of their leaders, enclosed within the more speculative, programmatic chapters that offer a Millsian analysis of the trajectory taken by U.S. capitalism and its political leadership, along with his own, barely covert "radical program for America today." The survey research itself, both the questions asked and the interpretation of the results, reflects a highly politicized probe into the mentality of the labor leadership. Mills, Hardman, and other like-minded observers wanted to know if an empirical basis existed for prodding the unions leftward if and when a new economic or political crisis hit. This was not value-free sociology.

Mills's survey research found that CIO union leaders were much younger than their AFL counterparts, that the industrial unionists were better educated, and that for most workers union activism was a more certain path to upward mobility than recruitment into the ranks of management. As Mills and his staff undoubtedly expected, a larger proportion of CIO unionists than those in the AFL were willing to contemplate formation of a labor party, but not before the 1948 presidential election. Leaders of both organizations still feared the power and intentions of big business, and Mills found that an extraordinary 69 percent of all industrial union leaders considered fascism to be a definite threat in the United States. The questionnaires Mills collected from hundreds of labor leaders lend little support to the idea that unionists and managers embraced a postwar "labor-management accord," at least not before 1948.

In June and July 1947 Mills finished what he described as "a fairly good draft" of a book then titled "The Labor Leader: Who He Is and What He Thinks." It was written at a ranch outside of Reno, Nevada, where Mills was staying while awaiting a divorce from his first wife, Freya, whom he had married when he was an undergraduate at the University of Texas. In the offing was marriage to twenty-four-year-old Ruth Harper, a Mount Holyoke College graduate whom

Mills met late in 1946 when he hired her to work on *White Collar*, for which he had already begun to assemble research data and interviews. Mills thrived in the high desert. Between jeep excursions, horseback rides, and sessions on a newly purchased guitar, Mills churned out the manuscript, 432 pages in five weeks. "It just rolls out," reported Mills to his parents. "Wrote it like free association," he told Dwight Macdonald. And it was in Nevada that Mills encountered an old Wobbly who provided the epigraph for the book's frontispiece. It's a "honey" he wrote to Ruth, "'WE AIN'T GOT NO LEADER. WE'RE ALL LEADERS.' That has just the right irony for a book on labor leaders."

The finished draft was not due at the publisher until early 1948, so Mills had time to send about half a dozen copies to friends and colleagues, including Macdonald, Gerth, Swados, Columbia's Robert Lynd, and William Miller, a historian of business who was one of Mills's best friends. We don't know precisely what revisions Mills made, but his attendance at the November 1947 convention of the United Automobile Workers had a large impact on the final book manuscript, especially the two last chapters, in which he is both more hopeful and more radical about the unions than either his introduction or his survey research might otherwise warrant. Mills was a partisan of Walter Reuther, an ex-socialist who had already fought his way to the UAW presidency, but when Nathan Glazer—then an assistant editor at *Commentary*—asked him to write an essay on the auto union, Mills became even more attentive to the outlook and ambience of the young intellectuals and labor militants who made up the general staff of the Reuther caucus within the million-member UAW.

To Mills "the most impressive thing about the United Auto Workers union is the spectacle it affords of ideas in live contact with power." His excitement was justified. In 1947 the UAW was the nation's largest trade union, confronting the very largest corporations in the world. The membership was militant and the leadership young, fractious, and highly political. Mills called it "a union amazed by itself." Indeed, the forty-year-old Reuther almost perfectly exemplified what Mills saw as the new union man of power. Mills was not uncritical of Reuther—he thought the UAW chief might well "become a 'human engineer' for some sort of state capitalism guaranteeing industry disciplined workers"—but he put these doubts aside to applaud the programmatically coherent victory of the Reuther caucus over the coalition of Communists and placeholders with whom they had been at war for a decade. Mills called Reuther's victory at the 1947 UAW convention "a democratic rank-and-file revolt against a disintegrating machine." It seems likely that when he retitled his book *The New Men of Power: America's Labor Leaders* sometime during the winter or spring of 1948, he was thinking of Reuther and his circle. Here Mills found the "union-made intellectuals," as opposed to the New York variety, whom he considered "intellectuals without fakery and without neuroticism." Among them were Nat Weinberg, the UAW's new research director, who came out of City College, and Jack Conway, Walter

Reuther's top assistant, who had studied for a PhD in sociology at the University of Chicago.

Mills saw such men as his natural audience, so in *The New Men of Power* he worked hard to avoid the language either of academic sociology or of the conventional left. Earlier, in applying for a Guggenheim grant, Mills asserted his wish "to rid myself of a crippling academic prose and to develop an intelligible way of communicating modern social science to nonspecialized publics." Mills also sensed the exhaustion of Marxian language in his time, and he tried to come up with alternate words and phrases, even if his ideas were still thoroughly meshed with those of the socialist tradition. We therefore find no reference in *The New Men of Power* to the bourgeoisie, imperialism, ruling class, the masses, and certainly nothing on the "labor lieutenants of capital." Instead we find phrases such as "the main drift" or "the grand trend" to describe the trajectory of a militarized capitalism. And in a letter to William Miller, who questioned the definition of the word "intellectual," much used in *The New Men of Power*, Mills responded, "By intellectual here we mean humanitarian socialist. What the hell else? So I'll say so in some innocent, hard-boiled way." He feared that because his book was "so very political," it would be pigeonholed as merely sectarian. Thus his search for a new language of class and politics was designed to win him the broader audience he craved. When Arthur Schlesinger Jr. endorsed it as "genuinely democratic and boldly radical . . . stimulating and fruitful," Mills sighed with relief: "Well! Anyway, it shows we can get away with it among the liberals."

Mills certainly put his politics front and center. This begins in the first chapter, "The Political Publics," where he offers a panoramic view of what he sees as the decisive points on the postwar political compass. The phrase "political publics" is important to this typology and in Mills's mind is quite distinct from the more passive, uninformed "public opinion." The political publics are more self-conscious, more politically alert communities either of ideology or interest that bring to bear a particular sensibility to the issues of the day. They formulate the ideas and programs that operate on the consciousness of the passive, atomized mass.

Mills describes five such publics, but they are of radically unequal weight. The first two, the "far left" and the "independent left," consist of but a few thousand individuals, and as Mills describes them, it is clear that he is talking about his friends, comrades, and erstwhile collaborators. But he is hardly uncritical of this milieu. Although Mills was ideologically close to Shachtman's Workers Party (Harvey Swados was a member), he found the Trotskyists to be "bureaucrats without a bureaucracy" and adherents to a "popish set of ideas." Thus Mills never joined up, even as he took a good bit of his ideological firepower from these neo-Leninists: the idea that labor had to see itself as a "third camp" that was hostile to both capitalism and Stalinism, the concept of a "permanent arms economy," the disdain for the liberal center, and the expectation that when the postwar slump finally came the ranks of the left might well multiply many-fold in the contest for power.

Mills is much harsher on the independent left. One suspects his animus is largely directed at Dwight Macdonald and the circle of *politics* writers and readers, of which he was once a founding member. By the late 1940s Mills thought Macdonald had moved to a political dead end: they both feared the encroaching power of a leviathan, corporate-military state, yet Macdonald had lost faith not only in the labor movement but in any political solution to the moral crisis enveloping the modern world. In stark contrast to the Reutherite intellectuals who had so hopefully come to power, Mills charged the *politics* circle with drift and hopelessness, "oscillating between lament and indignation." Thus Mills sharply attacked Macdonald's characterization of the unions as a "bureaucratic net ensnaring the people." Of course, Mills also foresaw the possibility of this Weberian devolution, which may account for the vitriol with which he attacked its premature proponents.

Mills identifies the Sturm und Drang of headline politics with the next two publics: the liberals, whom he finds "continuously excited and upset" but programmatically incoherent, and the practical right, who have no well-worked-out ideology but see politics as an immediate source of economic gain, legislative advantage, and antiunion muscle. The liberals read the *Nation* and the *New Republic*, pine for FDR, and look to Henry Wallace with some favor. (Mills wrote just before the liberal, anti-Communist assault on Wallace, who would run for president on a Communist-backed Progressive ticket, had begun in earnest.) The practical conservatives, identified with main-street business and small-town virtue, find their champions in Robert Taft and the congressional Republicans, who in 1946 had swept the Democrats out of power for the first time in sixteen years. Considering the extent to which these publics monopolized the overt world of mid-1940s politics, Mills gives them rather short shrift. He caricatures both the ardent liberals and the fervent conservatives, missing the nuances that divide each camp and underestimating their staying power, most notably that of the practical conservatives, whose influence would grow dramatically in the years after Barry Goldwater rose to prominence. Mills's relative disinterest derives from his expectation that when the postwar slump really came, these noisy combatants would fade from the scene, subordinating themselves to those who advance a more systematic set of political ideas. Power, writes Mills, will "shift toward those who are ideologically and strategically prepared for it."

Mills throws the Communists into the catfight between liberals and conservatives. Today most historians recognize that whatever the Communist Party's (CP's) relationship was to Soviet power, the party's social, cultural, and laborite ambitions represented something organic to the traditions of the American left. They were a motive force in the world of New Deal labor and 1940s liberalism, in the civil rights movement, and even in the nascent rebirth of feminism. Mills had to acknowledge some of this—he devotes an entire chapter to the CP's influence within the unions—but like so many of his friends on the anti-Stalinist left,

Mills was essentially contemptuous and dismissive. From his Columbia perch, he saw the party as composed of Union Square hacks and an ever-shifting pool of lower-middle-class enthusiasts whose influence was less on the labor movement, where they were being eliminated, than on the excitable liberals, to whose political sentimentality they appealed. Mills was an anti-Communist, but one who saw the enemy as pathetic rather than dangerous.

To Mills the most formidable public was that of the sophisticated conservatives, to whose analysis he returns throughout the book. These were the men who presided over the great New York law firms, the executives who led the largest corporations, and the editors of the nation's most respected papers. Mills does not use the term "power elite" in *The New Men of Power*, but these conservatives practically define it: "they work in and among other elite groups, primarily the high military, the chieftains of large corporations, and certain politicians. Knowing what they want, wanting it all the time, and believing the main drift is in their favor, these sophisticated conservatives try to realize their master aim quietly." Two decades later, New Left historians would label this kind of manipulation, which effectively created a consensus in so much of American politics, "corporate liberalism." Unlike the noisy right, this corporate-political elite sought not to destroy the unions, but to tame them by recruiting and rewarding a labor leadership willing to de-radicalize its own rank and file. Mills saw as their prime ideological weapons the new language of labor-management cooperation and the soporific rhetoric of contemporary liberalism, both of which served to demobilize labor and its leadership.

But these sophisticated spokesmen for American capitalism were hardly liberals themselves; indeed, Mills thought their victory led inexorably toward an American version of Franz Neumann's "Behemoth." The elite's effort to stabilize capitalism and buy off the labor movement contributed to the rise of an essentially authoritarian order, a garrison state sustained through a "permanent arms economy." These conservatives wanted "a New Deal on a world scale operated by big businessmen" that would keep open European and Latin American markets in order to forestall the coming depression.

To counter the main drift, Mills envisioned a new labor-based radicalism, outlined in his chapter "The Program of the Left." Here he borrows freely from the World War I–era guild socialists, from the circle of American Trotskyists associated with C.L.R. James, and from the left-wing Reutherites. Because he fears that the nationalization of industry, as in postwar Britain, will lead to just another form of bureaucratism, Mills posits the "socialization" of industry through a combination of both workers' control and centralized economic planning. Mills wants an independent labor party, of course, but he also seeks to infuse the labor-left with a syndicalist spirit. Consumer cooperatives, neighborhood price-control committees, and a thoroughgoing shop democracy are all part of his near-revolutionary vision. Mills knows that many readers will see sectarian utopianism here in the place of a more achievable, if prosaic, labor program. He justifies himself, however, by making an existential leap to those "who have decided to throw in with the 'little groups that cannot win.' In fact, the big groups never win; every group loses its insurgency; maybe that is all that is meant by winning. It is a question where one decides to keep placing one's weight."

The power and brilliance of C. Wright Mills lies in his effort to understand the social forces at play in midcentury America and the progressive calculus that might yet generate a democratic combination, even as he remains utterly aware of their reactionary potential. In the penultimate chapter, "The Power and the Intellect," he takes the measure of the salaried middle class. By 1948 Mills had already completed much of the research and some of the writing for *White Collar*, so his cautious optimism here is worth noting. The middle classes may well side with architects of the main drift, especially if and when the great slump arrives, but a bold labor program, designed to keep prices low and corporations on the defensive, might well forestall a white-collar flight to the right and in its place generate a far more inclusive and dynamic labor movement, one that could truly set the national agenda. Mills was hopeful that the burgeoning ranks of the salaried workforce might yet swell labor's power instead of being fodder for the fascists.

The labor intellectuals are crucial to this great turn, however, for without the ideas and program of engaged, practical union thinkers the labor leadership would drift with the conservative, bureaucratic tide. Mills writes that within the labor movement these professional intellectuals "act as leaven, lifting it beyond mere pork-chop contentment," so as to turn the unions into "vanguard organizations." Utopianism? Not if "the power and the intellect" are united. And that is why Mills found trade union leaders to be "the strategic elite in American society," even as he also warned on the very last page, "Never has so much depended upon men who are so ill-prepared and so little inclined to assume the responsibility."

When it appeared late in the fall of 1948 *The New Men of Power* won largely favorable reviews. The magazines and newspapers of the liberal center, like the *Progressive* and the *Nation*, though repeatedly skewered by Mills, offered the book a good send-off. In the academic journals Mills's book also won respectful readers, despite, or even because of, its politics. Ely Chinoy, then conducting the field research that would generate the classic sociological study of blue-collar mentality, *Autoworkers and the American Dream*, thought the book "demands and accepts a place for trained intelligence not only in providing piece-meal and limited solutions, but also in suggesting major alternatives for dealing with basic questions." Mills was probably most gratified by Irving Howe's piece in *Partisan Review*. Though not uncritical—Howe said the book suffered from a "certain lack of maneuverability in argumentation"—he nevertheless anointed Mills for resisting the pessimistic tide then sweeping the ranks of once-radical intellectuals. The book stood "in total opposition to such current inclinations as quietism, ideal-community building, advocacy of 'preventive' atomic war, [and] a truce with the right because of fear of Stalinism."

The radicalism of an Irving Howe or C. Wright Mills had little future in mid-century America. Even as Mills read the reviews of his book, he was turning his back on what he would later call the labor metaphysic. Given his cresting expectations, the deflation of his labor-left perspective was swift and thorough. Mills was sorely disappointed by President Truman's unexpected reelection. He had voted for Socialist Party candidate Norman Thomas, but his real hopes had lain with the possibility that Reuther and other CIO union leaders would take immediate steps to build a labor-based third party. Had the GOP's Thomas Dewey won the White House, Mills and a goodly number of others on the non-Communist left expected the Democrats to dissolve and a new labor party to come roaring forward. But in the wake of the election Mills saw such a prospect as "quite dead." And when it later became clear that no slump would materialize, the victory of the sophisticated conservatives was assured.

As these developments snuffed out the prospects for a more expansive set of laborite politics, Mills elevated to canonical status the conservative, but contested, trajectory he had hypothesized for the unions in *The New Men of Power*. Writing in mid-1949, in his last essay for *Labor and the Nation*, he argued that the unions were becoming just "another vested interest, an agency of political regulation at an economic price." Thus the organization of white-collar workers, which Mills had once seen as a key to a progressive transformation of the middle classes, would now become merely "unionization into the main drift: it will serve to incorporate them as part of the newest interest to be vested in the liberal state."

When Mills published *White Collar* in 1951, he wrote as if his political enthusiasms of the mid-1940s were some species of ancient incantation. "Trade unions," he wrote, "are the most reliable instruments to date for taming and channeling lower-class aspirations . . . The old radical faith that the mere enlargement of unions is good because it brings more workers into 'organizing centers' is now naïve, as is the belief that winning the white-collar people to unionism is necessarily 'a link to the middle class.'" By the time his last book, *The Marxists*, appeared in 1962, Mills had written off not just the unions but the Western working class as well. Looking with expectation to the Cuban Revolution and other third-world insurgencies, Mills now dismissed "wage workers in advanced capitalism [who] have rarely become a 'proletariat vanguard,' they have not become the agency of any revolutionary change of epoch."

There was, of course, much basis for such a doleful perspective. The defeat or expulsion of Communists from the CIO did not just eliminate an unpopular political current. It chilled all ideological debate and put further shackles on internal union democracy. Meanwhile, in 1950 the UAW, upon which Mills had staked such hopes, signed a five-year contract with General Motors. In *Fortune* Daniel Bell declared it "The Treaty of Detroit," whereby the Reutherites won a higher standard of living for blue-collar workers, but only in return for their assurance of industrial discipline and stability in GM factories. Then, as Mills's friend Harvey Swados would attest after his sojourn in a mid-1950s Ford plant, the working class itself seemed to have rejected, forgotten, or psychically buried any spark of radical opposition to the status quo. Even if the postwar economy did encounter the great slump Mills had prophesied, it was unlikely to generate the lurch leftward that he and so many other radicals had once expected.

It is therefore a tribute to Mills's courage that even as he turned away from the labor movement, he made no peace with what he conceived of as the main drift. Mills remained at odds with the power wielded by America's elite, at home and in the world. But without a powerful set of allies, or the prospect of such, his only stance was one of moral rectitude and intelligent dissection. He would "debunk, debunk, debunk," he wrote to his editor at Harcourt Brace, "go back to the Muckraker era, which may be one measure of our defeat." He soon transmuted this radical disappointment into what he held to be a "politics of truth." Writing in a 1955 issue of *Dissent*, Mills argued that the independent intellectual must serve as "the moral conscience of his society . . . asking serious questions, and if he is a political intellectual, he asks his questions of those with power." This was a worthy calling, and it would inspire a generation of New Left radicals a decade hence, but the Millsian perspective no longer sought the fruitful interpenetration of social power and critical intellect that had so animated *The New Men of Power*.

What remains of this book for our own day? As a historian and contemporary observer, Mills ignored or got some important things wrong. He was not interested in the social history of the working class: North or South, black or white, immigrant or native-born, women or men. He was unconcerned with the geographic mobility of capital and with the kind of technological change that has so dramatically transformed the nature of work and enterprise. Nor did Mills foresee the capacity of Keynesian fiscal policies to stabilize U.S. capitalism, at least in the first quarter century after World War II. Most important, Mills made too much of the distinction between the sophisticated conservatives and the practical right. Although the United States never became the kind of authoritarian society he believed the main drift would inexorably generate, he was much too sanguine about the labor policies of the managerial elite that ran America's largest corporations, staffed its most prestigious law firms, and sat on its highest courts. Mills feared that the fate of organized labor was one of a claustrophobic incorporation into a hierarchically structured political economy. Instead, after only a single generation of labor-capital accord, even the most internationalist and technologically advanced capitalists adopted the exclusionary union-free program, if not the polemics, of the entrepreneurial conservatives.

But *The New Men of Power* still bears a careful look by a new generation of unionists and social activists. If the unions are once again to become key elements of a new progressive movement, it is important to recognize that they are not in and of themselves radical institutions. Mills himself might well have avoided some of his own disillusionment if he had taken to heart the epigrammatic analysis put forth in the book's introduction. Trade unions are hybrid institutions—half monopoly seller of labor, half nascent social movement—and their leadership is just as mixed, though not always in the same personage: "an army general and a parliamentary debater, a political boss and an entrepreneur, a rebel and a disciplinarian." The unions alternately tilt their character toward stolid interest group or expansive social movement, but if and when they do move toward the latter, it is unlikely they will ever fully arrive there.

If the unions cannot substitute themselves for the left—an independent party is certainly needed, or at least an independent political voice—they are nevertheless essential to the health of the democratic polity. Mills saw the relationship between an organized working class and political democracy in stark Germanic terms, as in fact it had played out in 1933 and the years afterward. But the interwoven fate of the labor movement and a viable democracy need not be so Manichean. The erosion of democratic institutions in the contemporary United States is organically linked, at work and in the political arena, to the evisceration of the labor movement. When less than one-tenth of the private sector working class can speak directly on its own behalf, American politics begins to share some of the characteristics of those societies ruled by more overtly authoritarian regimes. Conversely, where democracy has been reborn in recent years—in Poland, South Africa, South Korea, Spain, and Brazil—its revitalization has been synonymous with the reemergence of a powerful, independent labor movement. In *The New Men of Power* we rediscover what Mills knew so well: the democratic stakes are always high when the labor movement charts its future.

CHAPTER 16

Harvey Swados

Harvey Swados died in 1972, just as Americans began to rediscover the world of work. But he helped prepare the way. His novels, stories, and spirited reportage in the last decade and a half of his life helped uncover the political and social drama that unfolds in the daily routine of every American workplace. Nothing he wrote accomplished this with more power and insight than the series of interconnected short stories called *On the Line*, which first appeared in the fall of 1957, a book, his wife remembers, that "Harvey dearly loved." This humane and sympathetic portrait of the psychological and social brutality inherent in midcentury factory work injected a moral urgency into the understanding of manual labor at a time, early in the postwar era, when most literary and political intellectuals were convinced that all meaning had been drained from the toil still required of so many millions. As Swados put it in his famous essay "The Myth of the Happy Worker," written just after the publication of *On the Line*:

> Sooner or later, if we want a decent society—by which I do not mean a society glutted with commodities or one maintained in precarious equilibrium by over-buying and forced premature obsolescence—we are going to have to come face to face with the problem of work . . . if we cling to the belief that other men are our brothers, . . . including millions of Americans who grind their lives away on an insane treadmill, then we will have to start thinking about how their work and their lives can be made meaningful.[1]

Here Swados prefigures so much that would come later: the empathic oral histories of Studs Terkel, the labor history of David Montgomery, the journalism of Barbara Garson, and the social psychology of Richard Sennett and Jonathan Cobb. The subtitle of one of the earliest and most influential of these studies, Harry Braverman's *Labor and Monopoly Capital: The Degradation of Work in the Twentieth Century*, reiterates the theme Swados sought to fictionalize in his collection of stories.[2]

Harvey Swados was born in Buffalo, New York, in 1920 of an upper-middle-class Russian Jewish family. His father was a physician with many working-class patients; his mother was a singer, pianist, and painter. Coming of age in the 1930s, this sensitive and intelligent youth not unexpectedly turned to radical politics, first as a Communist in high school and later, at the University of Michigan, as a recruit to the Trotskyist movement. At Ann Arbor, Swados enthusiastically followed the dramatic organizing victories of the new autoworkers union, and he participated in an unsuccessful effort to organize the radio factory where he had taken his first industrial job. Swados published several award-winning short stories in his college years and even then saw himself primarily as a writer. After his graduation in 1940, however, his political commitments drew him back to Buffalo, where he pounded rivets at Bell Aircraft, passed through a brief first marriage, and then moved on to New York to take another factory job in the big, turbulent Brewster Aviation plant in Long Island City, just across the East River from Manhattan.[3]

During these years, Swados gave his allegiance to the Workers Party, a small but extremely energetic and resourceful political group whose adherents he would later describe in *Standing Fast*, his 1970 novel that sympathetically recorded the exhilaration and despair of his political generation as it moved from the radical hopes of the late 1930s to a kind of acquiescent liberalism in the 1950s and 1960s. Despite his own drift away from the revolutionary expectations of his youth, much that would remain central to Swados's worldview was formed in these politically charged years of factory employment in the early 1940s.

An anti-Stalinist radical, Swados rejected the Soviet Union as any kind of model for the society he hoped to build. Instead, he—and others committed to his brand of Trotskyist politics—put their faith in a militant, international working class that would stand as a "third camp" opposed to the ruling classes in both capitalist and Communist regimes. To put their ideas into practice, they took factory jobs in the booming war plants of Detroit, Chicago, Buffalo, and New York. Here they defended the wildcat strikes that periodically erupted, pushed for a labor party, and attacked those in the labor movement, such as the Communists, who subordinated working-class aspirations for a better life and a more democratic workplace to the foreign policy interests of one of the big powers. The Workers Party had only a slight impact on the politics of American labor, but this wartime experience profoundly affected many in the generation of students and intellectuals who had "industrialized" in those years. For Swados, the imprint of such politics remained in his sensitivity to the psychology of everyday work, the unsentimental way he identified with the oppressed, and the enthusiasm with which he greeted the struggles of blacks and students in the 1960s. Until his premature death of an aneurysm at age fifty-two, Swados counted himself a socialist and a radical.

Politics aside, Swados found life in the wartime factories and in his tightly disciplined radical sect confining. At Brewster production was chaotic, the hours too long, and the boredom stupefying. So he did what thousands of young men had done for generations: he escaped to the sea, joining the merchant marine in 1943 as a radio operator and then traveling around the world, sometimes in dangerous waters. Returning to New York in 1946, he married Bette Beller and bought a house in Rockland County, twenty miles north of Manhattan. Between 1947 and 1955, Swados wrote furiously. Several short stories and a well-received novel, *Out Went the Candle* (1955), which focused on the family of a Jewish businessman who became a war profiteer in the 1940s, were published during this period.[4]

Finding time to write and to earn a living was always difficult. For a while Swados wrote and did public relations for the State of Israel's New York bonds office. He also wrote for television, in the process developing a lifelong animosity toward low-brow culture. In the mid-1950s he took his wife and three small children to the south of France, where a friend gave them a rent-free house, but he failed to finish his big novel of American life there. In need of work upon his return to New York, Swados found his efforts to land a college teaching job or win a writing fellowship unsuccessful. But he was nonetheless loathe to return to the world of speechwriting and public relations—a world he had never had much sympathy for, even when he worked in the middle of it.[5]

Fifteen miles from his home, the Ford Motor Company had just finished constructing the largest automobile assembly plant in the world, in Mahwah, New Jersey. This sprawling, single-story factory, big enough to cover seven football fields under a single roof, employed more than thirty-five hundred workers on two shifts. Built as part of Ford's gigantic postwar expansion and modernization plan, the new Mahwah factory was designed to turn out 800 Fords and Mercurys and 250 Ford trucks in each eight-hour shift. Like the other eighteen assembly plants Ford ran in the 1950s, the Mahwah facility contained no computers or robots, but Ford engineers had designed every part of the factory to ensure the most efficient and continuous production regime. The main building had ten miles of fifteen-foot-wide aisles, five miles of overhead conveyors, and two and a half miles of ground-floor assembly lines. A ninety-foot-wide runway for a double railroad track ran right under the forty-acre roof; outside, the parking lot had space for fifty-five hundred cars.[6] In *On the Line* Swados described the plant as a "vast, endless, steel and concrete world" through which "an endless succession of auto bodies slowly and inexorably" rolled past the workers "like so many faceless steel robots."

When Swados showed up at the Mahwah plant in February 1956, the personnel man was glad to see that he had had some blue-collar work experience, but he also found his job application strangely full of blank spots. When asked what he had been doing, Swados dodged: "Writing novels in the south of France." This little joke seemed to satisfy, so he was promptly assigned to the assembly line as a metal finisher, the same job he had mastered in the early 1940s when working in Buffalo. Some years later Swados remembered the shock of his return to factory labor: "I was appalled all over again but also tremendously excited, a selfish excitement because I said to myself, 'Good Lord, here they are! I have forgotten all about them. They have been here all these years, making all of these things, and here I am with them, but now I know what it is all about.'"[7]

Metal finishing is one of the more skilled production jobs on an assembly line. It requires a certain judgment and technique with a hammer and file. But the work is also exhausting, the hours long. Swados lost seventeen pounds in a couple of months, and by April, he reported, his right hand "crippled up from pushing a file against steel ten hours a night." However, he was excited as the idea of a new collection of short stories framed around the metal-finishing line in the body shop took shape. He talked with his workmates, took down their life stories, and told them he was a writer. They called him "Shakespeare."

"Everything has fallen into place for me," Swados wrote after two months on the job. "My earlier factory years have meaning now that they didn't before, and I think now I really know the pity and the vanity of American life from the inside." Writing a page or two each day before he set off for work on the night shift, Swados became increasingly enthusiastic about the collection. The stories were his best work yet: "I think when they are all done they will give an inkling of what has happened to the American dream. Even their titles are good!"[8]

Swados punched in at Mahwah at a time when many people saw the very existence of an American working class as up for grabs. The Census Bureau had just reported that for the first time in U.S. history the number of clerical, sales, and service ("white collar") workers outnumbered those who worked in factories, mines, and construction sites ("blue collar"). Moreover, with the demise of industrial violence, the steady increase in real wages, and the tidal wave of consumer goods available even to factory hands, the once-alien, politically charged character of the industrial working class seemed at an end. As *Fortune* put it in 1951, the misery and conflict of the Great Depression now belonged to a remote, barely believable past. Then, observed the influential business magazine, "bloodshed and hate stalked the streets of Gadsden, Toledo, Detroit and Aliquippa. Looking back . . . these memories seem almost incredible."[9]

Thanks to the success of the unions and to a pragmatic, enlightened management, class divisions had been reduced in the postwar years to virtual irrelevance. "We have no classes in this country," trade union leader Philip Murray boldly told a convention of the once-radical Congress of Industrial Organizations, "that's why the Marxist theory of the class struggle has gained so few adherents . . . the interests of farmers, factory hands, business and professional people, and white collar toilers prove to be the same."[10] The union, wrote the editors of *Fortune*, "has made the worker to an amazing degree a middle-class member of a middle-class society—in the plant, in the local community, in the economy."[11] Or as Swados himself put it, explaining this viewpoint in "The Myth of the Happy Worker," "If the worker earns like the middle-class, votes like the middle-class, dresses like the middle-class, dreams like the middle-class, then he ceases to exist as a worker."[12]

Indeed, workers as *workers* seemed on the verge of disappearance from the public imagination. Sociologist David Riesman's widely read *The Lonely Crowd* (1950) summarized much contemporary social science wisdom, arguing that with the shift from "an age of production to an age of consumption," work had ceased to be a central experience in the lives of American men and women. With craftsmanship in decline and production unproblematic, Americans had progressed to a point at which the "inner-directed" personality would give way to an "other-directed" personhood focused on the manipulation of symbols and people in a world of declining labor and greater leisure. Historian David Potter extended Riesman's argument in *People of Plenty: Economic Abundance and the American Character* (1954), arguing that consumption and the ability to collect it were not just recent phenomena but also the defining characteristics of American life.[13]

Autoworkers partook fully in this postwar sense of affluence. They were among the best paid of all American workers in the mid-1950s, and their union, the United Auto Workers (UAW), was without doubt the most powerful and imaginatively led of all labor institutions. Under the skillful leadership of ex-socialist Walter Reuther, the UAW had negotiated higher wages, company-paid pensions and health insurance, and in 1955 a supplemental income scheme designed to provide workers with a substantial portion of their income even if they were laid off. UAW members were buying tract houses, taking vacations, and agitating for more parking space in factory lots. Most important, the union had curbed the unfettered power of the shop bosses, bringing a measure of due process and industrial justice to the resolution of the daily conflicts that inevitably broke out on the shop floor of the thousand or more workplaces in which the UAW held bargaining rights.

Appearing in the midst of this celebration of American life, *On the Line* became—and still is—a powerful argument for the continued existence of an American working class. Despite high levels of consumption, unionization, and political complacency, Swados would later write, "there is one thing that the worker doesn't do like the middle-class: he works like a worker."[14] Swados thus returned his readers to one of Karl Marx's most important insights—namely, that class is not defined by income or consumption level, but by the relationship to the means of production, to the authority vested in those who own capital, and to subordination of the many to the authority of the few.

On the Line drives this point home in a series of eight short stories, each moving a different worker under the authorial spotlight, with a number of characters appearing shadowlike in two or three stories. There is no single protagonist, although Swados's story of Walter—the young, awkward metal finisher who is pounding and sweating his way toward college—has a clear autobiographical ring, as does his portrait of the itinerant radical named Joe. This old Wobbly, this "Vanishing American," becomes Walter's mentor, offering him a credo that would also guide Swados as a reporter and critic of industrial America: "Never mind the machinery. Remember the men. The men make the machines and they make their own tragedies too."

Swados revealed himself to be very much an intellectual of the 1950s—aware of injustice but incapable of pointing toward any fundamental resolution. In his emphasis on the alienation of modern work, rather than on the simultaneous possibilities for self-liberation, he shared much of the despair of such equally radical social critics as C. Wright Mills, his neighbor and friend, who even more than Swados came to see the American working class as essentially a powerless victim. The frustration of modern work can therefore rarely be translated into anything more than a cry from the heart.

But Swados overlooked something important at Mahwah: the inchoate solidarities and social norms that workers themselves create in even the most oppressive employment situations. This work culture, which arises organically out of the interplay between the natural rhythms of the work process and the ethnic and generational composition of the workforce, can provide a powerful basis for resistance and organization. The union picnic Swados described in *On the Line* offers a glimpse of such fraternity, but it is a pale vision of the solidarity that is episodically forged out of shop floor friendships and struggle.

Swados missed this, in part because he wasn't looking for it, but also because circumstances prevented him from full immersion in a rich factory work life. He was at Mahwah for less than a year, and he lived not in one of the working-class neighborhoods of northern New Jersey but in the more rural, small-town groves of Rockland County, New York. More important, perhaps, the Mahwah plant had just opened in a social wilderness at the confluence of two recently completed freeways. Although many workers had come from an older Ford plant in Edgewater, most of those on the less-desirable night shift where Swados worked were new to the factory, without the friendships and social contacts that would inevitably weave their dense web throughout the plant. "The absenteeism was fantastic," remembered Swados shortly after he quit. "You could never be sure of enough men to keep the line rolling except on payday."[15] All of this meant that, despite his keen powers of observation, his brief sojourn in the plant did not give him the time or the opportunity to fully discover the informal networks that almost always arise to texture the work lives of most blue-collar workers.[16]

Mahwah workers would in fact demonstrate a combativeness that was not atypical of autoworkers in this prosperous era. Like so many other workers, Mahwah unionists, organized into UAW Local 906, were engaged in a constant fight over the pace and content of their work. As early as December 1957, 80 percent of the local's membership voted to strike Ford if their numerous grievances over the company's violation of the health and safety provisions of the contract and over work standards—the amount of sheer physical labor each worker must put into his job—were not resolved.[17] Local 906 easily shut down the plant when the

UAW struck the Ford Motor Company in 1958, 1961, 1964, and 1967. But workers also "wildcatted" without going through the UAW's formal strike procedures. In July 1959, 178 workers walked out of the trim department to protest company efforts to discipline a union committeeman. Two years later, 2,000 workers shut down the entire plant during a September heat wave that drove temperatures above 90 degrees inside sections of the plant. Then in November 1962, all 4,350 members of Local 906 participated in an officially sanctioned strike over eighty-three unresolved grievances, many involving safety problems.[18]

Swados became loosely attached to the academy in the late 1950s, but he maintained his interest in the labor movement and the world of work. For many years he taught at Sarah Lawrence College and the University of Massachusetts at Amherst. His writing classes frequently visited the factory districts and union halls of New York and Boston. He was extremely productive, publishing two more novels, *False Coin* (1959) and *The Will* (1963), as well as stories, anthologies, and a biography of Estes Kefauver, *Standing Up for the People* (1972). Although he considered himself first and foremost a novelist, he had also become an experienced labor journalist, publishing long essays on the difficulties that mechanization had brought to coal miners and longshoremen. His 1958 essay "The Myth of the Powerful Worker" challenged the conventional wisdom that equated "big labor" with "big business." Many of his labor essays were collected in *A Radical's America* (1962), which enjoyed currency within the early New Left.

In one of his most important and controversial essays of the early 1960s, "The UAW—Over the Top or Over the Hill?" Swados returned to the condition of workers and their union in the auto industry. But in this 1963 investigation of what happened to the once-radical UAW, he was far more critical of the union than he had been in *On the Line*. Here, the alienation, humiliation, and speed-up experienced by automobile workers were seen less as the product of industrial life itself than as a consequence of the UAW's failure to fulfill the aspirations of its founding generation. Confronted with the financial and political strength of the most powerful American corporations, the UAW tempered its fight against job dissatisfaction, unemployment, and racial discrimination. Swados recognized that Walter Reuther was by far the most imaginative and progressive of contemporary trade union leaders, but in a critique of the Reuther circle that a generation of New Leftists would later make of other liberals, he declared that the union leadership hardly took its own reformist demands seriously anymore. Manipulation therefore replaced mobilization of the membership, and bureaucracy triumphed over locally initiated activism.[19]

At Mahwah itself, conflict between a liberal union and a radicalized section of the rank and file became increasingly manifest during the late 1960s and early 1970s. By the end of the decade, the plant was more than half African American. Inspired by the civil rights and Black Power movements sweeping so much of this community, black workers in the plant organized a brief but militant insurgency. A new group, the United Black Brotherhood of Ford Mahwah, attacked the local's white union leadership for its failure to defend black workers, and the group sparked strikes and walkouts for dignity and civil treatment in 1969. Much to the alarm of UAW officials, the Brotherhood on one occasion invited radicals from the Black Panther Party and Students for a Democratic Society to assist in picketing the plant.

Writing in the *New York Times*, Swados applauded the student-worker collaboration, seeing "signs that some students . . . are ridding themselves of glib antiunion attitudes and coming to the factories in search of allies, rather than simply as hip leafleteers on another kind of trip." Furthermore, he argued, their potential alliance raised the question with which he had struggled since the publication of *On the Line*: "If universities are to be humanized, why not factories and offices?"[20] The issue remains unresolved. But like so much of Harvey Swados's writing, the questions he posed command a moral response from all those who work or who know something of work's meaning.

CHAPTER 17

B. J. Widick

In the annals of American labor and its committed partisans, Branko J. Widick, who died on June 28, 2008, at the age of ninety-seven, is not a well-known figure. He deserves much recognition and admiration, however, because Widick was not only an activist at the very epicenter of the great strikes that launched the industrial unions in the 1930s, but he also remained a radical and an acutely honest observer throughout those postwar decades when the great organizations he had helped to build entered an era of stagnation and decline.

Known as "B. J." or "Jack," he was born on October 25, 1910, in the Serbian village of Okucani and was brought by his father to the United States just prior to World War I. Like other working-class families, the Widicks moved frequently, first to Serbian communities in Minnesota, then to Detroit, and finally to Akron in 1923. There B. J. graduated from the University of Akron and then found work as a journalist at the *Akron Beacon Journal* (1933–1936). He led a double life. In his day job he was a cocky reporter, nicknamed "Scoop" by the local police; off work he was a revolutionary, joining the Communist Party in the early 1930s but shortly thereafter aligning himself with the Trotskyists, whose forceful opposition to the dictatorship emerging in the Soviet Union and whose leadership of the 1934 Minneapolis General Strike made a large impression. All the while he plunged into work as a writer, researcher, and editor for the unions that were spawned by the working-class upsurge of that Depression era. He helped organize a chapter of the Newspaper Guild at the *Beacon Journal*, he set up a research department and newspaper for the United Rubber Workers in 1936, and then he assisted in the 1936–1937 Flint sit-down strike. In June 1937 he spent time in Mexico with Leon Trotsky as well as Diego Rivera and Frida Kahlo. Trotsky, who had read Widick's reportage from Flint, Akron, and other sites of the union upsurge, wanted to know if a prerevolutionary situation existed in the United States. It did not, but upon his return to the States Widick turned down offers to take a paid job with the new unions and instead spent the years until World War II as a writer, speaker, and organizer—first, for James Cannon's Trotskyist group, the Socialist Workers Party, and after 1940 for Max Shachtman's Workers Party, the anti-Stalinist political group, which was equally hostile to the Western capitalism and Soviet-style Communism.[1]

After serving as a sergeant in World War II, Widick settled in Detroit and got a job in an automobile plant, not unlike scores of other Trotskyists and hundreds of Communists who saw the United Automobile Workers as the most strategic venue from which American radicals could attempt to shift the politics of the unions and the working class. Widick was a forceful and attractive figure, a natural leader on the shop floor, and an autodidact who happily and heartily held his own among credentialed intellectuals on campus or on the union staff. The literary critic Alan Wald, who knew Widick for the last three decades of his life, described him as "self-assured, quick, energetic, expressive and warmhearted. Widick kept up affable ties to several generations of socialist activists on whom he eagerly bestowed advice. Although he was only five feet, four inches tall, his personality aura was powerfully etched in the minds of many who knew him well."[2]

B. J. Widick was among those men of the left, including the influential group who were influenced by Shachtman's "third camp" socialism, for whom the post–World War II United Auto Workers (UAW) became the institution into which they poured their passion, intellect, and organizational energies. For at least two decades the UAW filled the vacuum once occupied by the socialist or Trotskyist commitment that had formed their politics in the 1930s and early 1940s. For some this engagement with America's largest and most powerful trade union eased the way to an accommodation with a tepid brand of labor-liberalism and often to a set of politics far to the right even of that. As the writer Harvey Swados once put it, the problem with the UAW leadership and the circle of formerly left-wing intellectuals who sustained it was that they "did not take their own politics seriously."[3]

Widick shared an emotive fixation with the UAW and the leadership stratum that made Walter Reuther an icon of postwar liberalism. But if Widick saw the UAW as standing at the center of progressive politics for many years, he remained for much of that same time a sharp critic of Reuther and the bargaining regime over which he presided. As chief steward at Chrysler Local 7 from 1947 to 1959, Widick had the best possible vantage point from which to observe both the devolution of the UAW and the economic and racial transformations that would make Detroit the "city of race and class violence" he described in his 1971 history of the auto capital. Widick was a friend and collaborator with many of the former socialists who would later play influential roles in the UAW research department and in the Reuther "brains trust." But Widick himself never took a permanent post within the UAW apparatus, opting for an on-again, off-again career at Wayne State University and at Columbia University's Graduate School of Business in the years after 1962. Wald remembered that Widick invariably called this line of work "the professor racket." He told him, "If you're a radical and a trouble-maker, it can't be beat."[4]

Widick's critique of industrial America proved insightful on three fronts: his analysis of the rise of the Reutherite bureaucracy in the UAW; his views on the transformation of the union's role in the shop floor work regime; and his engagement with postwar racial and urban politics in both the UAW and in Detroit itself.

Although Widick spent the war years in military service, he supported Reuther and his caucus in their epic factional battle against those unionists whose political coloration was often shaped by the support they took from the sizable Communist group in the UAW. This perspective is found in the influential book *The UAW and Walter Reuther*, which Widick authored with Irving Howe in 1949. The authors celebrated the role of the union's wartime Rank and File Caucus, a group whose political guidance was often provided by the Shachtmanite Workers Party, but the authors also offered Reuther and his circle of ex-socialist supporters an equivocal appreciation, which was apparently not enough for the Reuther partisans in Solidarity House, who failed to give the book public notice in any UAW-controlled publication.[5]

In their portrait of Reuther, Howe and Widick found "a distinct quality of improvisation" in his recent political thinking; indeed Reuther had "slipped into the character mold of the American managerial type." They found a "disturbing *distance* . . . between the ultimate ideas tucked away in the back of his head and his immediate actions."[6] With C. Wright Mills, Howe and Widick thought that a new economic crisis might well shift the Reutherites to the left once again, including moves toward formation of an independent party of labor, but in the meantime the drift to bureaucracy went unchecked. This criticism became far sharper in the pages of *Labor Action*, in which Widick's pointed reportage appeared in the early 1950s. When the Reutherites put the big Ford Local 600, a sometime node of Communist influence, under an administratorship, Widick complained: "It's amazing! Walter Reuther points out a thousand times in a thousand speeches that Stalinism cannot be defeated by force alone—superior ideas and better program for the workers is the only answer! Yet in the UAW today, the only answer to Stalinism is bureaucratic force!"[7]

Widick's *Labor Today: The Triumphs and Failures of Unionism in the United States* (1964) reflected his critique of bureaucracy and political devolution throughout the entire union movement. In contrast to the expectant mood projected throughout *The UAW and Walter Reuther*, Widick now saw the industrial relations system as a fixed, if stolid, part of the body politic. Trade unions, he reported, "are a permanent feature of society," as functional to industrial capitalism as management itself. But the cost was enormous, for the unions were no longer a dynamic force in American life. Widick thought the prospects were "not very bright" that a still-ambitious figure like Walter Reuther could escape "the small role to which he had been restricted."[8]

Although he served as chief steward at Chrysler, the Big Three automaker in which stewards retained the greatest shop floor power, Widick proved a prescient observer of the ways in which the increasingly rigid and all-encompassing UAW collective bargaining contract constrained the capacity of the union to defend its members in their chronic daily battles with shop management. "Our contracts are becoming such legalistic documents as to be unworkable in terms of real, genuine labor relations," he asserted in 1954, "and we are getting this whole new body of law which is just fantastic." The shop steward, complained Widick, has become a "Philadelphia lawyer. It's embarrassing."[9]

For more than twenty years, such shop issues and the UAW's capacity to resolve them would stand near the center of Widick's politics and his increasingly prolific writing, now found in the pages of *Dissent* and the *Nation*. Indeed one might say that his socialist vision shifted from the grand politics in which the UAW was celebrated as a "vanguard" of the American working class to a much more constrained world in which issues of grievance handling and quality of working life became, if not more central, than at least somewhat amenable to reform. This era ended abruptly in the mid-1970s when issues of job loss and deindustrialization marginalized efforts to humanize the assembly line. Thereafter the "reform" of the shop floor work regime became largely a project of management, as publications such as *Labor Notes* have demonstrated in such convincing detail.

Indeed, by the 1970s Widick's own steward-centered solution to these problems had been eclipsed in his own thinking by a more psychologically attuned critique of alienated labor among industrial workers. This perspective is apparent in *Auto Work and Its Discontents,* a 1976 collection of essays that Widick edited. Although Widick had been teaching at Columbia since 1969, most of the contributors to his volume, including Bill Goode, Patricia Sexton, and Al Nash, were, like Widick, veterans of the Workers Party who had spent a number of years as stewards and activists within UAW-organized factories. Funded by the Ford Foundation, the Widick study came at the very end of an era of industrial stability in which laborite intellectuals of the center-left could seek to resolve these problems, if only in a reformist fashion.[10]

Although Howe and Widick had defended the Reutherite approach to racial issues within the UAW in their 1949 book, Widick soon became a critic of UAW inertia and outright racism. In 1943 when the Reuther caucus had opposed Communist efforts to create what we would today label an "affirmative action" program for moving blacks onto the UAW executive board, Widick agreed with the Reuther brothers that this was "reverse Jim Crow," a violation of color-blind socialist principles. But the intractable quality of racial discrimination in the auto industry and UAW soon pushed Widick to adopt positions once advocated by his Communist opponents. When Reuther ignored a report on racial problems in the UAW authored by Widick in the mid-1950s, he allied himself with the postwar generation of black militants who formed the Detroit chapter of A. Philip Randolph's Trade Union Leadership Council (TULC). Widick served on the TULC executive board, wrote speeches for Horace Sheffield and other black union leaders, and campaigned to put an African American unionist on the UAW executive board. That finally took place in 1962. Widick also played an important role in supporting the successful mayoral candidacy of Jerome Cavanagh, a racially progressive white reformer strongly supported by the TULC but opposed by most Detroit leaders of the UAW.[11]

Any optimism Widick might have held for the state of race relations in Detroit was shattered by the riots of 1967, after which he published *Detroit: City of Race and Class Violence*. Although he was rather disdainful of the radical black workers who had organized such militant groups as the Dodge Revolutionary Union Movement, the first edition of the book put forward the thesis that Detroit might well become a black metropolis, a vibrant center of black political and economic power. But by 1989, when he published another edition, Widick could see little hope for a city undergoing radical deindustrialization and increasingly bitter racial polarization.

B. J. Widick was an organic intellectual of the mid-twentieth-century working class who found his voice not only in the great upheavals of the late 1930s but also during the labor movement's long postwar era of institutional consolidation and political retreat. Widick was not a high theorist, but his authority as a writer and teacher was rightly enhanced by his rich engagement with the generation of shop militants who had built the great industrial unions and fought to maintain their democratic vibrancy. His voice was clear when he sought to frame for postwar labor-liberals key issues facing the unions in an era of racial tension, industrial conflict, and urban decline.

CHAPTER 18

Jay Lovestone

The Cold War is long gone, but the ghosts of that era still walk among us. This is because so many of the political and ideological battles of the twentieth century depended, and still depend, upon our evaluation of a set of regimes whose ideology, for those on the left, was seductively anticapitalist but whose authoritarian statecraft proved reprehensibly brutal.

The American labor movement was right in the middle of that fight, because the working class holds a special place in the political imagination of both leftists and reactionaries. Are the unions to be a strategically well-placed lever that can transform all society or, conversely, an ideologically powerful bulwark of the status quo? Thus, from the Bolshevik Revolution until the collapse of the Berlin Wall, no unionist could aspire to lead even a small slice of the movement without asserting his or her views on the character of world Communism, whether it be in Moscow or Milwaukee, Managua or Minneapolis. Communism was the inescapable question, especially in the two decades that bracketed World War II. It revealed itself in almost every election, strike, and organizing campaign; indeed, it was the issue that seared itself into the consciousness of the generation of unionists who passed from the scene only in the last decades of the twentieth century.

No man was more central to this argument than Jay Lovestone, who helped found the American Communist Party in 1919 and lived to see the Iron Curtain fall seventy years later. His life was consumed by the fate of world Communism, first as one of the American party's most energetic and creative leaders, then as a man burning in his hatred for the people and ideas to which he had once given such loyalty. Working behind the scenes at George Meany's AFL-CIO, Ted Morgan describes him at midcentury as "holed up in his office behind piles of reports, working the phones, hatching his plots, spreading his tentacles, whispering his orders."[1]

Morgan's biography of Lovestone is full of intimate detail and eye-popping revelation, but it will not be the last word on Lovestone and his times. Morgan has had access to an enormous Lovestone archive, now housed at Stanford University's Hoover Institution, and he has brought to light a good many machinations that

Lovestone himself sought to keep secret. This includes, above all, Lovestone's testy, quarter-century-long relationship with the Central Intelligence Agency, as well as much correspondence with his ambassadorial alter ego, Irving Brown, who actually handed out the clandestine cash packets to the foreign unionists whom Lovestone and the CIA sought to support. And Morgan offers up a juicy account of the serial love affairs undertaken by Lovestone, whose lifelong conduct remained true to the values of a leftish New York bohemian, circa 1919.

Unfortunately, Morgan, who has written popular biographies of Franklin Roosevelt and Winston Churchill, has a tin ear for historical context, especially when it comes to an evaluation of European or Asian labor politics. He largely adopts the shrill, Manichean assessments of Brown and Lovestone as his own. Especially during the crucial postwar decades, this distorts Morgan's capacity to see just how sectarian and self-serving was the Lovestonite worldview, not to mention the disastrous politics that flowed from it. Morgan is not uncritical of his subject—even Lovestone admirers were appalled at his "apparatchik mentality, deceitful and omissive"—but Morgan's biography remains essentially hagiographic in structure and sentiment.[2]

In 1907 Jacob Liebstein immigrated to the United States with his family. He was part of that enormously energetic, highly politicized generation of East European Jews who did so much to rejuvenate American radicalism and found the modern labor movement, or at least that large slice of it that flourished east of the Hudson River. Liebstein entered City College in 1915, became an active socialist, and by age twenty had already begun to play a leading role in the organization that would soon become the American Communist Party.

Jacob Liebstein shortly changed his name to Jay Lovestone. Like so many other immigrant Jews, Lovestone wanted to Americanize his persona, but the name change is also significant because, as a Communist, Lovestone was searching for a way that immigrant radicals could link themselves to the larger reform forces in American life. Lovestone, who was a full-time revolutionist, sought to break the party out of the immigrant ghetto, link up the radicalized Finns and Russians with English-speaking workers, and, in the parlance of the day, "burrow from within." This put him in opposition to William Z. Foster, the leader of the "proletarian" wing of the American Communist Party, who remained suspicious of alliances with either liberals or mainstream labor leaders.

And it plunged Lovestone into the struggle that arose out of Stalin's effort to consolidate his dictatorship in the Soviet Union. In the deadly infighting, Lovestone sided with Nikolai Bukharin, who argued that world capitalism had stabilized itself for the foreseeable future. Revolutionary vanguardism was therefore foolish or worse. In any event, argued Lovestone, American capitalism differed markedly from that of unstable Europe; moreover, American workers, divided by race and ethnicity and seduced by the abundance of mass production, were hardly in a revolutionary mood. This Lovestonite perspective came to be known as the theory of "American exceptionalism," an idea that in a later day would spawn a thousand dissertations.

But in 1929 there was nothing academic about it. At age twenty-nine Lovestone was a resourceful factionalist—his enemies labeled him "unscrupulous"—who had defeated Foster and won the majority of his party solidly behind him. But Lovestone could not outwit Joseph Stalin, who brought the whole weight of the Comintern down upon him when his faction journeyed to Moscow. "Who do you think you are?" shouted Stalin. "Trotsky defied me. Where is he? Zinoviev defied me. Where is he? Bukharin defied me. Where is he? And you! Who are you? Yes, you will go back to America. But when you get there, nobody will know you except your wives."[3]

And this is precisely what happened. In the Moscow maneuvering, Lovestone actually denounced Bukharin—Morgan calls it a "a complete abandonment of principle, a craven repudiation of his friend"—but it was not enough to forestall Stalin's dictate.[4] By the time he escaped from the Soviet Union in June 1929, Lovestone's American majority had simply melted away and he had been expelled from the party to which he had given a decade's commitment.

But for Lovestone Communism was not yet a god that had failed. He promptly gathered together his few friends and comrades and founded a new Communist Party (Opposition) to continue the struggle against "the anti-Leninist party-wreckers." He still thought of himself as an orthodox Leninist, a fulsome defender of Soviet collectivization and industrialization. Indeed, Lovestone cooperated with some of Stalin's overseas agents, and he actually voted for Earl Browder, the official Communist Party (CP) presidential candidate, in 1936.

His sect would have constituted little more than an historical footnote, a wannabe party, had not Lovestone gravitated during the 1930s into the orbit of David Dubinsky's International Ladies Garment Workers Union. Dubinsky was battling the Communists and left-wing socialists within his own union and in the world of New York politics, so he found Lovestone's critique of the American Stalinists useful. This became increasingly true in the late 1930s when Lovestone dropped all pretense of being any kind of Communist except that of an "anti." Morgan writes that it was Dubinsky who in 1941 introduced Lovestone to an even more powerful patron, George Meany, saying, "The son of a bitch is okay, he's been converted."[5]

Unfortunately, Lovestone's conversion left him with an entirely sectarian perspective on labor politics in the United States. These were the years when the CIO was on the march, when Communists, Socialists, Trotskyists and regulation trade unionists were organizing thousands of workers all across industrial America. It was an era of mass mobilization and ideological fluidity, but all Lovestone could see was the Communist threat.

This generated a near-disaster in the fledgling United Auto Workers (UAW). There Lovestone and his faction came to serve as the brains trust for union president Homer Martin, the Hollywood-handsome preacher whom even some Lovestonites declared "biologically incompetent." This was a "classic Lovestone operation," writes Morgan, with "Jay working behind the scenes, using surrogates, and coming to Detroit only in emergencies." Taking Lovestone's advice, Martin fired or demoted many of the radicals who had played key roles in actually building the UAW. These included some Communists but also socialists like the Reuther brothers, then working in tandem with the CP, as well as loyal followers of CIO president John L. Lewis, who was also ready to work with the Reds.[6]

Lovestone thought a Martin defeat would mean that "the Lewis dictatorship would become more arrogant than ever and the Stalinite stronghold would be strengthened in the CIO." He therefore pushed Martin to defy top CIO leaders, split the UAW, and accommodate the auto corporations. This was a monumental misjudgment but entirely in keeping with the Lovestonite political imagination. Lovestone ascribed diabolical powers to the union Communists; therefore any leadership alternative was preferable, no matter how maladroit or right-wing. As it turned out, the elimination of Homer Martin was essential to the revitalization of the UAW, the subsequent marginalization of Communist strength, and the emergence of Walter Reuther as the exemplar of progressive anti-Communism in midcentury America. Biographer Morgan neither reports nor understands any of this.[7]

Lovestone's energetic work on behalf of European trade unionists in the immediate postwar era constitutes the fulcrum upon which Morgan's biography turns. This was his "finest hour," writes Morgan, in which Lovestone deployed scarce AFL resources to rebuild a democratic labor movement in the face of Communist power and U.S. indifference. In this struggle he used everything he had learned as a Stalinist in the 1920s to fight the Communists on their own turf two decades later. Unlike so many liberals, enamored of Communist win-the-war fervor or Red Army heroism, Lovestone had no illusions about the postwar Soviets. "I couldn't have been a good anti-Communist," Lovestone often said, "if I had not been a good Communist." Indeed, Lovestone seemed to be fulfilling the prophecy made by the equally disillusioned Italian novelist Ignazio Silone: "The final conflict will be between Communists and ex-Communists."[8]

Lovestone orchestrated AFL (later AFL-CIO) foreign policy from 1944 to 1974. Like Lovestone himself, Ted Morgan is at pains to point out that the financial and political support the AFL offered European unionists had been ongoing for almost half a decade before the CIA itself became Lovestone's banker early in 1949. More importantly, the AFL's Free Trade Union Committee (FTUC), headed by Lovestone, took few political cues from the CIA or any other organ of the U.S. government; if anything, the political tutelage flowed in the other direction.

Indeed after 1950 Lovestone and his CIA handlers were embroiled in a constant tug of war. Lovestone wanted carte blanche funding, and he wanted the FTUC to monopolize U.S. trade union work abroad, cutting out both the rival CIO and the

CIA itself. Lovestone took to calling the youthful CIA case officers "Fizz Kids," effervescent but producing only bubbles. He finally found his CIA soul mate in the 1950s when Lovestone began working with the legendary counterintelligence chief James Jesus Angleton. They were "peas in pod," said a friend. And each was as hard-line and paranoid as the other. Both detested the "détente-mongers" in their respective backyards, and both believed any report of a thaw in the Cold War little more than a Communist ruse.[9]

But in the immediate aftermath of World War II Jay Lovestone was absolutely right about one important question. He insisted that the AFL denounce the Eastern Bloc "trade unions" for what they really were: "instruments of the state . . . that have enslaved millions . . . government-controlled, government-fostered, and government-dominated."[10] Lovestone was hardly alone in his analysis, but he kept pounding away. Thus the AFL would have nothing to do with the World Federation of Trade Unions, in which high-profile delegates from both the CIO and the British Trade Union Congress sat across the table from Soviet "unionists." And through George Meany, Lovestone vetoed for decades entry into the United States of those Eastern Bloc officials who claimed to speak for the working class.

This hard line became increasingly dysfunctional as the value of East-West diplomatic and political intercourse came to outweigh the danger, if it ever existed, that Western workers would somehow be duped into believing that the Communist unions were the real thing. Lovestone called this effort to thaw the Cold War "hands across the caviar," but the history of that conflict demonstrates that dissent in Eastern Europe had its greatest potential in precisely those moments when Cold War tensions were at an ebb. This was the basis for Willy Brandt's highly successful *Ostpolitik* (Eastern policy), which helped undermine the insularity of the East German regime, thus laying the basis for its implosion in 1989.[11]

But what about 1945 and 1946? Did the AFL really save Western European labor from Communist dominance? Echoing Lovestonite claims, biographer Morgan sees the work of Irving Brown and Jay Lovestone as crucial to the establishment of free, anti-Communist unions. In Germany Lovestone fought for the elimination of Communist influence—he called it "Hillmanism," a reference to CIO leader Sidney Hillman, who briefly cooperated with the Communists in American politics—within the U.S. occupation regime. He also stymied Red control of the German labor movement, where brave social democrats like Kurt Schumacher fought against overwhelming Soviet pressures.

This self-congratulatory story is largely a myth. As Denis MacShane and other historians have shown, a powerful anti-Communist brand of social democratic unionism quickly reemerged after the Nazi era. As early as 1945 and 1946 the Communists were overwhelmingly defeated in Western Zone trade union elections by those who remembered the disastrous role played by the Reds during the immediate pre–Nazi era (the Communist slogan then was "After Hitler Us!"). Moreover, British and American soldiers just happened to be in occupation of almost all of Western Germany. Just as we now know that there was little likelihood of a Soviet military invasion of this region, so too can we appreciate the indigenous strength of social democratic unionism there.[12]

This was even true in France and Italy, where mass Communist parties did exist and where the most important labor bodies were led by Communists or their allies. The "strategy here," Morgan writes, "was an international version of what Lovestone had tried to accomplish with Homer Martin's autoworkers in the 1930s—that is, to split the non-communist branch from the Communist tree."[13] Anti-Communist union federations did emerge in both countries, but the Lovestone-Brown influence was relatively minor at the time of the split itself. In France the emergence of the anti-Communist Force Ouvrière (Workers' Force) arose out of conflicts between the Communists and the Socialists dating back to 1920, and in any event it took place well before Irving Brown had a chance to spread much money around. Lovestone probably had more actual clout in Italy, in part because the American embassy provided more funds. Here, the AFL backed Giulio Pastore's Catholic labor federation, whose reach would always remain limited within an industrial working class steeped in the traditions of radical anticlericalism.

In all of this maneuvering, Lovestone could barely distinguish the fight against the CIO from that against European Communists. In 1946 he wrote to Brown, "The fight against Hillmanism in Europe must be made by the AFL." And when the State Department and the Marshall Plan set up posts for labor attachés, Lovestone and Meany did everything in their power to keep CIO men out, even after the expulsion of the Communist unions from the industrial labor federation in 1949. When Walter Reuther became president of the CIO—and later influential in the newly merged AFL-CIO—Lovestone waged war on a new front. Reuther had a natural affinity for the European socialists, endorsed the neutralism of Nehru's India, and challenged Meany's hard line in the Cold War. "Jay is obsessed with destroying Reuther," wrote one of Lovestone's most loyal friends. "He can think and talk of nothing else."[14]

This was not just a question of petty jealousy. Lovestone wrote speech after speech about "free trade unionism," but neither he nor Meany really trusted the social democrats of Western Europe. Thus Lovestone and Meany quickly found themselves at odds with most of the unionists who had joined the International Confederation of Free Trade Unions, the anti-Communist labor body the AFL did so much to establish in 1949. Lovestone claimed its leadership inept and corrupt, but their independence, their interest in moderating the Cold War, and their conception of trade unionism as a social movement of the broad left constituted the real crime.

Morgan admits that Lovestone's brand of Cold War intransigence had outlived its diplomatic usefulness by the 1960s. But he misses the far larger damage his subject was inflicting upon the labor movement, both at home and abroad. Lovestone and Brown backed unions that believed in "collective bargaining," not the "class struggle." But in Asia and Latin America, as well as most of Europe, U.S.-style business unionism generated the most ineffectual, blinkered kind of labor movement. (And the same would soon be apparent in the United States as well.)

Thus, the AFL-CIO helped ensure that when U.S.-based multinational corporations began their restless search for cheap labor and friendly governments, they would encounter few obstacles from a politically mobilized working class. In South Korea, South Africa, Japan, the Philippines, the Dominican Republic, much of Central America, Brazil, South Vietnam, and Venezuela, Lovestone sought to build foreign unions that aped American-style business unionism. This meant that the AFL-CIO often subsidized the most conservative, regime-dependent leaders of the working class in those countries where U.S. funding enabled it to function.

But Lovestone's influence was even more disastrous at home. U.S. unions appeared to be secure in the 1940s and 1950s, but even then their capacity for growth, even for survival, depended upon a certain elemental honesty, not to mention the kind of political vision that could link them to a new generation of radicals and a new set of social movements. But Lovestone was contemptuous of all this. When hard evidence of the extent to which the CIA had been funding AFL-CIO foreign operations broke into the headlines in 1967, Lovestone and Meany just stonewalled. If they admitted the connection, Lovestone advised Meany, "We shall have brought on our heads the wrath of every fake liberal and semiskilled intellectual."[15]

Thus Lovestone helped erect the ideological Iron Curtain that walled off the unions from an entire generation of New Left activists and civil rights militants whose energy and talent was essential to the health of a truly "free" labor movement. Instead, Lovestone and his friends turned their faces rightward, helping to drive the AFL-CIO into the arms of those neoconservative Democrats and Reaganite intellectuals whose opportunistic regard for the liberties of the Polish working class was nicely balanced by their indifference to the decline of living standards at home and the near-destruction of the American union movement in the years after 1981.

At his death in 1990 Lovestone's influence had just about exhausted itself. An old friend reported that at the AFL-CIO memorial service there were more mourners in attendance from the CIA than the labor movement. Then five years later AFL-CIO president Lane Kirkland, whose politics were just about as orthodox as Lovestone might have wanted, lost his job in a long-overdue housecleaning. Let's hope that Lovestone's ghost has finally been banished from our movement.

CHAPTER 19

Herbert Hill

Thurgood Marshall once described Herbert Hill as "the best barbershop lawyer in the United States."[1] That he was, and a whole lot more. Hill was a warrior, a strategist, a polemicist, a man who identified himself as "an unreconstructed abolitionist."[2] As labor secretary of the National Association for the Advancement of Colored People (NAACP), he was a combatant in a war against men and women who, by history, politics, and religion, should have been in his camp. So when he found them to be laggards or opponents of the civil rights impulse, he struck back with a ferocity that was determined and righteous. "My policy is to tell the truth and hit them hard," he said in 1963.[3]

Hill became labor secretary of the NAACP when the American trade union movement stood at its economic and organizational apogee right after World War II. Born in 1924, he graduated from New York University in 1945 and attended the New School for Social Research from 1946 to 1948, where he studied under the émigré political scientist Hannah Arendt. He was a member of the Socialist Workers Party in these years and a sometime organizer for the United Steelworkers. He frequented Harlem jazz clubs, read voraciously in what was then called Negro literature, and became as knowledgeable and comfortable with African American politics and culture as was possible for any white Jewish New Yorker.

Because of Hill's familiarity with radical politics and the labor movement, NAACP secretary Roy Wilkins hired him in 1949 to solicit contributions, conduct membership drives, and build political support for the NAACP's civil rights initiatives within the flush and muscular union locals that then occupied so many strategic points throughout the American industrial archipelago. He would also prove highly useful to the NAACP in the 1950s when the organization, under pressure from the Federal Bureau of Investigation and segregationist politicians, sought to purge Communists and other radicals from its ranks. In his travels to Youngstown, Erie, Toledo, and Detroit, Hill quickly found that after he had made his formal presentation to the local, and once the white local union officers had left the room, he was approached by stay-behind African American workers who poured out to him all the bottled-up frustrations and complaints that festered in even the most progressive of the midcentury industrial unions.

So Hill's work for the NAACP soon turned into one of persuasion and negotiation where possible, and litigation, denunciation, and protest where necessary, on behalf of African American workers who were trapped in the most insecure, segregated, and underpaid jobs. Hill was a brilliant and determined crusader who made the most of the limited legal remedies available against workplace discrimination in the 1950s and 1960s. He brought actions before the National Labor Relations Board to decertify unions that violated the nondiscrimination provision in federal contracts, and he carried cases against both labor unions and employers to state antidiscrimination commissions. Hill consciously fashioned this employment rights campaign after the larger NAACP fight to dismantle de jure segregation and discrimination in education, housing, and at the ballot box. He drafted an effective and widely distributed NAACP *Labor Manual* that described the complex gamut of discrimination tactics in the workplace and advised African Americans that the NAACP was ready to aid them in their fight against such inequities.[4]

Hill's insurgency took on the character of a civil war, not just within the top leadership of the labor-liberal civil rights coalition, but also among the old socialists, the erstwhile radicals, even the set of 1940s Trotskyist intellectuals who had done so much to politicize Hill in the first place. Some were now union officers and staffers: their resistance, equivocation, and hypocrisy fueled Herbert Hill's outrage for the rest of his life. Nothing infuriated him more than the complicacy, condescension, presumption, and outright racism that he found in the International Ladies Garment Workers Union (ILGWU). In 1960 the ILGWU still traded on its socialist roots, its pioneering role in the New Deal, and in some circles its Jewish and Italian communitarianism. Yet anyone who bothered to look could also see that a stratum of aging Jewish liberals was presiding over a trade union that systematically excluded African Americans and Puerto Ricans from advancement in both the shop and the union hierarchy.[5]

In his NAACP memoir, Gilbert Jonas, who worked with Hill in the 1950s and 1960s, recounted one of his friend's initial encounters with the ILGWU leadership, whose dissimulation, cozy relationship with employers, and presumption that Hill would "understand" enraged the NAACP labor secretary. In 1960 and 1961 Hill knocked his head against the ILGWU in an effort to get Ernest Holmes, a black Korean War veteran then working as a cutter's helper, the membership he had been denied in the union's well-paid but racially exclusive union of journeyman cutters. Everywhere he was told, "Don't make trouble. There is nothing to it." And by implication, all this fuss was bad for the Jews. Finally, Hill got an interview with one Moe Falikman, the president of the cutter's local, who told him that it was as a favor to an old union colleague, now an employer, that he had put Holmes on the cutting tables, but only as a temporary helper during the rush season. "So you see, Hill, it was all a misunderstanding, nothing to get excited about."[6]

Then, according to Jonas: "Hill rose up to his full height of six feet and leaned over Falikman's desk, replying in stentorian tones, 'But Falikman, you gave an employer permission to violate your own contract.' Falikman, alarmed at Hill's observation, replied, 'Hill, don't get excited, nothing to get excited about. Don't make me no trouble.' Hill, seizing the last word, shouted, 'Falikman, you don't know what trouble is. I haven't even *begun* to make trouble,' after which he stomped out of the union leader's office, slamming the door behind him."[7]

Hill would continue to make trouble, and if this was better accomplished with a hammer than a scalpel, all the better. As a litigator Hill had to drive home to judges and the larger public the racially discriminatory "pattern and practice" of those who conducted the affairs of some of the nation's most powerful unions. To win before the reluctant jurists of that era, Hill had to offer evidence that substantiated the NAACP contention that the union or company in question was guilty of monolithic, unproblematic, and willful conduct. Above all, his polemical, litigious presentations were designed to eviscerate the legal and moral standing of his opponents. Despite the problems with this kind of "history," we salute Hill's thirty-year artillery barrage for pushing and prodding a generation of liberals to put issues of union racism and structural subordination high on the agenda of reformers and scholars alike.

But there were historiographic and intellectual costs as well, which became evident as Herbert Hill transformed himself from an NAACP litigator to a University of Wisconsin historian in the late 1970s. These were the years in which the "new" labor history became influential within the humanities and when a reborn labor metaphysic captured the imagination of young intellectuals who had come out of the New Left. Hill seems to have interpreted much of this scholarship celebrating the Knights of Labor and the militants within the Congress of Industrial Organizations as a kind of retrospective endorsement of his trade union adversaries. In truth this new generation of labor historians, like their mentors Herbert Gutman and David Montgomery, were highly critical of contemporary trade unionism, including its racial apologias. But Hill chose to see any analysis that put the unions, or even the white working class, in anything but the most Manichean light as an endorsement of an ideological "workerism" that ignored or elided the hard kernel of late twentieth-century racism.

Hill condemned what he called the "revived populist neo-Marxism that advanced the ideology of working class consciousness and solidarity against the social realties of race." And as he put it in his critique of Gutman's study of the late nineteenth-century United Mine Workers, "The attempt to dissolve race in class thus emerged in the 'New Labor History' as a modern version of the old socialist dream: that the class struggle, joined by united workers, would in time resolve the persistent and ideologically vexing issue of race by rendering it irrelevant."[8] This was a perspective from which Hill rarely deviated. In a 2002 review of Judith Stein's book on the postwar history of steel unionism, Hill wrote that she "denies the record of union racism in order to sanitize labor history," along with many other labor historians who "find it necessary to minimize or deny racism in the labor movement because its existence conflicts with the useable past that they are constructing as labor history."[9]

This perspective caricatured both the contemporary politics and the historiographic thrust of Hill's ostensible opponents. And it denies the possibility that historians or unionists can modify their views and become more sophisticated and sensitive in their evolving analysis of the relationship among race, class, and union structure. Hill looked for a stark polarization within the ranks of labor historians and usually found it. For example, he once charged that the textbook *Who Built America?* which was indeed a product of a new generation of Gutmanesque scholars, abandoned considerations of racial identity once Reconstruction had passed. "Race in fact remains the fundamental and enduring division in the nation," wrote Hill, "whereas if we are to believe *Who Built America?* two hundred and fifty years of slavery were merely the prelude for the class struggle."[10] Needless to say, such a judgment mischaracterizes the textbook's first edition and all of those revised in its wake.

This thrust toward bipolarity was also at the heart of Hill's attack on my portrait of Walter Reuther. I wanted to show that the union and its leading personage were in flux, subject to a divergent set of forces that sometimes moved that institution toward a stolid defense of the existing racial order, but at other times opened the door to contestation and transformation. Hill would have none of this, at least not in his writings from the late 1990s, when he polemicized against what most reviewers saw as my highly critical biography of the UAW's leading mid-twentieth-century personality. Indeed, I actually agreed with most of Hill's analysis of how and why Reutherism devolved over time and why UAW racial liberalism never escaped a debilitating hypocrisy. But like so many other historians of American unionism, I also saw these institutions as a terrain of struggle. Hill knew this as well; he was intimately acquainted with the generation of African American insurgents—in steel, auto, trucking, and in the building trades—who challenged and prodded and sometimes won against the bureaucratic strata that had come of age in the Depression era. But in his written work, Hill downplayed or ignored the impact of these union rebels, as if to say that a concession to the view that the internal affairs of a union might be altered was also a step toward an argument that racial constructs within the working class might well be ameliorated by struggles within the working class itself.[11]

This may explain two things about Hill's understanding of historiography. He did not take chronology very seriously, or rather he saw it as marginal to the racial structures that he sought to expose. The latter were so entrenched,

so meta-historical, so pervasive that the evolution of working-class consciousness, union power, civil rights law, and capitalist development was eclipsed by
an overarching racial stasis. Hill took pains to reject arguments that called for
a consideration of what he called "the Zeitgeist"—that is, the ideological and
political structure of power and sentiment that influenced social action at any
given moment in historical time. Thus AFL efforts to exclude Asian workers in
the late nineteenth century are flattened into the fight against affirmative action
a century later, just as craft union bars against African Americans transmute
themselves into a rigid CIO defense of a racially coded seniority system a
generation later. Making such trans-generational connections is the historian's
job, but it requires nuance and care, the failure of which sometimes got Hill
a reprimand, even among those historians, such as Nick Salvatore and David
Roediger, who might be thought most friendly to his work.[12]

Hill's effort to ground his critique of union racial practices within a larger historical framework found sustenance in the 1990s with the emergence of whiteness
studies in labor history and cultural studies. Hill deployed the work of Roediger,
Eric Lott, Gwendolyn Mink, and Bruce Nelson, but the admiration was not entirely reciprocated. Historians of whiteness never quite embraced Hill's effort to
link trade union policies with white working-class mentalité. His outlook probably won a good deal more support from the nonacademic left and among some
social scientists.[13]

Indeed, when Hill did fieldwork for the NAACP, his own reports back to the
New York office sometimes reflected a more complex relationship between union
structure and working-class consciousness than his latter-day writings would
admit. The CIO was a racial advance from the AFL not just because the former
enrolled more minority workers but also because the regularization and bureaucratization of work relations brought a kind of "citizenship" to the shop floor, even
taking all the segregationist and discriminatory structures of power and privilege
into account. CIO-style unionism, with its signed contracts, clearly defined wage
scales, shop stewards, and grievance procedures, generated an industrial order
that stood against the paternalism, deferential subordination, and violence of the
old regime. This explains the remarkable union consciousness that characterized
many black workers in the years when industrial unions rejected the old AFL
labor market control strategy and began to recruit to its ranks the workforce of
an entire mine, mill, or factory.[14]

This was even true in Birmingham during the early 1950s, when Hill inves-
tigated conditions at Tennessee Coal and Iron. Ku Klux Klan (KKK) racism
saturated the union and the community, but Hill reported that

> on the level of day to day trade union operation in enforcing the union contract,
> officials of the Steelworkers Union vigorously defended the job rights of Negro
> workers. There was general agreement and praise for the CIO within the Negro

community on this matter . . . Mr. Davis (a black grievance man at the TCI Tin Mill) was most concerned about separate lines of progression for Negro workers employed in the steel mills and ore mine, and complained about the lack of up-grading of Negro workers into more skilled positions and the existence of segregated toilet facilities and drinking fountains within the plant. However, he paid tribute to the CIO because now "the company pays the job not the man."[15]

Any reference to the fate of African American workers in the steel industry, or to the other high-wage manufacturing industries that have been so devastated of late, forces us to consider the efficacy of any kind of legal, rights-based remedy, whatever its imperative moral and historic virtues. In *Running Steel, Running America*, Judith Stein sought to embed the reform of that industry's racial structures within a larger analysis of the economic and employment decline of the steel industry. Hill rejected this gambit as merely one of obfuscation and union apologia, but the affirmative action program that was eventually adopted in steel turned out to be a tool of insufficient power to open up or preserve the good-paying positions that African Americans had long struggled to occupy. The strategy championed by Hill and so many other civil rights militants provided little leverage when confronted by the economic catastrophe that overtook so much of American industry in the 1970s and subsequent decades. Likewise, in the nineteenth as well as the twentieth century, any effort to account for the status of minority or ethnic workers cannot be divorced from the trajectory of U.S. capitalism. Thus, in the years following the landmark 1974 consent decree in basic steel, the number of black steelworkers plunged, from more than thirty-eight thousand in 1974 to fewer than ten thousand in 1988. Segregated and separate seniority lines were broken open, generating a substantial rise in the proportion of racial minorities in the skilled trades. But this was a Pyrrhic victory, because industry shrinkage eliminated far more good jobs than were created as a result of the consent decree. Given such devastating statistics, Stein labeled the fight over affirmative action in that industry the "narcissism of small differences."[16]

But enough! I can imagine Herbert Hill's voice right now—objecting, rejecting, putting forth an exhaustively footnoted argument full of moral power and indignation. He would not just disagree; he would counterpoise another universe full of contrary lessons and imperatives useful for legal and political combat in our own time. It is a quality we should respect, indeed celebrate, even when we find ourselves on the blunt end of it.

Addendum: Late in 2012 historians Christopher Phelps and Trevor Griffey published essays and blog posts, largely based on FBI files they unearthed through the Freedom of Information Act, that found Hill acting as an episodic informant for the FBI during the years 1953 through 1955 and perhaps as late as 1962. Approached by the FBI he offered information on SWP members that he knew from his days in that organization. As William C. Sullivan, head of domestic intelligence for the

FBI observed in 1962, Hill " has [already] been contacted on several occasions by New York Agents and has been cooperative." On that 1962 occasion the FBI sought to use Hill to obstruct a rumored fraternization between the NAACP and a short-lived Committee to Aid the Monroe Defendants, an organization initiated by SWP members in support of the black militant and advocate of armed self-defense, Robert F. Williams, and the movement he led in North Carolina.[17]

What are we to make of Hill's complicit role in this ugliness? Not everyone approached by the FBI "named names," so does a certain moral cowardice and political hypocrisy attach itself to a man who defined himself as a militant advocate of civil rights and a principled civil libertarian?

I think not, or rather I think that whatever his failures and misjudgments, they were actually those of the NAACP itself, of which Hill was a loyal and committed operative. Because the organization had long feuded with the Communists and because the NAACP of the early 1950s feared that the government might well label it a subversive group, NAACP leaders like Walter White, Thurgood Marshall, and Roy Wilkins cooperated with the FBI and other government agencies to purge leftists and eschew radical demands and tactics. Hill, who had broken from the SWP because he thought it insufficiently activist on civil rights issues, had no reason to dissent from this posture. It therefore seems virtually certain that Roy Wilkins and other NAACP officials knew and approved of Hill's FBI contacts.[18] To the extent that all this drove a wedge between the nation's most important civil rights organization and the American left, the tragedy is hardly Hill's alone.

CHAPTER 20

Do Graduate Students Work?

Hundreds of thousands of graduate students grade millions of papers and blue books every year. The work is absolutely vital to the "product" put out by just about every American university, and of course they get paid for it, though not very much. Thousands of teaching assistants and research assistants are union members, and others would join if more statutes, on either the federal or state level, allowed. These unionized grad students negotiate with their university administration over pay, class size, and other working conditions. Sometimes they go on strike.

At the same time, these graduate students are also "in school." They are apprentice scholars whose teaching and grading tasks are integral to their learning experience, even as they put most of their effort into completing their own classes and moving on to a terminal degree. So how do we categorize these many thousands of young people: as workers or students, as fish or fowl? Or must we come down on one side or the other? The question has been up for grabs for several years in Congress, at the National Labor Relations Board (NLRB), and in the courts. The issue is important not just because such a decision will help advance or retard the enrollment of thousands of graduate students into trade unions. Rather, this is the kind of question that bedevils and confuses our understanding of the nature of work, of the purposes of the labor law, and of how we think about class in a society when the vast majority of people wear collars that are neither blue nor white.

The unionization rights of graduate students at public universities come under the jurisdiction of state law, so in traditionally liberal states like New York, California, Wisconsin, Massachusetts, and Illinois, thousands have successfully formed legally recognized trade unions. In contrast, the conditions under which employed students may form unions at private colleges and universities are determined by the NLRB, whose decisions have been highly politicized in recent years. After rejecting graduate employee unionization for decades, a new board with a majority of appointees chosen by President Bill Clinton ruled in the year 2000 that graduate students at private universities were indeed "employees" and hence covered under the national labor law. Four years later a GOP-dominated board reversed that decision, which may yet be revised once again as the set of board members appointed by President Barack Obama make their views known.

The NLRB's 2004 decision that excluded graduate students from the protections offered by federal labor law illuminates why a labor law designed for an earlier industrial era has proven so dysfunctional when it comes to the work lives of graduate students, but it also explains how that very legal ossification of a once radical labor law has proven so useful to twenty-first-century conservatives. That 2004 ruling, which was brought to the board by Brown University to discourage unionization of its teaching assistants, doomed to defeat the energetic organizing campaigns that teaching assistants had mounted at Brown and at other high-profile private universities such as Yale, Columbia, University of Pennsylvania, and New York University.[1] At one very important and consequential level, the Bush-era NLRB won another skirmish in the long and successful war that conservatives have waged to marginalize the labor movement and confine it to a shrinking blue-collar ghetto. For the better part of a decade, Bush administration appointees at the NLRB and the Labor Department were busy overturning Clinton-era rulings, like the 2000 New York University decision that declared working graduate students to be employees, or the rules that forced companies to bargain with, or pay overtime and benefits to, tens of thousands of employees whom management sought to label as "independent contractors" or exempt professionals.[2]

Is Barack Obama's administration likely to reverse this right-wing advance? He was elected president in 2008 with the enthusiastic and effective support of the unions, and like all other Democratic presidents, he has appointed labor-liberals to the NLRB; however, the courts, which normally rule on all important NLRB decisions, remain notably conservative when it comes to the organizing rights of American workers. Equally important, virtually the entire Republican establishment—from Congress to the U.S. Chamber of Commerce and on to the dozens of statehouses now in GOP control—remains intransigent when it comes to labor's organizing efforts. So even if the liberals who now hold a majority on the NLRB reverse Bush-era decisions that define graduate students as organizational ciphers, not much is likely to change in the world of work, academic or otherwise.

However, there is a larger issue at stake in the conservative effort to define the sociological category into which graduate students fall and then forcibly stuff them into it. What is the meaning and definition of work in the modern university? What is the relationship between teaching, learning, creativity, and the nature of education? And how is the idea of trade unionism, which once stood close to the imaginative heart of the American democratic ethos, to be restored to its former status? The stakes are huge, because if one explores the logic inherent within the opinion put forward by that Bush-era NLRB, then we are moving not just toward the extinction of the American labor movement, but into an Orwellian universe in which words like "individualism," "education," and "choice" turn into their negations.

In its 2004 decision ruling that graduate students were not covered by the American labor law, the Republican-dominated NLRB of that era ruled first and foremost that a clear difference exists between the educational and economic functions performed by graduate students. The board majority drew a sharp distinction between the roles teaching assistants (TAs) play as students and workers. They have to be one or the other. No multiple identities or subjective understandings, please!

Harking back to the original language of the New Deal–era Wagner Act, these Bush appointees embraced something close to a class-warfare reading of American labor law. The 1935 statute, they argued, has been "premised on the view that there is a fundamental conflict between the interests of the employers and employees" and that the "inequality of bargaining power between employees and employers was one of the central problems addressed by the Act." And, most importantly, these GOP appointees held that "the vision of a fundamentally economic relationship between employers and employees is inescapable."[3] Thus, if graduate students have something less than an antagonistic relationship with administrators and professors, if they are paid mainly to learn and not work, they are not employees and therefore not covered by the labor law.

This GOP Marxism flies in the face of the argument that conservatives have long made to declare both the labor law and the labor movement antique and obsolete. We've come a long way since the Depression, assert the corporate consultants. Both modern management and "postindustrial" technology have made for cooperative, non-adversarial, creative relationships within the world of work. High-tech firms like Microsoft declare unions unsuitable to their well-educated, hyper-creative employees, and even General Motors has asserted that it now rejects the production principles pioneered by Frederick Taylor and Henry Ford, correcting "the great flaw in the assembly line concept [that] tends to exclude the creative and managerial skills of the people who work on the line."[4] So if the conservatives on the Bush-era NLRB have returned us to a stark world of polarized classes, I hope that the government will soon inform millions of workers at Wal-Mart, K-Mart, Federal Express, and other antiunion firms of that fact, because managers at those firms are constantly bombarding their employees with a contrary message.

Of course, the reason the Bushite NLRB members have echoed these class-warfare polarities is to make the argument that grad students are at Brown, NYU, and other big universities not as employees but as nonworker learners. And like their hyper-industrial conception of the world of work, they also subscribe to a Victorian notion of education that is at once highly personal but also utterly authoritarian. Professors impart knowledge to grad students who soak it up; no backtalk, please, and no tilt toward the participatory, learning-by-doing aspirations of a John Dewey, a Paul Goodman, or the Antioch educator Arthur E. Morgan, who pioneered the cooperative, work-and-learn model of higher education.

In truth the advocates of graduate student unionism also see a dichotomy between the educational life of employed students and their function as the labor power that makes the big university go. Empirical reality undoubtedly lies far more on the union side of the debate, because TAs and RAs (research assistants), like all workers, really are paid for their work time, and because their labor now plays such a massive role in sustaining the instructional and research life of higher education. Perhaps 50 percent of all teaching hours are now performed by graduate students and other contingent teachers. And in both natural science and humanities departments, graduate students are responsible for 90 percent of the grading. Most important, however, is that tens of thousands of employed grad students *feel* like workers, which is one reason why so many of them have joined organizations that can collectively represent their interests.

But I think it is a dead end to argue that the proletarianization of graduate student life, or of any form of skilled, creative employment, will lead us to a revitalized union movement and a more densely woven social safety net. This is really playing on the right wing's turf. They are happy to consign the union idea to the most onerous, repetitive, and undignified forms of labor. The right argues that any job that contains a spark of creativity, a bit of authority, an element of education or apprenticeship, should be exempt from the labor law and the union compass. And then, of course, as the union idea becomes synonymous with the most undignified and repetitive jobs, these same ideologues argue that teachers, programmers, nurses, doctors, journalists, and writers would be crazy to link their fortunes with such unfortunates.

In truth all jobs, even the lowest-wage and lowest-skilled, require judgment, self-reliance, and initiative. All work can and should be dignified. But by the same measure, the labor movement needs to make it abundantly clear that you don't have to be a horny-handed proletarian to benefit from a collective defense of one's self-interest, which is why eighteenth-century printers, nineteenth-century craftsmen, and twentieth-century airplane pilots, screenwriters, and baseball players joined the house of labor. Union work rules and wage standards are best understood not as a depersonalizing straitjacket, but as code of workplace law—a practical instance of "equal protection under the law"—to which all men and women are rightly subject.

And this brings us back to the NLRB's spurious distinction between the educational and the employee aspects of graduate student existence. Although many universities have forged moneymaking alliances with corporations and the state, and although many research assistants provide a pool of cheap, talented labor for these enterprises, universities still measure their well-being by a standard that falls somewhat outside the capitalist marketplace. They are judged, and their students and faculty rewarded, not by how much money flows to the bottom line, but by the standing and prestige their researchers, teachers, and students generate. And sports teams, too, of course.

One might take a cynical approach to this, like Thorstein Veblen, and argue that all of this heavy academic lifting is merely designed to boost alumni self-esteem and undergraduate matchmaking. But I'd rather argue that the scholarship that takes place in the modern university, and upon which so much of its standing is measured, cannot be distinguished from the educational "work" itself. For example, when a research lab attracts outside funding, the status of the principal investigator, and her capacity to recruit excellent research assistants, is all part of the dollar-labor power exchange, even as the RAs are working on their PhDs. Likewise, when a graduate student in history writes a great dissertation and lands a prestige job, this accomplishment, while undoubtedly part of the great stream of disinterested scholarship, also redounds to the material credit of her university and her mentors. We have no trouble paying faculty for their career-boosting scholarship, so why not recognize that graduate education is also composed of a seamless web of teaching, learning, and research. The general health and well-being of the institution—in terms of its capacity to attract good students, recruit an excellent faculty, raise funds from the alumni, secure government and corporate funding—are all enhanced by the scholarship of the faculty and the educational apprenticeship of their students.

It is therefore futile for a government agency or a university administrator to construct a set of antiquated job categories and then stuff unwilling grad students into them. Instead we should celebrate their multiple identities, held not only by the men and women of the university but also by so many others whose democratic empowerment requires the legal and imaginative deconstruction of the stultifying and dysfunctional occupational hierarchy into which our current labor law seeks to consign them. Indeed, it was Karl Marx, our most famous student of class society, who looked forward to the day when we "hunt in the morning, fish in the afternoon, rear cattle in the evening, criticize after dinner . . . without ever becoming a hunter, fisherman, cowherd, or critic."[5]

CHAPTER 21

Why American Unions Need Intellectuals

Sixty-five years ago, in *The New Men of Power*, C. Wright Mills made a perceptive observation about the troubled relationship between labor leaders and radical intellectuals during an era of Cold War militarism and conservative advance. Wrote Mills: "To have an American labor movement capable of carrying out the program of the left, making allies among the middle class, and moving upstream against the main drift, there must be a rank and file of vigorous workers, a brace of labor intellectuals, and a set of politically alert labor leaders. There must be the power and the intellect."[1]

It did not happen. Labor leaders soon became entrapped within a stultifying bargaining regime, and the "working class" failed to fulfill its radical destiny. As for the intellectuals, they found careers and rewards aplenty in the midcentury academy. Indeed, Mills himself soon abandoned what he once called "the labor metaphysic" and launched a provocative quest for a new set of actors who might transform America and the world.

But today union leaders and intellectuals are more entangled than at any time since the 1940s. If one has a generous definition of "intellectual," it is easy to find lots of students, academics, researchers, journalists, and writers, many of radical pedigree, working in, around, and for the U.S. labor movement. Unions have long sought help from high-profile outsiders in support of their strikes, bargaining agendas, and political objectives, but today these connections have grown so dense that some of these figures, many pro-labor academics, now find themselves enlisted, at times even drafted, into the disputes that have recently wracked some of the nation's key unions. Not since the early Cold War split the labor movement and divided American liberals have otherwise independent writers and academics played such a public role inside the labor movement.

In 2008 top officials at the Service Employees International Union (SEIU), perhaps the country's most influential trade union, organized a conference call with more than two dozen academics to explain why a dissident California local, United Healthcare Workers West (UHW), posed an obstacle to the national union's health-care organizing strategy. In response UHW reached out to its own group of professors, and when they signed on to a letter of support, UHW spent several thousand dollars to publish it as an advertisement in the *New York Times*. In this dispute both sides also posted advertisements and Web links on Talking Points Memo and at the Huffington Post, blogs that had plenty of liberal readers but that spent little energy covering union affairs.

Meanwhile, in another dispute that divided UNITE HERE (the union for workers in the hotel, food service, laundry, warehouse, and casino gaming industries) and also pitted that union against the SEIU, both sides have been assiduous in courting and in some instances winning support from scores of pro-labor academics and outside activists. In the summer of 2009, partisans of John Wilhelm, the UNITE HERE president, secured nearly 250 signatures, many from members of the Labor and Working-Class History Association, on a "letter of concern" to the SEIU executive board lamenting that the big union was "dividing the progressive movement at a critical moment in history." In response the SEIU purchased the entire back page of the *Nation* to explain to that magazine's well-educated readers why the UNITE HERE leadership was actually the most disruptive element in the internal union dispute. All summer long a barrage of emails and phone calls from both sides sought to win over the academics, or at least neutralize their voice.[2]

My point here is not to evaluate the pros and cons of these internal trade union fights, or even to note the role played by the academic partisans. (I tended to be on the side of the SEIU's critics and competitors.) Rather, I want to explore how we got to this moment, where these academics and other such nonmembers seem to be playing a significant role in the life of the trade union movement.

In the nineteenth century when trade unions in Europe and North America were young, insecure, and often socialist, autodidactic intellectuals were everywhere. Many had been radicals, veterans of 1848 or 1905 expelled from the old country after revolutionary defeat or stepped-up repression. Mills dedicated *The New Men of Power* to J.B.S. Hardman, "Labor Intellectual," who had been cast out of Russia in 1907 by special vote of the czar's imperial cabinet. Such men and women were seen as interlopers by those steeped in the tradition of Samuel Gompers and other advocates of pure and simple unionism.

Selig Perlman, author of *A Theory of the Labor Movement*, denounced the labor intellectuals of his day for their incapacity to resist "an onrush of overpowering social mysticism" in their quest for a "new social order." Though Perlman was himself a University of Wisconsin professor, for all of his life he remained suspicious of those who came to the labor movement with an agenda that transcended the job-conscious collective bargaining he thought was the essence of modern unionism.[3] Thus, when he heard a particularly radical talk at a workers' education summer school late in the 1940s, Perlman spat out his worst epithet: "Who was that intellectual?" It turned out to be Emil Mazey, a high school drop-out, then secretary-treasurer of the United Auto Workers (UAW), who had learned his politics in the Depression-era socialist movement.[4]

Despite his confusion between the social role of an intellectual and his or her politics, Perlman ended up more right than wrong. In the postwar era the trade unions kept their distance from both the academy and the kind of people, like Harvey Swados and Sidney Lens, who wrote for *Dissent,* the *Nation,* and similar venues. Clark Kerr, Derek Bok, John Dunlop, George Shultz, and other high-profile economists founded an entire academic discipline, "industrial relations," which took as its subject the union contest with management. But these administrative mandarins—many would rise to occupy key university and cabinet posts—were the kind of analysts who took the existence of a trade union movement for granted and focused their academic and policy-making energies on how governments or corporations should regulate, resist, or reshape this large presence in American life. There were intellectuals who looked to labor in the 1950s and 1960s. But in a movement led by fierce anti-Communists like George Meany and pragmatic bargainers like Walter Reuther, there were few opportunities for pro-labor outsiders to play much of a role.

In the UAW, for example, virtually all organizers, officers, and other staffers had to come out of the ranks, putting in at least a year in an auto plant, before they could go on the union payroll. The rule was put in place to minimize the influence of the "politicals"—the Communists and Socialists—whose loyalties were thought to lie outside the union. Thus, in the mid-1950s, when Reuther was looking for a radical black activist to groom for higher office, he urged James Farmer, an anti-Communist active in the nascent civil rights movement, to take a job with the UAW. But first Farmer would have to spend a year on one of Ford's assembly lines.

With the civil rights movement gaining momentum, that was too long a wait for Farmer, so Reuther had to do without his talents and those of many others like him. Indeed, even in the years when the UAW remained a dynamic institution, it proved difficult to draw upon veterans of the 1960s social movements to vitalize the union's organizing staff. For the many autoworkers who did achieve a long-sought promotion out of the ranks, their new "organizing" jobs were akin to a preretirement perk.[5]

All this began to change in the 1980s and 1990s, creating the conditions under which students, professors, and writers might play a role more organic to the life of the labor movement. One morning in the spring of 1991, I picked up my phone at the University of Virginia (UVa), where I was teaching. On the line was Allison Porter, the first director of the AFL-CIO's new Organizing Institute. "Do you have any students who might like to enroll in our summer program?" she asked. I was flabbergasted. I'd been a labor historian for years, but I had never entertained such a query from anyone actually associated with an honest-to-God trade union. Indeed, back at Berkeley, where as a grad student I spent a lot of time on picket lines, even the more liberal Bay Area unions had been highly suspicious of student involvement. And why was Porter calling me at UVa, hardly known, then or now, as a center of labor education and activism?

Porter's call was part of a union effort to finally tap the new talent, activism, and passions necessary to survive in an increasingly hostile political and economic environment. John Sweeney would be elected AFL-CIO president on just such a platform. His fourteen-year presidency did little to stem the steady decline in numbers and bargaining clout, but he did play an important role in breaking down the Berlin Wall, which had long divided the trade unions from the main body of the American left, on the campus and elsewhere. He thereby ushered in an era when college activists—anti-globalization, anti-sweatshop, environmentally conscious, pro-immigrant—looked to the labor movement to advance their causes.

From the 1999 World Trade Organization protests in Seattle and elsewhere to the campaign against Nike and Wal-Mart, the unions now have gained new allies. In late 2009, Russell Athletic, a maker of university-branded clothing, bowed to the power of this alliance when it agreed to reopen a Honduras apparel factory and facilitate unionization of the workforce. Playing a decisive role in this unprecedented agreement, the campus-based Worker Rights Consortium persuaded ninety-six U.S. universities to cancel clothing contracts with Russell until the company guaranteed its workers freedom of association in all of its Honduras factories.[6]

This kind of campus-union alliance provides a model for the long delayed broadening of what constitutes a labor movement. You don't have to pay dues or work under a union contract to consider yourself a partisan. But such a movement also enhances the weight of experts, academics, researchers, writers, and students with plenty of free time, sometimes to the marginalization of the workers themselves. The use of such pressure tactics, boycotts, and embarrassing publicity began as innovative "corporate campaigns," during the Reaganite 1980s, when the traditional strike seemed to have become ineffective. Ray Rogers, who pioneered the strategy during the protracted strike against Hormel, was once anathema in many union circles. But his tactics have now been institutionalized in many unions, making the work of staff researchers and publicists organic to routine organizing and bargaining.

In fact, public policy, not the privatized world of collective bargaining, now constitutes the key arena in which unions and their opponents reshape the future. When Wal-Mart sought to defend its wages and pricing policy from union critics, it hired Global Insight, a Cambridge-based economic research firm, to organize an academic-style conference with papers and panels, not all in lockstep with the big retailer, to counter labor's barrage. And when the unions faced an onslaught of criticism from companies and Republican politicians denouncing as inherently coercive the card-check provisions of the Employee Free Choice Act, union allies commissioned Cornell's Kate Bronfenbrenner to conduct an empirical study. She found that in union organizing drives, virtually every instance of coercion, economic and even physical, arose from the employer efforts to thwart the union campaign. Her findings were released at a high-profile Capitol Hill press conference.[7]

This new relationship between unions and intellectuals became apparent to me, as well as to columnist Harold Meyerson, when on separate occasions we were both invited to address the HERE (Hotel Employees and Restaurant Employees Union) research staff during one of their weekend retreats in coastal California. When first invited I expected to talk to a just a handful of number crunchers. During its heyday, when the UAW represented a million and a half workers, the research staff consisted of Nat Weinberg and three or four of his friends, old socialist comrades of the Reuther brothers. They read the General Motors annual report and the *Wall Street Journal*, sized up the company's profitability, and then calculated what the UAW could demand without bankrupting Chrysler, whose balance sheet was always in much poorer shape.

So I was surprised when more than sixty young and energetic researchers awaited my talk, brought together by a union with less than two hundred thousand members. There was even a former student of mine whose experience in Virginia's living wage campaign had turned her on to the labor movement. What could they possibly do to occupy their time and justify the expense of keeping all of this ex-collegiate talent on the payroll?

Unfortunately, they had plenty of work. HERE's decision to create a cadre of corporate campaigners was based on the grimmest of circumstances. As Meyerson later wrote, "Traditional private-sector union organizing—signing up workers who want to join a union, winning a certification election conducted by the government, and securing a collective-bargaining agreement in negotiations with the employer—had become a dead-end." So HERE had to organize and bargain with as little recourse to the National Labor Relations Board as possible. The union used all of those researchers to dream up new and creative ways to pressure hotels and casinos, first to get to a card-check certification, and then to bargain a satisfactory contract.[8] If an antiunion casino in California wanted to expand, HERE's staffers would make sure there were plenty of zoning headaches; if a living wage ordinance was on the ballot in Santa Monica, the union would generate reams of economic data to prove it was needed.

The work of these researchers has blended seamlessly with that of the union's public relations operation and its political mobilizations. Indeed, today few union organizing drives can succeed without this kind of "air" game in which websites are built, newspaper and TV ads created, and the endorsement of politicians, clerics, academics, and celebrities solicited. Cesar Chavez and his farmworker union pioneered this kind of campaign in the 1960s and 1970s. It has been emulated by the unions that have sought to tarnish Wal-Mart's image, shame management at Smithfield Foods in North Carolina, organize university food service workers, and convince the public that executives at the Cintas Corporation mistreat their employees.

The result of all this activity is that academics, intellectuals, and their students and followers have become functional to American unionism in a fashion that would have surprised both Mills and Perlman. Their politics and cultural sensibilities no longer put them at odds with the main body of the American labor movement. The unions are no longer foreign policy hawks, and they have long since abandoned the culture wars once happily waged by some pro-labor neoconservatives against the remnants of the New Left. Meanwhile, union density in education, both for schoolteachers and professors, is far higher than for most other occupations. The largest UAW local west of the Mississippi represents teaching assistants, tutors, and readers on the University of California's ten campuses. And despite the fact that the leadership of many unionists, including that of the SEIU's former president Andy Stern, as well as the Teamsters' Jimmy Hoffa, has been found unimaginative or worse during the recent economic crisis, most liberals and academics today see existing trade unions as allies, agents, and leaders for the kind of America they hope to construct.

At the same time, unions face unprecedented hostility from virtually the entire business community and from almost every Republican officeholder. For their part, most national Democrats have long since forgotten how to defend the unions in any fashion designed to stir the soul, as both the bailout of the auto companies in 2009 and the right-to-work conflicts in Wisconsin, Indiana, and Michigan in 2011 and 2012 so graphically demonstrated. Organized labor is embattled, and not just at the bargaining table, but in a fundamentally ideological way that calls its very existence into question. In this context, academic intellectuals play a vital role as defenders, legitimizers, and even spokespeople for a movement that no longer quite knows how to explain itself to a larger public.

This is something the business community and free-market ideologues understand. They pump millions of dollars a year into public intellectual training programs designed to build the next generation of right-wing writers, journalists, and ideologues. The unions have nothing like this, which is why the AFL-CIO appealed with increasing desperation to the academic community to put out manifestos, petitions, and other statements during the fight over the Employee Free Choice Act. Many intellectuals and writers stepped up to the firing line, including historians Michael Honey, David Brody, John Logan, and Ruth Rosen, but they were outgunned by right-wing journalists, organizations, and public relations people who eviscerated union claims that the proposed law would advance the public welfare. Politics really is a war of ideas, so the union movement needs articulate men and women, not just to become effective operatives, but also to serve as forceful advocates in the public square. It matters if a Robert Reich, a Paul Krugman, or less notable wordsmiths believe that unionization is essential to remaking the American middle class.

In this context the university has become an essential recruiting ground for the current generation of union staffers, organizers, even top officials. At the SEIU's Washington headquarters, according to one well-placed observer, almost all the staffers who work in research, political/governmental affairs, and communications are relatively recent college graduates, many veterans of the student social justice movements that have flourished in the campus milieu. This is also largely true of the organizers in the field, even though the national union, and especially the locals, have made a concerted effort to hire rank-and-file workers for these jobs. In other unions the pattern is similar if not quite so pronounced: less evident in the old industrial unions, far more so in those unions that organize in the service sector.

Many of the most committed and effective ex-students were "turned on" to the unions by influential teachers or by the labor internship programs that have arisen at the University of Massachusetts, CUNY, UCLA, Rutgers, and other schools. At the more elite universities, including Columbia, NYU, Brown, and Yale, where campus administrations have resisted graduate student organizing efforts, chronic struggles to form a campus union have generated wave after wave of energetic militants, many of whom find their way onto union staffs.

But few become union "lifers." An extraordinarily high level of ideological and personal commitment is necessary to compensate for the constant travel, long hours, social isolation, and arduous work that is today the life of a labor organizer. Many are imbued with what one recent college graduate called a "cowboy mentality," a sense that their work was more than an ordinary job, even superior to other work within the labor movement itself.

Burnout and turnover are constant problems, but for those who stay even a few years, their employment is akin to a religious or ideological calling. It is a vocation that can only be sustained through continual reinforcement—from their peers, from their union higher-ups, and from those academics, writers, and outside activists who first made them think that a job in the labor movement was something special. Indeed, that is why Harold Meyerson and I were invited to the HERE retreats: to put their hard work in its larger political and historical context, to explain again why unionism is a crucial lever for social change in America, to tell these staffers that they were part of something big and bold.

So is this a good thing or not? Given the messy and contentious disputes that have convulsed American unions in recent years, one is tempted to urge the academics and writers to back off. But this may well be impossible, because the transformation of so many unions from insular collective bargaining agents into hybrid formations that put an unprecedented emphasis on policy and politics gives leverage and functionality to those whose job it is to trade in ideas and advocacy. This is not what either Perlman or Mills might have imagined, but it is a condition we are going to live with in the years ahead.

NOTES

Introduction

1. Clark Kerr, *The Uses of the University* (Cambridge, MA: Harvard University Press, 1963), 66; also see Kerr's autobiography, *The Gold and the Blue: A Personal Memoir of the University of California, 1949–1967* (Berkeley: University of California Press, 2003).

2. This was the wing of Trotskyism identified with Max Shachtman. See Peter Drucker, *Max Shachtman and His Left* (Atlantic Highlands, NJ: Humanities Press, 1994).

3. Nelson Lichtenstein, "Industrial Unionism under the No-Strike Pledge: A Study of the CIO during the Second World War" (unpublished PhD thesis, University of California, Berkeley, 1974).

4. Nelson Lichtenstein, *Labor's War at Home: The CIO in World War II* (New York: Cambridge University Press, 1982; repr. Philadelphia: Temple University Press, 2003).

5. Nelson Lichtenstein, "Defending the No-Strike Pledge: CIO Politics during World War II," *Radical America* 9 (July-August 1975): 49–75.

6. Charles Maier, *Recasting Bourgeois Europe* (Princeton, NJ: Princeton University Press, 1975); David Abraham, *The Collapse of the Weimar Republic: Political Economy and Crisis* (New York: Holmes and Meier, 1986); Howell Harris, *The Right to Manage: Industrial Relations Policies of American Business in the 1940s* (Madison: University of Wisconsin Press, 1982); Sanford Jacoby, *Employing Bureaucracy: Managers, Unions, and the Transformation of Work in American Industry, 1900–1945* (New York: Columbia University Press, 1985).

7. Herbert Gutman, "Work, Culture, and Society in Industrializing America, 1815–1919," *American Historical Review* 78 (June 1973): 531–88.

8. See W. W. Rostow, *The Stages of Economic Growth: A Non-Communist Manifesto* (Cambridge, UK: Cambridge University Press, 1960), where the author famously describes Communists and other radicals as "scavengers of the modernization process." Likewise, Clark Kerr also saw labor radicalism as a variable that was largely dependent on the particular stage of development in an industrial society and the relative isolation or integration of the workers into that larger society. Kerr, "The Interindustry Propensity to Strike: An International Comparison," in *Labor and Management in Industrial Society,* ed. Clark Kerr (Garden City, NY: Doubleday, 1964), 105–147.

9. Like the 1911 edition of the *Encyclopedia Britannica*, the first edition of *Who Built America* was the most distinctive and best remembered. It was "authored" less by individual writers than by a collective. The American Social History Project et al., *Who Built America? Working People and the Nation's Economy, Politics, Culture, and Society,* Vol. 2: *From the Gilded Age to the Present* (New York: Pantheon, 1992).

10. Martin Glaberman, "Walter Reuther and the Decline of the American Labor Movement," *International Journal of Politics, Culture, and Society* 11 (1997): 73–77; Herbert

Hill, "Lichtenstein's Fictions: Meany, Reuther, and the 1964 Civil Rights Act, *New Politics* 7 (Summer 1998): 82–107. Glaberman, a sometime follower of C.L.R. James, thought working-class militancy emerged from a spontaneous and unstructured context. He therefore rejected my close attention to the role played by veteran militants, whom he saw as ensnared within a union structure that was inherently antiradical.

11. For more of my thoughts on these matters, see the middle chapters of Nelson Lichtenstein, *State of the Union: A Century of American Labor* (Princeton, NJ: Princeton University Press, 2002).

12. Nelson Lichtenstein, ed., *American Capitalism: Social Thought and Political Economy in the Twentieth Century* (Philadelphia: University of Pennsylvania Press, 2006).

13. Nelson Lichtenstein, ed., *Wal-Mart: The Face of Twenty-First-Century Capitalism* (New York: New Press, 1996); and Lichtenstein, *The Retail Revolution: How Wal-Mart Created a Brave New World of Business* (New York: Picador, 2010).

Chapter 1. Writing and Rewriting Labor's Narrative

This essay was first published as "Introduction to the New Edition," *Labor's War at Home: The CIO in World War II* (Philadelphia: Temple University Press, 2003).

1. New Left skepticism toward both the UAW and GM during the 1970 strike is well captured in William Serrin, *The Company and the Union: The "Civilized" Relationship of the General Motors Corporation and the United Automobile Workers* (New York: Knopf, 1973).

2. The International Socialists, which now exists as Solidarity, traced its ideological roots to the 1940 division within the Trotskyist movement. Max Shachtman, Irving Howe, Dwight Macdonald, Hal Draper, and others then argued that the Soviet Union was not, as Trotsky held, a "degenerated workers state" worthy of critical support, but a "bureaucratic collectivist" regime, as repressive in its own way as any state in the capitalist world. See Peter Drucker, *Max Shachtman and His Left: A Socialist's Odyssey through the "American Century"* (Atlantic Highlands, NJ: Humanities Press, 1994). Solidarity was largely responsible for publication of the widely respected *Labor Notes*.

3. Important influences were C.L.R. James, *State Capitalism and World Revolution* (Detroit: Facing Reality, 1963); C. Wright Mills, *The New Men of Power: America's Labor Leaders* (1948; Urbana: University of Illinois Press, 2001); Stanley Aronowitz, *False Promises: The Shaping of American Working-Class Consciousness* (New York: McGraw-Hill, 1973); and Harvey Swados, "The UAW—Over the Top or Over the Hill?" *Dissent* (Fall 1963): 321–43. The 2001 edition of *New Men of Power* contains my appreciative introduction.

4. Hal Draper (1914–1990), a founder of the third camp Workers Party in 1940, had been a contributor and editor of *Labor Action* and a shipbuilder in Long Beach during World War II. A scholar of Marx and Marxism, his most widely read and influential work was the pamphlet *The Two Souls of Socialism*, first published in 1960. Stan Weir (1921–2001) was a seaman in World War II and a well-known internal union opponent of Harry Bridges in the International Longshore and Warehouse Union of the early 1960s. He later published Singlejack Books, which distributed shirt-pocket guides for rank-and-file militants.

5. Nelson Lichtenstein, "Industrial Unionism Under the No-Strike Pledge: A Study of the CIO during the Second World War," PhD diss., University of California, Berkeley, 1974. Richard Abrams was the chair of my dissertation committee, but political scientist Michael Rogin (1937–2001) exerted what little real interpretative guidance I accepted from anyone on the faculty.

6. See, for example, Joel Seidman, *American Labor: From Defense to Reconversion* (Chicago: University of Chicago Press, 1952); Richard Lester, *As Unions Mature* (Princeton, NJ: Princeton University Press, 1958); and Clark Kerr, Frederick Harbison, John Dunlop, and Charles Myers, *Industrialism and Industrial Man* (Cambridge, MA: Harvard University Press, 1960). As a dissertation, my book manuscript was rejected for publication by both Greenwood Press and University of Kentucky Press. The outside readers were from the world of industrial relations. Cambridge University Press decided to publish it because of a fortuitous political-generational shift. Steven Fraser had become the history editor at Cambridge; one of the readers to whom he sent the manuscript was Peter Friedlander, who had just published the pioneering social history *The Emergence of a UAW Local, 1936–1939: A Study in Class and Culture* (Pittsburgh: University of Pittsburgh Press, 1975).

7. See, in particular, Kim Phillips-Fein, *Invisible Hands: The Businessmen's Crusade against the New Deal* (New York: W. W. Norton, 2009); Elizabeth Tandy Shermer, *Sunbelt Capitalism: Phoenix and the Transformation of American Politics* (Philadelphia: University of Pennsylvania Press, 2013); Steven Fraser and Gary Gerstle, *The Rise and Fall of the New Deal Order, 1930–1980* (Princeton, NJ: Princeton University Press, 1989); Colin Gordon, *New Deals: Business, Labor, and Politics in America, 1920–1935* (New York: Cambridge University Press, 1994); David Plotke, *Building a Democratic Political Order: Reshaping American Liberalism in the 1930s and 1940s* (New York: Cambridge University Press, 1996); and Michael Brown, *Race, Money, and the American Welfare State* (Ithaca, NY: Cornell University Press, 1999).

8. See Lizabeth Cohen, *Making a New Deal: Industrial Workers in Chicago, 1919–1939* (New York: Cambridge University Press, 1991); Steve Babson, *Building the Union: Skilled Workers and Anglo-Gaelic Immigrants in the Rise of the UAW* (New Brunswick, NJ: Rutgers University Press, 1991); Bruce Nelson, *Divided We Stand: American Workers and the Struggle for Black Equality* (Princeton, NJ: Princeton University Press, 2000); Eric Arnesen, "Up from Exclusion: Black and White Workers, Race, and the State of Labor History," *Reviews in American History* 26 (March 1998): 146–74; and Gerald Zahavi, "Passionate Commitments: Race, Sex, and Communism at Schenectady General Electric, 1932–1954," *Journal of American History* 82 (September 1996): 514–48.

9. On this topic see the outstanding work of Gary Gerstle, *Working-Class Americanism: Industrial Unionism in a Textile Town* (New York: Cambridge University Press, 1991); Joshua Freeman, *In Transit: The Transport Workers Union in New York City, 1933–1966* (New York: Oxford University Press, 1989; repr. Philadelphia: Temple University Press, 2001); and in a different vein, Michael Denning, *The Cultural Front: The Laboring of American Culture in the Twentieth Century* (New York: Verso, 1996).

10. Much of the perspective is summarized in Nelson Lichtenstein, "From Corporatism to Collective Bargaining: Organized Labor and the Eclipse of Social Democracy in the Postwar Era," in Fraser and Gerstle, *Rise and Fall of the New Deal Order*, 122–52. And see more generally Nelson Lichtenstein, *State of the Union: A Century of American Labor* (Princeton, NJ: Princeton University Press, 2002), 98–140.

11. See especially Joseph A. McCartin, *Labor's Great War: The Struggle for Industrial Democracy and the Origins of Modern American Labor Relations, 1912–1921* (Chapel Hill: University of North Carolina Press, 1997), 94–119; and, of course, David Montgomery, *The Fall of the House of Labor: The Workplace, the State, and American Labor Activism, 1865–1925* (New York: Cambridge University Press, 1987), 330–410.

12. Martin Glaberman, *Wartime Strikes: The Struggle against the No-Strike Pledge* (Detroit: Bewick, 1980); George Lipsitz, *Rainbow at Midnight: Labor and Culture in the 1940s,* rev. ed. (1981; Urbana: University of Illinois Press, 1994), 69–99, 120–56, 253–334; Lichtenstein, *Labor's War at Home: The CIO in World War II* (1982; Philadelphia: Temple University Press, 2003), 44–81. The introduction and several essays touch on these issues in Sally Miller and Daniel Cornford, *American Labor in the Era of World War II* (Westport, CT: Praeger, 1995).

13. Robert Korstad, *Civil Rights Unionism: Tobacco Workers and the Struggle for De-mocracy in the Mid-Twentieth-Century South* (Chapel Hill: University of North Carolina Press, 2003); see also Michael Honey, *Southern Labor and Black Civil Rights: Organizing Memphis Workers* (Urbana: University of Illinois Press, 1993); Michelle Brattain, *The Politics of Whiteness: Race, Workers, and Culture in the Modern South* (Princeton, NJ: Princeton University Press, 2001); and Daniel Clark, *Like Night and Day: Unionization in a Southern Mill Town* (Chapel Hill: University of North Carolina Press, 1997).

14. Important books that take a relatively favorable view of the union dividend from such war-era labor relations agencies include Robert Zieger, *The CIO, 1935–1955* (Chapel Hill: University of North Carolina Press, 1995), 163–90; and Gilbert Gall, *Pursuing Justice: Lee Pressman, the New Deal, and the CIO* (Albany: SUNY Press, 1999), 113–91.

15. Lichtenstein, "From Corporatism to Collective Bargaining," 125; WLB quoted in Craufurd Goodwin, *Exhortation and Controls: The Search for a Wage Price Policy, 1945–1971* (Washington, DC: Brookings Institution, 1975), 13 (italics in original).

16. Christopher Tomlins, *The State and the Unions: Labor Relations, Law, and the Or-ganized Labor Movement in America, 1880–1960* (New York: Cambridge University Press, 1985), 328; James B. Atleson, *Labor and the Wartime State: Labor Relations and Law during World War II* (Urbana: University of Illinois Press, 1998), 1–2; Katherine Van Wezel Stone, "The Postwar Paradigm in American Labor Law," *Yale Law Journal* 90 (June 1981): 1517. I kick myself for not consulting the Stone essay before my first book appeared, but in the 1970s, when I did most of the research for *Labor's War at Home,* labor law scholarship, especially that involving the history of industrial relations, had become increasingly arid. Today no labor historian can afford to ignore the rich and plentiful work of the current generation of labor law scholars.

17. Nelson Lichtenstein, "Great Expectations: The Promise of Industrial Jurisprudence and Its Demise, 1930–1960," and David Brody, "Workplace Contractualism in Compara-tive Perspective," both in *Industrial Democracy in America: The Ambiguous Promise,* ed. Nelson Lichtenstein and Howell John Harris (New York: Cambridge University Press, 1993), 113–41, 176–205; and Steven Tolliday and Jonathan Zeitlin, "Shop-Floor Bargaining, Contract Unionism, and Job Control: An Anglo-American Comparison," in *The Automo-bile Industry and Its Workers,* ed. Steven Tolliday and Jonathan Zeitlin (Cambridge, UK: Polity Press, 1986), quote on page 112.

18. Clark, *Like Night and Day,* 4.

19. Judith Stein, *Running Steel, Running America: Race, Economic Policy, and the Decline of Liberalism* (Chapel Hill: University of North Carolina Press, 1998), 43; Roger Horowitz, *"Negro and White: Unite and Fight!": A Social History of Industrial Unionism in Meatpack-ing, 1930–1990* (Urbana: University of Illinois Press, 1997), 96. See also Honey, *Southern Labor and Black Civil Rights;* Brattain, *Politics of Whiteness;* and Korstad, *Civil Rights Unionism.*

20. Alan Brinkley, *The End of Reform: New Deal Liberalism in Recession and War* (New York: Knopf, 1995), 175–226; Steven Fraser, *Labor Will Rule: Sidney Hillman and the Rise of American Labor* (New York: Free Press, 1991), 407–94.

21. Brian Waddell, "Economic Mobilization for World War II and the Transformation of the U.S. State," *Politics and Society* 22 (June 1994): 165–94; Waddell quoted on page 170, Secretary of War Stimson quoted on page 173. The pioneering work of Paul A. C. Koistinen sustains Waddell's view. See Koistinen's "Mobilizing the World War II Economy: Labor and the Industrial-Military Alliance," *Pacific Historical Review* 42 (November 1973): 443–78. And see John C. Culver and John Hyde, *American Dreamer: The Life and Times of Henry A. Wallace* (New York: W. W. Norton, 2000), 266–303.

22. Howell Harris, *The Right to Manage: Industrial Relations Policies of American Business in the 1940s* (Madison: University of Wisconsin Press, 1982), 105–127, 177–204; Sanford Jacoby, *Modern Manors: Welfare Capitalism since the New Deal* (Princeton, NJ: Princeton University Press, 1997), 143–92 (on Thompson Products' diabolically successful resistance to the UAW during and just after World War II); Timothy Minchin, *What Do We Need a Union For? The TWUA in the South, 1945–1955* (Chapel Hill: University of North Carolina Press, 1996); James C. Cobb, *The Selling of the South: The Southern Crusade for Industrial Development, 1936–1990* (Urbana: University of Illinois Press, 1993), 96–121; Jefferson Cowie, *Capital Moves: RCAs 70-Year Quest for Cheap Labor* (Ithaca, NY: Cornell University Press, 1999), 1–40; and see the essays by Chris Nyland, Kyle Bruce, Tami Friedman, Michael Pierce, and Elizabeth Tandy Shermer in *The Right and Labor in America: Politics, Ideology, and Imagination,* ed. Nelson Lichtenstein and Elizabeth Tandy Shermer (Philadelphia: University of Pennsylvania Press, 2012).

23. Andrew Workman, "Manufacturing Power: The Organizational Revival of the National Association of Manufacturers, 1941–1945," *Business History Review* 78 (Summer 1998): 279–317.

24. Ira Katznelson, Kim Geiger, and Daniel Kryder, "Limiting Liberalism: The Southern Veto in Congress, 1933–1950," *Political Science Quarterly* 108 (Summer 1993): 283–306.

25. As quoted in Joseph Gaer, *The First Round: The Story of the CIO Political Action Committee* (New York: CIO-PAC, 1944), 22. See also Lawrence Samuel, *Pledging Allegiance: American Identity and the Bond Drive of World War II* (Washington, DC: Smithsonian Institution Press, 1997).

26. Gary Gerstle, "The Working Class Goes to War," *Mid-America* 75 (October 1993): 315. See also the essays by Lary May, Elaine Tyler May, Perry Duis, Reed Ueda, and Gary Gerstle in *The War in American Culture: Society and Consciousness during World War II,* ed. Lewis Erenberg and Susan E. Hirsch (Chicago: University of Chicago Press, 1996).

27. See, for example, Joshua Freeman, "Hardhats: Construction Workers, Manliness, and the 1970 Pro-War Demonstrations," *Journal of Social History* 26 (Summer 1993): 725–37.

28. I discuss this at greater length in Lichtenstein, "The Making of the Postwar Working Class: Cultural Pluralism and Social Structure in World War II," *Historian* 51 (November 1988): 42–63.

29. Mark Leff, "The Politics of Sacrifice on the American Home Front in World War II," *Journal of American History* 77 (March 1991): 1318.

30. Thomas Sugrue, *The Origins of the Urban Crisis: Race and Inequality in Postwar Detroit* (Princeton, NJ: Princeton University Press, 1996), 33–88; John T. McGreevy, *Parish Boundaries: The Catholic Encounter with Race in the Twentieth-Century Urban North* (Chicago: University of Chicago Press, 1996), 55–110; Kenneth Durr, "When Southern Politics Came North: The Roots of White Working-Class Conservatism in Baltimore, 1940–1964," *Labor History* 37 (Summer 1996): 309–31; and Nelson, *Divided We Stand,* 89–141,185–218.

31. For the skeptics, see Bruce Nelson, "Class, Race, and Democracy in the CIO: The 'New' Labor History Meets the 'Wages of Whiteness,'" *International Review of Social*

History 41 (Fall 1996): 351–74; Robert Norell, "Caste in Steel: Jim Crow Careers in Birmingham, Alabama," *Journal of American History* 73 (December 1986): 669–701; and Herbert Hill, "Black Workers, Organized Labor, and Title VII of the 1964 Civil Rights Act: Legislative Record and Litigation Record," in *Race in America: The Struggle for Equality,* ed. Herbert Hill and James E. Jones Jr. (Madison: University of Wisconsin Press, 1993), 263–341.

32. For an elaboration of this perspective, see Robert Korstad and Nelson Lichtenstein, "Opportunities Found and Lost: Labor, Radicals, and the Early Civil Rights Movement," *Journal of American History* 75 (December 1988): 786–811; August Meier and Elliott Rudwick, *Black Detroit and the Rise of the UAW* (New York: Oxford University Press, 1979); Gretchen Lemke-Santangelo, *Abiding Courage: African American Migrant Women and the East Bay Community* (Chapel Hill: University of North Carolina Press, 1996); Zaragoza Vargas, *The Union Makes Us Strong: Mexican American Workers, Unionism, and the Struggle for Civil Rights, 1929–1945* (Princeton, NJ: Princeton University Press, 2004); Honey, *Southern Labor and Black Civil Rights,* 177–213; and Horowitz, "Negro and White, Unite and Fight!" 145–74.

33. Eileen Boris, "'You Wouldn't Want One of 'Em Dancing with Your Wife': Racialized Bodies on the Job in World War II," *American Quarterly* 50 (March 1998): 83; Daniel Kryder, *Divided Arsenal: Race and the American State during World War II* (New York: Cambridge University Press, 2000), 88–132.

34. Of course, the gendered world of *production* politics is another story. Here, the dramatic massive influx of women into new jobs and new industries during the war has been well studied. But the institutional and social legacy was proportionally tepid because this demographic upheaval was unaccompanied by the kind of ideological legitimization that made the upgrading of black labor such a pivotal development. See Ruth Milkman, *Gender at Work: The Dynamics of Job Segregation by Sex during World War II* (Urbana: University of Illinois Press, 1987); Karen Anderson, *Wartime Women: Sex Roles, Family Relations, and the Status of Women during World War II* (Westport, CT: Greenwood Press, 1981); Nancy Gabin, *Feminism in the Labor Movement: Women and the United Auto Workers, 1935–1975* (Ithaca, NY: Cornell University Press, 1990), 50–51; and Alice Kessler-Harris, *A Woman's Wage: Historical Meanings and Social Consequences* (Lexington: University Press of Kentucky, 1990), 81–112. Gunnar Myrdal finished writing *An American Dilemma* by the end of 1942; it would take twenty-one more years for Betty Friedan, whose feminist politics were heavily influenced by her experiences in the 1940s labor left, to publish the equally influential *The Feminine Mystique.* See Walter Jackson, *Gunnar Myrdal and America's Conscience: Social Engineering and Racial Liberalism, 1938–1987* (Chapel Hill: University of North Carolina Press, 1987); Daniel Horowitz, *Betty Friedan and the Making of the Feminine Mystique: The American Left, the Cold War, and Modern Feminism* (Amherst: University of Massachusetts Press, 1998).

35. Meg Jacobs, "How About Some Meat? The Office of Price Administration, Consumption Politics, and State Building from the Bottom Up, 1941–1946," *Journal of American History* 84 (December 1997): 910–41; National Association of Manufacturers, "Would You Like Some Butter or a Roast of Beef?" (newspaper advertisement), reproduced in Jacobs, "How About Some Meat?" 935; see also Anne Stein, "Post-War Consumer Boycotts," *Radical America* 9 (July-August 1975): 156–61. In another context Marilynn Johnson captures the war-era flavor of an empowered citizenship in her striking essay "War as Watershed: The East Bay and World War II," *Pacific Historical Review* 63 (August 1994): 315–31.

36. Bruce Nissen, "A Post–World War II Social Accord?" *U.S. Labor Relations, 1945–1989: Accommodation and Conflict*, ed. Bruce Nissen (New York: Garland, 1990), 174–79; John Sweeney, *America Needs a Raise* (Boston: Houghton Mifflin, 1996), 17.

37. Timothy Willard, "Labor and the National War Labor Board, 1942–1945: An Experiment in Corporatist Wage Stabilization," PhD thesis, University of Toledo, 1984; Elizabeth Fones-Wolf, *Selling Free Enterprise: The Business Assault on Labor and Liberalism, 1945–60* (Urbana: University of Illinois Press, 1994); David A Horowitz, *Beyond Left and Right: Insurgency and the Establishment* (Urbana: University of Illinois Press, 1997).

38. A particularly good discussion of how Taft-Hartley's threat to union security generated a more privatized, interest-group labor movement is found in Brown, *Race, Money, and the American Welfare State*, 135–64.

39. See David Stebenne, *Arthur Goldberg: New Deal Liberal* (New York: Oxford University Press, 1996); and my own *Walter Reuther: The Most Dangerous Man in Detroit* (Urbana: University of Illinois Press, 1997).

Chapter 2. Supply-Chain Tourist

This essay was first delivered as a talk at the University of Maryland, November 14, 2005.

1. For some evocation of all this, see Nelson Lichtenstein, *Walter Reuther: The Most Dangerous Man in Detroit* (Urbana: University of Illinois Press, 1997), 16–17.

2. Author's interview with Hillary Claggart, April 29, 2005, Bentonville; Jeff Glasser, "Boomtown, U.S.A.," *U.S. News and World Report*, June 25, 2001, 17–20; Anne D'Innocenzio, "Wal-Mart Suppliers Flocking to Arkansas," *The State*, September 21, 2003, 1.

3. Nelson Lichtenstein, *The Retail Revolution: How Wal-Mart Created a Brave New World of Business* (New York: Picador, 2010).

4. Joseph Y. S. Cheng, *Guangdong: Preparing for the WTO Challenge* (Hong Kong: Chinese University Press, 2003); Michael Enright, Edith Scott, Ka-mun Chang, *Regional Powerhouse: The Greater Pearl River Delta and the Rise of China* (Singapore: John Wiley, 2005), Joe Studwell, *The China Dream* (London: Profile Books, 2005).

5. Robert Marquand, "China Coast as Factory of the World," *Christian Science Monitor*, December 16, 2003, 1; author's interview with Helen Du, Yantian International Container Terminal, September 13, 2005.

6. Peter F. Drucker, *Concept of the Corporation* (New York: John Day, 1946).

7. C. Wright Mills, *The New Men of Power: America's Labor Leaders* (Urbana: University of Illinois Press, 2001), 291.

8. "Wal-Mart, P & G Link up for Efficiency," *St. Louis-Post Dispatch*, February 14, 1989, 12B; Constance Hays, "What's behind the Procter Deal? Wal-Mart," *New York Times*, January 29, 2005, C1.

9. Edna Bonacich with Khaleelah Hardie, "Wal-Mart and the Logistics Revolution," in *Wal-Mart: The Face of Twenty-First-Century Capitalism*, ed. Nelson Lichtenstein (New York: New Press, 2006), 163–88. The etymology of the phrase "supply chain" is instructive. In the 1980s business consultants like Bain and Company coined the phrase "value chain management" or "supplier rationalization" to describe how components and materials were purchased and transformed into saleable goods. Industrial relations scholars Frederick Abernathy and John Dunlop used the phrase "commodity channels" as recently as 1999 to describe how apparel moved from Asian and Central American suppliers to North American retailers. In the twenty-first century, however, the artful "supply chain" has become the

pervasive terminology, especially in the hands of theorists such as Gary Gereffi and Gary Hamilton, who have emphasized the market-making potential of the contemporary buyer-driven supply networks in order to more clearly evaluate the hierarchy of power and profitability that characterizes contemporary global trade. For an overview of this literature, see Jennifer Bair, "Global Capitalism and Commodity Chains: Looking Back, Going Forward," *Competition and Change* 9, no. 2 (2005): 129–56; and Gary Gereffi and Miguel Korzeniewicz, eds., *Commodity Chains and Global Capitalism* (Westport, CT: Praeger, 1994), 95–122.

10. Lichtenstein, *Retail Revolution*, 1–9, 35–52. Excellent essays covering workers, entrepreneurs, and states in a single industry are found in Gary Gereffi, David Spender, and Jennifer Bair, eds., *Free Trade and Uneven Development: The North American Apparel Industry after NAFTA* (Philadelphia: Temple University Press, 2002).

11. Glenn Porter and Harold Livesay, *Merchants and Manufacturers: Studies in the Changing Structure of Nineteenth-Century Marketing* (Chicago: Ivan R. Dee, 1971), 29–34; Sven Beckert, "Merchants and Manufacturers in the Antebellum North," in *Ruling America: A History of Wealth and Power in a Democracy*, ed. Steve Fraser and Gary Gerstle (Cambridge, MA: Harvard University Press, 2005), 116–17.

12. This is a broad topic. For starters, see Thomas L. Haskell, "Capitalism and the Origins of the Humanitarian Sensibility, Part I," *American Historical Review* 90 (April 1985): 339–61; Richard McIntyre, *Are Workers Rights Human Rights?* (Ann Arbor: University of Michigan Press, 2008).

13. Among the many studies, see, especially, Pun Ngai and Yu Xiaomin, "Wal-Martinization, Corporate Social Responsibility, and the Labor Standards of Toy Factories in South China," in *Wal-Mart in China*, ed. Anita Chan (Ithaca, NY: Cornell University Press, 2011).

Chapter 3. Historians as Public Intellectuals

This essay was first published as "Public Intellectual: A View from the Minor Leagues," in *Maryland Historian* 30, no. 1 (2006), and was extensively revised in 2012.

1. Russell Jacoby, *The Last Intellectuals: American Culture in the Age of Academe* (New York: Basic Books, 1987).

2. On Mills, perhaps the iconic public intellectual of our times, see Howard Brick, "C. Wright Mills, Sociology, and the Politics of the Public Intellectual," *Modern Intellectual History* 8 (2011): 391–409; Daniel Geary, *Radical Ambition: C. Wright Mills, the Left, and American Social Thought* (Berkeley: University of California Press, 2009); and Stanley Aronowitz, *Taking It Big: C. Wright Mills and the Making of Political Intellectuals* (New York: Columbia University Press, 2012).

3. C. Wright Mills, *The New Men of Power: America's Labor Leaders* (1948; Urbana: University of Illinois Press, 2001), 13–27.

4. Steve Fraser, Nelson Lichtenstein, et al., "Hope for Labor," *New York Review of Books*, February 1, 1996.

5. Malcolm Gladwell, "Labor Love-In," *New Yorker* 72, no. 32 (1996): 77–78.

6. Steven Greenhouse, "Wal-Mart: A Nation Unto Itself," *New York Times*, April 17, 2004, B7. The papers from the conference were published in *Wal-Mart: The Face of Twenty-First-Century Capitalism*, ed. Nelson Lichtenstein (New York: New Press, 2006).

7. Simon Head, "Inside the Leviathan," *New York Review of Books* 51 (December 16, 2004); Lee Scott (president and CEO of Wal-Mart), "Wal-Mart's Impact on Society: A Key Moment in Time for American Capitalism," in *New York Review of Books*, April 7, 2005.

8. Among the collections thus far published are Nelson Lichtenstein, ed., *American Capitalism: Social Thought and Political Economy in the Twentieth Century* (Philadelphia: University of Pennsylvania Press, 2006); and Nelson Lichtenstein and Elizabeth Tandy Shermer, eds., *The Right and Labor in America: Politics, Ideology, and Imagination* (Philadelphia: University of Pennsylvania Press, 2012).

Chapter 4. Tribunes of the Shareholder Class

This essay was first given as a talk at the City University of New York Graduate Center, December 2002, and substantially revised in 2012.

1. Many of the insights in this essay are drawn from Thomas K. McCraw, "In Retrospect: Berle and Means," *Reviews in American History* 18 (1990): 578–96. The quotes above are from page 582.

2. Adolf Berle and Gardiner Means, *The Modern Corporation and Private Property* (New York: Macmillan, 1932), 66, 68.

3. As quoted in Jordan Schwarz, *Liberal: Adolf A. Berle and the Vision of an American Era* (New York: Free Press, 1987), 60.

4. Howard Brick, *Transcending Capitalism: Visions of a New Society in Modern American Thought* (Ithaca, NY: Cornell University Press, 2006), 65, 74.

5. McCraw, "In Retrospect," 590.

6. George J. Stigler and Claire Friedland, "The Literature of Economics: The Case of Berle and Means," *Journal of Law and Economics* 26 (June 1983): 241.

7. Julia Ott, *When Wall Street Met Main Street: The Quest for Investors' Democracy* (Cambridge, MA: Harvard University Press, 2011).

8. "Briefing: The Endangered Public Company," *Economist* 403 (2012): 27–30.

9. As quoted in Dalia Tsuk, "From Pluralism to Individualism: Berle and Means and Twentieth-Century American Legal Thought," *Law and Social Inquiry* 30 (Winter 2005): 196.

10. "Acceptance Speech for the Renomination for the Presidency," Philadelphia, Pennsylvania, June 27, 1936, at the American Presidency Project online archive, University of California, Santa Barbara.

11. McCraw, "In Retrospect," 589.

12. Berle and Means, *Corporation and Private Property*, 356.

13. As quoted in Bernard Beaudreau, *Mass Production, The Stock Market Crash, and the Great Depression: The Macroeconomics of Electrification* (Westport, CT: Greenwood, 1996), 64.

14. As quoted in Colin Gordon, *New Deals: Business, Labor, and Politics in America, 1920–1935* (New York: Cambridge University Press, 1994), 39.

15. Robert Wagner, "Proposal for Better Industrial Relations," in *American Labor since the New Deal,* ed. Melvyn Dubofsky (Chicago: Quadrangle Books, 1971), 59.

16. As quoted in Bryant Simon, *A Fabric of Defeat: The Politics of South Carolina Millhands, 1910–1948* (Chapel Hill: University of North Carolina Press, 1998), 88.

17. Jennifer Klein, *For All These Rights: Business, Labor, and the Shaping of America's Public-Private Welfare State* (Princeton, NJ: Princeton University Press, 2003), 115, 219.

18. Kenneth Casebeer, "Aliquippa: The Company Town and Contested Power in the Construction of Law," *Buffalo Law Review* 43 (Winter 1995): 618.

19. I discuss this Whiggish impulse in "Great Expectations: The Promise of Industrial Jurisprudence and Its Demise, 1939–1960," in *Industrial Democracy in America:*

The Ambiguous Promise, by Nelson Lichtenstein and Howell Harris (New York: Cambridge University Press, 1993); see also W. Jett Lauck, *Political and Industrial Democracy, 1776–1926* (New York: Funk and Wagnalls, 1926).

20. As quoted in William Forbath, "Cast, Class, and Equal Citizenship: An Essay for David Brian Davis," in *Moral Problems in American Life: New Perspectives on Cultural History,* ed. Karen Halttunen and Lewis Perry (Ithaca, NY: Cornell University Press, 1998), 167–200.

21. Peter Drucker, *Post-Capitalist Society* (New York: HarperCollins, 1993), 43. Although this quote is taken from one of Drucker's later books, his views on the managerial transition to postcapitalism have been consistent since he wrote *Concept of the Corporation* in 1945.

22. Mark Mizruchi, "Berle and Means Revisited: The Governance and Power of Large U.S. Corporations," *Theory and Society* 33 (2004): 583.

23. Ibid., 599.

24. Tsuk, "From Pluralism to Individualism," 215.

25. For a collection of papers on the influence of Ronald Coase, see Oliver Williamson and Sidney Winter, *The Nature of the Firm: Origins, Evolution, and Development* (New York: Oxford University Press, 1991); and see Alfred Chandler, *The Visible Hand: The Managerial Revolution in American Business* (Cambridge, MA.: Harvard University Press, 1977).

26. Gary Gereffi, John Humphrey, and Timothy Sturgeon, "The Governance of Global Value Chains," *Review of International Political Economy* 12 (February 2005): 79–82; and Nelson Lichtenstein, "The Return of Merchant Capitalism," *International Labor and Working-Class History* 81 (Spring 2012): 8–27.

Chapter 5. "The Man in the Middle"

This essay was originally published in Nelson Lichtenstein and Stephen Meyer, eds., *On the Line: Essays in the History of Auto Work* (Urbana: University of Illinois Press, 1989), and was revised in 2012.

1. Donald E. Wray, "Marginal Men of Industry: The Foremen," *American Journal of Sociology* 54 (January 1949): 298–301.

2. Laura Brown, "War of the Nurses: The Struggle for a Voice in *National Labor Relations Board v. Kentucky River Community Care, Inc.,* 532 U.S. 706 (2001)," *South Texas Law Review* 43 (Summer 2002): 885–919; Steven Greenhouse, "Board Redefines Rules for Union Exemption," *New York Times,* October 4, 2006, A16.

3. Jean-Christian Vinel, *Travails of the Worker* (Philadelphia: University of Pennsylvania Press, 2013).

4. Daniel Nelson, *Managers and Workers: Origins of the New Factory System in the United States, 1880–1920* (Madison: University of Wisconsin Press, 1975), 34–78; Stephen Meyer III, *The Five-Dollar Day: Labor Management and Social Control in the Ford Motor Company, 1908–1921* (Albany: State University of New York Press, 1981), 37–65; see also Thomas H. Patten Jr., *The Foreman: Forgotten Man of Management* (New York: McGraw-Hill, 1968), ch. 2.

5. Nelson, *Managers and Workers,* 140–62; Sanford Jacoby, "The Human Factor: An Historical Perspective on Internal Labor Markets in American Manufacturing Firms," Working Papers Series, no. 21, Institute of Industrial Relations, University of California, Los Angeles, May 1980.

6. "Hiring and Separation Methods," *Monthly Labor Review* 35 (November 1932): 1005–1017; Sanford Jacoby, *Employing Bureaucracy: Managers, Unions, and the Transformation of Work in American Industry, 1900–1945* (New York: Columbia University Press, 1985), 193–99.

7. As quoted in Meyer, *Five-Dollar Day*, 58–59.

8. Charles R. Walker, *The Foreman on the Assembly Line* (Cambridge, MA: Harvard University Press, 1956), 10.

9. Meyer, *Five-Dollar Day*, 56; David M. Gordon, Richard Edwards, and Michael Reich, *Segmented Work, Divided Workers: Historical Transformation of Labor in the U.S.* (New York: Cambridge University Press, 1982), 135.

10. M. J. Kane, *The Relation of the Foreman to the Personnel Department,* Production Executive Series, no. 40 (New York: American Management Association, 1926), 4.

11. "Hiring and Separation Methods," 1010–1011; W. Ellison Chalmers, "Labor in the Automobile Industry: A Study of Personnel Policies, Worker's Attitudes, and Attempts at Unionism," PhD diss., University of Wisconsin, 1932, 171–72; Chen-Nan Li, "A Summer in the Ford Works," in *Personnel and Labor Relations: An Evolutionary Approach,* ed. Allan Nark and John B. Miller (New York: McGraw-Hill, 1973), 477–78.

12. Blanch Bernstein, "Hiring Policies in the Automobile Industry," Works Project Administration Report, January 1937, in W. Ellison Chalmers Collection, box 1, Archives of Labor History and Urban Affairs, Wayne State University, Detroit, Michigan (hereafter, ALHUA); Jacoby, *Employing Bureaucracy*, 193–95.

13. Clayton W. Fountain, *Union Guy* (New York: Viking, 1948), 41.

14. Author's interviews with Robert Robinson, Ford Motor Company salary specialist, October 9, 1983, Sterling Heights, Michigan; and Robert Durfee, Essex Wire Company foreman, April 30, 1982, Berkeley, California.

15. National Industrial Recovery Administration, "Hearings on Regularizing Employment and Otherwise Improving the Conditions of Labor in the Automobile Industry," Detroit, December 15, 1934 (mimeo), 51, Department of Labor Library.

16. "Reminiscences of W. C. Klann," vol. 2, 153, in Ford Motor Company Archives, Henry Ford Museum, Dearborn, Michigan.

17. Frank Marquart, *An Auto Worker's Journal: The UAW from Crusade to One-Party Union* (State College: Pennsylvania State University Press, 1975), 31.

18. Stewart M. Lowery, *Selection and Development of Foremen and Workers*, Production Series, no. 127 (New York: American Management Association, 1940), 7; author's interview with Bertram Fenwick and Roy Campbell, former Ford foremen, August 4, 1983, Livonia, Michigan; Melvin Dalton, "Conflicts between Staff and Line Management Officers," *American Sociological Review* 15 (June 1950): 344.

19. For a discussion of ethnic cleavages in the factory workforce during the interwar years, see Peter Friedlander, *The Emergence of a UAW Local, 1936–1939: A Study in Class and Culture* (Pittsburgh: University of Pittsburgh Press, 1975), 3–37; Ronald Schatz, *The Electrical Workers: A History of Labor at General Electric and Westinghouse, 1923–60* (Urbana: University of Illinois Press, 1983), 80–99; William Kornblum, *Blue-Collar Community* (Chicago: University of Chicago Press, 1974), 38–67; Meyer, *Five-Dollar Day*, 149–94; Albert Sobey, *Foremen's Clubs*, Production Series, no. 45 (New York: American Management Association, 1926); William Musman, "Facts about Foremen's Clubs," *Management Record* (November 1946): 375.

20. Lynn Dumenil, "Brotherhood and Respectability: Freemasonry and American Culture, 1880–1930," PhD diss., University of California, Berkeley, 1981, 131–37, 269–76; Roy

Rosenzweig, "Boston Masons, 1900–1935: The Lower Middle Class in a Divided Society," *Journal of Voluntary Action Research* 6 (July-October 1977): 119–26.

21. Author's interviews with Fenwick, Campbell, and Robinson; Dumenil, "Brotherhood and Respectability," 379–84; see also Melvin Dalton, "Informal Factors in Career Advancement," *American Journal of Sociology* 56 (March 1951): 407–415. Dalton found Masonic membership a virtual requirement for worker promotion to supervisory ranks in the Chicago-area factory he studied in the mid-1940s. In an overwhelmingly Catholic workforce, he found that 75 percent of the foremen were Masons.

22. Author's interview with Fenwick, Campbell, and Ford R. Bryan, Ford technician, May 27, 1983, Dearborn, Michigan.

23. Dalton, "Conflicts between Staff and Line," 345, 348; author's interview with Theodore Bonaventura, former Ford foreman, February 12, 1984, Washington, DC.

24. L. A. Sylvester, *The Foreman as Manager*, Production Executives Series, no. 38 (New York: American Management Association, 1926), 10–11.

25. F. J. Roethlisberger, "The Foreman: Master and Victim of Double Talk," *Harvard Business Review* 23 (1945): 283.

26. Stanley B. Mathewson, *Restriction of Output among Unorganized Workers* (New York: Viking Press, 1931), 45.

27. Donald Roy, "Efficiency and the Fix: Informal Intergroup Relations in a Piecework Machine Shop," *American Journal of Sociology* 60 (November 1954): 261.

28. Walker, *Foreman on the Assembly Line*, 17. In the course of their famous Hawthorne observations, the Harvard University team headed by Elton Mayo also found this perspective common among first-line supervisors whose work put them in intimate contact with the employees they supervised. See F. J. Roethlisberger and William Dickson, *Management and the Worker* (Cambridge, MA: Harvard University Press, 1939), 453–67.

29. Chalmers, "Labor in the Automobile Industry," 159–60; see also Chen-Nan Li, "Summer in the Ford Works," 484.

30. Walker, *Foreman on the Assembly Line*, 47.

31. UAW-CIO, *How to Win for the Union: A Discussion for UAW Stewards and Committeemen* (Detroit: UAW, 1941), 8–9.

32. Marquart, *Auto Worker's Journal*, 78.

33. Don Lescohier, "The Foreman and the Union," *Personnel* 15 (August 1938): 18–21.

34. Testimony of Walter Nelson in *Murray Corporation v. Local 34 Foreman's Association of America*, November 4, 1943, 27, in Case 111-2882-D, National War Labor Board Collection, RG 202, National Archives, Suitland, Maryland.

35. Interviews with Durfree, Robinson, and Shelton Tappes, Rouge committeeman, October 7, 1982, Detroit, Michigan.

36. Harry Shulman, "Elimination of Semi-Supervisory Job (Yardmaster)," Opinion A-220, April 8, 1946, in *UAW-Ford Arbitration Awards* (Detroit: UAW, 1947).

37. Ford Rouge Plant Factory Counts, July 7,1935, October 29,1946, in box 196, accession 157, Henry Ford Museum; author's interview with Robinson.

38. U.S. Bureau of the Census, Historical Statistics of the United States, *Colonial Times to 1970*, part 1 (Washington, DC: U.S. Government Printing Office, 1975), 137, 138, 142.

39. Some observers have argued that the increasing complexity of production technology has itself been responsible for a rise in supervisory overhead, but as David Noble has shown, the character of workplace machinery cannot be divorced from the system of factory authority. See David Noble, *Forces of Production* (New York: Knopf, 1984), 265–323; and William A. Faunce, "Automation in the Automobile Industry: Some Consequences for

In-Plant Social Structure," *American Sociological Review* 67 (October 1959): 401–407. Faunce found a sharp increase in the foreman-to-worker ratio after the introduction of motor block transfer lines; he ascribed that not so much to the increasing complexity of the machinery but more to the need for continuous production and greater collective work discipline.

40. Ira B. Cross, "When Foremen Joined the CIO," *Personnel Journal* 18 (February 1940): 274–78; "New Allies in Guise of Foremen Keep Rallying to CIO Banner," *Kelsey-Hayes Picket*, June 6, 1939, in box 10, Joe Brown Collection, ALHUA.

41. Cross, "When Foremen Joined the CIO," 279.

42. Clarence Bolds, "Foremen Win Security, Labor Gains Ally in New CIO Union," *Michigan CIO News*, September 4, 1939.

43. Steve Jefferys, *Management and Managed: Fifty Years of Crisis at Chrysler* (Cambridge, UK: Cambridge University Press, 1986), 91–103; "Union Striking, Chrysler Says," *Detroit Free Press*, October 9, 1939, in vol. 17, Joe Brown Scrapbooks, ALHUA.

44. "Chrysler Slowdown," *Detroit Free Press*, October 11, 1939, in vol. 17, Joe Brown Scrapbooks, ALHUA.

45. "Weckler and Thomas Hurl Strike Charges," *Detroit News*, October 26, 1939; "Chrysler Talks Hit New Snag," *Detroit News*, November 22, 1939; "New Issues Debated in Auto Talks," *Detroit News*, November 23, 1939, all in vol. 17, Joe Brown Scrapbooks, ALHUA.

46. "Wait Ruling on Foremen," *Detroit News*, December 9, 1939, in vol. 17, Joe Brown Scrapbooks, ALHUA; Cross, "When Foremen Joined the CIO," 280–82.

47. T. Carl Cabe, "Foremen's Unions: A New Development in Industrial Relations," *University of Illinois Bulletin* 44 (March 1947): 20–28.

48. U.S. House of Representatives, Committee on Military Affairs, Part 68, *Full Utilization of Manpower*, 78th Congress, 1st Sess., 375–78; Desoto Wyoming Plant, "Foremen on Roll, December 31, 1940 through May 31, 1944," in File 111-8243-D, War Labor Board Collection, RG 202, National Archives.

49. Ernest Dale, "The Development of Foremen in Management," *AMA Research Report* 7 (1945): 9–59; Herbert R. Northrup, "The Foreman's Association of America," *Harvard Business Review* 23 (1945): 187–91; Packard supervisor quoted in U.S. Senate, Special Committee to Investigate the National Defense Program, part 28, *Manpower Problems in Detroit*, 79th Congress, 1st Sess., 13730.

50. Author's phone interview with Fred Temple, February 12, 1985; Fenwick and Campbell interview.

51. George Heliker, "Ford Labor Relations," 323, unpublished manuscript in Frank Hill Papers, Henry Ford Museum.

52. Charles P. Larrowe, "A Meteor on the Industrial Relations Horizon," *Labor History* 2 (Fall 1961): 259–87; author's interviews with Bonaventura, Fenwick; testimony of W. Allen Nelson, *Full Utilization of Manpower*, 496.

53. Robert Keys, "Union Membership and Collective Bargaining by Foremen," *Mechanical Engineering* 66 (April 1944): 251–52; Philomena Marquart, "Foreman's Association of America," *Monthly Labor Review* 62 (February 1946): 241–44.

54. Testimony of Carl Brown, U.S. House of Representatives, Committee on Education and Labor, *National Labor Relations Act of 1949*, 81st Congress, 1st Sess., March 21, 1949, 1232–33.

55. Keys, "Union Membership and Collective Bargaining," 251; Larrowe, "Meteor on the Industrial Relations Horizon," 270–85.

56. "Foremen Warm Up to Union," *Business Week*, November 17, 1942, 108; "Foremen's Cases," *War Labor Board Reports* 26 (July 23, 1945): 657–60.

57. "The Foreman Abdicates," *Fortune* 32 (September 1945): 38; Carl Brown interview with Howell Harris, Detroit, November 13, 1974, ALHUA; author's phone interview with Raymond Erickson, March 13, 1985; author's interview with Fenwick; trial examiner's transcript, *Packard v. FAA*, December 18, 1944, 36, 423, box 8314, RG 25, National Archives; National War Labor Board Panel Hearings, Chrysler Corporation (Case 111-4747-D), June 14, 1944, 35, RG 202, National Archives.

58. Author's interviews with Temple, Fenwick, and Bonaventura; Testimony of Robert Keys, U.S. House of Representatives, Committee on Education and Labor, 80th Congress, 1st Sess., *Hearings on Bills to Amend and Repeal the NLRA*, vol. 2, February 1947, 868.

59. As quoted in *Hearings on Bills to Amend and Repeal the NLRA*, 883.

60. National War Labor Board Panel Hearings, Packard Motor Company (Case 111-5436-D), June 14, 1944, 157, RG 202.

61. Robert Keys, "Foremen Have Organized," radio broadcast of March 16, 1944 (printed), FAA pamphlet in Sumner Slichter Papers, Baker Library, Harvard Business School.

62. "Membership Director's Column," *Supervisor* 2 (June 1944): 3.

63. Testimony of John Bugas, U.S. House, Committee on Education and Labor, 83rd Congress, 1st Sess., *Hearings on Matters Relating to Labor Management Relations Act of 1947*, part 7, April 16, 1953, 2492–96; "Foremen Challenge Ford II 'Human Relations' and Win," *Wage Earner*, October 11, 1946.

64. Author's interview with Bonaventura; Bugas testimony, *Hearings on Matters*, 2493.

65. U.S. House of Representatives, Committee on Education and Labor, 80th Congress, 1st Sess., *Hearings on Bills to Amend and Repeal the NLRA*, vol. 2, March 7, 1947, 2711.

66. Ibid., 2712–14. Similarly, in shipyards and in many steel mills, foremen and sub-foremen simply affiliated directly with the CIO unions in those industries. In the coal fields, an independent organization of mine foremen joined District 50 of the United Mine Workers of America. The International Association of Machinists organized several foremen's lodges, sometimes in CIO-represented factories but more often in facilities where the IAM had already organized the production worker rank and file.

67. "Summary of FAA Strike," *Supervisor* 2 (June 1944): 10–11; "Foremen's Cases," *War Labor Board Reports* 26 (July 23, 1945): 661.

68. "Union Wins More Foremen," *Business Week*, May 18, 1946, 95.

69. Virginia A. Seitz, "Legal, Legislative, and Managerial Responses to the Organization of Supervisory Employees in the 1940s," *American Journal of Legal History* 28 (January 1984): 218–35; Larrowe, "Meteor on the Industrial Relations Horizon," 285–87. General Motors succeeded in resisting large-scale foreman organization: first, the corporation had reformed its supervisory program and raised foreman pay in prewar years; and second, UAW shop floor organization at GM was somewhat less aggressive than at Ford, Chrysler, and the auto independents.

70. Howell John Harris, *The Right to Manage: Industrial Relations Policies of American Business in the 1940s* (Madison: University of Wisconsin Press, 1982), 84–87, 95–104.

71. William T. Gossett, Ford Motor Company counsel, as quoted in Harris, *Right to Manage*, 85.

72. Testimony of Edward Butler, *Full Utilization of Manpower*, 91; "Company's Comments on Panel Report," 33, in *Hudson Motor Company v. FAA*, NWLU Case No. 111-85-14-D, RG 202, National Archives.

73. Testimony of C. C. Coulton, *Full Utilization of Manpower*, 110.

74. Testimony of Walter McNally, Murray Corporation, *Hearings on Bills to Amend and Repeal the NLRA*, 717.

75. "The Foreman Abdicates," *Fortune* 32 (September 1945): 150.

76. Ibid., 150. See also Jürgen Kocka, *White-Collar Workers in America, 1890–1940: A Social-Political History in International Perspective* (Beverly Hills: Sage, 1980), 200–50. Mark McColloch, "White Collar: Electrical Machinery, Banking and Public Welfare Workers, 1940–1970," PhD diss., University of Pittsburgh, 1975; C. D. Snyder, *White-Collar Workers and the UAW* (Urbana: University of Illinois Press, 1973).

77. "Ford Gives 15% Raise to Foremen," *Supervisor* 4 (February 1946): 1; author interview with Bonaventura.

78. "Major Issues in Foremen's Strike at Fords Are Listed," *Supervisor* 5 (May 1947): 1; David Levinson, "Wartime Unionization of Foremen," PhD diss., University of Wisconsin, 1949, 298–302.

79. Levinson, "Wartime Unionization of Foremen," 303–307; author interviews with Fenwick, Campbell, Bonaventura. On the grounds that they had engaged in strike violence, Ford fired thirty-two FAA activists. Most were blacklisted throughout the industry, and many never worked as foremen again.

80. Robert Keys to Walter Reuther, June 17, 24, 1947, in box 96, Walter P. Reuther Collection, ALHUA; Special Session, UAW International Executive Board, July 1, 1947, in box 1, International Executive Board Collection, ALHUA; Seitz, "Legal, Legislative, and Managerial Responses," 239–41. The same trade-off took place in the coal industry, where John L. Lewis abandoned any effort to organize mine supervisors in return for industry contributions to a health and welfare fund. In the UAW the situation proved more complicated because a referendum of Ford workers rejected the 1947 pension plan, but it was successfully renegotiated in 1949. For more on UAW bargaining strategy, see Nelson Lichtenstein, "UAW Bargaining Strategy and Shop-Floor Conflict: 1946–1970," *Industrial Relations* 24 (Fall 1985): 360–81.

81. Larrowe, "Meteor on the Industrial Relations Horizon," 289–92; Levinson, "Wartime Unionization of Foremen," 308–27.

82. Jefferys, *Management and Managed*, 127–45; author's interview with Roger Erickson, Chrysler worker, May 13, 1985, Dearborn. Chrysler locals demanded the right to "discipline" authoritarian foremen when, during slack production, they returned to rank-and-file status. See "Foreman Tussle," *Business Week*, May 22, 1954, 151.

83. Author's phone interviews with Gary Bonaventura, former Ford foreman, January 23, 1985, and Wendy Thompson, GM committeewoman, May 31, 1985; Kenneth Hopper, "The Growing Use of College Graduates as Foremen," *Management of Personnel Quarterly* 6 (Summer 1967): 2–12.

84. For a history of black power politics in the workplace, see Don Georgakas and Marvin Surkin, *Detroit: I Do Mind Dying* (New York: St. Martin's, 1975); James Geschwender, *Race and Worker Insurgency; The League of Revolutionary Black Workers* (New York: Cambridge University Press, 1977); and Heather Thompson, *Whose Detroit? Politics, Labor, and Race in a Modern American City* (Ithaca, NY: Cornell University Press, 2004).

85. John A. Patton, "The Foreman: Most Mis-Used, Accused, and Abused Man in Industry," speech delivered before National Machine Tool Builders' Association, October 11, 1973, in "Foremen," vertical file, ALHUA. See also, "As a Ford Foreman, Ed Hendrix Finds He Is Man in the Middle," *Wall Street Journal*, August 9,1973; and Daniel Cook, "Foreman: Where Theory Collides with Reality," *Industry Week*, April 6, 1981, 74–80.

86. Leonard A. Schlesinger and Janice A. Klein, "The First-Line Supervisor: Past, Present, and Future," working paper, *Harvard Business School*, April 1983, 29.

Chapter 6. From Corporatism to Collective Bargaining

This essay was first published in Steve Fraser and Gary Gerstle, *The Rise and Fall of the New Deal Order, 1930–1980* (Princeton, NJ: Princeton University Press, 1989), 122–52.

1. Although not uncritical of the New Deal labor relations system, the most comprehensive example of pluralist scholarship remains Derek C. Bok and John T. Dunlop, *Labor and the American Community* (New York: Simon and Schuster, 1970), 207–28. More critical assessments of the postwar "settlement" include Michael Piore, "Can the American Labor Movement Survive Re-Gomperization?" *Proceedings, Industrial Relations Research Association Thirty-Fifth Annual Meeting*, 1982, 30–39; Samuel Bowles, David M. Gordon, and Thomas E. Weisskopf, *Beyond the Waste Land: A Democratic Alternative to Economic Decline* (Garden City, NY: Anchor Press/Doubleday, 1983), 70–75; Robert Kuttner, *The Economic Illusion: False Choices between Prosperity and Social Justice* (Boston: Houghton Mifflin, 1984), 26–49, 136–86; Mike Davis, *Prisoners of the American Dream* (London: Verso, 1986), 102–27; and David Brody's influential synthesis, *Workers in Industrial America: Essays on the Twentieth-Century Struggle* (New York: Oxford University Press, 1980), 173–257.

2. Leo Troy, "The Rise and Fall of American Trade Unions: The Labor Movement from FDR to RR," in *Unions in Transition*, ed. Seymour Martin Lipset (San Francisco, 1986), 75–89.

3. *Proceedings of the Seventh Constitutional Convention of the CIO*, Chicago, November 20–24, 1944, 313; Sumner Slichter, *The Challenge of Industrial Relations* (Ithaca, NY: Cornell University Press, 1947), 4.

4. For a discussion of the war years, see Nelson Lichtenstein, *Labor's War at Home: The CIO in World War II* (New York: Cambridge University Press, 1982); and George Lipsitz, *Class and Culture in Cold War America: "A Rainbow at Midnight"* (South Hadley, MA: J. F. Bergin, 1982), 37–86.

5. For contrasting discussions of the way in which state functions accommodated and influenced the new labor movement, see Theda Skocpol, "Political Response to Capitalist Crisis: Neo-Marxist Theories of the State and the Case of the New Deal," *Politics and Society* 10 (1980): 155–201; and Christopher Tomlins, *The State and the Unions: Labor Relations, Law, and the Organized Labor Movement in America, 1880–1960* (New York: Cambridge University Press, 1985), 197–328.

6. Of course, the term "corporatism" would not have been used in the 1940s to describe these structural arrangements because of corporatism's close identification with Fascist ideology. But on both sides of the Atlantic scholars have noted the presence of a corporatist strain within the body politic of liberal capitalist society, especially in northern Europe, where once-stable capital-labor accords have begun to crumble. See especially the work of Philippe Schmitter, "Still the Century of Corporatism?" in *Trends toward Corporatist Intermediation*, ed. Philippe Schmitter and Gerhard Lehmbruch (Beverly Hills: Sage, 1982); Wyn Grant, ed., *The Political Economy of Corporatism* (New York: Cambridge University Press, 1983); Leo Panitch, *Working-Class Politics in Crisis: Essays on Labor and the State* (London: Verso, 1986), 132–86; and Charles S. Maier, *Recasting Bourgeois Europe: Stabilization in France, Germany, and Italy in the Decade after World War I* (Princeton, NJ: Princeton University Press, 1975). For the United States, see the pioneering work of Ellis Hawley, *The New Deal and the Problem of Monopoly: A Study in Economic Ambivalence* (Princeton, NJ: Princeton University Press, 1966), as well as the comparative work of

Margaret Weir and Theda Skocpol, "State Structures and the Possibilities for a 'Keynesian' Response to the Great Depression in Sweden, Britain, and the United States," in *Bringing the State Back In,* ed. Peter B. Evans et al. (New York: Norton, 1984), 132–49.

7. U.S. Department of Labor, *Termination Report of the National War Labor Board* (Washington, DC: U.S. Government Printing Office, 1947), 150–55, 211–91, 338–402; Paul Sultan, *Labor Economics* (New York: Henry Holt, 1957), 71.

8. As quoted in Craufurd Goodwin, *Exhortation and Controls: The Search for a Wage Price Policy, 1945–1971* (Washington, DC: Brookings Institution, 1975), 13.

9. Philip Murray, "Industry Councils: The CIO Prosperity Program," October 22, 1946, in box A4, Murray Papers, Catholic University of America. See also Merton W. Ertell, "The CIO Industry Council Plan: Its Background and Implications," PhD diss., University of Chicago, 1955.

10. David Brody, "The New Deal in World War II," in *The New Deal: The National Level,* ed. John Braeman et al. (Columbus: Ohio State University Press, 1975), 281–86.

11. George R. Clark, "Strange Story of the Reuther Plan," *Harper's* 184 (1942): 649.

12. Alonzo Hamby, *Beyond the New Deal: Harry S. Truman and American Liberalism* (New York: Columbia University Press, 1973), 33–38; Norman D. Markowitz, *The Rise and Fall of the People's Century: Henry A. Wallace and American Liberalism, 1941–1948* (New York: Free Press, 1973), 124–54; Joseph Gaer, *The First Round: The Story of the CIO Political Action Committee* (New York: Duell, Sloan, and Pearce, 1944), 187–221.

13. *Proceedings of the Tenth Constitutional Convention of the CIO,* Portland, Oregon, November 22–26, 1948, 270.

14. Seymour E. Harris, ed., *Saving American Capitalism: A Liberal Economic Program* (New York: Knopf, 1948), 4; for an extended discussion of the shift in liberal thinking, see Alan Brinkley, "The New Deal and the Idea of the State," in *Rise and Fall of the New Deal Order, 1930–1980,* ed. Steve Fraser and Gary Gerstle (Princeton, NJ: Princeton University Press, 1989), 85–121.

15. Byrd L. Jones, "The Role of Keynesians in Wartime Policy and Postwar Planning, 1940–1946," *American Economic Review* 62 (1972): 125–33; "Washington Bureau of UAW to Fight on National Front," *United Automobile Worker,* March 1, 1943; John Moutoux, "Reconversion and Pricing Policies Assailed by CIO Groups as Unjust," *PM,* May 13, 1945; Joel Seidman, *American Labor from Defense to Reconversion* (Chicago: University of Chicago Press, 1953), 244–47.

16. Victor Reuther, *The Brothers Reuther and the Story of the UAW* (Boston: Houghton Mifflin, 1976), 247–48; Walter Reuther, "The Challenge of Peace," box 1, UAW Ford Department Collection, Archives of Labor History and Urban Affairs, Wayne State University (hereafter, ALHUA); *Proceedings of the Seventh Constitutional Convention of the CIO,* Chicago, November 20–24, 1944, 39.

17. *New York Times,* March 29, 1945; *CIO News,* April 1, 1945.

18. Howell Harris, *The Right to Manage: Industrial Relations Policies of American Business in the 1940s* (Madison: University of Wisconsin Press, 1982), 110; on Henry Kaiser, see Eliott Janeway, *The Struggle for Survival* (New Haven, CT: Yale University Press, 1950), 249–53; and Janeway, "Adventures of Henry and Joe in Autoland," *Fortune* 38 (1946): 96–103.

19. Barton Bernstein, "The Truman Administration and Its Reconversion Wage Policy," *Labor History* 4 (1965): 216–25.

20. Robert Carson, *The Democratic Party and the Politics of Sectionalism, 1941–1948* (Baton Rouge: Louisiana State University Press, 1974), 94–130.

21. Alan Wolfe, *America's Impasse: The Rise and Fall of the Politics of Growth* (Boston: South End Press, 1981), 18–21; Hamby, *Beyond the New Deal*, 53–85.

22. Bert Cochran, *Harry S. Truman and the Crisis Presidency* (New York: Funk and Wagnalls, 1973), 208.

23. Harris, *Right to Manage*, 111–18, 129–58; Robert M. C. Littler, "Managers Must Manage," *Harvard Business Review* 24 (1946): 366–76. See also David Brody, "The Uses of Power I: Industrial Battleground," in his *Workers in Industrial America*, 173–214; and Ron Schatz, *The Electrical Workers: A History of Labor at General Electric and Westinghouse, 1923–60* (Urbana: University of Illinois Press, 1983), 167–71.

24. U.S. Department of Labor, *The President's National Labor-Management Conference*, Bulletin 77 (Washington, DC: U.S. Government Printing Office, 1945), 12–24; *New York Times*, November 9, 1945; *CIO News*, November 26, 1945. For a larger analysis of the postwar corporate offensive, see Robert Griffith, "Forging America's Postwar Order: Politics and Political Economy in the Age of Truman," paper presented at the Harry S. Truman Centennial, Woodrow Wilson International Center for Scholars, September 1984.

25. U.S. Department of Labor, *Labor-Management Conference*, 18–19; Christopher L. Tomlins, "AFL Unions in the 1930s: Their Performance in Historical Perspective," *Journal of American History* 65 (March 1979): 1021–1042.

26. As quoted in Melvyn Dubofsky and Warren Van Tine, *John L. Lewis: A Biography* (New York: Quadrangle, 1978), 456–57.

27. Walter Reuther, "Our Fear of Abundance," in Henry Christman, ed., *Walter Reuther: Selected Papers* (New York: Macmillan, 1961), 13–21; Barton Bernstein, "Walter Reuther and the General Motors Strike of 1945–46," *Michigan History* 49 (September 1965): 260–77; Irving Howe and B. J. Widick, *The UAW and Walter Reuther* (New York: Random House, 1949), 97–101; Donald Montgomery, "The Product Standard in OPA Price Ceilings," January 16, 1945, and Montgomery to Philip Murray, March 6, 1945, both in UAW-Montgomery Collection, box 10, ALHUA.

28. "Report of the National Citizens Committee, December 1945," in file UAW-CIO, 1945, box 29, Paul Sifton Papers, Library of Congress; and "National Committee to Aid Families of General Motors Strikers," in file Labor Union Contributions, box A336, NAACP Papers, Library of Congress.

29. Barton Bernstein, "The Truman Administration and Its Reconversion Wage Policy," *Labor History* 6 (Fall 1965): 214–31. For a good discussion of the changing character of the liberal economic agenda, see Wolfe, *America's Impasse*, 13–79; and Brinkley, "New Deal and the Idea of the State."

30. Seidman, *American Labor from Defense to Reconversion*, 233–44.

31. James A. Gross, *The Reshaping of the National Labor Relations Board: National Labor Policy in Transition, 1937–1947* (Albany: State University of New York Press, 1981). See also Harris, *Right to Manage*, 121–25; and R. Alton Lee, *Truman and Taft-Hartley: A Question of Mandate* (Lexington: University of Kentucky Press, 1966), 236.

32. CIO, *Proceedings of the Ninth Constitutional Convention*, Boston, October 13–17, 1947, 22, 186, 189.

33. CIO, *Proceedings of the Eleventh Constitutional Convention*, Cleveland, October 31-November 4, 1949, 124.

34. Jack Bloom, *Class, Race, and the Civil Rights Movement* (Bloomington: Indiana University Press, 1987), 59–70; August Meier and Elliott Rudwick, *Black Detroit and the Rise of the UAW* (New York: Oxford University Press, 1979); Herbert Garfinkel, *When*

Negroes March: The March on Washington Movement in the Organizational Politics of FEPC (Glencoe, IL: Free Press, 1959); Michael Honey, "Labor, the Left, and Civil Rights in the South: Memphis, Tennessee, during the CIO Era, 1937–1955," in *Anti-Communism, the Politics of Manipulation,* ed. Gerald Erickson and Judith Joel (Minneapolis: University of Minnesota Press, 1987). Judith Stein offers a more sympathetic analysis of CIO racial politics in her *Running Steel, Running America: Race, Economic Policy, and the Decline of Liberalism* (Chapel Hill: University of North Carolina Press, 1998), 15–18, 41–65. For a contrary view that emphasizes a continuing pattern of CIO racial discrimination, see Robert Norrell, "Caste in Steel: Jim Crow Careers in Birmingham, Alabama," *Journal of American History* 73 (December 1986): 669–701.

35. Harold Preece, "The South Stirs," *Crisis* 48 (October 1941): 318.

36. "Murray Says Labor Should Be in Politics," *New York Times*, April 21, 1946; F. Ray Marshall, *Labor in the South* (Cambridge, MA: Harvard University Press, 1967), 225–27; Garson, *Democratic Party*, 1–54.

37. James Foster, *The Union Politic: The CIO Political Action Committee* (Columbia: University of Missouri Press, 1975), 28–29; Everett Carll Ladd Jr., *Negro Political Leadership in the South* (Ithaca, NY: Cornell University Press, 1966), 58–61; Winston-Salem Membership Report, July 31, 1946, box C141, file North Carolina State Conference, in NAACP Papers, Library of Congress.

38. "CIO Will Seek End of Poll Tax," *New York Times*, April 11, 1946, 30; "Unionized South Will Oust Reaction, Murray Declares," *Wage Earner*, April 12, 1946, 3; *Proceedings of 1946 Convention of the CIO*, November 18–22, 1946, 194.

39. Marshall, *Labor in the South*, 229–66, 276; Michael Honey, "Labor and Civil Rights in the Postwar South: The CIO's Operation Dixie," paper delivered at the Southern Labor Studies Conference, Atlanta, September 1982; see also Barbara Griffith, *The Crisis of American Labor: Operation Dixie and the Defeat of the CIO* (Philadelphia: Temple University Press, 1988), 22–45, 161–76.

40. Gavin Wright, *Old South, New South: Revolutions in the Southern Economy since the Civil War* (New York: Basic Books, 1986), 226–69; Weir and Skocpol, "State Structures," 143–45.

41. Quotation taken from Joseph Huthmacher, ed., *The Truman Years* (Hinsdale, IL: Franklin Watts, 1972), 111.

42. Griffith, *Crisis of American Labor*, 139–60; Anne Braden, "Red, White, and Black in Southern Labor," in *The Cold War against Labor*, ed. Ann Fagan Ginger and David Christiano (Berkeley, CA: Meiklejohn Civil Liberties Institute, 1987), 648–60.

43. Marshall, *Labor in the South*, 258–60; Neil Irvin Painter, *The Narrative of Hosea Hudson* (Cambridge, MA: Harvard University Press, 1979), 329–34). Hudson was a black Communist, purged by the CIO, whose graphic account of Southern labor illustrates both the potential and the tragedy of its history in the 1930s and 1940s. And see Stein, *Running Steel, Running America*, 41–65.

44. Brody, "Uses of Power II: Political Action," in *Workers in Industrial America*, 215–21.

45. Ibid., 222–25; *United Automobile Worker*, October 1, 1948. See also Mike Davis, "The Barren Marriage of American Labour and the Democratic Party," *New Left Review* 124 (1980): 72–74.

46. Hamby, *Beyond the New Deal*, 185–86; Michael Hogan, "American Marshall Planners and the Search for a European Neocapitalism," *American Historical Review* 86 (April 1981): 44–72; and Federico Romero, "Postwar Reconstruction Strategies of American

and Western European Labor," Working Paper no. 85/193, European University Institute, Department of History and Civilization, San Domenico di Fiesole, Italy.

47. Markowitz, *Rise and Fall of the People's Century*, 242–60.

48. CIO Executive Board Minutes, January 22–23, 1948, 220, ALHUA. See also Mary Sperling McAuliffe, *Crisis on the Left: Cold War Politics and American Liberalism, 1947–1954* (Amherst: University of Massachusetts Press, 1978), 3–47.

49. McAuliffe, *Crisis on the Left*, 41–47; Harvey A. Levenstein, *Communism, Anti-Communism, and the CIO* (Westport, CT: Greenwood Press, 1981), 280–97, 330–40; Brody, "Uses of Power," 226–28.

50. Foster, *Union Politic*, 199.

51. Davis, *Prisoners of the American Dream*, 97–100; The decline in working-class voting has been the most visible manifestation of this depoliticization process; see Thomas Edsall, *The New Politics of Inequality* (New York: W. W. Norton, 1984), 141–201; and Thomas Ferguson and Joel Rogers, *Right Turn: The Decline of the Democrats and the Future of American Politics* (New York: Hill and Wang, 1986), 61–67.

52. "Are We Moving toward a Government-Controlled Economy?" May 30, 1946; and UAW Press Release, December 7, 1946, in box 542, Walter Reuther Collection, ALHUA.

53. Lester Velie, *Labor, U.S.A.* (New York: Random House, 1958), 64.

54. Frederick Harbison, "The UAW-General Motors Agreement of 1950," *Journal of Political Economy* 58 (October 1950): 402.

55. Stephen Amberg, *The Union Inspiration in American Politics: The Autoworkers and the Making of a Liberal Industrial Order* (Philadelphia: Temple University Press, 1994).; Kathyanne El-Messidi, "Sure Principles midst Uncertainties: The Story of the 1948 GM-UAW Contract," PhD diss., University of Oklahoma, 1976, 48–107; Daniel Bell, "The Subversion of Collective Bargaining: Labor in the 1950s," *Commentary*, March 1960, 697–713.

56. W. S. Woytinsky, *Labor and Management Look at Collective Bargaining: A Canvas of Leaders' Views* (New York: Twentieth Century Fund, 1949), 105–109; El-Messidi, "Sure Principles," 60; "UAW Press Release on GM Contract," May 25, 1948, box 72, file 5, UAW-Montgomery Collection, ALHUA.

57. Russell Davenport, *U.S.A.: The Permanent Revolution* (New York: Fortune Magazine, 1951), 94; George Ruben, "Major Collective Bargaining Developments: A Quarter Century Review," reprinted from Bureau of Labor Statistics, *Current Wage Developments* (Washington, DC: U.S. Government Printing Office, 1974), 46–47.

58. Monte M. Poem, *Harry S. Truman versus the Medical Lobby* (Columbia: University of Missouri Press, 1979), 29–43; Woytinsky, *Labor and Management*, 128–40.

59. Vivian Vale, *Labour in American Politics* (London: Barnes and Noble, 1971), 97; Harold Wilensky, *The Welfare State and Equality* (Berkeley: University of California Press, 1975), 24–26.

60. Company-financed fringe benefits had been put on the union bargaining agenda during World War II, initially when such schemes were given important tax advantages (1942), and then more forcefully when the War Labor Board exempted the cost of "fringe" benefits from the government's wage ceiling in a politically adroit maneuver designed to derail union efforts to break the Little Steel formula (1944). See Sumner Slichter et al., *The Impact of Collective Bargaining on Management* (Washington, DC: Brookings Institution, 1960), 372–76; Donna Allen, *Fringe Benefits: Wages or Social Obligation?* (Ithaca, NY: Cornell University Press, 1964), 99–152; and Beth Stevens, "Blurring the Boundaries: How the Federal Government Has Influenced Welfare Benefits in the Private Sector," in

The Politics of Social Policy in the United States, ed. Margaret Weir, Ann Shola Orloff, and Theda Skocpol (Princeton, NJ: Princeton University Press, 1988), 123–48.

61. Dubofsky and Van Tine, *John L. Lewis,* 454–72; Edward Berkowitz and Kim Mc-Quaid, *Creating the Welfare State: A Political Economy of Twentieth-Century Reform* (New York: New York University Press, 1980), 137. The draft and the lure of higher-paying urban jobs also confronted Lewis with a dramatically older workforce in the coal fields. Average age rose from thirty-two to forty-five during the war, with more than eleven thousand men age sixty-five or over still working in 1944.

62. *Proceedings of the Eighth Constitutional Convention of the CIO,* Atlantic City, NJ, November 18–22, 1946, 186–87.

63. Peter Drucker, *The Unseen Revolution: How Pension Fund Socialism Came to America* (New York: W. W. Norton, 1976), 5–10; Ruth Glazer, "Welfare Discussion Down-to-Earth," *Labor and the Nation* (Spring 1950): 30–36; author's interview with Nelson Crunkshank, former AFL director of social insurance activities, July 18, 1984; Martha Derthick, *Policymaking for Social Security* (Washington, DC: Brookings Institution, 1979), 110–31. According to Crunkshank and Derthick, the AFL soon proved a stronger advocate of some social wage expenditures than did the CIO, because its influential craft unions found pension and health insurance systems difficult to establish in multi-employer industries. For a elaboration of many of these themes, with particular emphasis on the role played by private insurance companies, see Jennifer Klein, *For All These Rights: Business, Labor, and the Shaping of America's Public-Private Welfare State* (Princeton, NJ.: Princeton University Press, 2003), 204–257.

64. By the early 1970s private pension plans covered more than 30 million workers and amounted to almost $900 billion. U.S. Department of Commerce, *Statistical Abstract of the U.S.* (Washington, DC: U.S. Government Printing Office, 1975), 286.

65. Harold Levinson, "Pattern Bargaining: A Case Study of the Automobile Workers," *Quarterly Journal of Economics* (Spring 1959): 299.

66. Even at their greatest popularity in the late 1970s, only about 60 percent of all *union* contracts contained a COLA provision. See Louis Uchitelle, "A Labor Fight Looms over the COLA Concession," *New York Times,* June 14, 1987, E5. For a more extensive account of wage differentials within the working class, see Paul Blumberg, *Inequality in an Age of Decline* (New York: Oxford University Press, 1980), 65–107.

67. For additional discussion of these important issues, see Robert Gordon, Richard Edwards, and Michael Reich, *Segmented Work, Divided Workers* (New York: Cambridge University Press, 1982), 165–227; Jill Bernstein, "Employee Benefits in the Welfare State: Great Britain and the United States since World War II," PhD diss., Columbia University, 1980, 579; Hugh Mosley, "Corporate Benefits and the Underdevelopment of the American Welfare State," *Contemporary Crisis* 5 (1981): 139–54; Stevens, "Blurring the Boundaries," 145–48; and Dunlop, *Labor and the American Community,* 208–14.

Chapter 7. Communism On the Shop Floor and Off

This review essay was first published in *New Politics* (Winter 2004).

1. See John Earl Haynes and Harvey Klehr, *In Denial: Historians, Communism, and Espionage* (San Francisco: Encounter Books, 2003); Katherine A. S. Sibley, *Red Spies in America: Stolen Secrets and the Dawn of the Cold War* (Lawrence: University Press of Kansas, 2004); Richard Gid Powers, *Not Without Honor: The History of American*

Anticommunism (New Haven, CT: Yale University Press, 1998); and Sam Tanenhaus, *Whittaker Chambers: A Biography* (New York: Modern Library, 1997).

2. Judith Stepan-Norris and Maurice Zeitlin, *Left Out: Reds and America's Industrial Unions* (New York: Cambridge University Press, 2003).

3. Ibid., 23.

4. The classic text here is Irving Howe and Lewis Coser, *The American Communist Party: A Critical History* (New York: Praeger, 1957), 319–436.

5. Sidney Lens, *Left, Right, and Center: Conflicting Forces in American Labor* (Hinsdale, IL: Henry Regnery, 1949).

6. As quoted in Stepan-Norris and Zeitlin, *Left Out*, 4.

7. Max Kampelman, *The Communist Party vs. the CIO* (New York: Praeger, 1957).

8. Robin D. G. Kelley, *Hammer and Hoe: Alabama Communists during the Great Depression* (Chapel Hill: University of North Carolina Press, 1990), xi.

9. Michael Honey, *Southern Labor and Black Civil Rights: Organizing Memphis Workers* (Urbana: University of Illinois Press, 1993).

10. Ronald Schatz, *The Electrical Workers: A History of Labor at General Electric and Westinghouse, 1923–1960* (Urbana: University of Illinois Press, 1983).

11. Toni Gilpin cited in Stepan-Norris and Zeitlin, *Left Out*, 185.

12. Joshua Freeman, *Working-Class New York: Life and Labor since World War II* (New York: New Press, 2001).

13. Stepan-Norris and Zeitlin, *Left Out*, 57.

14. Ibid., 153.

15. Steve Jefferys, *Management and Managed: Fifty Years of Crisis at Chrysler* (New York: Cambridge University Press, 1986); Nelson Lichtenstein, "Life at the Rouge: A Cycle of Working-Class Militancy, 1940–1969," in *Life and Labor: Dimensions of American Working-Class History*, ed. Charles Stephenson and Robert Asher (Albany: State University of New York Press, 1986), 237–59.

16. As quoted in Nelson Lichtenstein, *State of the Union: A Century of American Labor* (Princeton, NJ: Princeton University Press, 2003), 116–17.

Chapter 8. Opportunities Found and Lost

This essay was first published as Robert Korstad and Nelson Lichtenstein, "Opportunities Found and Lost: Labor, Radicals, and the Early Civil Rights Movement," *Journal of American History* 75 (December 1988): 786–811.

1. Richard M. Dalfiume, "The 'Forgotten Years' of the Negro Revolution," *Journal of American History* 55 (June 1968): 90–106; Steven Lawson, "The Second Front at Home: World War II and Black Americans," paper delivered at the Sixth Soviet-American Historians Colloquium, September 24–26, 1986, Washington, DC (in Nelson Lichtenstein's possession). This view has recently been reinforced by the television documentary "Eyes on the Prize," which begins abruptly in 1954. Juan Williams, *Eyes on the Prize: America's Civil Rights Years, 1954–1965* (New York: Viking, 1986). However, a few sociologists have broken with the orthodox periodization: Aldon Morris, *The Origins of the Civil Rights Movement: Black Communities Organizing for Change* (New York: Free Press, 1984); and Jack Bloom, *Class, Race, and the Civil Rights Movement* (Bloomington: Indiana University Press, 1987).

2. Harold M. Baron and Bennett Hymer, "The Negro in the Chicago Labor Market," in *The Negro in the American Labor Movement*, ed. Julius Jacobson (New York: Doubleday,

1968), 188. See also Gavin Wright, *Old South, New South: Revolutions in the Southern Economy since the Civil War* (New York: Basic Books, 1986), 239–57. For a discussion of black proletarianization, see Joe William Trotter Jr., *Black Milwaukee: The Making of an Industrial Proletariat, 1915–1945* (Urbana: University of Illinois Press, 1985); Steven Lawson, *Black Ballots: Voting Rights in the South, 1944–1969* (New York; Columbia University Press 1976), 134; Henry Lee Moon, *Balance of Power: The Negro Vote* (Garden City, NY: Doubleday, 1949), 146–96; and Dalfiume, "'Forgotten Years,'" 99–100.

3. Dalfiume, "'Forgotten Years,'" 100; Harold Preece, "The South Stirs," *Crisis* 48 (October 1941): 318.

4. James A. Gross, *The Reshaping of the National Labor Relations Board' National Labor Policy in Transition, 1937–1947* (Albany: State University of New York Press, 1981), 5–41; Gary Gerstle, "The Politics of Patriotism: Americanization and the Formation of the CIO," *Dissent* 33 (Winter 1986): 84–92. Racist discrimination in hiring, promotion, and seniority were hardly eliminated by the new CIO unions; see Robert J. Norrell, "Caste in Steel: Jim Crow Careers in Birmingham, Alabama," *Journal of American History* 73 (December 1986): 669–701.

5. Herbert R. Garfinkel, *When Negroes March: The March on Washington Movement in the Organizational Politics of FEPC* (Glencoe, IL: Free Press 1959); *Louis Kesselman, The Social Politics of FEPC: A Study in Reform Pressure Movements* (Chapel Hill: University of North Carolina Press, 1948); William Harris, "Federal Intervention in Union Discrimination: FEPC and West Coast Shipyards during World War II," *Labor History* 22 (Summer 1981): 325–47.

6. Horace Huntley, "Iron Ore Miners and Mine Mill in Alabama: 1933–1952," PhD diss., University of Pittsburgh, 1977; Michael Honey, *Southern Labor and Black Civil Rights: Organizing Memphis Workers* (Urbana: University of Illinois Press, 1993); Nell Irvin Painter, *The Narrative of Hosea Hudson: His Life as a Negro Communist in the South* (Cambridge, MA: Harvard University Press, 1979); Rick Halpern, *Down on the Killing Floor: Black and White Workers in Chicago's Packinghouses, 1904–54* (Urbana: University of Illinois Press, 1997); Dennis C. Dickerson, "Fighting on the Domestic Front: Black Steelworkers during World War II," in *Life and Labor: Dimensions of American Working-Class History*, ed. Charles Stephenson and Robert Asher (Albany: State University of New York, 1986), 224–36; Toni Gilpin, "Left by Themselves: A History of United Farm Equipment and Metal Workers, 1938–1955," PhD diss., Yale University, 1988.

7. Nannie M. Tilley, *The Bright-Tobacco Industry, 1860–1929* (Chapel Hill: University of North Carolina Press,1948); Nannie M. Tilley, *The R. J. Reynolds Tobacco Company* (Chapel Hill: University of North Carolina Press, 1985).

8. Robert Korstad, "Those Who Were Not Afraid: Winston-Salem, 1943," in *Working Lives: The Southern Exposure History of Labor in the South*, ed. Marc Miller (New York: Pantheon, 1980), 184–99; and Robert Korstad, *Civil Rights Unionism: Tobacco Workers and the Struggle for Democracy in the Mid-Twentieth-Century South* (Chapel Hill: University of North Carolina Press, 2003), 142–200.; Tilley, *R. J. Reynolds Tobacco Company*, 373–414.

9. *Winston-Salem Journal*, July 14, 1943, 6, and July 25, 1943, 6; Horace R. Cayton and George S. Mitchell, *Black Workers and the New Unions* (Chapel Hill: University of North Carolina Press, 1939), 372–424.

10. *Winston-Salem Journal*, July 14, 1943, 6; July 16, 1943, 6; July 17, 1943, 6; and July 25, 1943, 6.

11. Robert A. Levett to David C. Shaw, August 22, 1944, in R. J. Reynolds Tobacco Company, Case 5-C-1730 (1945), Formal and Informal Unfair Labor Practices and Representation Cases

Files, 1935–48, National Labor Relations Board, RG 25 (National Archives); *Winston-Salem Journal*, November 17, 1943, 1.

12. "Directive Order, R. J. Reynolds Tobacco Company and the Tobacco Workers Organizing Committee," October 18, 1944, Case No. 111-7701-D, Regional War Labor Board for the Fourth Region, RG 202 (National Archives).

13. "Discussion Outline for Classes in Shop Steward Training," Highlander Folk School, n.d. (in Robert Korstad's possession); Velma Hopkins interview by Robert Korstad, March 5, 1986.

14. Ruby Jones interview by Korstad, April 20, 1979.

15. *Worker's Voice*, August 1944; January 1945, 2; April 1945, 2; Viola Brown interview by Korstad, August 7, 1981 (in Korstad's possession). The United Cannery, Agricultural, Packing and Allied Workers of America (UCAPAWA) changed its name to reflect the increasing number of tobacco locals within it.

16. Junius Scales interview by Korstad, April 28, 1987 (in Korstad's possession); Ann Matthews interview by Korstad, February 1986. See also Junius Irving Scales and Richard Nickson, *Cause at Heart: A Former Communist Remembers* (Atlanta: University of Georgia Press, 1987), 201–219; and Robin D. G. Kelley, *Hammer and Hoe: Alabama Communists during the Great Depression* (Chapel Hill: University of North Carolina Press, 1990), 296–311.

17. Roger Keeran, *The Communist Party and the Auto Workers Unions* (Bloomington: Indiana University Press, 1980), 234; Painter, *Narrative of Hosea Hudson*, 306–312; Nat Ross, "Two Years of the Reconstituted Communist Party in the South," *Political Affairs* 26 (October 1947): 923–35; Wilson Record, *Race and Radicalism: The NAACP and the Communist Party in Conflict* (Ithaca, NY: Cornell University Press, 1964), 84–168; Irving Howe and B. J. Widick, *The UAW and Walter Reuther* (New York: Random House, 1949), 223–25.

18. Saul Wellman interview by Lichtenstein, November 10, 1983 (in Lichtenstein's possession); Mark Naison, *The Communist Party in Harlem* (Urbana: University of Illinois Press, 1984), 23–34.

19. William H. Chafe, *Civilities and Civil Rights: Greensboro, North Carolina, and the Black Struggle for Freedom* (New York: Oxford University Press, 1980), 29–30; Lucille Black to Sarah March, March 28, 1945; Winston-Salem, 1945–55 file, box C140; Gloster Current to C. C. Kellum, November 19, 1947; Memorandum, February 9, 1942; Membership Report, July 31, 1946, North Carolina State Conference file, box C141; all in National Association for the Advancement of Colored People Papers, Manuscripts Division, Library of Congress.

20. *UCAPAWA News*, August 1, 1944, 2, and September 1, 1944, 5; *Worker's Voice*, October 1944, 3, and March 1946, 4. For politics in the pre-union era, see Bertha Hampton Miller, "Blacks in Winston-Salem, North Carolina, 1895–1920: Community Development in an Era of Benevolent Paternalism," PhD diss., Duke University, 1981, 6–74; *Worker's Voice*, October 1944, 3.

21. *Pittsburgh Courier*, June 3, 1944.

22. Board of Aldermen, Winston-Salem, North Carolina, Minutes, vol. 30, 278, and vol. 32, 555; both in City Hall, Winston-Salem, NC.

23. Herbert R. Northrup, *Organized Labor and the Negro* (New York: Harper, 1944), 186–88; August Meier and Elliott Rudwick, *Black Detroit and the Rise of the UAW* (New York: Oxford University Press, 1979), 3–7.

24. Meier and Rudwick, *Black Detroit*, 8–22.

25. Ibid., 39–87.

26. Shelton Tappes interview by Herbert Hill, October 27, 1967, February 10, 1968 (Archives of Labor History and Urban Affairs, Wayne State University, Detroit, Michigan).

27. Robert Robinson interview by Lichtenstein, October 9, 1983; Ed Lock interview by Peter Friedlander, December 1976; Walter Dorach interview by Lichtenstein, October 14, 1982 (all interviews in Lichtenstein's possession); Meier and Rudwick, *Black Detroit*, 106–107.

28. Wellman interview; Paul Boatin interview by Lichtenstein, October 12, 1982 (in Lichtenstein's possession); Keeran, *Communist Party and the Auto Workers Unions*, 33–67; U.S. Congress, House, Committee on Un-American Activities, *Communism in the Detroit Area*, 82 Cong., 2nd sess., March 10–11, 1952, 3036–45 and 3117–35.

29. Meier and Rudwick, *Black Detroit*, 175–206; Alan Clive, *State of War: Michigan in World War II* (Ann Arbor: University of Michigan Press, 1979), 144–51.

30. "20,000 Members in 1943," *Crisis* 50 (May 1943): 140–41; Dominic J. Capeci Jr., *Race Relations in Wartime Detroit: The Sojourner Truth Housing Controversy of 1942* (Philadelphia: Temple University Press, 1984), 75–99, 111–13.

31. "20,000 Members in 1943," 141; "All Out for Big Demonstration against Discrimination," file 1943, box C86, NAACP Papers; Meier and Rudwick, *Black Detroit*, 114–17; Howe and Widick, *UAW and Walter Reuther*, 103.

32. Meier and Rudwick, *Black Detroit*, 136–56.

33. Richard Deverall to Clarence Glick, "UAW-CIO Local 190 Wildcat Strike at Plant of Packard Motor Co.," Richard Deverall Notebooks (Catholic University of America, Washington); "Negro Workers Strike to Protest 'Hate Strike,'" *Michigan Chronicle*, November 18, 1944, Fair Employment Practices vertical file (Archives of Labor History and Urban Affairs); Meier and Rudwick, *Black Detroit*, 162–74.

34. Capeci, *Race Relations in Wartime Detroit*, 78–82, 164–70; Meier and Rudwick, *Black Detroit*, 164.

35. "Addes-Frankensteen to Support Proposal for UAW Board Member," *Michigan Chronicle*, September 25, 1943; "[Reuther] Slaps Addes for Stand on Race Issues," *Michigan Chronicle*, October 2, 1943; "UAW Leaders Assail 1,400 Hate Strikers," *Michigan Chronicle*, April 29, 1944; "Split in Ranks of Officials Aid to Cause," *Michigan Chronicle*, September 16, 1944; "Reuther Urges Support of NAACP Membership Campaign," *Detroit Tribune*, June 1, 1946; all in Fair Employment Practices vertical file, Archives of Labor History and Urban Affairs; George Crockett interview by Hill, March 2, 1968 (Archives of Labor History and Urban Affairs); William Dodds interview by Lichtenstein, June 12, 1987 (in Lichtenstein's possession); Martin Halpern, "The Politics of Auto Union Factionalism: The Michigan CIO in the Cold War Era," *Michigan Historical Review* 13 (Fall 1987): 66–69.

36. Harvard Sitkoff, "Harry Truman and the Election of 1948: The Coming of Age of Civil Rights in American Politics," *Journal of Southern History* 37 (November 1971): 597–616. See also Peter J. Kellogg, "Civil Rights Consciousness in the 1940s," *Historian* 42 (November 1972): 18–41.

37. "Labor Drives South," *Fortune* 34 (October 1946): 237; *Wage Earner*, April 12, 1946, 3; *New York Times*, April 21, 1946, 46; *Final Proceedings of the Eighth Constitutional Convention of the Congress of Industrial Organizations, November 18, 19, 20, 21, 22, 1946, Atlantic City, New Jersey* (Washington, DC, n.d.), 194; Barbara Sue Griffith, *The Crisis of American Labor: Operation Dixie and the Defeat of the CIO* (Philadelphia: Temple University Press, 1988).

38. Paul Sifton to Victor G. Reuther, "Revised Civil Rights Memorandum," June 13, 1958, Civil Rights Act of 1958 file, box 25, Joseph Rauh Collection (Library of Congress).

39. Sumner Rosen, "The CIO Era, 1935–55," in *The Negro in the American Labor Movement*, ed. Julius Jacobson (Garden City, NY: Anchor Books, 1968), 188–208; Herbert Hill, "The Racial Practices of Organized Labor: The Contemporary Record," in Jacobson, *Negro in the American Labor Movement*, 286–357.

40. *Worker's Voice*, January 1947, 2; Tilley, *R. J. Reynolds Tobacco Company*, 485–88; Everett Carll Ladd, *Negro Political Leadership in the South* (Ithaca, NY: Cornell University Press, 1966), 61. See also Howell John Harris, *The Right to Manage: Industrial Relations Policies of American Business in the 1940s* (Madison: University of Wisconsin Press, 1982), 96, 157.

41. *Winston-Salem Journal*, May 19, 1947, 1; Tilley, *R. J. Reynolds Tobacco Company*, 400–401; U.S. Congress, House, Committee on Un-American Activities, *Hearings Regarding Communism in Labor Unions in the United States*, 78 Cong., 1 sess., July 11, 1947, 63–122; *Winston-Salem Journal*, July 12, 1947, 1.

42. Jack Fry interview by Korstad, October 16, 1981 (in Korstad's possession).

43. Harvey A. Levenstein, *Communism, Anticommunism, and the CIO* (Westport, CT: Greenwood Press, 1981), 286–87.

44. *Winston-Salem Journal*, July 15, 1947, 14; Robert Black interview by Korstad, March 4, 1985 (in Korstad's possession).

45. *Winston-Salem Journal*, March 18, 1950, 1; March 22, 1950, 1; March 25, 1950, 1; and April 6, 1950, 1; Tilley, *R. J. Reynolds Tobacco Company*, 404–412.

46. Reginald Johnson to Lester Granger, memorandum, January 28, 1946, Community Relations Project, Winston-Salem, North Carolina, file, box 27, series 6, National Urban League Papers (Library of Congress); *Winston-Salem Journal*, November 16, 1947, sec. 3, p. 1.

47. Ladd, *Negro Political Leadership*, 121–27, 134–35; Black to March, January 25, 1950, 1946–55 file, box C140, NAACP Papers; Tilley, *R. J. Reynolds Tobacco Company*, 410; Aingred Ghislayne Dunston, "The Black Struggle for Equality in Winston-Salem, North Carolina: 1947–1977," PhD diss., Duke University, 1981, 59.

48. Tilley, *R. J. Reynolds Tobacco Company*, 412–14, 454–58, 463–71.

49. Dunston, "Black Struggle for Equality," 61–161.

50. Ibid., 270–71.

51. John Barnard, *Walter Reuther and the Rise of the Auto Workers* (Boston: Little, Brown, 1983), 101–117; Martin Halpern, "Taft-Hartley and the Defeat of the Progressive Alternative in the United Auto Workers," *Labor History* 27 (Spring 1986): 204–26.

52. Crockett interview; Tappes interview; Studs Terkel, *Division Street, America* (New York: Pantheon, 1971), 328–30.

53. Walter Reuther, "The Negro Worker's Future," *Opportunity* 23 (Fall 1945): 203–206; William Oliver to Roy Reuther, "Status of UAW Officers and NAACP Memberships," February 21, 1961, file 24, box 9, UAW Citizenship Department (Archives of Labor History and Urban Affairs); Herbert Hill interview by Lichtenstein, June 20, 1987 (in Lichtenstein's possession).

54. Martin Halpern, "The Disintegration of the Left-Center Coalition in the UAW, 1945–1950," PhD diss., University of Michigan, 1982, 237–40, 273–74, 433–37; Tappes interview.

55. William D. Andrew, "Factionalism and Anti-Communism: Ford Local 600," *Labor History* 20 (Spring 1979): 227–36; Dorach interview. See also Nelson Lichtenstein, "Life

at the Rouge: A Cycle of Workers' Control," in Stephenson and Asher, *Life and Labor*, 237–59.

56. Tappes interview; Oliver to Roy Reuther, "Ford Plant, Indianapolis," December 20, 1957, file 29, box 8, UAW Citizenship Department (Archives of Labor History and Urban Affairs); Oliver to Walter Reuther, "Preliminary Analysis of Allegations Made against UAW by the NAACP Labor Secretary Which Were Unfounded," November 1, 1962, file 10, box 90, Walter Reuther Collection.

57. Dudley W. Buffa, *Union Power and American Democracy: The UAW and the Democratic Party, 1935–72* (Ann Arbor: University of Michigan Press, 1984), 133–73; B. J. Widick, *Detroit: City of Race and Class Violence* (Chicago: Quandrangle Books, 1972), 151–55.

58. *Proceedings, Fourteenth Constitutional Convention, International Union, United Automobile, Aerospace, and Agricultural Implement Workers of America (UAW), March 22–27, 1953, Atlantic City, New Jersey* (n.p., [1953]), 264; Philip Foner, *Organized Labor and the Black Worker* (New York: International, 1981), 295–309.

59. Herbert Hill to Roy Wilkins, December 23, 1949, Hill-1949 file, box C364; "Graphic Representation of Detroit Branch NAACP Campaigns, 1941 to 1948," Detroit file, box C89; "Memorandum for Gloster Current on Rehabilitation of Detroit Branch," April 20, 1950, Detroit file, box C89; all in NAACP Papers; Record, *Race and Radicalism*, 132–231; Lerone Bennett Jr., *Confrontation: Black and White* (Chicago: Johnson Publishing Company, 1965), 213.

60. Widick, *Detroit*, 138–40; "UAW Fair Practices Survey-1963," file 12, box 90, Reuther Collection; Robert Battle to James Brown, "RE: Civil Rights Hearing," December 13, 1960, file 13, box 50, also Reuther Collection.

61. William Gould, *Black Workers in White Unions* (Ithaca, NY: Cornell University Press, 1977), 371–88; Jack Stieber, *Governing the UAW* (New York: Wiley, 1962), 83–88; "UAW Fair Practices Survey-1963."

62. Horace Sheffield, "Bitter Frustration Gave Added Impetus to Trade Union Leadership Council," *Michigan Chronicle*, May 28, 1960, Horace Sheffield vertical file (Archives of Labor History and Urban Affairs); B. J. Widick interview by Lichtenstein, August 6, 1986 (in Lichtenstein's possession).

63. Buffa, *Union Power*, 139–42; Widick, *Black Detroit*, 151–56. The UAW made an all-out, but ultimately unsuccessful, effort to stop George Crockett's reentry into mainstream political life. See Nadine Brown, "Crockett Supporters Charge Union 'Takeover' in First," *Detroit Courier*, October 6, 1966: and Morgan O'Leary, "Hectic '49 Trial Haunts Crockett's Bid for Bench," *Detroit News*, October 7, 1966; both in George Crockett vertical file, Archives of Labor History and Urban Affairs.

64. Nelson Jack Edwards and Willoughby Abner, "How a Negro Won a Top UAW Post," *Detroit Courier*, April 4, 1964, vertical file, Trade Union Leadership Conference (Archives of Labor History and Urban Affairs); "Reuther Outlines UAW Position on Sheffield Assignment," file 9, box 157, Reuther Collection; Hill interview; Widick interview.

65. Foner, *Organized Labor and the Black Worker*, 423.

66. Notes on E. P. Thompson, speech in support of European peace movement, July 8, 1983, Berkeley, California (in Lichtenstein's possession). The notion that protest movements have a limited time frame in which to make their impact felt is also put forward by Frances Fox Piven and Richard A. Cloward, *Poor People's Movements: Why They Succeed, How They Fail* (New York: Pantheon, 1977), 14–34.

67. David Garrow, *Bearing the Cross: Martin Luther King, Jr., and the Southern Christian Leadership Conference* (New York: William Morrow, 1986), 431–624.

Chapter 9. The Lost Promise of the Long Civil Rights Movement

This essay was originally published as "Recasting the Movement and Reframing the Law in Risa Goluboff's *The Lost Promise of Civil Rights*," *Law and Social Inquiry* 35, no. 1 (2010): 243–60.

1. Jacquelyn Hall, "The Long Civil Rights Movement and the Political Uses of the Past," *Journal of American History* 91 (March 2005): 1233–63. In April 2009 Hall and her colleagues convened a major conference at Chapel Hill, "The Long Civil Rights Movement: Histories, Politics, Memories," which confirmed the paradigm.

2. Richard M. Dalfiume, "The 'Forgotten Years' of the Negro Revolution," *Journal of American History* 55 (June 1968): 90–106; Harvard Sitkoff, *A New Deal for Blacks: The Emergence of Civil Rights as a National Issue* (New York: Oxford University Press, 1978).

3. Timothy Tyson, *Radio Free Dixie: Robert F. Williams and the Roots of Black Power* (Chapel Hill: University of North Carolina Press, 2001); Martha Biondi, *To Stand and Fight: The Struggle for Civil Rights in Postwar New York City* (Cambridge, MA: Harvard University Press, 2006); Patricia Sullivan, *Race and Democracy in the New Deal Era* (Chapel Hill: University of North Carolina Press, 1996); Barbara Ransby, *Ella Baker and the Black Freedom Movement: A Radical Democratic Vision* (Chapel Hill: University of North Carolina Press, 2005).

4. Nancy MacLean, *Freedom Is Not Enough: The Opening of the American Workplace* (Cambridge, MA: Harvard University Press, 2006).

5. Charles M. Payne, "'The Whole United States Is Southern!': *Brown v. Board* and the Mystification of Race," *Journal of American History* 91 (June 2004): 83.

6. Ibid.

7. Mary Dudziak, "*Brown* as a Cold War Case," *Journal of American History* 91 (June 2004): 32–42.

8. Ibid.

9. Sundiata Keita Cha-Jua and Clarence Lang, "The 'Long Movement' as Vampire: Temporal and Spatial Fallacies in Recent Black Freedom Studies," *Journal of African American History* 92 (Spring 2007): 265.

10. Eric Arnesen, "Reconsidering the 'Long Civil Rights Movement,'" *Historically Speaking* (April 2009): 32.

11. W.E.B. DuBois, *Black Reconstruction in America, 1860–1880* (New York: New Press, 1935, 1998), 55–84.

12. Sean Wilentz, *Chants Democratic* (New York: Oxford University Press, 1982); Alan Dawley, *Class and Community: The Industrial Revolution in Lynn* (Cambridge, MA: Harvard University Press, 1975); David Montgomery, *The Fall of the House of Labor* (New York: Cambridge University Press, 1988); Herbert Gutman, *Work, Culture, and Society in Industrializing America* (New York: Vintage, 1977).

13. David Roediger, *The Wages of Whiteness* (New York: Verso, 1991).

14. Michelle Brattain, *The Politics of Whiteness: Race, Workers, and Culture in the Modern South* (Princeton, NJ: Princeton University Press, 2001); Bruce Nelson, *Divided We Stand: American Workers and the Struggle for Black Equality* (Princeton, NJ: Princeton University Press, 2001); Shelley Sallee, *The Whiteness of Child Labor Reform in the New South* (Athens: University of Georgia Press, 2004).

15. Robert Korstad and Nelson Lichtenstein, "Opportunities Found and Lost: Labor, Radicals, and the Early Civil Rights Movement," *Journal of American History* 75 (December 1988): 811.

16. Risa L. Goluboff, *The Lost Promise of Civil Rights* (Cambridge, MA: Harvard University Press, 2007).

17. Ibid., 45.

18. Ibid., 50.

19. Ibid., 5.

20. Ibid., 85.

21. Jerold S. Auerbach, *Labor and Liberty: The La Follette Committee and the New Deal* (Indianapolis: Bobbs-Merrill, 1966), 1.

22. Ibid., 86.

23. Gary Gerstle, "The Protean Character of American Liberalism," *American Historical Review* 99, no. 4 (1994): 1070.

24. Daniel Geary, " Carey McWilliams and Antifascism, 1934–1943," *Journal of American History* 90 (December 2003): 912–34.

25. Goluboff, *Lost Promise*, 128.

26. Ibid., 146.

27. James Gray Pope, "The Thirteenth Amendment versus the Commerce Clause: Labor and the Shaping of American Constitutional Law, 1921–1957," *Columbia Law Review* 102 (January 2002): 30–38.

28. Ibid.

29. Ibid., 48.

30. Ibid., 49.

31. Ibid.

32. Nelson Lichtenstein, "Taft-Hartley: A Slave Labor Law?" *Catholic University Law Review* 47, no. 3 (1998): 766.

33. George Meany, "The Taft-Hartley Law: A Slave Labor Measure," *Vital Speeches of the Day* 14 (December 1, 1947): 119.

34. Lichtenstein, "Taft-Hartley," 767.

35. Goluboff, *Lost Promise*, 186.

36. Ibid., 192.

37. Ibid., 187.

38. Ibid., 209.

39. Ibid.

40. Kenneth Clark, *Prejudice and Your Child* (Boston: Beacon Press, 1955).

41. Ellen Herman, *The Romance of American Psychology: Political Culture in the Age of Experts* (Berkeley: University of California Press, 1995), 174–207; Daryl Michael Scott, *Contempt and Pity: Social Policy and the Image of the Damaged Black Psyche, 1880–1996* (Chapel Hill: University of North Carolina Press, 1997), 71–91; Goluboff, *Lost Promise*, 243.

42. Goluboff, *Lost Promise,* 261.

43. Lani Guinier, "From Racial Liberalism to Racial Literacy: *Brown v. Board of Education* and the Interest-Divergence Dilemma," *Journal of American History* 91 (June 2004): 95.

44. Goluboff, *Lost Promise*, 237.

45. Sophia Lee, "Forum: 'Poking Holes in Balloons': New Approaches to Cold War Civil Rights: Hotspots in a Cold War: The NAACP's Postwar Workplace Contractualism, 1948–1964," *University of Illinois Law and History Review* 26 (Summer 2008): 331.

46. Ibid., 333.

47. Laura Kalman, introduction to Lee, "Forum," 319; Lee, "Forum," 375–77.

48. Nelson Lichtenstein, "Herbert Hill in History and Contention," *LABOR: Studies in Working-Class History of the Americas* 3, no. 2 (2006): 25–31; Goluboff, *Lost Promise*, 260.

49. Nelson Lichtenstein, *The Retail Revolution: How Wal-Mart Created a Brave New World of Business* (New York: Henry Holt, 2009), 118–48.

Chapter 10. A New Era of Global Human Rights

This essay was first delivered as a talk at the Institute for Human Sciences, Vienna, June 2002.

1. International Labour Organization, *World Labour Report, 1997–98* (Geneva: International Labour Office, 1997), 4–8, http://www.ilo.org.

2. K. D. Ewing, "Human Rights and Industrial Relations: Possibilities and Pitfalls," *British Journal of Industrial Relations* 40, no. 1 (2002): 139.

3. James A. Paul, "NGOs and Global Policy-Making," June 2000, *Global Policy Forum*, http:/www.globalpolicy.org/ngos/analysis/ana100.htm.

4. Lance Compa, "Wary Allies: Trade Unions, NGOs, and Corporate Codes of Conduct," *American Prospect* 12 (July 2, 2001): 8–12; Debora Spar, "The Spotlight on the Bottom Line: How Multinationals Export Human Rights," *Foreign Affairs* 77 (March-April 1998): 7–13.

5. Doug Cahn and Tara Holeman, "Business and Human Rights," *Forum for Applied Research and Public Policy* 14 (Spring 1999): 52–58. Cahn and Holeman are executives at Reebok.

6. Human Rights Watch, *Unfair Advantage: Workers' Freedom of Association in the United States under International Human Rights Standards* (Washington, DC: Human Rights Watch, 2000), 6.

7. Steve Watkins, "Racism du Jour at Shoney's," *The Nation* 257 (October 18, 1993): 424–26; "Shoney's Co-Founder Quits Board, Sells Stock after Multimillion Bias Decision," *Jet* 83 (March 29, 1993): 4; quote found in Jeff Seinstein, "Shoney's 'Workforce 2000' Courts Minority Employees," *Restaurants and Institutions* 101 (March 6, 1991): 26.

8. Bill Mesler, "Hotline to the White House: Sprint, Blatantly Anti-Union, Has Drawn N.L.R.B. Censure but Bill Clinton's Praise," *The Nation* 264 (June 30, 1997): 20–24; Kim Phillips-Fein, "A More Perfect Union Buster," *Mother Jones* 23 (September-October 1998): 62–66.

9. A larger discussion of this history is found in Nelson Lichtenstein, *State of the Union: A Century of American Labor* (Princeton, NJ: Princeton University Press, 2002), 25–38, 59–60.

10. C. Wright Mills, *White Collar: The American Middle Classes* (New York: Oxford University Press, 1951), 318; John Kenneth Galbraith, *The New Industrial State* (Boston: Houghton Mifflin, 1967), 274.

11. Reinhold Niebuhr, "'End of an Era' for Organized Labor," *New Leader* (January 4, 1960): 18.

12. David Brody, "Labour Rights as Human Rights: A Reality Check," *British Journal of Industrial Relations* 39, no. 4 (2001): 601–695.

13. Reed Larson, "Is Monopoly in the American Tradition?" *Vital Speeches of the Day* 39 (June 15, 1973): 527–28. And see Sophia Z. Lee, "Whose Rights? Litigating the Right to Work, 1940–1980," in *The Right and Labor in America: Politics, Ideology, and Imagination,* ed. Nelson Lichtenstein and Elizabeth Tandy Shermer, 139–59 (Philadelphia: University of Pennsylvania Press, 2012).

14. Reuel Schiller, "From Group Rights to Individual Liberties: Post-War Labor Law, Liberalism, and the Waning of Union Strength," *Berkeley Journal of Employment and Labor Law* 20 (1999): 328–30.

15. David Abraham, "Individual Autonomy and Collective Empowerment in Labor Law: Union Membership Resignations and Strikebreaking in the New Economy," *New York University Law Review* 63 (December 1988): 1281, 1314–23.

Chapter 11. *The United States in the Great Depression*

This essay first appeared as a talk given at the conference "Routes into the Abyss: Coping with Crises in the 1930s," sponsored by Verein für Geschichte der Arbeiterbewegung, Vienna, February 2009.

1. Sinclair Lewis, *It Can't Happen Here* (New York: New American Library, 1935).

2. Philip Roth, *The Plot against America* (New York: Random House, 2004).

3. Wolfgang Schivelbusch, *Three New Deals: Reflections on Roosevelt's America, Mussolini's Italy, and Hitler's Germany, 1933–1939* (New York: Metropolitan Books, 2006), 1–15; Kenneth O'Reilly, "A New Deal for the FBI: The Roosevelt Administration, Crime Control, and National Security," *Journal of American History* 69, no. 3 (1982): 638–58.

4. As quoted in Schivelbusch, *Three New Deals*, 41.

5. Ibid., 19.

6. Edward Robb Ellis, *A Nation in Torment: The Great American Depression, 1929–1939* (New York: Coward-McCann, 1970), 330–64; Colin Gordon, *New Deals: Business, Labor, and Politics in America, 1920–1935* (New York: Cambridge University Press, 1994), 166–203; and see also the long-neglected essay by John Garraty, "The New Deal, National Socialism, and the Great Depression," *American Historical Review* 78, no. 4 (1973): 907–944.

7. Melvyn Dubofsky, *The State and Labor in Modern America* (Chapel Hill: University of North Carolina Press, 1994), 107–128.

8. As quoted in Schivelbusch, *Three New Deals*.

9. Ibid., 32.

10. Ibid., 37.

11. Gordon, *New Deals*, 128–65, 204–239; Stanley Vittoz, *New Deal Labor Policy and the American Industrial Economy* (Chapel Hill: University of North Carolina Press, 1987); and see the highly useful Theda Skocpol, "Political Response to Capitalist Crisis: Neo-Marxist Theories of the State and the Case of the New Deal," *Politics and Society* 10 (1980): 155–201.

12. Lizabeth Cohen, *Making a New Deal: Industrial Workers in Chicago, 1919–1939* (New York: Cambridge University Press, 1990), 251–321; Nelson Lichtenstein, *State of the Union: A Century of American Labor* (Princeton, NJ: Princeton University Press, 2002), 20–53.

13. Dubofsky, *State and Labor*, 128–36.

14. For a review of the early literature on this brand of American fascism, see Leo Ribuffo, "Fascists, Nazis and American Minds: Perceptions and Preconceptions," *American Quarterly* 26, no. 4 (1974): 417–32.

15. Steve Babson, *Building the Union: Skilled Workers and Anglo-Gaelic Immigrants in the Rise of the UAW* (New Brunswick, NJ: Rutgers University Press, 1991); Stephen Norwood, *Strikebreaking and Intimidation: Mercenaries and Masculinity in Twentieth-Century America* (Chapel Hill: University of North Carolina Press, 2002), 171–227; Bryant Simon, *A Fabric of Defeat: The Politics of South Carolina Millhands, 1910–1948* (Chapel Hill: University of North Carolina Press, 1998), 188–236.

16. Among the outstanding books that explore these issues are Alan Brinkley, *Voices of Protest: Huey Long, Father Coughlin, and the Great Depression* (New York: Oxford University Press, 1982); Steven Fraser, *Labor Will Rule: Sidney Hillman and the Rise of American Labor* (New York: Free Press, 1991); Joshua Freeman, *In Transit: The Transport Workers Union in New York City* (New York: Oxford University Press, 1989); and Peter Friedlander, *The Making of a UAW Local: A Study of Class and Culture* (Pittsburgh: University of Pittsburgh Press, 1975).

17. As quoted in Gordon, *New Deals*, 286.

18. Kim Philips Fein, *Invisible Hands: the Making of the Conservative Movement from the New Deal to Reagan* (New York: W. W. Norton, 2009); Alan Brinkley, *The End of Reform: New Deal Liberalism in Recession and War* (New York: Random House, 1996); David A. Horowitz, *Beyond Left and Right: Insurgency and the Establishment* (Urbana: University of Illinois Press, 1997).

19. All histories of the New Deal contain an account of FDR's "court-packing" debacle. A fine one is found in David Kennedy's *Freedom from Fear: The American People in Depression and War, 1929–1945* (New York: Oxford University Press, 1999), 331–40. For the shifting nature of American populism, see Michael Kazin, *The Populist Impulse: An American History* (New York: Oxford University Press, 1993); Catherine McNicol Stock, *Main Street in Crisis: The Great Depression and the Old Middle Class on the Northern Plains* (Chapel Hill: University of North Carolina Press, 1992).

20. Ira Katznelson, Kim Geiger, and Daniel Kryder, "Limiting Liberalism: The Southern Veto in Congress, 1933–1950," *Political Science Quarterly* 108, no. 2 (1993): 283–306; Michael Brown, *Race, Money, and the American Welfare State* (Ithaca, NY: Cornell University Press, 1999), 99–134; Michelle Brattain, *The Politics of Whiteness: Race, Workers, and Culture in the Modern South* (Princeton, NJ: Princeton University Press, 2001), 18–85.

Chapter 12. Market Triumphalism and the Wishful Liberals

Another version of this essay appears in Ellen Schrecker, ed., *Cold War Triumphalism: The Misuse of History after the Fall of Communism* (New York: Free Press, 2004).

1. As quoted in Tom Frank, *One Market under God: Extreme Capitalism, Market Populism, and the End of Economic Democracy* (New York: Anchor Books, 2000), 5.

2. Ibid., 23–40; James Arnt Aune, *Selling the Free Market: The Rhetoric of Economic Correctness* (New York: Guilford Press, 2001), 8. And see Angus Burgin, *The Great Persuasion: Reinventing Free Markets since the Depression* (Cambridge, MA.: Harvard University Press, 2012).

3. Gilder quoted in Frank, *One Market under God*, 3; Frances Fukuyama, "The End of History," *National Interest* (Spring 1989): 14–15. Fukuyama's essay and his subsequent books have generated a considerable historiography. See, for example, Philip Abbott, "'Big' Theories and Policy Counsel: James Burnham, Francis Fukuyama, and the Cold War," *Journal of Policy History* 14 (Fall 2002): 417–30.

4. "The National Security Strategy of the United States of America," September 17, 2002, National Security Council, White House, http://www.whitehouse.gov/nsc/nssall.html.

5. As quoted in William Greider, *One World Ready or Not: The Manic Logic of Global Capitalism* (New York: Touchstone Books, 1998), 212.

6. Frank, *One Market under God*, 211.

7. Michael Lewis, "Why You?" *New York Times Magazine*, September 23, 2001, 70–71.

8. "Second Presidential Debate Full Transcript," ABC News online, October 17, 2012, http://abcnews.go.com/Politics/OTUS/2012-presidential-debate-full-transcript-oct-16/ story?id=17493848.

9. Michael Cox, "American Power before and after 11 September: Dizzy with Success?" *International Affairs* 78, no. 2 (2002): 289–91.

10. Bennett Harrison and Barry Bluestone, *The Great U-Turn: Corporate Restructuring and the Polarizing of America* (New York: Basic Books, 1988), 3–52; Godfrey Hodgson, *The World Turned Right Side Up: A History of the Conservative Ascendancy in America* (Boston: Houghton-Mifflin, 1996), 186–215; Robert Kuttner, *Everything for Sale: The Virtues and Limits of Markets* (New York: Knopf, 1997), 68–109; Thomas and Mary Edsall, *Chain Reaction: The Impact of Race, Rights, and Taxes on American Politics* (New York: W. W. Norton, 1991), 154–97.

11. David Pilling, "Japanese Companies: How Could a Corporate Sector that Dominated the World a Decade Ago Have Become so Unproductive?" *Financial Times*, April 21, 2003, 9; Paul Krugman, *The Return of Depression Economics* (New York: W. W. Norton, 1999). The once vaunted "Four Tigers"—South Korea, Hong Kong, Taiwan, and Singapore— also had their troubles, but South China, whose labor relations and regulatory regime resembles that of nineteenth-century Pittsburgh, has roared ahead. It is fast becoming the twenty-first-century workshop of the world.

12. Hodgson, *World Turned Right Side Up*; see especially chapter 8, "The Strange Death of John Maynard Keynes," 186–215.

13. Howard Brick, "Talcott Parson's 'Shift Away from Economics,' 1937–1946," *Journal of American History* 87, no. 2 (2000): 511.

14. See most recently, and from the right, Aaron Frieberg, *The Spectre of a Garrison State* (Princeton, NJ: Princeton University Press, 2000).

15. The *Times Literary Supplement* names the book as one of the one hundred most influential books to appear since the end of World War II. A new edition appeared in 2000, in which Bell asserts "the resumption of history" along with the continuing "end of ideology" at the dawn of the twenty-first century. Daniel Bell, *The End of Ideology: On the Exhaustion of Political Ideas in the Fifties* (Cambridge, MA: Harvard University Press, 1960, 2000), xi–xxviii.

16. Howard Brick, "Talcott Parsons's 'Shift Away,'" 507, 511; Brick, *Age of Contradiction: American Thought and Culture in the 1960s* (New York: Twayne, 1998), xiv–xv, 54–57.

17. Jordan Schwarz, *Liberal: Adolf A. Berle and the Vision of an American Era* (New York: Free Press, 1987), 60.

18. Richard Pells, *Radical Visions and American Dreams: Culture and Social Thought in the Depression Years* (New York: Harper and Row, 1973), 69–70; Schwarz, *Liberal: Adolf A. Berle*, 59. See also Thomas K. McCraw, "In Retrospect: Berle and Means," *Reviews in American History* 18 (1990): 578–96.

19. Schwarz, *Liberal: Adolf A. Berle*, 353. The Twentieth Century Fund mission statement is from 1948, when Berle was a board member. He would serve as chair from 1950 to 1970.

20. Adolf Berle, "Property, Production, and Revolution: A Preface to the Revised Edition," *The Modern Corporation and Private Property* (New York: Harcourt, Brace, and World, 1968), xxvi. Tellingly, Berle relied on the old socialist slogan (in italics here)

to define the direction of contemporary social change. I thank Howard Brick for this reference.

21. John Medearis, "Schumpeter, the New Deal, and Democracy," *American Political Science Review* 91, no. 4 (1997): 819–33.

22. Joseph Schumpeter, *Capitalism, Socialism, and Democracy* (New York: Harper and Row, 1975, 1942), 134, 143; see also Arnold Heertje, *Schumpeter's Vision: Capitalism, Socialism, and Democracy after 40 Years* (New York: Praeger, 1981), especially Tom Bottomore, "The Decline of Capitalism Sociologically Considered," 22–44; and Arthur Smithies, "Schumpeter's Predictions," 130–49.

23. Volker Berghahn, *America and the Intellectual Cold Wars in Europe* (Princeton, NJ: Princeton University Press, 2001), 96–113; Hugh Wilford, *The CIA, the British Left, and the Cold War: Calling the Tune* (London: Frank Cass, 2003).

24. Peter Drucker, *The Concept of the Corporation* (1946; New York: John Day Company, 1972), 8.

25. Ibid., 12; and nearly fifty years later Drucker still held much the same evolutionary view. See Peter Drucker, *Post-Capitalist Society* (New York: HarperBusiness, 1993), 4–9.

26. Drucker, *Concept of the Corporation*; this viewpoint was given a powerful, comparative elaboration by another influential, émigré theorist of industrial society. See "The Bureaucratization of Economic Enterprises" in Reinhard Bendix, *Work and Authority in Industry* (Berkeley: University of California Press, 1956, 1974), 198–253.

27. For much more along this theme, see Howard Brick, *Transcending Capitalism: Visions of a New Society in Modern American Thought* (Ithaca, NY: Cornell University Press, 2006).

28. Arthur Schlesinger Jr., *The Vital Center* (Boston: Houghton Mifflin, 1949), 173. The book is still in print, still in the news, and in his autobiography endorsed once again half a century after it first appeared. Arthur Schlesinger Jr., *A Life in the 20th Century: Innocent Beginnings, 1917–1950* (Boston: Houghton Mifflin, 2000), 522.

29. Schlesinger, *Vital Center*, 154, 174.

30. James Cochrane, *Industrialism and Industrial Man in Retrospect: A Critical Review of the Ford Foundation's Support for the Inter-University Study of Labor* (New York: Ford Foundation, 1979), 61–80.

31. Richard M. Bissell Jr., *Reflections of a Cold Warrior: From Yalta to the Bay of Pigs* (New Haven: Yale University Press, 1996), 30–79; Evan Thomas, *The Very Best Men: Four Who Dared: The Early Years of the CIA* (New York: Simon and Schuster, 1995), 87–97; see in particular two excellent essays: Nils Gilman, "Modernization Theory, the Highest State of American Intellectual History," and David Engerman, "West Meets East: The Center for International Studies and Indian Economic Development," both in Engerman, Gilman, Mark H. Haefele, and Michael E. Latham, *Staging Growth: Modernization, Development, and the Global Cold War* (Amherst: University of Massachusetts Press, 2003), 47–80, 199–224.

32. Cochrane, *Industrialism and Industrial Man*, 92–95.

33. Kerr, Dunlop, et al., "Industrialism and Industrial Man Reconsidered: Some Perspectives on a Study over Two Decades of the Problems of Labor and Management in Economic Growth," typescript 1974, in Clark Kerr papers, unprocessed, Institute of Industrial Relations, UC Berkeley. It is difficult to calculate total expenditures over the two decades, especially when home institution funds are added it. The Ford Foundation's first full grant came to more than $400,000, which is over $4 million in 2010 dollars.

34. Ibid., 80–95, 118–19; Clark Kerr, John T. Dunlop, Frederick Harbison, and Charles A. Myers, *Industrialism and Industrial Man* (Cambridge, MA: Harvard University Press,

1960), 12; see in particular chapter 3, "The Industrializing Elites and Their Strategies," and chapter 9, "The Rule Makers and the Rules," 47–76, 234–63. John Dunlop is generally recognized as the author of the concept of a "web of rules." See his highly influential *Industrial Relations Systems* (Cambridge, MA: Harvard University Press, 1958). Some twelve books and twenty articles were published during the 1950s alone under the auspices of the Kerr-Dunlop Inter-University Study. Bruce Kaufman, *The Origins and Evolution of the Field of Industrial Relations in the United States* (Ithaca, NY: ILR Press, 1993), 94–95.

35. Paddy Riley, "Clark Kerr: From the Industrial to the Knowledge Economy," in *American Capitalism: Social Thought and Political Economy in the Twentieth Century,* ed. Nelson Lichtenstein (Philadelphia: University of Pennsylvania Press, 2006), 71–87.

36. C. Wright Mills, *The New Men of Power: America's Labor Leaders* (Urbana: University of Illinois Press, 1948, 2001), 233, 237. On Franz Neumann, whose work greatly influenced Mills, see H. Stuart Hughes, "Franz Neumann between Marxism and Liberal Democracy," in *The Intellectual Migration: Europe and America, 1930–1960,* ed. Donald Fleming and Bernard Bailyn (Cambridge, MA: Harvard University Press, 1969), 446–62.

37. Scholarship on C. Wright Mills is once again flourishing. For two of the best short studies, see Kevin Mattson, *Intellectuals in Action: The Origins of the New Left and Radical Liberalism, 1945–1970* (University Park: Pennsylvania State University Press, 2002), 43–96; and Daniel Geary, *Radical Ambition: C. Wright Mills, the Left, and American Social Thought* (Berkeley: University of California Press, 2009).

38. This perspective, which denies the hegemony of a postwar labor-management accord or a consensus liberalism, is advanced in Rick Perlstein, *Before the Storm: Barry Goldwater and the Unmaking of the American Consensus* (New York: Hill and Wang, 2001); Meg Jacobs, *Pocketbook Politics: Economic Citizenship in Twentieth-Century America* (Princeton, NJ: Princeton University Press, 2005); and Nelson Lichtenstein, *State of the Union: A Century of American Labor* (Princeton, NJ: Princeton University Press, 2002), 98–140.

39. This idea was first brought to my attention in Maurice Isserman and Michael Kazin, "The Failure and Success of the New Radicalism," in *The Rise and Fall of the New Deal Order, 1930–1980,* ed. Steve Fraser and Gary Gerstle (Princeton, NJ: Princeton University Press, 1989), 225–26.

40. Adolf Berle Jr., *Power without Property: A New Development in American Political Economy* (New York: Harcourt, Brace and Company, 1959), 11–26; Robert Booth Fowler, *Believing Skeptics: American Political Intellectuals, 1945–1964* (Westport, CT: Greenwood Press, 1978), 176–86.

41. James Miller, *"Democracy Is in the Streets": From Port Huron to the Siege of Chicago* (New York: Simon and Schuster, 1987), 232–33.

42. John Kenneth Galbraith, *The New Industrial State* (Boston: Houghton Mifflin, 1967), 263–64, 274, 280–81.

43. Virginia Postrel, "Looking Forward," *Forbes,* September 18, 2000, 108.

44. As quoted in Mark Gerson, *The Neoconservative Vision: From the Cold War to the Culture Wars* (Lanham, MD: Madison Books, 1996), 221.

45. Daniel Bell, *The Coming of Post-Industrial Society: A Venture in Social Forecasting* (1973; New York: Basic Books, 1999), 298.

46. Francis Fukuyama, "Getting It Right," *National Interest* (Winter 1999): 130.

47. The Tofflers had been Communists, or close to the party, during the late 1940s. They were members of that youthful cohort who worked for Henry Wallace and then industrialized. By the time they came out of a Cleveland factory in the 1950s, they had

repudiated Marxism, but not its sense that history moves by grand socio-technical stages. Gingrich had been a fan since the early 1970s. See the excellent essay by John Judis, "Newt's Not-So-Weird Gurus: In Defense of the Tofflers," *New Republic* 213 (October 9, 1995): 16–24.

48. Jeffery Halprin, "Getting Back to Work: The Revaluation of Work in American Literature and Social Theory, 1950–1985," PhD diss., Boston University, 1987, 42–89, 114–67, Dublin quoted at 57; Clark Kerr, "The Prospect for Wages and Hours in 1975" (1958), in Kerr, *Labor and Management in Industrial Society* (Garden City: Doubleday, 1964), 203–31.

49. Brick, *Transcending Capitalism*, 208–209.

50. Charles Sabel and Jonathan Zeitlin, "Alternatives to Mass Production," *Past and Present*, revised and updated in Zeitlin and Sabel, *Worlds of Possibilities: Flexibility and Mass Production* (New York: Cambridge University Press, 1994); Michael Piore and Charles Sabel, *The Second Industrial Divide: Possibilities for Prosperity* (New York: Basic Books, 1984), 19–48.

51. Piore and Sabel, *The Second Industrial Divide*, 133–64.

52. Robert Reich, *The Next American Frontier* (New York: Penguin, 1983), 246.

53. Piore and Sabel, *Second Industrial Divide*, 261, 305–306. And see also Shoshana Zuboff, *In the Age of the Smart Machine: The Future of Work and Power* (New York: Basic Books, 1984). Piore, Sabel, and Zuboff stood on the left, but their faith in a technocratic progressivism fed rather easily into the Reaganite optimism of such techno-market futurists as George Gilder and Ben Wattenberg.

54. As quoted in Kim Moody, *Workers in a Lean World: Unions in the International Economy* (New York: Verso, 1997), 43–44.

Chapter 13. Did 1968 Change History?

This essay first appeared as "Did 1968 Change History?" in *New Politics* (Summer 2009).

1. Philipp Gassert and Martin Klimke, "1968: Memories and Legacies of a Global Revolt," *Bulletin of the German Historical Institute*, Supplement 6 (2009).

2. David Caute, *The Year of the Barricades: A Journey through 1968* (New York: Harper and Row, 1988), 91, 254.

3. Ibid., 71; and see Paul Berman's *A Tale of Two Utopias: The Political Journey of the Generation of 1968* (New York: W. W. Norton, 1996), 195–219.

4. Paul Ormerod, "Bourgeois Fools," *Prospect Magazine*, May 2008, as part of an online symposium, "1968: Liberty or Its Illusion?"

5. Denis MacShane, "The Heaven of 1968," *Prospect Magazine*, May 2008.

6. Timothy Garton Ash, "This Tale of Two Revolutions May Yet Have a Twist," *Guardian*, May 8, 2008, online edition.

7. Michael Denning, *The Cultural Front: The Laboring of American Culture in the 20th Century* (New York: Verso, 1997); Gary Gerstle, *American Crucible: Race and Nation in the Twentieth Century* (Princeton, NJ: Princeton University Press, 2001); Peter Levy, *The New Left and Labor in the 1960s* (Urbana: University of Illinois Press, 1994).

8. Much of this discussion of party politics is taken from Mark Stricherz, "Primary Colors: How a Little-Known Task Force Helped Create Red State/Blue State America," *Boston Globe* online edition, November 23, 2003.

9. Jeremi Suri, *Power and Protest: Global Revolution and the Rise of Détente* (Cambridge, MA: Harvard University Press, 2003), 2.

10. Ibid., 261; Rick Perlstein, *Nixonland: The Rise of a President and the Fracturing of America* (New York: Scribner, 2008), 417–44.

11. Suri, *Power and Protest,* 249–50; see also Stephen Kotkin, "The Kiss of Debt: The East Bloc Goes Borrowing," in *The Shock of the Global: The 1970s in Perspective,* ed. Niall Ferguson et al. (Cambridge, MA: Harvard University Press, 2010), 80–96.

12. Julian Zelizer, *On Capital Hill: The Struggle to Reform Congress and Its Consequences, 1948–2000* (New York: Cambridge University Press, 2004), 33–62.

13. Mark Lilla, "A Tale of Two Reactions," *New York Review of Books* 45, no. 8 (1998).

14. Myron Magnet, *The Dream and the Nightmare: The Sixties' Legacy to the Underclass* (San Francisco: Encounter Books, 1993), 1.

15. Daniel Bell, *The Cultural Contradictions of Capitalism: 20th Anniversary Edition* (New York: Basic Books, 1996).

16. Michael Kazin, "1968: Lessons Learned," *Dissent* (Spring 2008): 16. For a more thorough evocation of Kazin's perspective, see his *American Dreamers: How the Left Changed a Nation* (New York: Knopf, 2011), 209–251.

17. Tom Frank, *The Conquest of Cool: Business Culture, Counterculture, and the Rise of Hip Consumerism* (Chicago: University of Chicago Press, 1998); *One Market under God: Extreme Capitalism, Market Populism, and the End of Economic Democracy* (New York: Doubleday, 2000); Nelson Lichtenstein, *The Retail Revolution: How Wal-Mart Created a Brave New World of Business* (New York: Metropolitan Books, 2009), 70–111.

18. Lichtenstein, *Retail Revolution,* 99–104; see also Bethany Moreton, *To Serve God and Wal-Mart: The Making of Christian Free Enterprise* (New York: Harvard University Press, 2009), 106–24.

19. Nelson Lichtenstein, "Why Was SDS Founded at an AFL-CIO Summer Camp?" in *The Port Huron Statement: Reflections on the Sources and Legacies of the New Left's Founding Manifesto,* ed. Richard Flacks and Nelson Lichtenstein (forthcoming from the University of Pennsylvania Press).

Chapter 14. Bashing Public Employees and Their Unions

This essay was first delivered as a talk at the University of Cambridge, May 24, 2012.

1. Amy Traub, "War on Public Workers," *Nation,* July 5, 2010, 4–6.

2. Bradley Blackburn, "New Jersey Governor Chris Christie Calls His State's Teachers Union 'Political Thugs,'" ABC News online, April 6, 2011; Scott Walker, "Striking the Right Bargain in Wisconsin," *Washington Post,* online edition, March 16, 2011.

3. This schema was first suggested to me in Steve Fraser and Joshua B. Freeman's illuminating intervention, "In the Rearview Mirror: A Brief History of Opposition to Public Sector Unionism," *New Labor Forum* (Fall 2011): 93–96.

4. Joseph Slater, *Public Workers: Government Employee Unions, the Law, and the State, 1900–1962* (Ithaca, NY: Cornell University Press, 2004), 26.

5. Francis Russell, *A City in Terror: The Boston Police Strike* (New York: Viking Press, 1975), 131–204; Wilson is quoted on 170.

6. FDR quoted in Slater, *Public Workers,* 83. Rarely does a contemporary right-wing attack on public sector unionism pass without a reference to this famous presidential rejection of collective bargaining in the federal sector. I only wish that right-wing opponents of the welfare state, of unionism in the private sector, of Social Security, or of

government regulation of Wall Street would take some of FDR's other pronouncements with equal deference and respect.

7. Missouri Supreme Court quoted in Wilson R. Hart, "Government Labor's New Frontiers through Presidential Directive," *Virginia Law Review* 48 (1962): 902–903; *City of Springfield v. Clouse*, S.W. 2d 539 (Mo. 1947) (en banc).

8. Stanley Aronowitz, *From the Ashes of the Old: American Labor and America's Future* (Boston: Houghton Mifflin, 1998), 140; Marjorie Murphy, *Blackboard Unions: The AFT and the NEA, 1900–1980* (Ithaca, NY: Cornell University Press, 1990), 196–226.

9. Wilson R. Hart, *Collective Bargaining in the Federal Civil Service* (New York: Harper and Brothers, 1961), 3.

10. Ibid., 9.

11. As quoted in Daniel Disalvo, "The Trouble with Public Sector Unions," *National Affairs* (Fall 2010): 3.

12. Joseph A. McCartin, "'A Wagner Act for Public Employees': Labor's Deferred Dream and the Rise of Conservatism, 1970–1976," *Journal of American History* (June 2008): 126.

13. Allen J. Matusow, *Nixon's Economy: Booms, Busts, Dollars and Votes* (Lawrence: University Press of Kansas, 1998), 160.

14. Joshua Freeman, *Working-Class New York: Life and Labor in New York City since World War II* (New York: New Press, 2000), 256–90; Alice O'Connor, "The Privatized City: The Manhattan Institute, the Urban Crisis, and the Conservative Counterrevolution in New York," *Journal of Urban History* 34 (January 2008): 333–53; Kim Moody, *From Welfare State to Real Estate: Regime Change in New York City, 1974 to the Present* (New York: New Press, 2007).

15. Joseph McCartin, *Collision Course: Ronald Reagan, the Air Traffic Controllers, and the Strike that Changed America* (New York: Oxford University Press, 2011), 290, 338–51.

16. Joseph A. McCartin and Jean-Christian Vinel, "'Compulsory Unionism': Sylvester Petro and the Career of an Anti-Union Idea, 1957–1987," in *The Right and Labor in America: Politics, Ideology, and Imagination*, ed. Nelson Lichtenstein and Elizabeth Tandy (Philadelphia: University of Pennsylvania Press, 2012), 244.

17. Ibid., 242–43.

18. Ibid., 245.

19. Eileen Boris and Jennifer Klein, *Caring for America: Home Health Workers in the Shadow of the Welfare State* (New York: Oxford University Press, 2012), 183–209.

20. Ibid., 212.

21. Steven Malanga, *Shakedown: The Continuing Conspiracy against the American Taxpayer* (New York: Ivan R. Dee, 2010); for a contrary view, see Robert Kuttner, "Land of the Free, Home of the Turncoats: In Its Nihilistic Demonization of Government, the Right Has Declared War on America," *American Prospect*, September 20, 2011.

22. Scott Walker, "Striking the Right Bargain in Wisconsin," *Washington Post*, online edition, March 16, 2011.

23. David Brooks, "The Paralysis of the State," *New York Times*, October 12, 2010, A31; see also Disalvo, "Trouble with Public Sector Unions," 1–2.

24. Sylvia Allegretto, Ken Jacobs, and Laurel Lucia, "The Wrong Target: Public Sector Unions and State Budget Deficits," *Policy Brief*, UC Berkeley Labor Center, October 2011.

25. Marisa Lagos, "Public Workers Highly Paid? Not Exactly," *San Francisco Chronicle*, October 19, 2010.

Chapter 15. C. Wright Mills

This essay was originally published as "Reconsiderations: *The New Men of Power*" in *Dissent* (Fall 2001): 121–30. The essay quotes extensively from *C. Wright Mills: Letters and Autobiographical Writings*, ed. Kathryn Mills with Pamela Mills (Berkeley: University of California Press, 2000); *Power, Politics, and People: The Collected Essays of C. Wright Mills*, ed. Irving Louis Horowitz (New York: Oxford University Press, 1962); and from letters and manuscripts held in the Mills papers at the University of Texas. A longer version appears as the introduction to the University of Illinois Press edition of C. Wright Mills's *The New Men of Power*, published in the fall of 2001.

Chapter 16. Harvey Swados

This essay was originally published as "Introduction" in Harvey Swados, *On the Line* (Urbana: University of Illinois Press, 1990), vii–xxvii.

1. Harvey Swados, "The Myth of the Happy Worker," in Swados, *On the Line*, 247. The essay was first published in the *Nation*, August 17, 1957.

2. Richard Sennett and Jonathan Cobb, *The Hidden Injuries of Class* (New York: Knopf, 1972); Harry Braverman, *Labor and Monopoly Capital: The Degradation of Work in the Twentieth Century* (New York: Monthly Review Press, 1974).

3. For more on Swados, see Alan Wald, *The New York Intellectuals: The Rise and Decline of the Anti-Stalinist Left from the 1930s to the 1980s* (Chapel Hill: University of North Carolina Press, 1987), 334–39.

4. Ibid., 335; Harvey Swados, *Out Went the Candle* (New York: Viking Press, 1955).

5. Swados's efforts to earn a living are recounted in Harvey Swados, "Some Social Implications of Automation," ms. dated April 19, 1966, box 23, Swados Collection, University of Massachusetts; and in a Lichtenstein telephone interview with Robin Swados, July 25, 1989.

6. "First Ford Rolls in Mahwah Plant," *New York Times*, July 17, 1955, 53.

7. Quoted in U.S. Department of Labor, "Seminar on Manpower Policy and Program," box 23, Swados Collection.

8. Harvey Swados to Stuart and Barbara Schulberg, April 5, 1956, box 33, Swados Collection.

9. Quoted in Russell Davenport, *USA: The Permanent Revolution* (New York: Time-Life, 1951), 91.

10. *Proceedings*, Congress of Industrial Organizations, November 1948, 234.

11. Quoted in Davenport, *USA: The Permanent Revolution,* 91.

12. Swados, *On the Line*, 237.

13. For further discussion, see Jeffrey Halprin, "Getting Back to Work: The Revaluation of Work in American Literature and Social Theory, 1950–1985," PhD diss., Boston University, 1987, 46–52.

14. Swados, *On the Line*, 237.

15. Harvey Swados, *A Radical's America* (New York: World Publishing, 1962), 118.

16. Lichtenstein telephone interview with Stan Weir, October 14, 1988.

17. "Ford Strike Is Voted," *New York Times*, December 11, 1957, 23.

18. "Ford Workers Quit," *New York Times*, September 6, 1961, 28; "Ford Mahwah Plant Halted by Walkout," *New York Times*, November 28, 1962, 62.

19. Harvey Swados, "The UAW—Over the Top or Over the Hill?" *Dissent* (Fall 1963): 321–43.

20. "Topics: Workers and Students—Enemies or Allies?" *New York Times*, August 30, 1969, 20. Unfortunately, Ford Motor Company had the last laugh. Complaining of poor workmanship, it permanently closed down the big factory in the summer of 1980.

Chapter 17. B. J. Widick

This essay was first published as "B. J. Widick, 1910–2008," *New Politics* 12, no. 2 (2009): 41–44.

1. Much analysis of Widick's political commitments in the 1930s can be found in Alan Wald, "B. J. Widick, 1910–2008," *Against the Current* 126 (September-October 2008). Available online at http://www.solidarity-us.org/node/1893.

2. Ibid.

3. Harvey Swados, "The UAW—Over the Top or Over the Hill?" *Dissent* (Fall 1963): 342–44.

4. Author's interview with B. J. Widick, July 22, 1989, Ann Arbor; Wald, "B. J. Widick."

5. Irving Howe and B. J. Widick, *The UAW and Walter Reuther* (New York: Random House, 1949), 117–25, 183.

6. Ibid., 200–201 (italics in original).

7. Walter Jason [B. J. Widick], "Union Democracy under Attack in UAW-Ford Trial," *Labor Action*, October 16, 1950.

8. B. J. Widick, *Labor Today: The Triumphs and Failures of Unionism in the United States* (New York: Houghton Mifflin, 1964), vii, 206.

9. B. J. Widick, "A Shop Steward on the Frustrations of the Contract System, 1954," in *Major Problems in the History of American Workers,* ed. Eileen Boris and Nelson Lichtenstein (Lexington, KY: D. C. Heath, 1991), 506.

10. B. J. Widick, ed., *Auto Work and Its Discontents* (Baltimore: Johns Hopkins University Press, 1976).

11. B. J. Widick, *Detroit: City of Race and Class Violence* (1972; Detroit: Wayne State University Press, 1989).

Chapter 18. Jay Lovestone

This essay was first published in *Working USA* 3, no. 2 (1999): 90–96.

1. Ted Morgan, *A Covert Life: Jay Lovestone, Communist, Anti-Communist, and Spymaster.* (New York: Random House, 1999), 372.

2. Ibid. This was the view of Pagie Morris, one of Lovestone's closest and oldest friends.

3. Ibid., 99.

4. Ibid., 81.

5. Ibid., 141.

6. Ibid., 125–26.

7. For the other side of the story, see Nelson Lichtenstein, *Walter Reuther: The Most Dangerous Man in Detroit* (Urbana: University of Illinois Press, 1997), 104–131.

8. Morgan, *Covert Life,* 140.

9. In agreement with Morgan, but with a more subtle understanding of the CIA, is Hugh Wilford, *The Mighty Wurlitzer: How the CIA Played America* (Cambridge, MA: Harvard University Press, 2008), 51–69.

10. Morgan, *Covert Life*, 152.

11. Timothy Garton Ash, *In Europe's Name: Germany and the Divided Continent* (New York: Vintage, 1994).

12. Denis MacShane, *International Labor and the Origins of the Cold War* (Oxford: Clarendon Press, 1984).

13. Morgan, *Covert Life*, 177.

14. Ibid., 164, 288.

15. Ibid., 339.

Chapter 19. Herbert Hill

This essay was first published in *LABOR: Studies in Working-Class History of the Americas* 3, no. 2 (2006): 25–31.

1. Stephen Steinberg, "Herbert Hill Remembered," *New Politics* 10, no. 2 (2005): 113.

2. "Herbert Hill Dies, Fought Racial Discrimination in Labor," *Public Employee Press* (District 37, American Federation of State Country and Municipal Workers), January 2005, 4.

3. Ibid.

4. Hill's work was, of course, marginal to the general thrust of NAACP litigation from the late 1940s through the 1960s. But as Risa Goluboff demonstrates in her illuminating study of NAACP litigation strategy, this had not always been the case. During World War II NAACP lawyers considered employment discrimination as important as that in education, and it seemed possible that the desegregationist precedents that would later culminate in *Brown v. Board of Education* might well have come in the employment field, including that in which discriminatory trade unions played a large role. However, the onset of the Cold War and the devaluation of working-class issues shifted the attention of the NAACP legal team away from labor and toward an almost exclusive focus on school desegregation. This transformed the modern meaning of "civil rights" and may well have made Hill's work both more difficult and more lonely. Risa Lauren Goluboff, "'Let Economic Equality Take Care of Itself': The NAACP, Labor Litigation, and the Making of Civil Rights in the 1940s," *UCLA Law Review* 52, no. 5 (2005): 1393–1486.

5. Hill's 1960s critique and a labor response can be found in Herbert Hill, "The Racial Practices of Organized Labor: The Contemporary Record," and Gus Tyler, "Contemporary Labor's Attitude toward the Negro," in *The Negro and the American Labor Movement,* ed. Julius Jacobson (Garden City, NY: Doubleday, 1968), 286–379.

6. Gilbert Jonas, "Herbert Hill and the ILGWU," *New Politics* 10, no. 2 (2005): 119.

7. Ibid.

8. Herbert Hill, "Myth-Making as Labor History: Herbert Gutman and the United Mine Workers of America," *Politics, Culture, and Society* 2, no. 2 (1988): 133.

9. Herbert Hill, "Race and the Steelworkers' Union: White Privilege and Black Struggles. Review Essay of Judith Stein's *Running Steel, Running America,*" *New Politics* 8, no. 4 (2002): 174.

10. Herbert Hill, "The Problem of Race in American Labor History," *Reviews in American History* 24, no. 2 (1996): 191. Hill was referring to an epilogue from volume 1 of the textbook, which was notable for the discussion and sheer number of pages devoted to the dual labor systems, free and slave, that had emerged out of colonial America. Volume 2 continued to problematize the class and racial consciousness of American proletarians.

11. For the polemics, see Herbert Hill, "Lichtenstein's Fictions: Meany, Reuther, and the 1964 Civil Rights Act," *New Politics* 7, no. 1 (1998): 82–107; Nelson Lichtenstein, "Walter Reuther in Black and White: A Rejoinder to Herbert Hill," *New Politics* 7, no. 2 (1999): 133–47; Herbert Hill, "Lichtenstein's Fictions Revisited: Race and the New Labor History," *New Politics* 7, no. 2 (1999): 148–63.

12. See in particular the replies offered by Roediger and Salvatore, as well as by David Brody, Kenneth Waltzer, and myself, in a 1987 *New Politics* symposium, responding to Hill's "Race, Ethnicity and Organized Labor: The Opposition to Affirmative Action," *New Politics* 1, no. 2 (1987): 31–82. The replies and Hill's rejoinder are found in "Discussion: Race, Ethnicity and Organized Labor," *New Politics* 1, no. 3 (1987): 22–71.

13. See in particular "In Memorial: Herbert Hill, 1924–2004," a selection of elegies at his October 2004 memorial service, in *New Politics* 10, no. 2 (2005): 113–23.

14. Relying upon the scholarship of Roger Horowitz, Timothy Minchen, Robert Korstad, and Gilbert Gall, I expand on this point in my *State of the Union: A Century of American Labor* (Princeton, NJ: Princeton University Press, 2002), 103–107.

15. Herbert Hill, "Confidential Memorandum to Walter White," May 8–17, 1953, A4–15, Philip Murray Collection, Catholic University of America (courtesy of Judith Stein).

16. Judith Stein, *Running Steel, Running America: Race, Economic Policy, and the Decline of Liberalism* (Chapel Hill: University of North Carolina Press, 1998), 195.

17. Christopher Phelps, "Herbert Hill and the Federal Bureau of Investigation," *Labor History*, 53, no. 4 (Novermber 2012), 561–570; Trevor Griffey, "Was Herbert Hill, NAACP's Labor Secretary, an FBI Informer?" Labor and Working Class History Association, LaborOnline, January 25, 2013. The Sullivan quote is from Phelps, "Herbert Hill and the FBI" 564.

18. Phelps, "Herbert Hill and the FBI," 566–67; In a 1992 interview with the author, held in Madison, Wisconsin, Hill made clear that he never acted on any important issue without the approval and backing of Roy Wilkins.

Chapter 20. Do Graduate Students Work?

This essay was first published as "Graduate Education Is a Seamless Web of Learning and Work, Not Class Warfare," *Chronicle of Higher Education*, August 6, 2004, and was revised in 2012.

1. *Brown University and UAW AFL-CIO*, Case 1-RC-21368, 342 NLRB No. 42, July 13, 2004, 483–500.

2. Toss Runkel, "NLRB Reversals during the Bush Administration," LawMemo.Com, June 16, 2004.

3. *Brown University and the UAW AFL-CIO*, 488.

4. Mike Parker, "Team Production by Stress," in *Industrial Democracy: The Ambiguous Promise*, ed. Nelson Lichtenstein and Howell John Harris (New York: Cambridge University Press, 1991), 103–137.

5. This famous quotation is taken from Marx, *The German Ideology* (New York: International Publishers, 1947), 53. The book was originally published in 1846.

Chapter 21. Why American Unions Need Intellectuals

This essay was originally published in *Dissent* (Spring 2010): 69–73.

1. C. Wright Mills, *The New Men of Power: America's Labor Leaders* (1948; Urbana: University of Illinois Press, 2001), 291.

2. The dispute generated an enormous amount of reportage and comment. For a sample, see Max Fraser, "Labor's Conundrum: Growth vs. Standards," *New Labor Forum* (Winter 2009): 49–57; Max Fraser, "The SEIU Andy Stern Leaves Behind," *Nation*, July 5, 2010, 20–24; Randy Shaw, "SEIU Wages War on Progressives," BeyondChron: San Francisco's Alternative Online Daily News, November 17, 2009; Steve Early, "The Progressive Quandary about SEIU: A Tale of Two Letters to Andy Stern," *WorkingUSA* 12 (December 2009): 611–28.

3. Quote taken from Selig Perlman, *A Theory of the Labor Movement* (1928), as excerpted in *Theories of the Labor Movement,* ed. Simon Larson and Bruce Nissen (Detroit: Wayne State University Press, 1987), 170.

4. Leon Fink, *In Search of the Working Class: Essay in American Labor History and Political Culture* (Urbana: University of Illinois Press, 1994), 221.

5. I discuss these developments in greater detail in my *Walter Reuther: The Most Dangerous Man in Detroit* (Urbana: University of Illinois Press, 1997), 299–326.

6. Steven Greenhouse, "Labor Fight Ends in Win for Students," *New York Times*, November 18, 2009, B1.

7. Kate Bronfenbrenner, "No Holds Barred: The Intensification of Employer Opposition to Organizing," Economic Policy Institute Briefing Paper, no. 235, May 20, 2009; Steven Greenhouse, "Study Says Antiunion Tactics Are Becoming More Common," *New York Times*, May 20, 2009, B5.

8. Harold Meyerson, "Where Are the Workers?" *American Prospect* 20, no. 2 (2009), 20.

INDEX

NELSON LICHTENSTEIN is MacArthur Foundation Professor in History at the University of California, Santa Barbara, where he also directs the Center for the Study of Work, Labor, and Democracy. His books include *The Retail Revolution: How Wal-Mart Created a Brave New World of Business*, *State of the Union: A Century of American Labor*, *Walter Reuther: The Most Dangerous Man in Detroit*, and *American Capitalism: Social Thought and Political Economy in the Twentieth Century*.

THE WORKING CLASS IN AMERICAN HISTORY

The University of Illinois Press
is a founding member of the
Association of American University Presses.

———————————————————————

Composed in 10.5/13 Minion Pro
by Lisa Connery
at the University of Illinois Press
Manufactured by Cushing-Malloy, Inc.

University of Illinois Press
1325 South Oak Street
Champaign, IL 61820–6903
www.press.uillinois.edu